The Master-Servant Doctrine

# The Master-Servant Doctrine

*How Old Legal Rules Haunt the Modern Workplace*

Elizabeth Chika Tippett

UNIVERSITY OF CALIFORNIA PRESS

University of California Press
Oakland, California

© 2025 by Elizabeth Chika Tippett

All rights reserved.

Library of Congress Cataloging-in-Publication Data

Names: Tippett, Elizabeth C. author
Title: The master-servant doctrine : how old legal rules haunt the modern workplace / Elizabeth Chika Tippett.
Description: Oakland, California : University of California Press, [2025] | Includes bibliographical references and index.
Identifiers: LCCN 2025019679 (print) | LCCN 2025019680 (ebook) | ISBN 9780520382312 cloth | ISBN 9780520382329 paperback | ISBN 9780520382336 epub
Subjects: LCSH: Labor laws and legislation—United States | Industrial relations—United States
Classification: LCC KF3319 .T57 2025 (print) | LCC KF3319 (ebook) | DDC 344.7301—dc23/eng/20250506
LC record available at https://lccn.loc.gov/2025019679
LC ebook record available at https://lccn.loc.gov/2025019680

GPSR Authorized Representative:
Easy Access System Europe,
Mustamäe tee 50, 10621 Tallinn, Estonia,
gpsr.requests@easproject.com

34  33  32  31  30  29  28  27  26  25
10  9  8  7  6  5  4  3  2  1

publication supported by a grant from

**The Community Foundation for Greater New Haven**

as part of the *Urban Haven Project*

*For my family*

# Contents

Introduction — 1

### PART I. THE RIGHT TO CONTROL

1. Physical Control — 13
2. Termination — 27
3. Pay — 38
4. Time Management — 52

### PART II. THE RIGHT TO GOVERN

5. Unions — 69
6. Equal Opportunity — 83
7. Human Resources — 101

### PART III. THE DUTY OF SUPPORT

8. Benefits — 117
9. Left Behind — 133
10. Policy Interventions — 145

Conclusion                                    159
Epilogue                                      163


Acknowledgments                               165
Notes                                         167
Bibliography                                  247
Figure Credits and Sources                    275
Index                                         277

# Introduction

Maetta Vance worked as a catering assistant at Ball State University in Indiana for more than a decade. For most of that time she was the only Black employee in the department.[1] The catering department worked on a variety of projects, from small group lunches to large banquets in the community. Vance worked the early morning baking shift so she could make it to a second job in the afternoon.

In 2001 a white coworker named Saundra Davis "hit Vance on the back of the head without provocation" in an argument over whether a client needed extra deli meat.[2] Vance later testified that she complained to management, Davis admitted to the slap, and then Davis was sent home.[3]

At the time, Vance was worried that Ball State did not take her complaint seriously and that management was unduly focused on whether she and Davis were "friends," rather than on the severity of Davis's conduct.[4] Her boss even allegedly asked Vance to reenact the slap.[5] (In litigation, management denied having any recollection of any of these events.)[6]

Ball State did not fire Saundra Davis. Instead, Davis was transferred to another department.[7]

However, in 2005 Davis returned to the catering department. Management assigned Davis some supervisory duties, although her authority over Vance was somewhat murky.[8] At this point—according to the 7th Circuit Court of Appeals—"things took a turn for the worse."[9] Davis threatened to "do it again" while blocking Vance from getting off an elevator.[10] Vance also learned through the grapevine that a coworker named Connie McVicker had referred to Vance using the n-word and bragged about having relatives in the Ku Klux Klan.[11]

Vance reported Davis and McVicker to human resources (HR). McVicker received a written warning.[12]

The university did not discipline Davis because she had lodged her own complaint against Vance for using profanity.[13] An internal management email stated, "I believe we can only *counsel* [Vance and Davis] as to showing proper respect for one another, never using unacceptable language, and taking problems to management for solution."[14]

The harassment did not stop. Vance complained to HR that McVicker called her a "monkey."[15] On another occasion, Vance reported that McVicker threatened "payback" when stepping off an elevator, while McVicker insisted that Vance had profanely warned her that it was "just beginning."[16] Ball State investigated but did nothing, citing the absence of third-party witnesses.[17]

Vance filed a complaint with the Equal Employment Opportunity Commission (EEOC) and then filed a lawsuit. This only made things worse. While the lawsuit was pending, Davis's daughter and husband accosted Vance and a coworker.[18] The daughter and husband hurled racial epithets at them, and the daughter threatened to "kick [Vance's] ass."[19]

In a handwritten complaint to the National Association for the Advancement of Colored People (NAACP), Vance wrote: "If these people were at all fair I would or could have gotten at least an apology back then. Instead they, I felt were bent on trying to make me leave, like so many others had done. But I love what I do in catering and have never caused any trouble in 16 years of service.... I feel that I have to constantly work in a hostile environment. My rights have been violated. My dignity as a Black woman and individual have been stripped.... I'm afraid to be at work."[20]

Vance lost her harassment case against Ball State on summary judgment. The court ruled that Davis did not qualify as Vance's supervisor,[21] which meant that Vance's case was treated as a coworker harassment claim. Consequently, the university would only be liable if it had been negligent, and its various investigations and written warning to McVicker demonstrated that it had exercised reasonable care.[22] Vance appealed the case to the Seventh Circuit and lost again.[23]

A team of law students from the University of Virginia led by Professor Daniel Ortiz appealed the case to the Supreme Court.[24] By the time the Supreme Court granted certiorari, *Vance v. Ball State* was a husk of a case, limited to the technical question of whether Davis qualified as a "supervisor" under Title VII of the Civil Rights Act of 1964.[25]

At the November 2012 hearing, Professor Ortiz had barely begun his oral argument when Chief Justice John Roberts interrupted him: "Let's say you have a work room. There are five people who work there. And the employer has a rule that the senior employee gets to pick the music that's going to play all day long."[26] Roberts continued, "And the senior employee says to one of the other employees—'you know, if you don't date me—I know you don't like country music; if you don't date me, it's going to be country music all day long.'"[27] Would that senior employee be considered a supervisor?

Ortiz started to explain, but Roberts interrupted again, followed by Justice Antonin Scalia, who suggested country music was a far worse punishment than "hard rock."[28] The transcript shows laughter.[29]

Vance lost her Supreme Court case.

Although the Court was interpreting a federal statute, the opinion relied on much older principles of common law, providing that "'masters' are generally not liable for the torts of their 'servants'" if the conduct was "outside the scope of the servant's employment."[30] Rather than holding companies strictly liable for harassment,[31] as they are for discrimination claims, the court applied a series of exceptions and affirmative defenses depending on whether the harasser was a supervisor or a coworker. For coworker harassment, the plaintiff must show that the employer was negligent. For supervisor harassment, the company will be strictly liable. However, the company can assert an affirmative defense that it took "reasonable care to prevent and correct" harassment, and that the plaintiff failed to make use of internal channels to complain.[32]

This loophole in harassment law removes employers from accountability and oversight.[33] As in Vance's case, companies can avoid liability without doing anything meaningful or effective to stop or prevent harassment. Instead, they need only create internal policies and procedures regarding harassment, essentially their own internal "law" that governs the workplace.[34] Courts then largely defer to those internal policies and the employer's judgments regarding their application[35]—almost as if the employer were a mini-state[36]—rather than focusing on whether unlawful harassment occurred.

. . .

Why is the Supreme Court so tempted to resort to old concepts of "master" and "servant" in a modern employment dispute involving a twentieth-century civil rights statute? Vance's case is not unique in this regard.[37] Concepts of master and servant remain central in determining whether an employment relationship exists, as articulated in a 1992 Supreme Court ruling, *Nationwide v. Darden*, discussed in greater detail in chapter 1.[38]

The terms "master" and "servant" likewise appeared in a 2003 case deciding whether medical partners should be counted as employees or employers. The court reasoned that the "common law's definition of the master-servant relationship" offered "helpful guidance."[39] In a 2019 case, *New Prime Inc. v. Oliveira*, the Supreme Court conducted its own historical analysis of the term "employee."[40] The opinion, written by Justice Neil Gorsuch, concludes that the word "employee" came to be widely used in the twentieth century because it "didn't suffer from the same historical baggage" of the word "servant."[41] Another 2019 Supreme Court case, about a sailor injured on a ship, made frequent reference to the ship owner as the "master."[42] The terms "master" and "servant" likewise appear in a 2022 wage and hour case involving a cargo supervisor for Southwest Airlines.[43]

The terms "master" and "servant" also appear in current legal treatises and other secondary sources. *Black's Law Dictionary* defines "employment" as the "relationship between master and servant."[44] The authors of the *Restatement of Employment Law*, pointedly chose to use the terms "employer" and "employee" over "master" and "servant,"[45] but nevertheless could not avoid using the latter terms repeatedly.[46] The term "master" appears twenty-three times in the *Restatement*, and "servant" appears forty-nine times.

Indeed, the field of employment law used to be understood as master-servant law.[47] A famous 1877 treatise by Horace G. Wood, which is periodically blamed for the at-will employment doctrine, was titled *A Treatise on the Law of Master and Servant*.[48] A variety of other treatises published between 1852 and 1913 bore titles that included the phrase "the law of master and servant."[49]

The master-servant principles described in this book are based on Robert Steinfeld's and Karen Orren's respective legal-historical descriptions of feudal employment relations in early modern England, when employment centered on the household.[50] Steinfeld explained that feudal master-servant relations relate to the concept of *parens patriae*: the idea that the king is "the father of his people."[51] By extension, the male head of household governed those within. "When contemporaries spoke of household or family government, they did not mean to be taken metaphorically," writes Steinfeld. "They meant quite literally that the household was a polity, like other polities and that it, like other polities was governed."[52]

This feudal system of government was one of shared jurisdiction. The king ceded certain matters of local governance to towns. And likewise, towns and even the court system ceded some jurisdiction to the head of the household. The household unit also included employees who lived in the master's residence, such as servants and apprentices.[53] These individuals also fell within the master's jurisdiction.[54]

The master had the right to direct a servant's activities (the "right to control").[55] The master could also enforce his will through violence or the threat of violence—a form of police power that is otherwise reserved to the state—because he was considered the sovereign of the household (the "right to govern").[56] Individuals who were not affiliated with a household and not otherwise economically independent could be punished through vagrancy laws that forced them into service.[57] Local governments enforced vagrancy laws and other poor laws because it relieved them of the obligation to support the poor, having nominally shifted that obligation onto the master (the "duty of support").[58]

This book illustrates the ways in which modern employment law and workplace practices have been influenced by a related set of concepts known as the "master-servant doctrine." Broadly, the doctrine stands for the idea that the state defers to the authority of the employer to govern those within the workplace.[59] From this authority, employers derive (1) the *right to exercise control* over workers, and (2) the *right to govern* the workplace. In turn, employers have (3) a *duty to provide material support* to workers, in the form of wages or benefits.

Throughout this book, I also use the term "master-servant system," which refers to the respects in which the state relies upon employers to deliver social welfare benefits, the incentives that push individuals toward employment relationships rather than other forms of work,[60] and the ways in which employers exploit the dependence of the state—and of workers themselves—to retain power and authority over the workplace. In doing so, I am not suggesting that American employment arrangements are inherently feudal in nature. On the contrary, examples throughout this book illustrate the respects in which master-servant concepts ultimately align with capitalism and have been successfully leveraged by corporate employers to resist legislative efforts to constrain their power and authority.

## CONTEXT FOR THIS BOOK

Researchers have examined master-servant concepts in a variety of contexts, principally with reference to concepts of servitude. Political scientist Karen Orren documented the feudal influence of master-servant principles on judicial rulings over hundreds of years.[61] Legal historians such as Christopher Tomlins, Lea VanderVelde, and James Schmidt analyzed master-servant principles in nineteenth-century labor and employment law.[62] Historian Amy Dru Stanley examined the relationship between master-servant principles, contract law, and the subordination of women in the nineteenth century.[63] Legal historian Catherine Fisk noted the historical influence of master-servant principles on intellectual property law in the workplace.[64] And labor historian Jean-Christian Vinel conducted in-depth research on the development of the term "employee" and how it came to replace older master-servant terminology in American law.[65]

Contemporary legal scholars also make frequent references to master-servant principles in law review articles, often as background context to explain a particular principle of current law.[66] Legal scholar James Atleson devoted the most sustained attention to the continued influence of master-servant principles in a 1983 book on modern labor law (the law governing labor unions, labor organizing, and collective bargaining).[67] Atleson argued that many of the "underlying assumptions" of labor law derive from master-servant principles, and that these old ideas account for "many decisions which otherwise seem odd, irrational, or at least inconsistent with the received wisdom."[68]

Building on that prior scholarship, this book aims to explore the influence and remarkable hold of master-servant concepts in a broader and more expansive manner across American employment law. Secondarily, the book highlights a theme that has received relatively less sustained attention in prior scholarship: the complicated relationship between master-servant law and slavery.[69]

Slavery was not solely a property regime; it was also a labor regime. Indeed, recent work by historians (discussed in chapter 1) treats slavery as a violent and racialized form of capitalist labor exploitation.[70] Although the law of slavery was distinct from other areas of American law, it was not entirely sealed off.[71] Instead, it formed a part of the broader historical ecosystem of labor regulation in the United States. Southern courts readily applied master-servant concepts to slavery without regard to whether it technically conformed to English common law.[72]

In this way, the law of slavery became an extreme variant of master-servant law.[73] The law of slavery was also relevant to free workers, as legal scholar Lea VanderVelde argued, because it served as an unspoken comparator for all other employment rights in the antebellum South.[74]

Historian Nell Irvin Painter thus advises "recast[ing] the labor history of the United States" by "including enslaved workers as part of the American working classes."[75] Doing so both informs and enlivens the broader picture, not just to the suffering that enslaved people experienced, but also to their voices, contributions, and achievements. Consequently, this book includes slavery as relevant historical context for understanding the master-servant doctrine, along with other historical examples from the nineteenth and twentieth centuries, as well as more contemporary case studies.

OVERVIEW OF CHAPTERS

The book proceeds in three parts, each devoted to a different component of the master-servant doctrine: the right to control (part I), the right to govern (part II), and the duty of support (part III). While the book is organized topically, each part is organized roughly chronologically, with the oldest historical material appearing in earlier chapters within that part.

Part I begins with an exploration of the most overt manifestation of the master-servant doctrine—the employer's right to control—and in particular, workplace incursions on bodily integrity. Chapter 1 explains how modern law gives employers nearly exclusive control over the workplace, using meatpacking workers at Tyson Foods as a modern case study. It summarizes the modern "control test" for employment status and provides historical context for understanding violence and danger in the workplace.

Chapter 2 focuses on the employer's right to terminate the employment relationship, as illustrated by *Guz v. Bechtel*, a famous California case involving an office worker laid off in a corporate reorganization. The chapter explores the implicit connection between slavery, antebellum contract law for free workers, and the subsequent rise of the employment-at-will doctrine, which enables companies to terminate employees without notice and for any reason.

Chapters 3 and 4 examine more subtle manifestations of control based on pay and time management. Chapter 3 describes how industrial employers used pay rates to control employee productivity, by revisiting the famous "Hawthorne experiments" of the 1920s, in which scientists monitored female factory workers. In the early twentieth century, employers retained control over pay through court rulings declaring wage and hour laws unconstitutional. The chapter then recounts the history of the 1938 Fair Labor Standards Act (FLSA)—which mandates minimum wage and overtime pay—and describes how the law was pared back to accommodate racial and gender-based hierarchies.

Chapter 4 illustrates employer resistance and adaptation to legal rules, enabling them to reassert control over workers. Following the passage of the FLSA, employers shifted their focus from controlling worker pay to controlling time. Worker time became an asset to be maximized. The chapter compares legal conceptions of working time—as illustrated in the 1946 Supreme Court decision in *Anderson v. Mt. Clemens*—to Taylorism and scientific management. It also contrasts the Japanese concept of *kaizen* and just-in-time production with the American implementation of those ideas at Amazon.

Part II explores employer claims to exclusive governance over the workplace, that is, the power to set workplace policies and other terms and conditions of employment, as well as the processes by which hiring, firing, compensation, and promotion occur. Two landmark pieces of twentieth-century legislation are discussed: the National Labor Relations Act of 1935 (NLRA) and Title VII of the Civil Rights Act of 1964 (Title VII), which imposed important limits on employer sovereignty. But like the FLSA, companies have persistently undermined those limits through a combination of litigation and management practices.

Chapter 5 is devoted to the NLRA, which limits employer governance by empowering unions to bargain collectively over the terms and conditions of work. However, to reap the full benefits of the NLRA, employees must vote to join a union. In 2024 only 9.9 percent of American workers were members of a union.[76] Chapter 5 recounts the rise and fall of union membership in the United States since the late nineteenth century, using Starbucks as a contemporary case study.

Chapter 6 and 7 are devoted to Title VII, which prohibits discrimination on the basis of "race, color, religion, sex, or national origin."[77] The law constrains employer governance by regulating discriminatory hiring, firing, promotion, and compensation decisions. However, Title VII did not force employers to restructure segregated worksites or implement merit-based systems. Chapter 6 uses military contractor Lockheed Martin to illustrate the respects in which antidiscrimination law rewarded employers for routinizing and documenting their employment practices. The chapter covers the development of Title VII jurisprudence and the limited reach of even favorable Supreme Court cases like *Griggs v. Duke Power* and *McDonnell Douglas v. Green*.

Chapter 7 places Title VII jurisprudence within the broader context of the growth of human resources policies and complaint systems, using *Bostock v. Clayton County* as a case study. The chapter traces the origins of those systems and explains why they predominantly serve to produce valuable documentation to defend against litigation.[78] In the context of harassment claims, master-servant principles operate through judicial deference to internal processes and policy. In discrimination law, courts tend to look beyond formal polices and processes to assess the motives of the manager responsible for the decision. Even so, master-servant principles apply through a variety of doctrines that defer to managerial prerogative in employment decisions.

Part III examines the role of the duty of support within the broader master-servant system. Chapter 8 returns to the law of slavery, describing how slavery apologists falsely portrayed the institution as a reciprocal relationship based on the enslaver's duty to provide material sustenance. Although the true dependency ran in the other direction—enslavers were economically dependent upon the revenue produced by the labor of enslaved people—the duty of support served as rhetorical justification for governance and control over enslaved people.

In a modern context, "an extraordinary range" of social welfare benefits are channeled through "work relationships,"[79] like sick leave, vacation pay, family leave, unemployment insurance, retirement savings, and most of all, health care. This structure creates state dependence on corporate employers to relieve the financial burden of social welfare benefits. Individuals likewise rely on employers to deliver those benefits. Both forms of dependency confer power on the employer and justify corporate claims of sovereignty over workers.

Chapter 8 examines this facet of the system on a small scale, noting the ways in which employers have used workplace benefits to control workers inside and outside the workplace since the nineteenth century. Chapter 9 considers the problem more broadly by examining the gig economy and what it reveals about the incentives that companies face, the choices and desires of gig workers, and cultural attitudes toward independent work.

Chapter 10 examines how employment law might be reformed without inadvertently conferring additional power on employers through the imposition of additional social welfare obligations. The chapter uses

Obamacare as a case study for this principle and proposes several legal reforms.

Although the ecosystem of employment laws has changed many times since the Civil War, the continued influence of the master-servant doctrine is discernible wherever we continue to see employer discretion unchecked. Employers aggressively defend their sovereign territory from legislative intervention. Even when they fail, companies resist accountability through the development of favorable case law and management practices that reassert control and authority.

This book charts the territory that employers have claimed over time and questions whether we have ceded too much ground to the companies that govern our lives at work.

. . .

Before proceeding, it is worth noting a few methodological limitations and qualifications. First, the case studies in this book do not reflect a random or representative subset of all leading employment law cases. They reflect the practical realities of the attorneys and parties I was able to locate, the willingness of individuals to speak on the record, and the accessibility of briefs and supporting documents many years after a case was litigated. In several cases—identified in the endnotes—I did not receive a response from attorneys representing the employer, or the company did not give its attorney permission to speak with me. For those cases, the perspective of management can only be inferred from the arguments the attorneys made in briefs.

Second, this book is not a comprehensive legal historical treatment of American employment law. Instead, it attempts to translate and synthesize legal history for modern legal audiences, with a particular focus on the historical context relevant to landmark legislative and jurisprudential developments in employment law. As such, important dimensions of labor history do not receive the depth of treatment they would deserve in a more comprehensive format, particularly relating to immigrant labor; feminist histories; and the roles of Latin Americans, Asian Americans, and Native Americans in shaping the workplace and labor struggles over time. Nevertheless, it is my hope that the historical context provided in this book sparks readers to further explore the rich scholarly literature presenting other historical windows into the American working experience.[80]

PART I

# The Right to Control

CHAPTER 1

# Physical Control

If any American company should have been prepared for the COVID-19 epidemic, it was Tyson Foods. One of the largest global food companies,[1] Tyson Foods had chicken processing operations in China when COVID first surfaced in January 2020.[2] According to a lawsuit filed against the company, Tyson quickly implemented a variety of stringent COVID-related protocols at its Chinese operations by February 2020, including "masks ... temperature checks ... air filtration ... quarantine," and social distancing in "cafeterias and break rooms."[3]

When COVID arrived in the United States, the company was remarkably slow to implement protections for American meatpacking workers. On March 20 an internal memo containing "key messages" for Tyson workers made no reference to safety protocols beyond a promise that they would "soon" conduct temperature checks and emphasized that frontline workers should "come to work as planned, despite stories about 'shelter in place.'"[4]

In early April local officials in Waterloo, Iowa, became alarmed by growing evidence of community spread in connection with a nearby Tyson pork processing plant.[5] The local emergency management commission, led by the county's public health director, Nafissa Cisse Egbuonye, traced an outbreak in a nursing home to staff members with family who worked at the Tyson plant.[6] The commission requested a tour of the plant.[7]

Sheriff Tony Thompson served on the emergency commission. He visited the plant on April 10 and recalled that the tour was curated to reflect what Tyson wanted them to see.[8] Even so, he was shocked by the scene: workers "elbow to elbow" and "working over the top of each other."[9] He explained, "[B]ecause the line moves so quickly, there is no personal space. [Workers] have seconds to do whatever [they] are responsible for on that carcass."[10] Thompson noticed Tyson lacked even basic protocols such as hand sanitizer, which could be readily procured at that time.[11] They saw "people wearing bandanas, not masking at all, [or] using sleep masks as masks."[12]

The commission begged the company to shut down the plant for twenty-four to forty-eight hours in order to sanitize the plant and implement new protocols.[13] Officials also offered to help procure protective equipment.[14] Tyson declined. Thompson concluded the company "truly believed they were too big to be governed at a local level."[15]

Many of the workers at the plant were refugees who relied on Tyson interpreters to translate for them.[16] Attorney Mel Orchard, who represents plaintiffs in several lawsuits against the company, explained, "We had lots of workers who were not sure about what was happening . . . and most of them don't have access to media and television."[17] Orchard claims that management instructed interpreters to reassure workers that everything was fine.[18]

As COVID spread throughout the plant, several managers started a betting pool on the number of workers who would test positive.[19] A subsequent congressional investigation revealed that nearly twelve hundred of the plant's twenty-eight hundred workers were infected.[20] On April 21 the company finally decided to shut the plant down temporarily—not for safety reasons but because it didn't have enough healthy workers to stay open.[21]

Five workers at the Waterloo plant died of COVID. They included Sedika Buljic, a Bosnian refugee; Félicie Joseph, a fifty-nine-year-old mother and Haitian refugee who held various butchering jobs at the plant;[22] and José Ayala, a forty-four-year old Texas native who worked as a mechanic at the plant.[23] Ayala's brother described him as inquisitive and high-energy: "always on the move, always doing something."[24] As a child, Ayala carefully disassembled the family video game system and VCR.[25] In Iowa, he "kept a garden with cherry and peach trees, cilantro and tomatoes."[26]

Ayala's family had hoped to visit in recent years but couldn't afford to travel. They stayed in touch over the phone.[27] In any event, COVID protocols prohibited Ayala's family from entering the hospital.[28] Like countless families at the time, their final words to Ayala occurred over a video call.[29]

Their estates sued Tyson for fraudulent misrepresentation, vicarious liability, and punitive damages.[30]

## THE RIGHT TO CONTROL

Part I of this book examines the different ways in which employers exercise control over the workplace today and in decades past. Control is the essence of the employment relationship, both as a practical matter and—in many cases—as a legal matter. Virtually all legal protections available to workers today are limited to those who qualify as "employees," including unemployment insurance, workers' compensation, antidiscrimination protections, wage and hour laws, whistleblower protections, and workplace benefits.[31] By contrast, independent contractors are entitled to no more than what the contract says they are owed.

Legislators and regulatory agencies are free to define who qualifies as an employee for the purpose of particular legal rights.[32] A law or regulation might define "employee" based on whether the worker is economically dependent on the business or has a separate business entity. However, if the statute does not offer a meaningful definition of employee, courts will apply what is known as the common law "control" test, addressed in a 1992 Supreme Court ruling, *Nationwide v. Darden*.[33]

The case involved a dispute between an insurance company and one of its longtime agents, Robert Darden, who began selling competitor policies after Nationwide terminated his contract of eighteen years. During that period, Darden accrued nearly $100,000 in retirement benefits,[34] which the company refused to pay, claiming Darden had violated a noncompete provision.[35] Darden sued under a 1974 law, the Employee Retirement Income Security Act (ERISA), which protected employee retirement benefits from forfeiture. However, ERISA only covers employees, and Nationwide claimed Darden was an independent contractor.

In deciding Darden's case, the Supreme Court resorted to the common law control test to determine whether he qualified as an employee.[36] The multifactor test examines whether the company has the right to exercise control over the "manner and means" by which the work is performed.[37] The test considers the worker's skill level, the location of the work, whether the company supplies tools, who sets the hours of work, and the duration of working relationship. The test also considers whether the work is part of the company's regular business, whether the company can assign additional projects, and whether the worker can hire their own assistants.[38]

The test serves to detect sources of employer power, as those forms of power have been exercised by employers over time: control over the physical premises, work assignments, pay, and hours.[39] The control test and related legal tests are also trying to detect the presence of[40]—to quote the Supreme Court in *Darden*—a "master-servant relationship,"[41] as opposed to more traditional artisanal relationships, in which the artisan operated independently. In the same way that feudal English laws made a distinction between independent tradespeople and unemployed "vagrants," the control test seeks to distinguish an individual who derives their livelihood from wage labor from one who is economically independent. As labor historian Jean-Christian Vinel explained, "[R]emnants of feudalism were ... visible in Post-Civil War labor law" through the "employer's right to control the work of those they employed."[42]

This chapter considers the most overt and oldest form of workplace domination: physical control over workers. It provides historical context for a modern legal regime that gives employers jurisdiction over workers themselves, primarily through control over a physical environment that can threaten the health or safety of workers. As the Tyson Foods case illustrates, many nonunionized workers have surprisingly few legal avenues to protect their bodies from external threats posed by the workplace.[43] Under modern law, workers' compensation regimes provide a remedy for workers after they are injured but afford them no say in the prevention of such injuries. Likewise, the federal Occupational Safety and Health Act of 1970 imposes certain safety-related rules that can only be enforced by the government and do not provide a self-help remedy for workers.

The paternalistic legal framework of modern workplace safety laws can be traced to older legal ideas, in particular, master-servant principles under British common law, which gave the master a measure of sovereignty over the bodies of servants. The law of slavery represented an extreme application of this general concept, authorizing extreme violence against enslaved people on the basis of the enslaver's purported sovereignty over the enslaved.[44] Since the Civil War, the primary bodily harms that workers face are workplace hazards and injuries. Nevertheless, the legal regime that would emerge in response to the problem of industrial accidents—workers' compensation—has surprising parallels to the law of slavery.

## SOVEREIGNTY OVER THE BODY

Perhaps the best illustration of a master's sovereignty over a servant comes from eighteenth-century jurist William Blackstone.[45] Under traditional British common law, Blackstone explained, a master had quasi-police powers over his workers, which served as an exception to tort law, which would have otherwise authorized the worker to bring an assault or battery claim against a violent master.[46]

The master's jurisdiction over the servant conferred upon him the state's right to engage in violence against the servant. The law treated violence by the master as a form of punishment, authorized by his status as the king of his familial empire.[47] A master who struck his wife or child was the legal equivalent of a police officer throwing a pickpocket in jail. It was within his jurisdiction.[48]

The English master-servant system imposed some limits on workplace violence. A master could "correct" an apprentice through force but was "not entitled to beat his apprentice."[49] If such "correction" proved insufficient, the master could bring a claim to the justice of the peace, who could minister further "due Correction and Punishment."[50] Likewise, masters were authorized to moderately "chastise" a servant "for negligence or other misbehavior."[51]

The United States inherited its legal precedent, known as the common law, from Britain. But American jurists treated British law less like scripture and more like a salad bar, picking and choosing the parts they found useful.[52] In the American context, the master's police power to engage in assault and battery as a form of "correction" proceeded on two tracks, with one set of rules applying to free white workers and another applying to enslaved Black workers.

The historical trajectory for white workers in the United States was of increasing worker protection from corporal punishment at the hands of the employer. According to scholar Robert Steinfeld, courts started placing limits on employer violence against white adults in the eighteenth century,[53] and by the nineteenth century they started intervening to protect minors as well.[54] For example, in 1805 a court in the District of Columbia overturned a local justice's decision to whip an Irish indentured servant for running away.[55] Similarly, a Pennsylvania court in 1828 declared that a factory overseer could not strike a white fourteen-year-old with a leather strap.[56]

The legal regime was vastly different as applied to enslaved Black workers. As historian Nell Irvin Painter observed, "[S]lavery rested on the threat and the abundant use of physical violence" such that "any sojourn in southern archives covers the researcher in blood."[57] Indeed, enslaver violence against enslaved people was authorized by law. "Unconditional submission is the general duty of the slave," wrote a North Carolina court, "unlimited power is, in general, the legal right of the master."[58] Even laws prohibiting the murder of enslaved people included an exception for "death ... by accident in giving such slave moderate correction."[59]

Enslavers had virtually unlimited power to engage in violence because they had a legal status on a par with the state itself with respect to enslaved people they owned. The 1857 Supreme Court decision *Dred Scott v. Sanford* can be understood as an articulation of the master-servant doctrine under slavery.[60] In that case, the Supreme Court refused citizenship to Dred Scott, an enslaved man who lived in free territory with his enslaver for some years before being moved back to Missouri.[61] The Court went to great lengths to examine the source of citizenship as understood by the framers of the Constitution.[62] Citizenship and its associated rights and freedoms, the court declared, is a privilege granted by the state,[63] and the founders declined to confer citizenship on African American slaves.[64] Instead, the framers delegated sovereignty to enslavers, who stood in the shoes of the state to govern enslaved people within their jurisdiction.[65]

In this conception of the law, the enslaver's right with respect to slaves like Mr. Scott was implicitly the right of the sovereign (the enslaver) to retain jurisdiction over his subject (the enslaved person) even when traveling to a state or territory that does not recognize slavery.[66] Thus, the master stood on equal footing to the state itself—like a treaty between Canada and the United States.[67]

Other aspects of the law and ideology of slavery conceived of the enslaver as a sovereign. For example, the president of the Mississippi Planter's College, E. N. Elliott, proclaimed, "The master, as the head of the system, has a right to the obedience and labor of the slave, but the slave has also his mutual rights in the master.... He has also a right in his master as the sole arbiter in all his wrongs and difficulties, and as a merciful judge and dispenser of law to award the penalty of his misdeeds."[68] Here, the master stands in for the state itself, the "dispenser of law" with a monopoly on violence. The enslaved person had no meaningful recourse or protection through the state. "Plantation spaces were, in a sense 'privatized'" writes historian Caitlin Rosenthal, "held outside the law but within the master's control."[69]

Southern judges likewise assigned quasi-sovereign status to enslavers, insisting in many instances that the court had no power to intervene in cases of enslaver violence. Instead, courts deferred to the master's judicial decisions over his domain. "That there may be particular instances of cruelty and deliberate barbarity, where, in conscience the law might properly interfere, is most probable," wrote South Carolina Judge Ruffin, "But we cannot look at the matter in that light... The slave, to remain a slave, must be made sensible, that there is no appeal from his master; that his power is in no instance usurped[.]"[70]

The enslaver's ultimate authority was a lived reality for enslaved people. Abolitionist Frederick Douglass was enslaved as a child. His enslaver, Colonel Lloyd, presided over an estate with twenty farms.[71] "The seat of government" was Lloyd's home plantation, wrote Douglass, "All disputes among the overseers were settled here. If a slave was convicted of any high misdemeanor, became unmanageable, or evinced a determination to run away, he was brought immediately here, severely whipped ... and sold to [a] slave-trader, as a warning to the slaves remaining."[72] So complete was the master's jurisdiction over enslaved people that those who went to other plantations at night to visit their spouses were said to be going "abroad."[73]

In summary, the law of slavery served as the ultimate extreme of the master-servant doctrine, wherein courts delegated jurisdiction and sovereignty wholesale to the enslaver.

## THE ECONOMICS OF VIOLENCE

Popular culture tends to depict violence against enslaved people as arbitrary and sadistic, a system that indulged the bloodlust of the worst actors. This portrayal obscures the economic purpose that violence served: to extract the labor of enslaved people and line the pockets of enslavers. As legal historian William Fisher observed, "[A]ll aspects of slave law were shrewdly designed to serve the interests of the master class—specifically, to enable masters to extract as much labor as possible from their slaves, to enhance masters' ability to discipline their slaves, and to protect masters' property interests in their slaves."[74]

Violence was routine. It was planned, threatened, and meted out in combination with other management techniques to maximize profit. Violence was such an integral part of the machinery of slavery that enslavers in Charleston, South Carolina, could outsource their whipping to the county jail or the workhouse "for a fee."[75]

Research by historians Edward Baptist and Caitlin Rosenthal illustrates the ways in which enslaver violence served the profit motive. Overseers whipped the fastest cotton pickers with the greatest frequency, on the premise that they had the most potential to accelerate further.[76] Overseers also assigned enslaved workers a daily picking quota. If the worker came up "short" of the quota, the overseer demanded repayment by whip.[77] One witness wrote, "The overseer meets all hands at the scales, with lamp, scales and whip. Each basket is carefully weighed and the nett [sic] weight of cotton set down upon the slate, opposite the name of the picker."[78] In a later testimonial, a formerly enslaved woman named Adeline reported that she "couldn't stand to watch clerks weighing the meat she bought at the grocery store,"[79] because it reminded her of the daily cotton reckoning.[80]

Enslaved workers tended to calibrate their picking speed to barely exceed the quota, lest their quota be increased. Enslavers raised the quota anyway.[81] Through this "calibrate[d] torture" enslavers extracted a 400 percent rise in productivity per worker between 1790 and 1860[82]—from an average of twenty-eight pounds per day to more than one hundred.[83] Some enslaved workers picked far more. Plantation records revealed that an enslaved man in Natchez, Mississippi, named Oskar picked 3,160 pounds of cotton over the course of a week, which would have yielded $474 in revenue (nearly $14,000 in today's dollars) for the enslaver.[84]

Enslavers also used violent threats in combination with surveillance, and occasionally rewards, to alter the behavior of enslaved workers on plantations. One such technique involved placing the fastest worker at the front of the picking row and forcing others to keep up. Not only did this method impose an unforgiving pace, it enabled overseers to surveil many workers at once by visually identifying breaks in the line.[85] Another tactic consisted of offering a prize—such as money or sugar—to the worker who could pick the most.[86] The contest was a ruse to figure out a worker's maximum picking speed, which could then be used to set quotas enforced by the whip.[87]

Enslaved workers did not always comply with attempts to control their behavior, despite the grave risks associated with resistance.

Historian Mary Turner characterized such acts of resistance as "forms of collective labour bargaining customarily associated with industrial wage labourers."[88] For example, experienced workers generally recognized the true purpose of picking contests and would warn others not to fall for the ruse.[89] On other occasions, enslaved workers engaged in covert slowdowns, a practice that landscape architect Frederick Olmsted observed during a visit to the South. Olmstead referred to the slowdowns as "sogering"—"pretending to work, and accomplishing as little as possible."[90] Enslaved workers were careful about how and when they sogered.[91] Enslaved women who cooked or cleaned in the enslaver's household, for example, would serve meals to out-of-town guests at irregular times by pretending they couldn't read the household clock.[92]

Historian Caitlin Rosenthal analyzed preprinted accounting books that enslavers used to track productivity.[93] The books contained "daily record of cotton picked," which listed each enslaved person's name, the weight of the daily picking, and the week's total.[94] "On plantations," she wrote, "the soft power of quantification supplemented the driving force of the whip."[95] Rosenthal, who previously worked as a management consultant, concluded that large plantations were not so far off from big business as we might assume: enslavers "built large and complex organizations, conducted productivity analysis akin to scientific management, and developed an array of ways to value and compare human capital."[96]

## PERIL AT WORK

Emancipation and the Thirteenth Amendment removed physical violence from the available legal methods for influencing workers' behavior. However, it did not remove workers from danger.

In the decades following the Civil War, the United States transformed from a primarily agricultural society—in which most people lived and worked on farms—to an industrialized country where workers traded their time and sweat for wages.[97] In an industrial workplace, the primary threat to bodily integrity was industrial accidents.

In the first decade of the twentieth century, one in every fifty workers suffered a fatal or potentially disabling injury at work.[98] A 1912 study estimated that accidental injuries caused 82,500 deaths per year.[99]

Unlike slavery, industrial injury and death was not visited exclusively on African Americans. Black workers were commonly excluded from coveted industrial jobs, even though skilled Black tradespeople vastly outnumbered their white counterparts in the South at the end of the Civil War.[100] As historian John Hope Franklin observed, their employment prospects tended to be limited "to perform[ing] the domestic chores for the white men and women who found jobs in the new stores, factories, and mills."[101]

The problem of industrial accidents was not that injury and death were impossible to avoid. According to legal historian John Fabian Witt, companies simply had no incentive to invest in safer machinery.[102] Injured workers (or surviving family members) who attempted to bring tort claims against employers faced hostile courts that erected a variety of legal doctrines meant to limit their prospects.[103] For example, in an influential 1842 case, *Farwell v. Boston and Worcester Rail Road*, Massachusetts Supreme Court Justice Lemuel Shaw declared that workers had no recourse for injuries caused by the negligence of coworkers, a principle that came to be known as the "fellow servant doctrine."[104]

The *Farwell* decision presumed an excess of freedom and choice on the part of individual workers. Justice Shaw claimed that workers like Farwell, who lost a hand in a railroad accident, accepted the risk of dangerous jobs and received higher wages in exchange.[105] Workers should also avoid injury by "observ[ing] ... the conduct of others ... giv[ing] notice of any misconduct ... and leav[ing]" if they aren't satisfied with working conditions.[106] As Witt argues, the ruling reflected the ideology of free labor, which drew a sharp distinction between paid labor and slavery.[107]

Companies took advantage of the weak tort system and continued to use dangerous equipment.[108] Railroads, for example, could have used lighter railroad cars, as the British did.[109] Instead, American railroad companies hired manual hand brake operators, who sat atop the train to run the brakes and were frequently injured or killed in the process.[110] A departmental record book from the Switchmen's Union of North America hinted at the grisly deaths and injuries, including various forms of being "run over" by a car or train. It also included vague references to "railroad accidents," "amputation of leg," and a "fractured skull."[111]

In the early 1900s some industrial employers started offering workers' compensation insurance as a workplace benefit, which would compensate them for injuries or death regardless of fault. Those decades represented a period of experimentation with workplace benefits, which companies used to improve morale and deter union organizing.[112] However, unlike other popular benefit offerings of the time, workers' compensation insurance rapidly transformed into a legal mandate under state law. By 1920 some forty-two states had adopted a workers' compensation statute.[113] Through workers' compensation, injured workers could receive guaranteed benefits in the event of a work-related injury. However, they would also be barred from bringing a claim in court. Scholars today sometimes refer to this trade-off as the "grand bargain" of workers compensation law.[114]

Witt's extensive historical study of the history of workers' compensation law suggests that state legislators viewed the laws as a modern solution to an industrial problem.[115] An influential 1910 report by labor advocate Crystal Eastman advocated importing a no-fault system for workplace injuries from Western Europe.[116] Workers' compensation was also presented as a form of "scientific management"—part of a broader effort, discussed in greater detail in chapter 4—to improve efficiency in the workplace through greater managerial control.[117] Workers' compensation further promised to restore the injured family man to his former status as a breadwinner for his otherwise destitute wife and dependent children.[118]

While Western Europe's no-fault system offered an appealing narrative from a marketing standpoint, it was not the only legal precedent available to state lawmakers. In 1900, seven years before Eastman released her report, labor lawyer Isaac Hourwich testified before the U.S. Industrial Commission on fixing the problem of industrial accidents. Hourwich proposed "a brutally frank" approach to reforming tort law: to treat injured workers' claims "as [they] would be treated in the old days of slavery."[119] That is, if a "slave was injured, it was so much injury to the owner of the slave."[120] Unsurprisingly, Hourwich's pitch does not seem to have caught on politically.[121]

Whatever its rhetorical deficiencies, Hourwich's argument was legally sound. The closest American legal antecedent to the workers' compensation system was the law of slavery. Enslavers commonly leased enslaved workers to third parties for a fixed period in exchange for a fee.[122] Through third-party hiring, enslaved workers could be assigned to dangerous jobs on steamboats, railroads, sawmills, or ironworks.[123] When those workers were severely injured or killed in the course of that dangerous work, the enslaver would sue the third-party hirer for the loss in value associated with the injury or death.[124]

Southern law generally favored the enslaver's claim against the third-party hirer and did not recognize the various tort doctrines that enabled industrial employers to escape liability.[125] As a Georgia court explained in the 1846 case of *Scudder v. Woodbridge*, a tort defense like the "fellow servant doctrine" was impractical in the context of slavery.[126]

Enslaved workers could not meaningfully object to their working conditions; they "dare not interfere with the business of others" and must instead "silently serve out their appointed time ... submitting to whatever risks and dangers are incident to employment."[127]

In assigning fault among an absent enslaver, an enslaved worker, and the third-party hirer who directed the worker to perform the dangerous task, Southern courts considered third-party hirers the most blameworthy. In that sense, today's workers' compensation system echoes the law of slavery: it allocates liability to the party that controls the work environment (the employer) and does so without an intensive fact-based inquiry into the immediate cause of the accident.

The law of slavery offered no benefits to the enslaved person or their surviving family. It only protected the economic interests of enslavers. By contrast, workers' compensation pays the affected worker. The workers' compensation system also proved more effective at reducing injury than the prior tort system because it gave employers an incentive to invest in safety measures. By 1920 both fatal and nonfatal injuries were cut by half or more.[128]

Yet the parallel between the law of slavery and workers' compensation illustrates the passivity it assumed—and imposed—on the part of workers then and today.[129] Workers' compensation law imposes no mechanism for employee involvement in injury prevention or complaints about workplace hazards. The workers' compensation system, as in the antebellum case of *Scudder v. Woodbridge*, presumes that workers "silently serve out their appointed time" and apply for benefits after they are injured. Meanwhile, the employer retains control over the worksite.

## THE OCCUPATIONAL SAFETY AND HEALTH ACT

In the path-dependent development of American employment law, legal reforms tend to be either defined in opposition to past law or patched together to fill in the holes. The Occupational Safety and Health Act of 1970 was a gap filler.[130]

Workers' compensation laws provided a remedy for injured workers but no safety requirements for employers. It operates through incentives rather than mandates, which employers can choose to ignore. The 1970 law filled the gap by creating a federal agency, the Occupational Safety and Health Administration (OSHA), which is responsible for issuing workplace safety standards. OSHA imposes both a general duty to provide a safe workplace and highly specific regulations, such as requirements for guard rails and safety nets or toilets in the workplace.[131]

The act treats workplace safety as a matter of expertise. This approach to safety makes a certain amount of sense—a nonexpert might not know how to handle dangerous chemicals or how to limit workers' hearing damage.[132] In doing so, OSHA also incorporated the paternalistic assumptions underlying the workers' compensation system, in which workers do not play an active role.

The law made OSHA exclusively responsible for the enforcement of workplace safety violations through investigations and fines, rather than providing workers with the right to bring a lawsuit against employers with unsafe conditions.[133] An employee's role in the enforcement structure of OSHA begins and ends with a complaint to the agency, which the agency is then responsible for investigating. However, OSHA fines are rarely sufficient to meaningfully deter bad actors or spur employers to step up their compliance efforts.

Neither workers' compensation laws nor OSHA encourages workers to engage in self-help to prevent or address workplace hazards. OSHA does not authorize workers to refuse work in the face of hazardous conditions, because the law assumes they "will ordinarily be corrected by the employer, once brought to his attention."[134] Instead, workers can only walk off the job if the employer fails to fix the problem and the hazard would mean "subjecting himself to serious injury or death."[135] In modern law, only the NLRA assigns workers an active role in workplace safety, empowering unions to strike over safety and for nonunionized workers to act together to address safety conditions.[136]

. . .

In summary, the physical worksite remains a domain over which employers retain substantial power and authority. If the employer is a sovereign, the worksite comprises its territory. Beyond whatever property rights the employer has in the worksite, its sovereignty extends to the workers, the work they perform, and ultimately the hazards they face in doing so.

In a modern context, employer sovereignty is not absolute; workers can invoke government regulation through an OSHA complaint or collectively resist safety hazards under NLRA. Nevertheless, the broader structure of workplace safety law treats workers as passive subjects rather than constituents empowered to hold employers accountable. Workers incur the risk of injury and pay the price with their bodies, to be compensated later through the workers' compensation system. The hazardous pandemic conditions at the Waterloo Tyson plant serve as a case in point.

Because both workers' compensation and OSHA concede physical control over the worksite to employers and limit enforcement for safety violations to OSHA, workers had few viable options to protect themselves from exposure to COVID. OSHA failed to issue emergency regulations during the pandemic, leaving workers to fend for themselves. OSHA also lacked the resources to respond to the thousands of safety complaints that poured in. Indeed, a 2019 report by the AFL-CIO estimated that "federal OSHA has enough inspectors to inspect workplaces only once every 165 years."[137]

Following complaints about the absence of protective equipment and failure to implement social distancing at the Tyson facility, the state OSHA agency conducted an investigation and found no violations.[138] The lawsuit against Tyson has not fared much better: the trial court dismissed the case, concluding the claim was preempted by workers' compensation.[139] If the plaintiffs lose on appeal, the surviving relatives of the Tyson workers who died of COVID would be limited to a fixed recovery through the workers' compensation system.

Sheriff Thompson may have been right that Tyson considered itself beyond local governance. But then again, Tyson was too—the company was in fact exempt from meaningful safety-related oversight.

CHAPTER 2

# Termination

John Guz had "kind of an Abe Lincoln" look, recalled his lawyer, Stephen Murphy; he was "very down to earth," and "honest as can be."[1] In 1971 Guz was hired to work as an administrative assistant at Bechtel National Inc., an engineering company that cleans up environmental disasters and toxic waste. His department provided financial information and forecasts to other departments.[2] Over his twenty-year career at Bechtel, Guz received seventeen merit raises, a promotion, and a performance award "for saving the company $1.7 million."[3]

However, a rival department within the company performed a similar function. In 1992 Bechtel fired Guz, along with everyone else in his department. As Bechtel's outside lawyers explained to me in an interview, the firing wasn't personal.[4] Guz had been a good employee. The company simply needed to be reorganized and "somebody is left standing when the music stops."[5]

California, like other states, had long recognized a principle known as employment-at-will, which authorized the employer to terminate the employment relationship without cause or notice.[6] Employment at-will is a legal presumption that employees have no fixed contract of employment. Instead, courts presume there are no limits on an employee's ability to quit or the company's ability to terminate an employee for any reason at any time.

But California case law in the 1980s and 1990s suggested that workers could overcome the at-will presumption with evidence relating to their performance, their long tenure, oral assurances, and similar evidence.[7] This was known as an "implied-in-fact contract claim" and was the basis for Guz's lawsuit against Bechtel.

Guz claimed his long record of service and track record of success, combined with the company's practice of only terminating workers for cause, meant that the employment-at-will doctrine didn't apply. The company president even admitted at his deposition that employees were only terminated with "good reason" or for "lack of available work."[8]

However, Guz did not have a contract that promised he would only be terminated for cause. Instead, he could only point to a variety of contradictory policies, some of which disclaimed any "employment agreements guaranteeing continuous service," while others promised progressive discipline for poor performers and a ranking system for layoffs.[9]

At the time, implied-in-fact contract claims forced employers to reconsider terminating workers without cause, particularly if the employee was a strong performer with a long history at the company. Paul Cane, one of Bechtel's outside lawyers, recalled that in the 1990s business owners would inquire about potentially firing an employee and ask, "Do I have an implied contract?"[10] Cane couldn't say for sure. The answer depended on too many factors.

Stephen Murphy, now a judge in California, offered a similar analysis of the law at the time. When he took on Guz as a client, Murphy had not lost an implied-in-fact contract case on summary judgment. He had every reason to believe Guz's case could make it to a jury, which would then decide the outcome of the case.[11]

Instead, the case ended up before the California Supreme Court. The case was argued in the old Sacramento courthouse, to commemorate the court's 150th anniversary. "It almost looked like a movie set." Cane recalled.[12] It seemed an incongruous setting for a modern employment dispute. Yet the debate over whether and when employees could be terminated without cause was not so different from similar such cases 150 years prior.

This chapter examines a second dimension of the right to control: control over whether and when employment should be terminated. If the worksite represents the employer's sovereign territory, control over termination represents the power to exile. And although employment-at-will is theoretically reciprocal—an employee can likewise quit at a moment's notice—the historical context relating to the rise of the at-will doctrine illustrates the considerable power that the doctrine gives employers.

## ANTEBELLUM CONTRACT DISPUTES

Today, virtually all American workers are employed at-will. Although at-will arrangements have existed since the early days of the republic—legal historian Deborah Ballam uncovered evidence that free agricultural day laborers preferred at-will arrangements at that time[13]—they were far less common prior to the Civil War.[14] The at-will employment presumption replaced a much more varied legal ecosystem, in which some workers enjoyed much stronger contractual protections from courts than they do today, while others labored under far more coercive conditions.

Antebellum employment law was racially stratified, particularly in the South. Although white workers could be subject to certain unfree employment statuses in the early 1800s, there was no equivalent to slavery for white workers. White workers could be bound to indentured servitude, a contractual arrangement through which an immigrant worker might repay their transatlantic travel costs in exchange for years of service. However, the transatlantic market for European indentured servants collapsed around 1820.[15] Indentured servitude then lingered for a period in Northern states, primarily as a "device gradually to move black people along the spectrum of unfreedom toward complete legal freedom."[16] It also persisted until the mid-nineteenth century through indentured Chinese laborers hired to work in railroads and mining.[17]

In the early 1800s white workers could also be bound to service as an apprentice. Apprenticeship arrangements were typically made between parents and a skilled artisan or tradesperson, who would agree to teach a child or young adult a trade in exchange for unpaid labor, typically lasting seven years.[18] Although apprentices could not leave during the period of their apprenticeship, the arrangement was limited in time and originated in a voluntary contract.[19] Upon completion of their apprenticeship, they gained entry into the privileged ranks of skilled artisans or tradespeople.

In other words, there were certain elements of reciprocity and voluntariness to even the most unfree statuses applied to white workers: a fixed term of service to work off a loan (indentured servitude) or a fixed term of service for training (apprenticeship).

Slavery was neither reciprocal nor time limited. Enslaved people were bound to perpetual unpaid servitude for their lifetimes and the lifetimes of their descendants. Enslavers could sell an enslaved person at any time, without cause and without notice, for any reason or no reason at all. The only meaningful limits on an enslaver's property rights arose from third parties claiming their own property interests in an enslaved person, such as those with future property interests or debtholders.[20]

Within this legal context, at-will employment and fixed term employment contracts were a privileged status. Free white day laborers, for example, preferred at-will status, so they could leave to pursue higher wages.[21] However, fixed term contracts—often for a one-year period—tended to predominate over at-will arrangements among free workers.[22] Fixed term contracts provided "a right to security for both employers and workers" whereby the worker would be entitled to wages if terminated without just cause.[23] Although free workers who left a contract early might forfeit wages for work already performed,[24] they were generally able to walk away.[25]

In deciding contract disputes involving free labor, courts would instruct juries to determine whether the termination decision was reasonable, insisting that the employer "cannot be the final arbiter in his own behalf."[26] Terminations based on poor performance typically required employers to present a pattern of conduct. As Horace Wood explained in his 1877 treatise, "Generally a single act of negligence will not be sufficient. . . . [B]ut it must be habitual rather than occasional" unless great care is required in the job.[27]

This approach was far more protective of workers than a contract dispute involving at-will employment, where the employer's basis for termination is not scrutinized. Instead, both courts and juries served to restrain employer power over the termination of free laborers. They routinely applied their own independent judgment regarding whether a termination was justified, rather than deferring to the employer's proffered reason. Courts also sought to give free workers some latitude to perform work in their own way without risking termination.

For example, in the 1856 Vermont case *Paul v. School District in Hartland*, a teacher successfully sued for breach of contract despite community dissatisfaction with his performance.[28] The Court largely ignored complaints about the teacher, declaring that "in all the relations of life, where it becomes necessary to exercise control over others, complaints will often arise without any just cause."[29] According to the court, an employee who "persist[s] in his right" should be provided a remedy unless the school proves "his incompetency or unfaithfulness."[30] "Dissatisfaction with a teacher, or any one called to exercise authority" should be "considered" but is "no[t] sufficient ground for removal."[31]

Courts protected both white collar workers and manual laborers, such as agricultural workers and domestic servants, from arbitrary discharge before the end of their contract.[32] Servants could be dismissed for acts of moral turpitude, provided those acts "produce[d] an actual injury to the master's business, or [were] of such a character as to operate as a continuous misconduct, and injur[y] . . . to the reputation of his family."[33] Likewise, "if a servant teaches the master's trade, or reveals his secrets to another, this is a violation of the implied provisions of the contract of hiring, and he may be discharged therefor."[34] Disloyalty was a misdeed to be tolerated to a point, beyond which the employer could invoke his right to control and exact punishment.[35]

Within the racial hierarchy of the South, robust contractual protections for free white workers came at the expense of enslaved Black workers. Although slavery was rarely, if ever, mentioned in disputes involving free white workers, it was the unstated reference point against which freedom for white workers was defined.[36] As sociologist Orlando Patterson wrote, "[S]lavery and freedom are intimately connected, [and] contrary to our atomistic prejudices it is indeed reasonable that those who most denied freedom, as well as those to whom it was most denied, were the very persons most alive to it."[37] Unfettered and unreviewable employer decision-making was a central legal feature of slavery. Defining white workers' rights in opposition to that standard meant protecting white workers from unjustified termination.[38]

The racial hierarchy of employment rights under antebellum law is most starkly illustrated through contract claims brought by plantation overseers.[39] Plantation overseers were generally members of the white working class hired on a contract basis by enslavers to supervise and mete out violence against enslaved workers.[40] Although overseers had somewhat fewer contractual rights than workers in the North, both courts and juries placed limits on an enslaver's authority to terminate overseers.[41]

Overseers terminated before the end of their contracted term could expect to reach a jury on the question of whether they were terminated "for sufficient cause."[42] In an 1847 Alabama case, *Martin v. Everett*, an overseer sued for breach of contract when the enslaver terminated him for "inflict[ing] cruel punishment on the defendant's slave" four months prior.[43] The jury awarded the overseer his entire year's wages. The Supreme Court of Alabama agreed, declaring that the enslaver waived his right to terminate the overseer by keeping him on the payroll following his acts of cruelty.[44] In other cases, juries sided with "uncontrollably" violent or even murderous overseers.[45] Appellate courts generally upheld such jury verdicts, although they would sometimes reduce the damage awards.[46]

The law that Southern courts applied to overseers was somewhat anomalous within the broader landscape of the law of slavery. In general, Southern courts protected the interests of wealthy enslavers, which would have meant restricting the rights of overseers.[47] But judicial allegiance to enslavers could not overcome the stringent racial hierarchies that entitled white overseers to protection from their employers. The right to challenge an employer's termination decision was part of what Southern courts considered integral to workplace freedom for white workers.

In summary, antebellum employment law was marked by racial hierarchy and sharp divisions with respect to contractual rights. Particularly in the decades leading up to the Civil War, courts provided stronger contractual protections for free white workers than they do today, partly because white wage laborers occupied a relatively privileged status within the hierarchy of the time.

## JUDICIAL WITHDRAWAL FROM CONTRACT DISPUTES

How did courts shift from protecting wage laborers to deferring completely to employer preferences, allowing companies to terminate workers for any reason without notice? The simplest answer is that the abolition of slavery—enshrined in the Thirteenth Amendment—protects a worker's right to quit.[48] But it doesn't explain how free workers went from having robust contractual protections to a legal presumption that they had no contract at all.

Jurist Horace Wood has been a convenient target of blame for the rise of the at-will presumption,[49] based on two sentences in his 1877 treatise, *The Law of Master & Servant*: "A general or indefinite hiring is prima facie a hiring at will, and if the servant seeks to make it out a yearly hiring, the burden is upon him to establish it by proof. A hiring . . . no time being specified, is an indefinite hiring . . . at the rate fixed for whatever time the party may serve."[50]

However, Wood's treatise also devotes scores of pages to jurisprudence relating to contract disputes. And as previously noted, Wood did not invent at-will employment; it was a common arrangement between farmers and free agricultural day laborers.[51] Historian James Schmidt also documented labor arrangements that resembled at-will employment for northern textile workers,[52] although the contracts were "nominally" for a year and were terminable upon notice.[53]

Legal historian Lea VanderVelde offered an alternate hypothesis: that the decline of corporal punishment for white workers in the decades leading up to the Civil War incentivized employers to locate new ways to exercise control over their workers.[54] "How did workplace corporal punishment reach its quiet end?" she writes. "Perhaps with a substitute: the at-will doctrine."[55] Legal scholar Jay Feinman likewise attributes the rise of the at-will employment doctrine to capitalism, a method for corporate employers to expand their power and influence over workers.[56] However, legal scholar Andrew Morriss conducted an empirical analysis of the timing associated with adoption of the at-will doctrine and found that states that industrialized early did not necessarily adopt the at-will doctrine earlier than others.[57]

My own review of the case law in the decades following the Civil War suggests that adoption of at-will employment was somewhat intermittent and at times punctuated by an intermediary approach, in which courts retreated from aggressive scrutiny over whether the employer had a basis for termination. These in-between cases, decided in the late 1800s, were characterized by a judicial stance of increasing deference toward employers regarding their basis for termination. These cases also illustrate how that judicial withdrawal confers power upon the employer over a worker's daily activities.

The judicial withdrawal from intervention in unjustified terminations occurred slowly and somewhat inconsistently.[58] As late as 1883, a Michigan jury returned a verdict in favor an inept steamboat captain fired for crashing into a bridge.[59] The Michigan Supreme Court upheld the verdict, declaring, "[W]e think there is neither reason nor law for making employers, in such cases, final judges in their own behalf of the propriety of dismissing their employe[e]s during the term of their employment."[60] Likewise, in 1886 a court sided with a worker terminated for disobedience, ruling that employers are not entitled to punish "every act of disobedience ... by the penalty of dismissal."[61]

However, by the 1890s courts were increasingly unwilling to serve as an intermediary between wage laborers and employers. Instead, they began deferring to employer judgments and demands for loyalty and obedience. The 1892 case of *Matthews v. Park Bros.* is emblematic of the shift.[62] The case involved a factory worker terminated for disobeying instructions on how to best degrease the equipment. The trial court judge instructed the jury that Matthews was properly terminated if his disobedience was "willful," defined as "a bad purpose, or has malice."[63]

An appellate court invalidated the instructions, declaring that the trial court judge set the standard for willfulness too high. Any disobedient act that was "intentional or voluntary . . . not accidental" qualified as cause for termination.[64]

The standard articulated by the appellate court in *Matthews*, which presumed that the employer's directives were sound and that any failure to follow those directives was unjustified, was a substantial departure from precedent. Previously, termination for noncompliance with an employer's directives would trigger a fact-based inquiry into the reasonableness of the order, the relative importance of the directive, and whether the employee engaged in a pattern of insubordinate conduct.[65] The *Matthews* case signaled a subtle shift, but one that transferred power and discretion to the employer.

Likewise, in the 1895 Colorado case *Koll v. Bush*, the court adopted a highly deferential stance toward employer judgments. The case involved a dispute between a chef and restaurant owner over a new gas stove.[66] The owner claimed that Koll had been secretly leaving the new gas stove on after dinner service to protest the new equipment. The owner claimed he had confronted Koll "in a very quiet way,"[67] while Koll testified that the owner told him to "pack up your things and get out of here," but changed his mind when the restaurant staff seemed inclined to quit in solidarity.[68]

A jury awarded Koll $413 in damages, which was reversed on appeal. On remand, the trial court ruled that the owner's testimony was "conclusive" on the question of "whether the plaintiff's services were satisfactory."[69] On a second appeal, the appellate court once again ruled for the employer, concluding that Koll breached his contract to "give his entire time and attention to the business for which he is employed and to render good and satisfactory service."[70]

Under antebellum principles of employment law—which the trial court initially followed—cases like *Koll v. Bush* would permit the jury to determine whether the termination was justified.[71] *Koll v. Bush* is notable not just for its departure from precedent but because it removed employer decision-making from scrutiny. The court would now defer to the employer's own assessment of whether termination was justified.

According to the appellate court, the contract was an "agreement on the part of the plaintiff that his services should be satisfactory. To whom [should the services be satisfactory] if not to his employers?"[72] The court then insisted that its involvement would only be justified if the contract included a clause providing for judicial scrutiny over what qualifies as "satisfactory."[73] This interpretation represented a stark departure from courts that ten years before had insisted that employers could not be "final judges in their own behalf."[74]

As with many important legal shifts, the court in *Koll v. Bush* did not acknowledge its departure from precedent. Nevertheless, the opinion reflected a growing judicial concern for preserving the authority of business owners. It wasn't Koll's cooking skills that justified the termination; it was his failure to submit and obey to the commands of the restaurant owner: "The business of defendants was so intimately dependent upon the chief cook and his subordinates that any want of harmony or laxity of discipline was of necessity destructive of business."[75] In this frame, it is not workers who are deserving of protection from overreaching employers, but capitalists whose investment was at risk.

A series of cases from Pennsylvania around 1900 further illustrate the trend in contract disputes. In one case, a salesman was fired for failing to complete his sales route for lack of funds. The court declared his failure to be a form of insubordination: "[W]hen a servant undertakes to do such things as are deemed necessary to advance the interests of his master, it is for the master and not the servant to determine what is necessary."[76]

In another Pennsylvania case, a publishing manager was fired for refusing to switch offices.[77] The court declared that although the plaintiff was "employed to be manager of a department . . . he was to be subordinate to a higher one: that of his employer, the corporation that had reserved to itself the right to supervise all."[78] Likewise, a case involving a tailor who used "profane and disrespectful language" led the court to declare that "[a] master is not compelled to keep an employee, hired for a given term, in his service until the master's business has suffered pecuniary loss."[79] The presence of master-servant language in these cases is noteworthy, particularly as applied to managers and other white collar workers,[80] who would not previously have been considered servants.[81]

The shift in judicial stance has important implications for the right to control. Even though *Koll* and similar cases had not yet adopted an at-will stance, they undermine workers' ability to challenge managerial judgment or exercise independence in their work. Workers who resist managerial command—however unreasonable—will lose both their jobs and the ability to challenge their termination in court. And as corporate employers expand the bases upon which they can rightfully terminate contracted workers for cause, their power to control and direct the activity of workers grows.[82]

The broader context of postbellum race relations may also have hastened the judicial retreat from intervention in contract disputes. Although the cases described here involved white workers, the social status of "wage laborer" was not as privileged as it had been during slavery. Black workers now joined the ranks of wage laborers and faced considerable racial resistance. The 1890s was a period in which Jim Crow laws were ascendant and were validated by the Supreme Court in *Plessy v. Ferguson*.[83] Lynchings were at an all-time high. Civil rights historians refer to the 1890s and early 1900s as the "nadir"—low point—in civil rights, as the progress of Reconstruction was replaced with racial segregation.[84]

Judges may have been less sympathetic to working-class interests once they were untethered from whiteness. As Amy Dru Stanley observed, "Only in the United States did full-scale industrial capitalism develop simultaneously with, and literally alongside, the consolidation and overthrow of chattel slavery."[85]

The intermediary approach to contract disputes did not last. It would prove to be a temporary waystation on the road to at-will employment: the logical extension of judicial retreat from cause determinations. As Andrew Morriss argued, the at-will presumption was attractive to judges because it served as a gatekeeping device.[86] The at-will presumption enabled courts to dismiss contract cases at an early stage, on the basis that there was essentially no contract to adjudicate.

The at-will principle gained considerable momentum in the 1890s.[87] "At some point early in [the twentieth] century," Morriss writes, "the at-will rule became the generally accepted default rule in the United States. A lengthy period of relative quiet ensued."[88] Today, the only state that has not adopted the at-will doctrine in some form is Montana.[89]

## *GUZ V. BECHTEL*

One hundred years later, California contract law drifted, ever slightly, toward contract law resembling that intermediate phase. Although the at-will principle had long been codified in a California statute, a series of cases in the 1980s and 1990s recognized an exception to at-will employment that empowered courts to consider promises and assurances made by employers as potential contracts.

Consequently, John Guz's attorney had good reason to believe that his evidence—a long period of service, exemplary performance, and various raises and promotions from the company—would be enough to create an "implied in fact" contract.

But Guz's evidence fell short.[90] The idea that a termination might be challenged as unjust, even if it was not discriminatory or retaliatory, posed too great a threat to employer authority. In a sprawling forty-four-page decision, the California Supreme Court reminded litigants that the "courts have not deemed it to be their function, in the absence of contractual, statutory or public policy considerations, to compel a person to accept or retain another in his employ."[91] Rather "the privilege [to terminate] is absolute, and the presence of ill will or improper motive will not destroy it."[92]

Guz lost on his claim that he had a right to only be terminated for cause; the company had an absolute right to eliminate his department generally, and his job specifically. The company's "motive and lack of care in doing so are, in most cases at least, irrelevant."[93] Only a thin slice of Guz's lawsuit survived the California Supreme Court: his claim that Bechtel breached its written policies, which included layoff procedures and reassignment assistance.[94]

Following the Supreme Court ruling, the case was remanded to the Court of Appeals to resolve Guz's remaining claim. The parties settled. For how much, Bechtel's lawyers wouldn't say.[95] Either way, Bechtel's lawyers succeeded at protecting their clients' interests. For proof that the *Guz* decision has held up over time, Bechtel's lawyers explained, "[Y]ou just don't see those claims brought anymore."[96]

*Guz v. Bechtel* remains today the most frequently cited case relating to the at-will presumption.[97] As such, the employer's authority to control the workplace, through the looming threat of termination—for any reason, or no reason at all—remains intact.

CHAPTER 3

# Pay

One of the first concepts taught in introductory psychology courses is the "Hawthorne effect": people alter their behavior when they are watched. The Hawthorne effect is considered undesirable in social science. In the ideal world of a social scientist, individuals would be unaffected by supervision, allowing the researcher to change the environment and measure its effect on behavior.

The "Hawthorne effect" was an inadvertent scientific finding. Starting in 1924, the National Research Council organized a series of studies on the effects of lighting on productivity, largely at the urging of electric companies hoping to increase lightbulb sales.[1] An "elite group of academic and industrial engineers" ran the experiments on workers at a subsidiary of AT&T known as Western Electric.[2]

The male scientists did more than experiment with lighting. As Richard Gillespie explains in his book, *Manufacturing Knowledge: A History of the Hawthorne Experiments*, the experiments were a years-long study on productivity, which involved intense scrutiny and observation of a handful of female workers who assembled small electric relays used to amplify telephone signals.[3] The relays were assembled like Lego sets, with workers snapping several pieces together at a breakneck pace.

The experimenters devised an elaborate method to figure out the exact rate at which each woman worked by placing a chute next to each work station. When a worker sent a finished relay down the chute, the relay would engage a lever that left a notch on some ticker tape. The ticker table could be used to quantify each woman's pace of work. Experimenters would then alter some aspect of the working environment and measure its effect on productivity.

The ticker-tape system wasn't so different, however, from the usual method used to calculate pay and productivity at the time, known as "piece-rate" pay. Rather than paying workers for the time that they worked, companies paid workers for the number of pieces they produced. Western Electric even had an employee on staff whose job consisted of analyzing piece-rate production.[4]

The Hawthorne research experiments didn't turn out as planned. Better lighting seemed to have a positive effect on productivity but so did worse lighting. In fact, some assembly workers could maintain high levels of productivity in near darkness—the equivalent of moonlight—because they relied mostly on tactile sensation and muscle memory to do their work. It wasn't lighting, but supervision and scrutiny from the researchers that had the largest effect on behavior.[5]

. . .

Although at-will employment remains a potent source of power and authority for employers, the threat of termination is a blunt instrument. It might ensure compliance with managerial edict but does not necessarily guarantee productivity. Compensation, by contrast, is periodic and variable, and therefore promised to alter behavior on a more regular basis. Control over pay helped to preserve the master-servant right to control workers through measurement, surveillance, punishment, and reward. Absolute employer discretion over pay also helped to preserve gender and racial stratification in the workplace, through discriminatory pay rates.

In the late nineteenth and early twentieth centuries, state legislators attempted to limit employer discretion over wages and hours but were met with aggressive resistance by employers, who challenged those laws in court as unconstitutional. As this chapter recounts, the Supreme Court consistently sided with employers in those lawsuits. Although the courts superficially claimed to be protecting the liberty of workers, other language in the rulings about preserving employer sovereignty reveal their underlying managerial allegiance.

Employers did not ultimately succeed in retaining exclusive power over wage setting. Instead, Congress passed the Fair Labor Standards Act in 1938, which imposed a minimum wage and overtime premium for eligible workers. The FLSA, like the NLRA and Title VII, represents a significant constraint on employer sovereignty. Nevertheless, the FLSA also retained—and thus preserved—certain racial, gender, and class-based hierarchies of the 1930s.

Employers also adapted to the FLSA by shifting from using pay to control worker behavior to a system of managerial surveillance focused on increments of time. These adaptations are the focus of chapter 4. Later chapters will explore employer resistance and adaptation to the NLRA and Title VII. Chapter 5 describes how employers resisted unionization directly through a variety of legal and extralegal practices, while chapter 8 recounts how they did so indirectly through favorable benefits meant to deter workers from joining unions. Employers likewise sought to blunt the impact of Title VII through defensive employment practices, as described in chapters 6 and 7.

### CONTROL THROUGH PAY

In the early twentieth century there were few limits on how employers could pay workers.[6] As described in chapter 2, workers could be employed on an annual or quarterly basis and be paid infrequently. Workers might also be paid a set daily rate for their work.[7]

In an unregulated environment, piece-rate pay was especially attractive to industrial employers.[8] Piece-rate pay originated in preindustrial, artisanal forms of production, in which an artisan or tradesperson would receive raw materials and convert them to the next stage in the production process.[9] For example, a skilled artisan might be compensated for tanning raw leather on a piece-rate basis. Piece rate could also involve "home work," typically craft projects completed by women and compensated as unskilled labor.[10] "Home work" even adapted to industrial forms of production; the Hand Knitcraft Institute, for example, "sold yarn to their ten thousand employees" and then "purchased" it back in the form of knitted infant clothing.[11]

Piece-rate pay enabled industrial employers to share the cost of doing business with workers. Time that workers spent on preparatory tasks, maintaining equipment, or transitions between tasks was effectively unpaid because it did not directly contribute to the completion of a "piece." Likewise, damaged or imperfect pieces, even if not attributable to the worker's mistake, could be unpaid or deducted from a worker's pay. But unlike a preindustrial artisan, an industrial pieceworker in a factory was unlikely to be in a position to negotiate the piece rate or to receive profits from the enterprise.

Industrial employers used the carrot of pay and the stick of discipline to prod workers to produce at a certain pace. Anna Haug, a relay assembler from the Hawthorn experiments, complained, "Out there [on the factory floor, rather than the experiment room], there are too many bosses.... When I didn't make my rate I was afraid to come down the next day."[12] A coworker agreed, recalling how she would "ge[t] bawled out about our rates."[13]

In theory, employees stood to make more money by working quickly. But as legal scholar James Atleson explained, "As employees increased production to take advantage of piece-work rates, the rates were routinely cut back" by employers.[14] Relay assemblers at Western Electric resented the fastest worker, a single woman named Jennie Sirchio, because they worried that the company would reduce the piece rate to match Sirchio's pace of work.[15] Sirchio had no choice but to maximize her take-home wages: she needed the money to support her extended family following her mother's death.[16]

Indeed, supporting a family would have been challenging for a woman like Sirchio. Jobs were segregated by gender, and the unregulated pay rates reflected the social hierarchies of the time. White men's wage rates presumed they were supporting a family, while women's wage rates were presumed to be "pin money," referring to small amounts of money husbands would give their wives for incidental expenses.[17]

In an 1896 article, "A Piece-Rate System," aspiring management consultant Frederick Winslow Taylor challenged the managerial orthodoxy of reducing the piece rate whenever workers increased production.[18] Taylor argued that workers were aware of the practice and maintained a deliberately slower pace to avoid rate cuts.[19] Taylor proposed an alternate two-tiered pay structure: those who produced quickly and in "perfect condition" would receive a premium rate,[20] meant to encourage them to produce to the best of their abilities. Those who produced slowly or in a defective manner would receive a lower rate,[21] meant to encourage them to find a new job.

Managers and investors were skeptical of Taylor's proposal. They considered him a naïve technocrat and worried that his system would increase labor costs.[22] Over time, Taylor developed a better elevator pitch, claiming he could identify the true "scientific" rate at which work could be completed and that his system would discourage workers from unionizing.[23] Instead of labor unrest, Taylor's scientific management promised "a most friendly feeling between the men and their employers."[24]

As discussed in chapter 4, Taylor's ideas would eventually spread. His ideas complemented the broader ascendance of the managerial class in the early twentieth century, when professional middle-class managers supplanted the working-class foremen who previously had managed industrial workers.[25] Taylorism became a shorthand for the idea that managers held the key to worker productivity and that they were best positioned to determine how workers should spend their time.

## PRESERVING EMPLOYER CONTROL OVER PAY

As chapter 2 recounted, the rise of the at-will doctrine in the late nineteenth century can be understood as a judicial shift, in which courts no longer viewed themselves as intermediaries between free workers and employers in contract disputes. Instead, they shifted toward protecting managerial discretion and authority. Judicial allegiance to management continued into the twentieth century in a different domain: wage and hour law.

In the late nineteenth and early twentieth centuries, state legislatures enacted laws to improve working conditions and wages. For example, Illinois passed a law requiring certain industrial employers to pay earned wages within six days.[26] Another Illinois law prohibited factories from employing women for more than eight hours a day.[27] Nebraska passed an overtime law requiring that all nonfarm and nondomestic labor be paid double time after eight hours of work in a day.[28] In 1891 Massachusetts passed a law to prohibit textile mills from withholding workers' wages to punish them for weaving defects.[29]

State courts declared these laws an unconstitutional restriction on the right to contract and the worker's property right in his own labor.[30] "Labor is property," wrote the Illinois Supreme Court, "and the laborer has the same right to sell his labor, and to contract with reference thereto, as has any other property owner."[31] A man's property right in his own labor was meaningless without the freedom to dispose of that labor through contract. "'Liberty' as that term is used in the constitution, means, not only freedom of the citizen from servitude and restraint but . . . the right of every man to be free in the use of his power and faculties, and to adopt and pursue such vocation or calling as he may choose."[32] The Nebraska Supreme Court declared the state's overtime law unconstitutional on similar grounds.[33]

In striking down a law prohibiting wage deductions for weaving mistakes, the Massachusetts Supreme Court seemed particularly aggrieved that the law would limit employer control over employee performance. The law "requires him [the employer], under a penalty, to pay the contract price if the employe[e] does his work negligently, and fails to perform his contract."[34] The court reasoned that an employer should not have to resort to the courts for an employee's "derelictions,"[35] suggesting that the employer instead has a constitutional right to impose sanctions and penalties as they see fit.

This line of judicial thought also extended to the U.S. Supreme Court, exemplified by its 1905 ruling in *Lochner v. New York*.[36] The case involved a New York law that limited the number of hours that bakers could work to ten hours per day and sixty hours per week. New York passed the law following an exposé by a union newspaper describing immigrant-run bakeries in the basements of tenement buildings. The article "included tales of cockroaches on the walls and on baking utensils, flour mixed in a tub that had been used to wash a sick child's clothes[.]"[37]

The Supreme Court declared the New York law an unconstitutional deprivation of "life, liberty, or property without due process of law" under the Fourteenth Amendment.[38] "The right to purchase or to sell labor is part of the liberty protected by this amendment,"[39] wrote Justice Peckham. Capping employee hours impaired both the employee's right to work additional hours for additional wages and the employer's right to hire him for doing so.[40]

Although cloaked in the language of worker freedom, other language in the opinion suggested the Court considered the law an intrusion on the employer's prerogative to govern the workplace. To permit New York to regulate hours, the Court reasoned, would enable the state to "assume the position of a *supervisor, or pater familias*, over every act of the individual."[41] The Court's reference to paterfamilias harkens back to feudal conceptions of master-servant, in which the master was the sovereign of the household. As sovereign, the master held the police power of the state to discipline those within it and to promulgate the internal laws that would apply to the household.

Political scientist Karen Orren blames the judiciary for the continued relevance of master-servant principles, arguing that courts engaged in a "concerted" effort to "defen[d] ... the labor remnant of feudal governance against legislative encroachment."[42] *Lochner* exemplifies Orren's claim.[43] The Court surmises that "the real object and purpose [of the law] were simply to regulate the hours of labor between the master and his employees ... in a private business." However, "the freedom of the master and employee to contract ... cannot be prohibited or interfered with, without violating the Federal Constitution."[44]

Legal scholar Charles McCurdy argued that "freedom of contract" represented a form of constitutional scrutiny that courts applied predominantly to labor and employment law.[45] By contrast, courts treated state restrictions on other types of contracts, such as insurance regulation and debt rules, as "unquestionably constitutional."[46] The Supreme Court's hypocrisy with respect to its commitment to freedom of contract principles is further illustrated by its 1896 decision in *Plessy v. Ferguson* to uphold state segregation laws, which interfered with the rights of both train passengers and train companies to freely contract for tickets regardless of race.[47]

The freedom of contract principles upon which courts invalidated wage and hour laws are substantially more interventionist than the at-will presumption discussed in chapter 2. While the at-will presumption reflects a judicial withdrawal from contract disputes, the freedom of contract cases entailed judicial interference with legislation. Moreover, because freedom of contract cases relied on constitutional grounds, rather than on statutory interpretation or an evidentiary presumption, legislatures could not amend or avoid them. Freedom of contract was nonnegotiable.

By 1918 the Supreme Court had developed a different legal basis for invalidating workplace legislation coming out of Congress: the commerce clause of the Constitution.[48] That clause gives the federal government the right to "regulate commerce ... among the several states," whereas general police powers to enact laws for general health and welfare would be reserved to the states.[49] In other words, if a particular federal law does not relate to interstate commerce (and is not otherwise authorized under another provision of the Constitution), it lies beyond the authority of the federal government.

In *Hammer v. Dagenhart*, the Supreme Court invalidated a federal law that prohibited the transportation of goods produced through child labor.[50] The law was an indirect means of regulating child labor: companies would be discouraged from hiring child labor if the product of their labor could not be transported out of state. The child labor law seemed tailor-made for the constraints imposed by the commerce clause because it only applied when goods crossed state lines. Yet the Court struck down the law because child laborers did not themselves cross state lines.[51]

Even President Franklin D. Roosevelt's early efforts to shore up wages at the height of the Great Depression were felled by the Supreme Court.

In 1933 Congress passed the National Industrial Recovery Act (NRA) to staunch the "downward spiral of hourly earnings."[52] The NRA was relatively modest by modern standards. It enabled the government to convene meetings among industry leaders, labor organizers, and the public to set wage rates, hours rules, child labor restrictions, and safety standards.[53] If such fractious groups reached a deal, the president could enforce it as industry code. But the Supreme Court declared the NRA unconstitutional, holding that a New York industry code for poultry workers did not implicate the "flow" of interstate commerce because "the poultry had come to a permanent rest within the State."[54]

The early twentieth century marked the high-water mark of judicial resistance to legislative interference in employer sovereignty over pay. Under this regime, few state employment laws survived. The workers' compensation laws described in chapter 1 survived constitutional scrutiny because they were structured as insurance rather than wage and hour restrictions. In addition, female-specific legislation intended to protect women's "biological role," such as "seating laws, rest period, night work prohibitions and prohibitions of female employment in some occupations" tended to have more success at avoiding constitutional challenge.[55] However, these laws tended to "yield policies of questionable value for working women."[56]

## THE FAIR LABOR STANDARDS ACT

In 1933 Roosevelt appointed a white woman, Frances Perkins, as his secretary of labor. She was the first woman to be appointed to the U.S. Cabinet.[57] Perkins was a controversial pick, not only because "she was a woman among trade unionists who prized their manliness" but because she "lacked both personal and institutional links to the labor movement."[58] Instead, both Perkins and Roosevelt were broadly focused on the needs of "all working people."[59] Wage and hour laws were just the type of reform that could benefit workers regardless of union membership.

Perkins and the Labor Department attempted to draft wage and hour legislation that would survive constitutional scrutiny.[60] For example, the bill limited the law to businesses operating in "interstate commerce," which would cover women in textile sweatshops but not the many women in the service industry, such as laundries, hotels, salons, and restaurants.[61] Perkins eventually gave up and stashed the document in a drawer.[62]

FIGURE 1. Secretary of Labor Frances Perkins, the first woman to be appointed to the U.S. cabinet.

Nevertheless, by 1936, after campaigning on wage and hour legislation and winning by a landslide, President Roosevelt was ready to give it another shot. He asked Perkins, "What happened to that nice unconstitutional bill you had tucked away?"[63] Roosevelt then revealed his plan to reshape the geriatric Supreme Court by adding on a new justice for every incumbent justice over age seventy who refused to retire. The plan would have resulted in six new appointments.

Roosevelt's court-packing plan was a legislative failure but famously ushered in the "switch in time that saved nine": the 1937 *West Coast Hotels v. Parrish* decision. In *West Coast Hotels*, the court upheld a state minimum wage law and repudiated freedom of contract principles in favor of a model in which "liberty ... requires the protection of law against the evils which menace the health, safety, morals and welfare of the people."[64] (Scholars disagree over whether the switch was prompted by Roosevelt's threat, because *West Coast Hotels* was drafted before Roosevelt announced his court-packing plan.)[65] Nevertheless, *West*

*Coast Hotels* did not entirely remove the risk that wage and hour legislation would be declared unconstitutional, as it was not yet known whether the judicial shift would persist over time.

The "nice unconstitutional bill" in Perkins's drawer would become the Fair Labor Standards Act of 1938 (FLSA). The legislation prohibited child labor.[66] It also established a phased-in hourly minimum wage for workers covered by the law—25 cents an hour—which would increase to 40 cents an hour by 1945.[67] Roosevelt argued that a minimum wage would stimulate the economy by improving workers' purchasing power.[68] "Political and social harmony requires that every state and every county not only produce goods for the nation's markets but furnish markets for the nation's goods."[69]

The FLSA does not impose a cap on hours, perhaps to avoid the same freedom-of-contract challenge that doomed the New York law in *Lochner*. Although the FLSA has a section labeled "maximum hours," the provision refers to an overtime premium, which requires employers to pay time-and-a-half for hours worked in excess of forty hours per week.[70]

The FLSA also did not prohibit piece-rate work. However, because it imposed an hourly wage, workers paid on a piece rate would need to be topped off if their hourly pay fell below the minimum wage or if they did not receive an overtime premium. This structure was no accident; Perkins hoped to extinguish certain abusive labor practices, particularly industrial "home work."[71] Over time, the FLSA largely succeeded at discouraging piece rate pay, at least for those workers covered by the law.[72]

In 1940 the Supreme Court upheld the constitutionality of the FLSA, declaring that Congress had the power to regulate goods transported across state lines, even if the purpose of doing so was to regulate labor.[73] Nevertheless, the compromises embedded in the law to assure its constitutionality in 1938 persist today, with remarkably few amendments.[74]

THE FLSA HIERARCHY

As economist Ellen Mutari observed, wage setting is not just an economic decision; it is also a social practice "organized by gender, class, and race-ethnicity."[75] Implicit assumptions about the types of workers considered worthy of minimum wage and overtime likely influenced legislative compromises in the FLSA.[76] These social distinctions are evident in the FLSA's many exemptions and exclusions, which produced an implied hierarchy of workers.

At the bottom of the FLSA hierarchy were workers entirely excluded from coverage: agricultural workers and domestic workers.[77] Scholar Juan Perea wrote, "During the New Deal Era, the statutory exclusion of agricultural and domestic employees was well-understood as a race-neutral proxy for excluding blacks from statutory benefits and protections made available to most whites."[78] Legal historian Marc Linder similarly concluded that the exclusion for agricultural workers was a concession to Southern landholders, who were opposed to a national wage that made no distinction based on race or gender.[79] Florida Representative Mark Wilcox, for example, argued in favor of a race-based wage scale, insisting, "You cannot put the Negro and the white man on the same basis and get away with it."[80]

Although Congress did not include a race-based or geographic exclusion in the FLSA, the exception for agricultural workers "disproportionately" affected Black and Latino workers.[81] In the South, more than half of Black men in 1940 worked in agriculture, compared to one-third of white men.[82] Likewise, most of the farmworkers in California were Latino.[83] President Roosevelt conceded the issue, lamenting, "even in the treatment of national problems there are geographic and industrial diversities which practical statesmanship cannot wholly ignore."[84] The FLSA was amended decades later to extend the minimum wage, but not overtime, to farmworkers.[85]

Similarly, the FLSA's exception for domestic workers served to exclude many women, especially Black women, from the minimum wage.[86] Legislators painted domestic labor as unskilled women's work, doubly cursed for being performed and supervised by women.[87] They argued that housewives could not properly account for the hours and pay of domestic workers, claiming it was beyond their skill level.[88]

This narrative continued even into the 1970s, when Congresswoman Shirley Chisholm successfully pushed to expand the minimum wage provision to domestic workers.[89] Those opposing the amendment claimed it was "bringing the federal bureaucracy into the kitchen of the American housewife."[90] In 1973 the secretary of labor went even further, warning, "Your wife will want to get paid.... That means you or I or we have to pay her. So we have to be very careful unless we are ready to do the dishes."[91]

The next rung in the ladder of the FLSA hierarchy consisted of workers eligible for the hourly minimum wage and overtime. For these workers, the FLSA offered a measure of equality previously absent

FIGURE 2. Representative Shirley Chisholm, the first Black woman elected to Congress, successfully pushed to expand the FLSA's minimum wage provision to domestic workers.

from wage and hour practices; it set one wage rate across the country, rather than setting a lower wage rate for women, immigrant workers, or Black workers,[92] or setting different regional rates.[93] A fixed minimum wage meant that employers could not pay eligible women or minority workers a subminimum wage or deny them overtime pay. At that time, however, employers were legally free to discriminate with respect to any wage scale above minimum wage.[94]

The top of the FLSA ladder is occupied by salaried "white-collar" workers who qualify for an exemption as "professionals," "administrators," and "executives."[95] As long as these workers are paid a salary above a certain threshold and meet certain duty-based requirements, they are not entitled to overtime or minimum wage.[96] Although the exclusion seems unfavorable to workers—and considerable litigation in recent decades seeks unpaid wages for misclassifying workers as exempt[97]—the white-collar exemptions represent a favored status in workplaces. These workers are paid the same amount without regard to the "quality or quantity of the work" they perform.[98] They need not keep track of their hours and are subject to substantially less surveillance. Indeed, it is these classes of workers who are typically doing the surveilling, measuring, and managing of nonexempt hourly workers.

Legal scholar Deborah Malamud conducted an in-depth study of the legislative history of the white-collar exemptions. She found the legislative history revealed little about why legislators wanted to include the exemptions; how they settled on the exemptions that they did;[99] or what Congress even meant by "executive, administrative, and professional" employees.[100] Because the exemptions distinguished between manual and nonmanual work,[101] Malamud surmised that it may have reflected class divisions between the "working class" and the "business class."[102] The exemptions also served to codify the practices of the time, whereby supervisors and professionals were paid a salary.[103] Malamud concluded that white-collar workers may have preferred to be exempt from overtime: a limit on working hours would be "contrary to their own interest" in distinguishing themselves and moving up the corporate ranks.[104]

Broadly, the FLSA illustrates how the hierarchies of the past paved the way for new iterations of that hierarchy.[105] Legislators representing Southern states, where the master-servant system had existed in its most extreme form, aggressively lobbied for exclusions to the law and succeeded in securing one for farmworkers.[106] Likewise, domestic workers, who were most closely associated with traditional "servants," were readily abandoned on the road to the federal minimum wage. In drafting the

FLSA, Perkins and the Labor Department also likely curtailed their ambitions for the legislation based on concerns about its constitutionality, regulating only wages and not hours. Malamud's research further suggests that existing hierarchies were also cemented by incorporating existing employment practices in white-collar exemptions.

In other words, the legislative branch has played a constructive but limited role in reforming the master-servant system.[107] The FLSA substantially curtailed employer authority, but also carved out space for employers to continue inequitable pay practices. Although Congress would later address discriminatory pay practices through Title VII and the Equal Pay Act, the hierarchical structure of the FLSA remains.

Moreover, Congress rarely has the final say in defining the contours of employer power and authority.[108] After a bill is passed, both employers and employees use the court system to attempt to blunt or expand the scope of the law.[109] Employers play an underrecognized role in this dynamic by adapting their practices in response to new legislation. Although some of these adaptations serve to comply with the law, others attempt to reassert power and control over workers.

And while the FLSA might have constrained employer efforts to manage workers through pay, companies quickly settled on another lever to exert control over workers: time.

CHAPTER 4

# Time Management

When Ball State University hired Maetta Vance in 1989,[1] harassment law was in its infancy. Only three years prior, the Supreme Court had issued its first decision recognizing harassment claims under Title VII of the Civil Rights Act of 1964: *Meritor Savings Bank v. Vinson et al.* The case involved a Black bank manager who was propositioned, fondled, and raped by her supervisor.[2] The Court ruled in Mechelle Vinson's favor, declaring that a hostile work environment can qualify as a form of discrimination.[3] The decision mentioned only Vinson's sex, not her race,[4] but the ruling applied to harassment based on all categories protected by Title VII: race, sex, color, religion, and national origin.

Ten years later, when Vance reported that Davis hit her in the head,[5] harassment law had evolved considerably. Two cases from 1998—*Burlington Industries v. Ellerth* and *Faragher v. Boca Raton*—drew a distinction between harassment committed by a supervisor and harassment from coworkers.[6] If the harasser was a coworker, the plaintiff would need to show the employer had been negligent in its response.[7] If the harasser was a supervisor, the employer would be strictly liable, though in some cases would be able to assert an affirmative defense.[8]

The legal distinction between a coworker and a supervisor was at the center of Vance's Supreme Court case. If Saundra Davis was merely a coworker, Vance would have the burden to prove that Ball State had been negligent in its response.

The case forced the Supreme Court to define the nature of managerial power and authority in the workplace. Justice Roberts's hypothetical during oral arguments about who "gets to pick the music that's going to play all day long" was an attempt to pin down what distinguishes a supervisor from a coworker.[9] The Supreme Court ultimately settled on a bright-line rule: a supervisor is an individual employed "to effect a significant change in employment status, such as hiring, firing, failing to promote, reassignment with significantly different responsibilities, or a decision causing a significant change in benefits."[10]

The Court defined "supervisor" narrowly. It privileged an employer's formal designations of supervisory authority over the day-to-day experiences of workers like Maetta Vance, whose work might be directed by an unofficial supervisor without the power to hire or fire.

In a concurring opinion in the 1986 *Meritor* case, Justice Thurgood Marshall offered an alternate definition of supervisory power. He wrote, "A supervisor's responsibilities do not begin and end with the power to hire, fire, and discipline employees" but "with the day-to-day supervision of the work environment. . . . There is no reason why abuse of the latter authority should have different consequences than abuse of the former."[11] In Justice Marshall's view, a manager is someone who controls how you spend your time.

This chapter examines managerial control over time and how definitions of productive working time have changed, using four examples from the twentieth century. This chapter is less about the respects in which master-servant principles have been embedded in law and more about how they persist ideologically, particularly as embodied in managerial principles and practices.

Master-servant ideology, as applied to twentieth-century management, is the employer's claim to ownership of workers' time and the prerogative to maximize the profit associated with that time. This idea has been most closely associated with business guru Frederick Winslow Taylor. But as historians Caitlin Rosenthal and Edward Baptist observed, time-based management was prevalent during slavery.[12] From an economic standpoint, ownership of a human being was not so different from ownership of a life's worth of time.

The chapter describes how, even in the early years of the FLSA, companies tried to claim extra unpaid minutes at the start and end of each workday, as illustrated by the 1946 case, *Anderson v. Mt. Clemens*. It then compares and contrasts Taylor's ideas with the Japanese management philosophy of *kaizen*—what we would today call "just-in-time" production—and how the Americanized version of *kaizen* stripped away the more measured and democratic aspects of the philosophy.

While master-servant principles persist in law, their continued vigor depends on corporate persistence in defending managerial power and authority, whether in court cases, legislative battles, or the workplace itself.

## FREDERICK WINSLOW TAYLOR'S RISE TO FAME

Taylor, whose early career is discussed in chapter 3, is famously credited for popularizing time-based management techniques. Yet Taylor may never have reached management guru status without the help of Louis Brandeis, a prominent progressive lawyer who would later serve as a justice on the U.S. Supreme Court.

In 1910 railroads were regulated by the Interstate Commerce Commission (ICC) and could not raise shipping rates without the ICC's permission. Shipping rates were a matter of concern to consumers because an increase in rates would affect prices at their local stores.[13] When railroads sought an increase in rates to offset $3.5 million in additional wage costs and compliance with legal rules,[14] Brandeis was incensed. He believed that the railroads were an inefficient mess and could easily offset their increased costs with better management. Brandeis decided to challenge the proposed rate hike before the ICC.[15]

At the time, industrial workplaces were not necessarily organized to maximize efficiency. Factory organization in the late nineteenth century was often modeled after artisanal models of production, with small fiefdoms overseen by foremen who were themselves skilled artisans.[16] Foremen tended to be focused on work within their own unit, rather than on coordination with other units in the business or with the company managers or owners. In addition, the work itself—preparing raw materials and operating industrial equipment—did not always correspond to traditional trade skills. In industrial operations, expertise in a craft mattered less than knowledge about the operation and maintenance of the equipment and managing the flow of goods from one step of the process to the next.

As historian Ruth Schwartz Cowan explained, industrialization gave rise to a new class of engineers responsible for designing and organizing production.[17] The early twentieth century also marked the rise of a managerial class that disrupted and displaced artisanal fiefdoms, replacing them with the managerial hierarchy familiar in today's workplace.[18]

Taylor and other self-appointed management experts promised to "rationalize" the workplace through management.[19] Taylor claimed that laborers lacked the incentive to work hard and needed guidance from management on efficient performance. He argued that workers adopted a deliberately slow pace, which he called "soldiering," a term that, according to historian Caitlin Rosenthal, bore a striking resemblance to "sogering," used by Southern planters to refer to deliberate work slowdowns by enslaved workers.[20]

As described in chapter 3, Taylor claimed he could identify the true "scientific" production rate, by breaking a job down into separate movements and timing the amount of time it took to complete the work. The symbol of a Taylorist approach came to be a stopwatch, used to measure the time associated with the most efficient performance of a task.[21] According to Taylor, merely observing workers offered an insufficient benchmark for performance, because it was in "the workman's interest then to go just as slowly as possible."[22]

This approach was already known to enslavers and overseers, who sought to quantify the "maximum sustainable pace of labor."[23] As historian Edward Baptist noted, Taylor was far from the first to use a stopwatch to measure worker performance and set an associated standard.[24] John Brown, a former slave, recalled that his enslaver "would stand with his watch in his hand, observing [the movements of the fastest workers] whilst they hoed or picked across a certain space he had marked out."[25] The results would be used to set a quota.[26] Taylor also proposed a system of intense work punctuated by periods of rest, which resembled one developed by a Georgia planter decades earlier, who had provided a five-minute break for every thirty minutes of work to maximize productivity.[27]

Brandeis's argument before the ICC rested heavily on Taylor's ideas.[28] At the hearings, Brandeis cited Taylor's claim that his scientific management techniques enabled a single worker to haul forty-seven tons of iron in a single day.[29] A *New York Times* headline the next day read, "[Rail]roads Could Save $1,000,000 a Day: Brandeis Says Scientific Management Would Do It."[30] The hearings rocketed Taylor to fame,[31] making him the most prominent of a "generation of managerial engineers" that would reshape the organization of industrial work.[32]

But as with many management gurus, Taylor's claims were almost certainly too good to be true. His techniques were rarely fully implemented in industrial workplaces. Taylor's professional track record also suggests that the early twentieth-century sources of efficiency were less dramatic and could be found in equal measure from operational changes. At a paper mill, Taylor's system resulted in only "marginal improvement" to the company's bottom line.[33] At a ball bearing company, his primary contribution was to its accounting practices, not management.[34] And at a shipbuilding company, Taylor's primary contribution was through improvements to the toolrooms and heavy machinery.[35]

Taylor may also have exaggerated or fabricated the most sensational claims in his famous 1911 book, *The Principles of Scientific Management*.[36] In 2000, two business historians attempted to reconstruct Taylor's famous claim that his method enabled a worker to haul forty-seven tons of pig iron in one day.[37] The story did not stand up to scrutiny. The researchers concluded that Taylor's method for hauling the iron was so sloppy that it would have damaged the equipment used to transport the iron and cost more money than the purported labor savings.[38]

Taylor's portrayal of workers as lazy and slow also ignored the harsh working conditions of the day. One of his contemporaries, women's rights activist Josephine Goldmark, published a book arguing that industrial workers were tapped well beyond their maximum sustainable pace.[39] Entitled *Fatigue and Efficiency*, Goldmark's book described how young women in textile factories monitored twelve sewing machine needles simultaneously.[40] "Her attention cannot relax a second while the machine runs. . . . [F]or at the breaking of any one of the 12 gleaming needles or the 12 darting threads, the power must instantly be shut off."[41] She also described banks of telephone operators "perhaps one hundred young women seated side by side" facing switchboards with receivers strapped to their ears, plugging and unplugging cords while maintaining a written call registry.[42]

Taylorism nevertheless seeped into the prevailing business culture, shorthand for the idea that managers held the key to worker productivity, and that managers were best positioned to determine how workers should spend their time. As legal historian John Fabian Witt observed, "Taylorism and accompanying varieties of management engineering worked a thorough transformation in the ways in which Americans conceived of work."[43]

## WORKING TIME UNDER THE FLSA

The FLSA did not invent the hourly wage; laborers were commonly paid on an hourly basis prior to the law.[44] However, the FLSA rendered the hourly wage the increment by which compliance would be measured for nonexempt workers. Any worker subject to the law was entitled to a minimum wage based on hours worked. Overtime was likewise pegged to weekly hours worked. And once minimum pay was affixed to time, employers had an even greater incentive to exercise surveillance, control, and measurement over how those workers spent their working time.

The 1946 Supreme Court case *Anderson v. Mt. Clemens* and its subsequent fallout illustrates how employers accustomed to piece-rate pay resisted paying workers in full measure for the hours they worked.[45] The Mt. Clemens Pottery Company was a large pottery factory in a small town. The factory employed twelve hundred workers, who churned out mass-market consumer dishware in a variety of colors and patterns. The dispute between the company and the pottery workers started out as a labor dispute, in which the named plaintiff, Steve Anderson, led his fellow pottery workers in a walkout and was promptly fired.

No local lawyer would take on the case, but it caught the attention of Ted Lamb, a pugnacious labor-side lawyer from out of town.[46] Lamb specialized in wage and hour cases, and he realized that Anderson and his colleagues were sitting on a valuable wage and hour lawsuit.[47] He brought an FLSA case on behalf of three hundred workers, taking the case on contingency and ploughing his own money into it.[48]

The central issue in the case was the number of hours the potters worked. Workers clocked in and out of their shifts using a punch card machine. Although the technology of the time would have enabled the company to calculate workers' punch time down to the minute,[49] the company didn't use the punch cards to calculate pay.[50] Instead, the pottery company persisted in using a piece-rate pay structure that did not comply with the FLSA.

The *Mount Clemens* case forced the trial court to define what qualified as working time: which tasks were "compensable" under the FLSA. A lot of activity occurred between the moment someone punched in and the whistle indicating the start of the shift. Depending on the job, workers might walk to their workstation, put on an apron, grease their arms, sharpen tools, or set up equipment.[51] Under a piece-rate system, workers were not paid for any of that time; they were only paid for what they produced.

The presiding judge was so overwhelmed by the complexity of the case that he delegated the fact-finding portion of the case to an outside expert known as a special master. The proceedings generated more than thirty thousand pages of testimony.[52]

At first the company claimed that none of the potters' preparatory work was compensable and that employees performed preparatory tasks extremely slowly. One official even testified that workers walked to their stations at "a rate of less than one mile per hour."[53] But when it became clear that workers would need to be paid for at least some of that time, the company took the opposite position, claiming that workers hustled to their workstations and got right to work.[54]

Lamb realized that all of the walking, waiting, and preparatory work could add up to fifty-six minutes a day—or fourteen thousand minutes over the course of a year[55]—awarded to each of the three hundred workers in the class action.[56] The damages would be enormous. In his autobiography, Lamb claimed the company tried to bribe him to drop the case.[57] Lamb refused the bribe and appealed the case to the Supreme Court.

In 1946 the Supreme Court ruled that "the statutory workweek includes all time during which an employee is necessarily required to be on the employer's premises, on duty or at a prescribed workplace" such that "the time spent in these activities must be" paid.[58] All that walking was not for workers' own "convenience or needs" but for the "necessities of the employer's business."[59] Likewise, the court declared the potters' preparatory activity—putting on uniforms, preparing tools, starting up machines—to be compensable work.[60]

The *Mount Clemens* case opened the floodgates to copycat suits.[61] Workers at the Bethlehem Steel Company, for example, filed a wage and hour claim for $200 million.[62] Lamb's firm filed more than two hundred wage and hour lawsuits.[63] The victory would be short lived, however. The Mount Clemens case was not completely over; the Supreme Court had remanded certain questions of fact down to the lower court.

The attorney general of the United States intervened in the trial court case, filing a brief arguing that all of the lost time was de minimis, a trifling amount unworthy of calculation.[64] It was a bold legal claim, since the attorney general sought to intervene precisely because it believed the implications for industrial operations to be ruinous, not trifling.[65] Nevertheless, the trial court judge followed the attorney general's recommendations, and the workers at Mount Clemens recovered nothing.[66]

Despite the attorney general's intervention at the trial court level, the Supreme Court's ruling in *Mount Clemens* remained good law. A year later, Congress sided with business interests and passed the Portal-to-Portal Act. The law amended the FLSA, declaring preliminary and postliminary tasks noncompensable unless they were "indispensable" to the "principal activities" of the work.[67]

The exclusion in the Portal-to-Portal Act only applied to activities at the start and end of an employee's shift. During a shift, the clock would keep running even if an employee was engaged in nonproductive or minor tasks. The rule gave companies added incentive to squeeze economic value out of every minute that hourly workers spent on the clock.

## REDUCING "WASTE"

Pressures to increase efficiency do not always originate from management. In the 1980s, foreign competition imposed added pressure on American manufacturers to reduce costs. Japan was viewed as a competitive rival to American industrial production, much in the way China is viewed today. And American business leaders were interested in understanding the business philosophy and practices of rising Japanese manufacturers like Toyota, Honda, and Sony.

Masaaki Imai's 1986 book, *Kaizen*, promised to reveal the manufacturing practices that were "the key to Japan's competitive success."[68] *Kaizen*, Imai explained, is a Japanese cultural idea about incremental and continual improvement.[69] While American corporate leaders might be focused on market disruption and great leaps of innovation, Imai claimed that similar, if not superior, outcomes can be achieved over time through gradual process improvements.[70]

Imai characterized these process improvements as identifying and reducing *muda*—the Japanese word for "waste."[71] *Muda* refers to any activity that consumes resources but is unnecessary or non-value added. *Muda* might refer to wasted time, effort, or raw materials. Much of what Imai characterizes as "waste" are forms of excess: too much inventory, too much production, product defects, or workers waiting around with nothing to do.

The *kaizen* model is familiar in American business today as "just-in-time production." Toyota often serves as a prototypical example of the approach for its practice of ordering raw materials needed at a particular time, rather than needlessly stockpiling extra inventory. In the *kaizen* model, unnecessary labor is also a source of waste. Workers moving product across the building from one department to the other are generating *muda* if management could have instead moved the departments to be adjacent to one another.[72] Workers are likewise engaged in *muda* if they are producing goods more quickly than the goods can be processed in the next chain of production.⁷³ In Imai's model, such a mismatch is just as wasteful as buying too much inventory.

The parallels between *kaizen* and a Taylorist mode of thinking are hard to miss: both are focused on finding hidden sources of efficiency. And indeed, the two approaches may be related. In 1913 a Japanese banker published Taylor's book, *The Principles of Scientific Management*, in Japan, only two years after its first publication in the United States. And in the 1920s Mitsubishi sent its managers to a Westinghouse factory in the United States to study scientific management techniques and brought those ideas home to Japan.⁷⁴ Taiichi Ohno, the "father of the vaunted Toyota production system" also cited his "intellectual debt to scientific management."⁷⁵

At the same time, the *kaizen* model was far more democratic both in theory and implementation than Taylor's top-down approach. Imai urged managers to make frequent visits to the worksite, to better understand the work being performed.⁷⁶ The *kaizen* model presumed that innovation originated from workers, who knew their job best and were always coming up with ways to improve. Imai urged managers to observe workers carefully, not for surveillance or control, but to identify innovations. Workers had likely already identified shortcuts and improvements to tools, the method of work, and organizing their workstation. These improvements, once identified, might be rolled out by management across the company, multiplying their effect.

Like Taylorism, the *kaizen* model had certain management-centric qualities. Even when managers selected worker innovations, they would eventually impose them on other workers through company-wide systems. Nevertheless, the *kaizen* model presumed that workers, rather than management, had the most expertise in how best to perform their jobs. The famous symbol of *kaizen* implementation at Toyota—a cord that any worker could pull to stop the production line and fix a mistake—was as much about deference and respect for frontline workers as it was about quality control.⁷⁷ Continual improvement was a shared responsibility, rather than a form of managerial surveillance, measurement, and control.

Even the implementation of scientific management in the 1920s at the Mitsubishi factory in Japan reflected a different sensibility toward workers. According to scholar Satoshi Sasaki, engineers used time and motion studies to calculate the average—rather than the optimal—time needed to perform a task.⁷⁸ Their estimates of average time also included "reasonable delays" for "personal needs, fatigue, and so on," as well as maintenance tasks, such as "sharpening tools, arranging belting and machines, and waiting for materials."⁷⁹ Sasaki also notes that management introduced a committee to represent workers in the 1920s following a surge of labor activity and retaliatory layoffs.⁸⁰ This, Sasaki argued, sensitized management to the concerns of workers and limited managerial overreach.

The Japanese approach also took a more moderate stance toward compensation. Mitsubishi used the time and motion studies to set pay but also looked at the cost of living and the pay rates for other employers in the region. They systematized pay rates—albeit based on gender, position, skill, and seniority—in a way that built in a pay increase.⁸¹ Sasaki noted, "[I]t may therefore be concluded that the reason why the new wage system was accepted by the workforce without difficulty is that . . . [it] had taken the standpoint of workers into consideration."⁸² Productivity increased moderately, but so did wages.

The *kaizen* example thus illustrates the respects in which management ideology and practices reflect cultural assumptions and context. Indeed, in his book, Imai insisted that *kaizen* was not a management practice so much as a cultural idea adapted to management.⁸³ The *kaizen* philosophy incorporated Japanese cultural assumptions about interdependence, gradual improvement, mutual respect, and deference to authority. By contrast, Taylorism reflected American cultural ideas dating back to slavery, of a zero-sum contest between those who perform the work and those who oversee it. Taylorism assumed that workers lack intrinsic skill, expertise, or motivation, and that only money and surveillance would overcome worker resistance.

## AMERICAN *KAIZEN*

The more recent American incarnation of *kaizen* abandons the democratic and balanced dimensions of the Japanese approach. In its most extreme forms, American implementations of a just-in-time management philosophy treats nonproductive time—and to some extent even the basic needs of workers—as a form of "waste."

Amazon's warehouse management practices embody this philosophy. As of 2024, Amazon pays its warehouse workers comparatively well, at $22 an hour, as well as benefits.⁸⁴ And because consumer demand for Amazon orders is so high, the company can offer warehouse workers plentiful hours of work. These financial inducements—competitive pay and benefits and generous hours—come at the cost of an unrelenting pace of work.

Journalistic accounts of Amazon's practices report that the company requires warehouse workers to pack or fetch a minimum number of units in an hour, which workers refer to as "making rate."[85] Because the company collects reams of data on worker productivity, it is able to set the rate for a given day at the average pace for workers in a particular position (e.g., ninety items per hour).[86] A hundred years ago, the relay assemblers at Western Electric used remarkably similar language to describe their own quotas, complaining that they would "ge[t] bawled out about our rates,"[87] or that they were scared to report to work if they didn't "make [their] rate" the day before.[88]

In a 2021 exposé of Amazon warehouses, the *New York Times* revealed that the "rate" was more benchmark than disciplinary threat, particularly as the company struggled to attract and retain workers during the pandemic.[89] However, the advisory nature of the rate was never communicated to workers, who suffered varying degrees of bodily discomfort and pain to meet the target.[90]

Amazon has also explored technology to push the envelope even further. The company was granted a patent in 2018 for a haptic wristband, which used cameras and sensors to locate the worker's arm in space.[91] The wristband could vibrate to alert a worker that they were about to put an item in the wrong spot.[92] Commentators criticized the wristband as "dystopian" and claimed that Amazon's goal was to "turn people into machines."[93]

In a way, the wristband exemplifies American *kaizen*. While Imai's philosophy might have counseled reorganizing the space to be more favorable to workers or developing assistive technology in collaboration with workers, the Amazon wristband reflects American corporate culture. It is an overly technical solution developed by an engineer who was likely far removed from the warehouse floor.[94] In the most generous interpretation of the inventor's mindset, the wristband might have been genuinely useful by eliminating the need for workers to scan bar codes.[95] Yet the punitive dimension of the wristband, even if not intentional, was nevertheless deemed tolerable or necessary to the wristband's operation.

Unlike more oppressive periods in American history, Amazon workers can quit anytime. And they do. The *New York Times* documented an astounding rate of employee turnover at Amazon: about 150 percent a year.[96] "That rate" the reporters note, is "almost double that of the retail and logistics industries, [and] has made some executives worry about running out of workers across America."[97]

Yet Amazon is far from the only company to have adopted aggressive employment metrics and unrealistic productivity standards. Sherriff Tony Thompson, who observed the conditions at the Tyson plant in April 2020, explained that the working conditions were partly a function of the rapid line speed of the pork carcasses and conveyer belts, forcing workers into crowded and awkward positions to grasp and cut the meat as it flew by their workstations.[98]

Food service and retail outlets also subject their workers to unforgiving metrics behind the scenes. Jessica Jaszewski, who worked as a Starbucks barista for five years, said that the company kept track of the "drive time" that elapsed between a customer order and pickup at the drive-thru windows. The metrics were displayed on a screen where the baristas input the order.[99] She recalled, "[Y]ou're constantly looking at it. How fast are you going? How fast can you be going? How fast were you 30 minutes [ago]?" According to Jaszewski, management emphasized "getting your drive times down," while also instructing baristas to "bring your best self to work" and "make human connections with these customers." Over time, Jaszewski came to feel that they were just "cogs in a machine"; "there's no appreciation . . . you know, it's never good enough" and "it's not like you're getting paid more" for making the metrics.

Food service and retail companies also squeeze workers through just-in-time scheduling software. The software matches worker schedules to the precise business need for labor, cutting labor to match customer traffic during the day, within the week, or even with the weather. Scheduling software might, for exempt, recommend a split shift, in which an employee works a few hours and is sent home, only to return a few hours later. Scheduling software can also assign workers to a "clopener"—a closing shift followed by an opening shift.

Just-in-time scheduling wreaks havoc on workers' lives. The trimmed schedules reduce the pay of hourly workers, many of whom are already paid at the lower end of the wage scale. As scholars Charlotte Alexander and Anna Haley-Lock observe, "[T]he reality faced by many low-wage jobholders today is no longer one of overwork, but rather of underwork," where "one form that work-hour insecurity may take is work-hour inadequacy, where workers are scheduled for fewer hours than they wish to work."[100]

The unpredictable and ever-changing nature of these schedules makes it nearly impossible to arrange child care, attend school, or work a second job.[101] A few states have sought to discourage just-in-time scheduling by passing laws requiring advanced notice or requiring companies to schedule (or pay) workers for a minimum number of hours.[102] And some employers have pledged to discontinue the practice.[103] However, nonunionized workers otherwise remain at the beck and call of their employers. Just-in-time scheduling can also have the follow-on effect of pushing workers into the gig economy (discussed in chapter 9), either as a primary source of income or to supplement income from an unpredictable job.

Overtime hours have likewise become a form of "waste" to be avoided at all costs. In a 2010 class action lawsuit against McDonald's, an assistant manager testified that the store goal was less than ten hours of cumulative overtime at the franchise per month.[104] The manager further elaborated that higher-level managers would "demand explanations from restaurant managers any time the restaurant had more than ten hours of overtime in any given week," and that the company "provided its salaried managers with a bonus that was largely based on reduced payroll and overtime compensation."[105] Store managers then had a strong incentive to instruct workers to perform work off the clock or shave employee time records after the fact.[106] In similar cases against companies like Wal-Mart, Applebee's, Chipotle, Dollar General, and CVS, managers were accused of altering employee time records to avoid paying workers.[107]

Indeed, the 2016 Wells Fargo scandal, involving workers who opened unauthorized customer accounts, may have been related to the company's productivity standards and wage and hour practices.[108] When workers failed to meet their quotas for opening new accounts, managers would clock them out but instruct them to keep working. Opening fake accounts may have served as another way to meet the quota without logging overtime.

Companies are also increasingly focused on limiting hourly schedules to avoid paying the escalating cost of health care, which large employers must offer to 95 percent of full-time workers under the Affordable Care Act to avoid a tax penalty.[109] By keeping workers well under the thirty-hour threshold for coverage,[110] employers can limit both their labor costs and the associated cost of benefits.

FREE TIME

It is tempting to ascribe Amazon's management practices to an ideological commitment to efficiency. However, Amazon's interest in reducing waste is limited to time spent on the clock. When it comes to unpaid time, Amazon is even less efficient than the Mt. Clemens Pottery Company eighty years earlier, when workers waited in line for "a minimum of 8 minutes" just to punch their time cards.[111]

In the 2014 Supreme Court case *Integrity Staffing v. Busk*, workers at an Amazon subcontractor sued to recover wages for time spent waiting in line for security screenings at the start and end of their shifts: around twenty-five minutes a day.[112] The security screenings are not intended to benefit workers but to prevent them from stealing merchandise. The subcontractor refused to pay for that time, insisting that the Portal-to-Portal Act rendered waiting in line noncompensable time. The Supreme Court agreed. Security screenings were not "indispensable" to the warehouse workers' jobs, even though they were mandated by the employer.[113] The Supreme Court disregarded the inefficient nature of the security screenings, noting that it was irrelevant whether the employer could have reduced the amount of time spent waiting in line.[114] The Portal-to-Portal Act was meant to save businesses money. It also removed any incentive for employers to assign value to all that waiting time. For them, the time is free.

Employers can also avail themselves of "free" time when it comes to their salaried workers. As described in chapter 3, certain white-collar workers are exempt from the FLSA, provided they perform certain types of exempt duties and are paid a minimum salary.[115] Salaried workers are paid the same amount, at regular intervals, regardless of the duration or quality of their work. This rule is baked into current law—an employer that attempts to dock a salaried employee's compensation for showing up late or for producing shoddy work risks losing the FLSA exemption that allows the employer to avoid paying overtime.[116]

Employers have the opposite incentive for salaried workers as for hourly workers. When paying a fixed salary, companies want to extract as many hours as possible. The lavish perks that prepandemic Silicon Valley firms offered to their salaried workers—from free food to dry cleaning and nap pods—served primarily to cajole workers to stay in the office a few more hours. Amazon likewise has a reputation for pushing its salaried workers to work extreme hours.[117] A 2015 *New York Times* exposé of Amazon's employment practices interviewed the spouse of one such employee, who reported driving to the office each night at 10:00 p.m. to cajole his wife to go home.[118]

The FLSA includes no maximum hours provision.[119] It regulates hours only indirectly through the overtime premium, which was meant to serve a work-spreading function:[120] companies could hire more workers to work for fewer than forty hours and avoid having to pay the overtime premium. But what the drafters of the FLSA may not have contemplated was the way it would eventually enable employers to redistribute work from hourly to salaried employees.

Economists estimate that most income inequality in the United States is attributable to wage inequality—that is, some workers being paid vastly more than others when calculated on a per-hour basis.[121] However, hours inequality between hourly and salaried workers also contributes to the gap.[122] Legal scholar Daniel Markovits notes a decades-long growth in hours among the highest earning workers, with the top 1 percent in income growing from an average of forty-six hours per week in 1940 to around fifty-three hours in the 2010s.[123] In contrast, workers in the bottom 60 percent in terms of income have seen their average hours per week decline from forty-nine hours per week to just over forty.[124] In other words, overtime is most concentrated among the more highly compensated workers, who are predominantly paid on a salary basis.

Of course, the extra hours extracted from high-wage workers are not actually free. High-wage workers pay for those hours with their time, in the same way that hourly workers lose the time spent waiting in a security line. Further, Markovits argues that the unequal distribution of hours has a corrosive effect on American culture, leading to resentful entitlement on the part of the rich, who are dreadfully afraid their children will fall on the wrong side of the all-or-nothing wealth distribution. In the zero-sum game of American *kaizen*, overtime hours are conferred on rich workers who don't want them, and are inaccessible for many hourly workers cobbling together part-time work to approximate a whole.

There is another Japanese word for waste: *mottainai*. The term refers to treating something precious as if it were worthless. The concept has a communal underpinning and a pejorative meaning—invoking, for example, a child who serves themselves a large portion of a carefully prepared family dinner, then eats only a bite.

Imai's book does not include the word *mottainai*, but perhaps it should have. Forcing workers to wait in line for nearly half an hour without paying them is *mottainai*. Assigning an employee to work a "clopener" is *mottainai*, as is expecting workers to organize their lives around capricious, last-minute scheduling software.

Time has value, even and maybe especially when companies haven't paid for it.

PART II

# The Right to Govern

CHAPTER 5

# Unions

Baristas Ian Meagher (they/he) and Jessica Jaszewski (she/her) trace the union organizing drive at their Eugene, Oregon, Starbucks location to a meeting with their district manager.[1] It was around December 2021, not long after a Starbucks in Buffalo, New York, became the first U.S. location to unionize.[2] The district manager called a store meeting, and according to Jaszewski and Meagher, conveyed "the overarching feeling" that "we value you" and "want you to feel like your work is appreciated" but "you don't need a union."[3] Meagher said that the best way to make them feel valued would be to pay them more.[4] The manager demurred.

Meagher went home and googled "how to start a union."[5] Within weeks Meagher, Jaszewski, and their colleagues managed to gather enough signatures on union cards to trigger a secret ballot election through the National Labor Relations Board (NLRB).

They were part of a broader wave of unionization at Starbucks that gained steam in 2022, where workers in more than three hundred stores across the country filed petitions with the NLRB for a union vote.[6] Marina Multhaup, a labor lawyer representing Workers United, was cautiously optimistic about how Starbucks would respond. "Starbucks had this really progressive reputation," Multhaup recalled, "and I remember thinking at that point . . . maybe they're going to be chill about this."[7]

Multhaup was wrong. Starbucks managed to delay elections in many Oregon stores by contesting the size of the bargaining unit.[8] The company also launched an aggressive internal campaign to persuade workers in Eugene to vote against the union. Managers warned workers that unionizing meant that managers would stop helping out during their shifts, and that they wouldn't be able to borrow workers from other stores.[9] Management also posted a "visual guide of the voting ballot" in the back of the store and advised them "to mark 'NO' on the ballot" if they wanted to "kee[p] their direct relationship with Starbucks."[10]

Local managers began strictly enforcing the corporate dress code. The long-standing dress code prohibited shirts that were brightly colored, patterned, or with large "logos, writings or graphics."[11] However, management in Eugene had previously been lax about enforcing the dress code, in one case ignoring a tie-dyed shirt with a penguin graphic.[12]

The impetus for the crackdown appears to have been a "Starbucks Workers United" shirt that workers began wearing under their aprons.[13] Both Meagher and Jaszewski were repeatedly hassled, and later disciplined, by management for wearing the Workers United shirt, despite their protestations that their actions were legally protected.[14] At one point Meagher even directed the manager to a government poster in the back of the store, prohibiting retaliation for "wearing union . . . t-shirts."[15] The language on the poster seemed to give the manager pause. He excused himself to make a phone call.[16] However, upon the manager's return, he reiterated that Meagher had violated the dress code and sent them home to change.[17]

The union filed a complaint with the NLRB challenging Starbucks's anti-union activity as an unfair labor practice. But the dispute was almost academic at that point; the secret ballot election over unionization was long over.

. . .

Part I of this book addressed control over workers through the work site, compensation, working time, and termination of the relationship itself. In the late nineteenth century, courts conferred power over termination to the employer through the employment-at-will doctrine. In the early twentieth century, courts likewise sought to preserve employer power over hours and wages by declaring wage and hour laws unconstitutional. The passage of the FLSA in 1938 represented a meaningful constraint on employer discretion, but it also solidified workplace hierarchies and increased employer incentives to engage in managerial surveillance and control over hourly employees.

Part II explores a related dimension of the master-servant doctrine: the power to govern. As described in the introduction, the feudal conception

FIGURE 3. Ian Meagher wearing their Starbucks Workers United T-shirt.

of the master-servant doctrine was one of governance, in which "the household was a polity, like other polities, and that it, like other polities was governed."[18] For enslaved people, governance was both legal and lived reality, as when Frederick Douglass referred to his enslaver's main plantation as "the seat of government."[19] The law of slavery ensured

FIGURE 4. Jessica Jaszewski.

that there would be no appeal from the enslaver's decree, that his power was "in no instance, usurped."[20]

I use the term "governance" to refer to the power to set workplace policies and other terms and conditions of employment, as well as the processes by which hiring, firing, compensation, and promotion occur.

Certain aspects of the workplace discussed in part I relate to governance. For example, the at-will employment doctrine could be viewed as a form of governance because it gives the employer the power to banish an individual from the workplace. Part II focuses on the nature of rules that employers impose and the limits of an employer's power to set those rules.

The vast majority of individual workers—with the exception of executives and other sought-after workers who negotiate their employment contracts—have very little control in setting the terms and conditions of their employment. As philosopher Elizabeth Anderson wrote, "Most workplace governments in the United States are dictatorships ... [B]osses govern in ways that are largely unaccountable to those who are governed. They don't merely govern workers; they dominate them."[21]

Under current law, employers do not have an exclusive, unencumbered right to governance over the workplace. Two landmark pieces of twentieth-century legislation placed substantial limits on the employer's right to govern: the National Labor Relations Act of 1935 (NLRA) and Title VII of the Civil Rights Act of 1964 (Title VII).[22] The NLRA imposed a form of power sharing on employers, forcing them to deal with elected unions in setting terms and conditions of employment and determining a process by which workplace grievances would be resolved. Likewise, Title VII and related laws constrain employer power regarding hiring, firing, promotion, and compensation.[23]

At the same time, neither the NLRA nor Title VII lived up to its early promise. This chapter focuses specifically on the rise and fall of union membership in the United States over the last century. As of 2024, only 9.9 percent of American workers were members of unions, according to the Bureau of Labor Statistics (BLS).[24] The factors that have led to the decline of union membership are complex and somewhat disputed among labor historians, labor law scholars, and economists.

Certain aspects of the story parallel other legal developments described in part I. Like the growth of at-will employment in the nineteenth century, employers in the twentieth century persuaded courts to incorporate master-servant principles into labor law. The presence of master-servant principles in labor law was well documented by labor scholar James Atleson, whose work is discussed in greater detail later in this chapter.[25] And like the wage and hour context, discussed in chapters 3 and 4, employers developed a variety of practices to blunt the impact of labor law. In addition, exclusionary and discriminatory practices by unions in the first half of twentieth century may have also weakened their ability to resist the changing economic landscape in the latter half.

## FROM GUILDS TO STRIKES

Historians trace labor unions back to preindustrial guilds and journeymen's associations.[26] Guilds were self-governing trade organizations for workers who completed an apprenticeship and bore the seal of the master craftsman. Although apprenticeships were coercive—often involving service by a minor for a fixed period of years—apprentices graduated into one of the most vaunted statuses of preindustrial America.[27]

Trade guilds reflected the labor hierarchies of the time. Enslaved tradespeople had none of the privileges of their white counterparts. Based on the 1865 Census, historian Juliet E. K. Walker estimated that skilled Black tradespeople in the South outnumbered skilled white tradespeople five to one.[28] Frederick Douglass was one such skilled craftsperson; he learned the trade of caulking through shipbuilding work while enslaved.[29] Case law during slavery made frequent references to enslaved people with trade expertise, such as coach makers, carpenters, tailors, bricklayers, blacksmiths, shoemakers, and saddle makers.[30]

As Ronald Lewis documented in his book *Coal, Iron and Slaves*,[31] the presence of enslaved workers in industrial settings could provoke labor unrest. For example, in 1847 white workers in a Virginia iron mill went on strike over the decision to place enslaved workers in high-skill positions.[32] The strike failed. Newspaper editorials sided with the mill owners, insisting that "in a slave-holding state" the employer must not be "prevented from making use of slave labor."[33]

Between 1870 and 1920, technological, social, and economic changes altered the prospects of American workers in various ways. Industrialization eroded the market power of skilled craftsmen, who lacked the capital to start their own large industrial operations.[34] Some craftsmen found work in industrialized workplaces, where, on occasion, they operated in a similar structure to their independent shops, supervising and training other workers.[35] However, mechanization enabled lower skilled workers to perform similar factory work without years of intensive training, a process historians refer to as "deskilling."[36]

In the late nineteenth and the early twentieth centuries, unions represented the strongest and most persistent threat to the corporate master's domination of the workplace.[37] Although unions had little to no legal protection[38]—operating in what legal historian Christopher Tomlins described as a legal "twilight zone"[39]—they were economically powerful. They could cripple industrial operations through strikes, boycotts, work slowdowns, and violence.[40]

During this period, courts protected corporate authority to rule over the workplace.[41] They claimed that strike activity violated antitrust laws and interfered with interstate commerce.[42] By the late nineteenth century, courts started using labor injunctions more broadly to put a quick end to strikes.[43] Courts also used enticement and conspiracy claims to sue labor organizers for "enticing" workers to stop work.[44] This "judicial antipathy" toward unions continued well into the twentieth century.[45]

### RACE- AND GENDER-BASED HIERARCHIES

The late nineteenth and early twentieth centuries were also a period of rampant discrimination, segregation, and workplace exclusion on the basis of race and gender. The 1896 Supreme Court decision in *Plessy v. Ferguson* authorized state-mandated racial segregation.[46] Although Black workers "formed unions and staged strikes to defend their jobs against the attempts of white workers to drive them from desirable trades," their efforts were overwhelmed by a "wave of terror ... directed at eliminating the rights of black people."[47]

Both employers and labor unions engaged in discriminatory employment practices.[48] In 1888 Black jurist David Augustus Straker called out trade unions "whose ostensible object is to protect labor against the oppression of capital but whose hidden purpose is to shut and keep shut the doors of industry against a class of people on account of their race."[49] Likewise, in multiple speeches between 1899 and 1914, Mary Church Terrell, the president of the National Association of Colored Women, denounced "flagrant discrimination against Colored youth, particularly against the girls, [that] must be abhorrent to all fair-minded people," as well as wage discrimination and exclusion from labor unions.[50] Companies exploited racial hierarchy and resentment, as in Chicago, where management that otherwise refused to hire Black workers sometimes hired them as strikebreakers.[51]

Women occupied a subordinate position in the workplace, which was reflected in wage discrimination and occupational segregation. In the nineteenth century, employment options for women were often confined to low-wage occupations like domestic service, sewing, and laundry.[52] At that time, having a wife who did not work outside the home was viewed as a marker of status for the male breadwinner.[53] Employers thus justified paying far lower wages to women than men on the basis that women's work merely served to supplement a man's wages.

Labor force participation was higher for women in immigrant and Black families to compensate for high rates of race- and ethnicity-based wage discrimination.[54] A 1900 study of New York households found that 33 percent of married Black women worked outside the home, compared to 4 percent of white women.[55] Likewise, a 1930s study of Mexican households in San Diego found that about half of wives worked, but their work only contributed about 20 percent of the household income.[56]

Male-dominated unions had an ambivalent relationship with female workers.[57] Unions considered high rates of female labor force participation a threat to union wages, because companies treated women as a cheap substitute for male labor.[58] Consequently, many prominent labor leaders argued that a woman's proper place was in the home.[59] In 1906 Samuel Gompers, the first president of the powerful American Federation of Labor (AFL), proclaimed, "It is the so-called competition of the unorganized defenseless woman worker, the girl and the wife, that often tends to reduce the wages of the father and husband."[60] Many unions formally or informally excluded women entirely.[61] Unions could also exclude women from prized industrial positions, contributing to occupational segregation in the workplace.[62]

On the other hand, in sectors where women worked in significant numbers, such as the garment industry, women could add to the membership rolls and reduce the threat of nonunionized female competition.[63] Thus, even the AFL "half-heartedly" employed a female labor organizer and called for equal wages on the basis of gender—primarily "to protect the earning power of men."[64] However, women were rarely given leadership positions in unions,[65] and their interests were often overlooked or undermined.[66] Scholar Alice Kessler-Harris recounted how male leadership would discourage women from active involvement in the union by "locating meetings in saloons, scheduling them at late hours, and ridiculing women who dared to speak."[67]

This underrepresentation of women in leadership persisted over time. In 1975 the BLS reported that the "Ladies' Garment Workers"—a union that was 80 percent female—could count only one woman among its twenty-six board members.[68]

## THE NATIONAL LABOR RELATIONS ACT

The NLRA brought labor out of the legal "twilight zone" and defined a protected sphere of activity for unions.[69] The NLRA protected workers from retaliation for engaging in union organizing. It provided a democratic process for representation, wherein a majority of workers within a company unit could elect a union by secret ballot. It required employers to deal with unions in good faith and negotiate a collective bargaining agreement over "pay, wages, hours of employment, or other conditions of employment."[70] If the union and the employer reached an impasse, the law authorized workers to strike[71]—a potent threat that forced employers to take the union's requests seriously. (Notably, the law did not prohibit unions from discriminating on the basis of gender or race.)[72]

In other words, through collective bargaining, the terms and conditions of employment are no longer at the employer's whim. Instead, both the union and the employer have a say over central aspects of the employment relationship: safety, termination, hours, and pay. As labor historian Melvyn Dubofsky argued, the NLRA "introduced federal power directly, deeply and coercively into realms heretofore regarded as private and voluntary."[73] Collective bargaining agreements also commonly provide a grievance process for workers, in which they can dispute an employer's decision with help from the union. When those grievances are not resolved informally, a union can help workers appeal their case through labor arbitration.

The NLRA was a boon for union membership. Unions saw membership climb from 3.7 million in 1935 to 6.5 million four years later.[74] By 1947, union membership had grown to 14.5 million—roughly 32 percent of the nonfarm labor force.[75]

Unions produce many indirect benefits for workers not covered by a collective bargaining unit. The looming threat of labor organizing was the original impetus for many industrial employers to provide more favorable working conditions and better pay and benefits.[76] The presence of unions in an industry has been shown to increase the wages of nonunionized workplaces.[77] And even within an organization, nonunion members can free ride from the benefits of a collective bargaining agreement.[78]

However, labor law does not operate in a vacuum. Scholar James Atleson argued that master-servant principles have contaminated labor law jurisprudence over time.[79] Atleson highlighted the 1938 case *NLRB v.*

*Mackay Radio & Telegraph Company*, which permits employers to permanently replace workers on strike.[80] Once a company has hired replacement workers, striking workers may find they have no job to return to after the strike is over.[81] Not only does the *Mackay* rule serve as a deterrent against exercising the right to strike, it also fills the workplace with nonunionized workers.[82] Atleson concluded that the "long tenure" of the right to replace and the "impossibility of rationalizing" it within labor jurisprudence "suggest[s] the doctrine is based on some deep-seated notion of employer prerogatives and rights."[83]

The 1950 case *Elk Lumber Co.* similarly reflected assumptions about labor hierarchy, according to Atleson.[84] The case involved a lumber mill that employed workers to haul lumber on a piece-rate basis. Management reorganized the job so that workers could perform the work much more quickly, but switched the workers to an hourly pay rate that substantially reduced their take-home pay. Workers responded with a covert slowdown, loading the lumber at the original pace prior to the reorganization. The NLRB declared the covert slowdown unlawful.[85] By siding with the employer, the NLRB was tacitly incorporating master-servant principles, in which the employer retains sole discretion over the pace of work. As such, the pace of work would not be a matter of shared governance between the union and the employer.[86]

Atleson argued that similar principles have been applied to workers' "refusa[l] to work overtime ... partial strikes, or intermittent work stoppages."[87] All are "thought by employers to interfere with their right to control the work process."[88] Judicial hostility toward employee self-help even extends to worker opposition to health and safety risks, because it "directly challenge[s] employer control over the quality of the work process."[89] Courts assume that "employers, having purchased labor power, have a right to direct and control that power, and concurrently, employees have no right to participate in the planning or operation of the production process."[90]

### THE DECLINE OF UNIONS

Starting in the 1950s, union membership experienced a steady decline in the private sector. By 2022, union membership had fallen to levels not seen since the 1930s, before the NLRA became law.[91]

Scholars have offered a variety of explanations for the decline. Labor scholar Paul Weiler argued that labor unions were poorly adapted to the more diverse workforces ushered in by the civil rights movement.[92] The

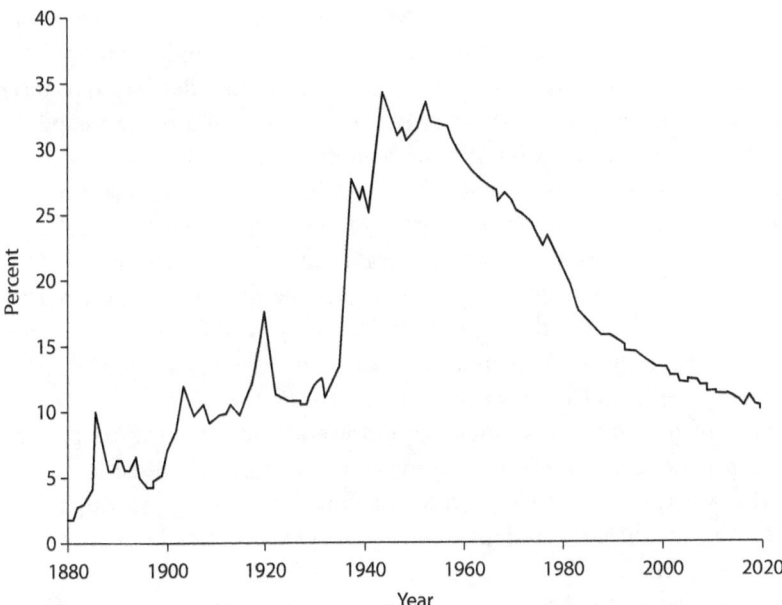

FIGURE 5. U.S. union membership as a share of nonagricultural employment, 1880–2022.

exclusionary practices of overwhelmingly male, white, and blue-collar unions became a source of weakness as more women entered the workforce and the country became more diverse.[93]

However, as Michael Goldfield argued, it is a mistake to assume that women and people of color are not interested in union organizing.[94] In polling dating back to the 1970s, women and workers of color have been highly receptive to unionizing.[95] Indeed, "the female share of union membership has expanded rapidly" in recent decades, particularly in sectors like education, health care, and government administration.[96] Today, although women remain underrepresented in union leadership, they have had marked success in rising up the ranks in unions with high proportions of female members.[97] Similarly, workers of color—and women of color especially—have strongly supported unionization in recent years, and workplaces where people of color are in the majority are more likely to vote for unionization than those with majority white workers.[98]

Macroeconomic factors—in particular, the global competition that fueled deindustrialization—have also been blamed for decreases in union membership.[99] Global competition meant the loss of jobs in the heavily unionized manufacturing sector. New jobs shifted to the service sector and office work, which historically had lower rates of unionization.[100] "It is not surprising," Weiler argued, "that an institution developed to meet the needs of one kind of worker in the factory would prove unappealing to quite another kind of worker in an office."[101] Economists, however, contest Weiler's account. Other developed economies like Canada, Germany, and France faced competitive pressures similar to those in the United States but did not experience a decline in unionization rates.[102]

Another point of contrast for assessing the decline of union density over time has been the surprising durability of public-sector unions, which represent workers in local, state, and federal government.[103] Because government workers are not covered by the NLRA, the development of public-sector unions has followed a different trajectory than for private-sector workers.[104] Prior to the 1950s, public-sector unions did not have formal legal protections: "no right to strike, to bargain, or to arbitrate disputes, and government workers could be fired simply for joining a union."[105]

The precise timing of the growth of public-sector unions is difficult to estimate due to gaps in the data from the BLS and changes in the way the BLS counted union membership in the public sector.[106] Figure 6 includes estimates of the missing BLS data and suggests that public-sector union density rose rapidly throughout the 1960s, when many states extended some labor law protections to government employees.[107] Federal workers also gained the right to organize in 1962.[108]

Remarkably, public-sector unions have not experienced the same decline as private-sector unions, even as legal protections under state law tend to be less robust than the NLRA.[109] Public-sector union membership has stayed relatively steady, at around 35 percent: higher than private-sector union membership at its peak.[110]

Economists believe that an increase in employer resistance to unions in the private sector has driven the decline in union membership.[111] Economist Richard Freeman charted a steep rise in unfair labor practices by private-sector employers between 1950 and 1980, based on filings with the NLRB.[112] Employers use a variety of tactics to discourage workers from joining or voting for a union, including firing union organizers, waging aggressive informational campaigns leading up to an election, refusing to bargain in good faith with unions, and filing decertification petitions.[113] Although retaliating against organizers and refusing to bargain are both unfair labor practices, the economic benefits

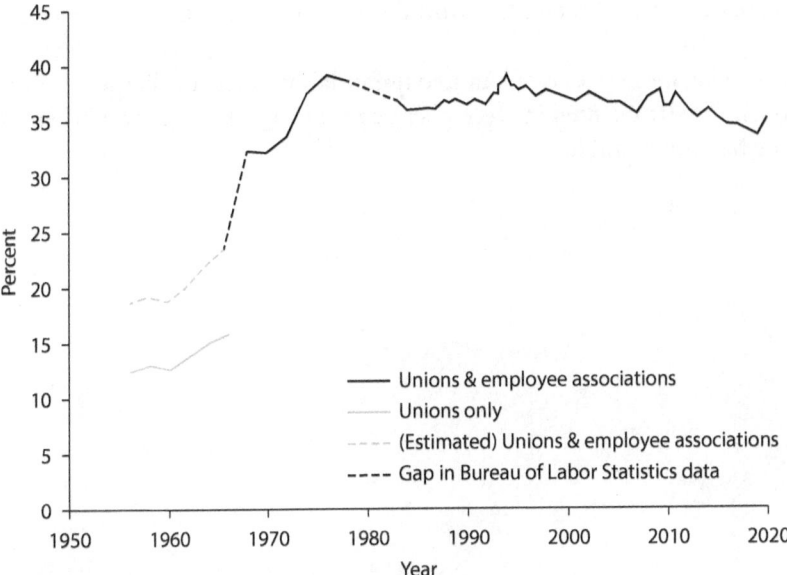

FIGURE 6. Union membership as a share of government employees, 1950–2020.

of doing so tend to far outweigh the penalties imposed by the NLRA months or years later.[114] By contrast, government employers do not face the same competitive market pressures as private employers and therefore have less incentive to thwart unions.[115]

The union drive in the Eugene-based Starbucks stores illustrates both the promise and limits of the NLRA in restraining employer misfeasance. Despite the company's anti-union tactics, all but one of the Starbucks locations in Eugene voted to unionize. More than a year after disciplining Meagher and Jaszewski, an administrative law judge determined that the company's sudden crackdown on the dress code violated the NLRA and ordered Starbucks to reverse their disciplinary record.[116]

Nevertheless, Starbucks and other private-sector employers have an overwhelming economic incentive to commit unfair labor practices. Although workers at nearly four hundred Starbucks locations voted to unionize between 2021 and 2023,[117] the company flatly refused to engage in collective bargaining—another apparent unfair labor practice—which forced the union back into litigation before the NLRB.[118] Whatever the legal merits of the company's position, it was a profitable one, allowing the company to defer the expense of bargaining, as well as any increased wage or benefits workers would obtain through collective bargaining.

Facing more than one hundred unfair labor practices charges,[119] Starbucks finally relented in December 2023 and agreed to meet workers at the bargaining table.

CHAPTER 6

# Equal Opportunity

Harry Hudson was the first Black supervisor at the segregated Lockheed plant in Marietta, Georgia. Following his death, Hudson's family discovered his unpublished memoir in the attic, which was published posthumously in 2015.[1]

In 1952 Hudson and nine other Black college graduates were recruited by the aerospace company to shore up its dismal hiring statistics. Lockheed was a military contractor subject to a series of executive orders prohibiting employment discrimination by federal contractors. Although the company was based in California, its operations in the segregated South presented a particular compliance challenge. By hiring a handful of Black college graduates for skilled labor positions at its segregated Georgia plant, the company hoped to improve its prospects for future military contracts.

Lockheed, however, fell far short of implementing the federal antidiscrimination mandate. Hudson's experience serves as a case in point: he faced discrimination from the moment he set foot in the plant. Unlike white college graduates, who were automatically given jobs in management or salaried positions,[2] Hudson and his fellow recruits were assigned to perform skilled labor. And even in the distribution of skilled work, they were placed at the bottom of the hierarchy, working as glorified riveters.[3]

In his book, Hudson describes his experiences at Lockheed with a dry wit, itemizing the many ways the company wasted Black expertise.

Hudson lamented the lost potential of a Black college classmate with a master's degree, who had been assigned a manual labor job. He wrote that the "top scientists we had were so wrapped up in their own importance that they would not have recognized talent if they were drowning in it."[4]

Lockheed put Hudson's team through an intensive but segregated training program. Although Hudson found some aspects of the program useful, others were comically elementary—particularly a fourth-grade math course in which the Black trainees knew far more than their ostensible trainer.[5] This would become a recurring theme in Hudson's career, during which he and other Black workers were subject to excessive and unnecessary training programs as a condition for advancement, while their white counterparts were simply awarded the jobs for which they were qualified.[6]

Lockheed assigned Hudson and the other Black recruits to a single team, which served to improve the company's hiring statistics without integrating the recruits into the department. A variety of obstacles seemed to follow Hudson's crew around the plant. Other workers assigned the crew a nickname that included the n-word. When a white plant inspector was instructed to sandbag their rivets, he found the work product so meticulous that he decided to measure it in micrometers rather than the more typical measurement of inches or centimeters.[7] Hudson also recounted numerous occasions on which his team solved tricky engineering problems in real time, while the all-white "engineers and methods people" stood around watching and "doing some deep thinking."[8]

Hudson would eventually be promoted to team leader and then supervisor, but the organization was nowhere close to meritocratic. At one point, Hudson recognized two white office workers from an earlier training program.[9] Over the course of a year, they had progressed several levels beyond Hudson in the hierarchy. Hudson also noticed that the original foreman for his crew—a white man—seemed tainted by association and was relegated to a dead-end job despite the team's success.[10]

Although Hudson was frequently trotted out by Lockheed as a success story, his career stalled. His boss denied his requests for a promotion to assistant manager because he could not fathom the idea of a Black man directing hundreds of white men.[11] In the 1960s, after Hudson had served in management for eight years,[12] an executive persuaded him to take a job in purchasing, claiming it would be a path to higher management. Three weeks later, Lockheed installed a white man in the assistant manager role Hudson had requested.[13]

Although Hudson would eventually shoulder substantial responsibility in the purchasing department, he was not meaningfully promoted within or beyond the department.[14] He retired from the company in 1987.

In comparing his own career to that of the executive who had enticed him to take the purchasing job, Hudson wrote, "What he did not mention was the fact that he was a vice president and my chances of ever reaching that position were about as possible as two grains of sand raising the ocean levels a foot."[15]

. . .

Harry Hudson's lifetime spanned a transformation from a legal regime in which workplace segregation was allowed, to one where defense contractors would be required to take affirmative action to address discrimination under Executive Order 11246.[16] Hudson's career also encompassed the changes wrought by Title VII of the Civil Rights Act of 1964, which prohibited discrimination by virtually all private employers and unions. Though his career was evidence of that progress, it also reveals the limits of the law and the practices employers implemented to comply with it.

While it might be tempting to characterize Lockheed as a particularly bad actor, the company was well ahead of many other companies in the South.[17] Indeed, Lockheed's 1961 approach to addressing discrimination would be used as a model for other defense contractors with affirmative action obligations in the early 1960s.[18] Following the passage of Title VII, watered-down versions of those defense contractor practices would be widely adopted by private employers.

Like the NLRA, Title VII would prove to be an important but ultimately limited restriction on employer discretion. Some limitations arose from legislative compromise embedded in the legislation itself. The Supreme Court has played an inconsistent role, in some instances expanding the scope of Title VII and in others creating loopholes that defer to employer governance. Over time, employers have also engaged in a subtle but powerful form of resistance through human resources policies and practices that create the appearance of fairness and equity while primarily serving the employer's interests.

Employment practices are shaped by the law but not exclusively determined by them. As part I illustrated, wage and hour practices were shaped by the FLSA, but also reflect the economic interests and preferences of management and the social hierarchies of the time. Although the FLSA forced employers to change some practices (e.g., piece-rate pay), it also authorized employers to continue prior practices (e.g., salary pay for white-collar workers).

Similarly, hiring, pay, promotion, and termination practices have been shaped by antidiscrimination laws. However, companies would ultimately decide how to alter their practices in a way that would pass muster under Title VII, as well as subsequent antidiscrimination laws, such as the Pregnancy Discrimination Act, the Age Discrimination in Employment Act, and the Americans with Disabilities Act. By focusing on equal opportunity rather than workplace integration, Title VII authorized employers to make only incremental changes to their practices.

This chapter recounts the trajectory of federal antidiscrimination laws before and after the passage of the Civil Rights Act of 1964. The earliest antidiscrimination mandates applied to federal contractors like Lockheed, which adopted an incrementalist approach to desegregation. Despite consistent public opposition from the NAACP, Lockheed was heralded by the Kennedy administration as a leader and innovator in compliance measures. Lockheed's approach would be imitated by countless other companies in the decades that followed.

Title VII likewise imposed a model of incremental change in the private sector, as it was organized around equality of opportunity, rather than desegregation. Various amendments to the original bill also served to limit the types of reforms employers would have to adopt to comply with the law. I illustrate the limited nature of Title VII using two landmark Supreme Court cases, *Griggs v. Duke Power* and *McDonnell Douglas v. Green*. The slow pace of workplace desegregation evident from early Supreme Court jurisprudence would continue over the next fifty years, as documented in empirical research by sociologists Kevin Stainback and Donald Tomaskovic-Devey. These trends provide additional context for the individual experiences of Harry Hudson.

LOCKHEED'S PLAN FOR PROGRESS

In 1941 President Roosevelt issued an executive order that prohibited discrimination on the basis of "race, creed, color, or national origin" in federal employment and defense contracts.[19] The 1941 order included no enforcement mechanism, although a follow-up order in 1943 included a complaint process and public hearings.[20] Harry S. Truman and Dwight D. Eisenhower later issued similar orders, also with limited enforcement capabilities.[21] Executive Order 10925, issued by President John F. Kennedy in 1961, added a requirement that contractors engage in "affirmative action" and included an enforcement mechanism that could result in termination of a government contract.[22]

Because these federal executive orders preceded later civil rights laws that applied to the private sector, defense contractors like Lockheed did not have much precedent to work with. That also meant they could drag their feet, changing some practices while leaving many other systems in place. In his study of the Georgia Lockheed plant, historian Randall Patton concluded that the company had limited interest in integrating the plant during the 1940 and 1950s.[23] A 1957 report by the NAACP recounted Lockheed's failure to hire Black workers and its segregation of those workers into two departments in entry-level positions.[24] The report further described the exclusion of Black workers from an apprenticeship program jointly administered by the company and the union.[25] The limited progress the company made in the 1950s was also "largely erased" through downsizing, leaving Lockheed in a poor position in 1961 when Kennedy took office.[26]

The company was nowhere close to complying with the federal nondiscrimination order even before Kennedy's more stringent executive order in March 1961.[27] The Georgia plant did not employ any Black women.[28] Its janitorial staff was exclusively Black.[29] And although the nearby population was 21 percent African American,[30] Black workers only made up 4 percent of its workforce (four hundred of ten thousand workers).[31] Black workers had even been refused service in a "white-designated" Lockheed cafeteria.[32]

In April 1961 the Kennedy administration announced that it had been awarded a $1 billion contract to Lockheed Martin. The NAACP was incensed, telling the *New York Times* the contract was "shameful mockery" of the recent executive order.[33] The NAACP argued that Black workers were "limited to the unskilled and semi-skilled job classifications" and denied promotions "beyond certain limited job classifications."[34] The organization submitted thirty-six affidavits from Black workers to challenge the defense contract.[35]

Lockheed insisted that it had "very conscientiously and vigorously done everything humanly possible to comply in all regulations in the operations of this facility" and that it had "made more progress than any individual employer in the South."[36] In his own analysis, historian Randall Patton concluded that Lockheed's claims of comparative progress were largely accurate, which mostly speaks to the lack of progress across the South in the 1950s.[37] Moreover, segregation was not limited to the South. Sociologists Kevin Stainback and Donald Tomaskovic-Devey documented high rates of segregation on the basis of race and gender nationwide as late as 1966, concluding that at that time "black men, white women, and black women were nearly totally excluded from both managerial and professional jobs, and nearly all women were excluded from skilled craft production jobs."[38] The *New York Times* job ads in 1966 still had a separate section for "help wanted male" and "help wanted female."[39]

Determined to keep its billion-dollar contract, Lockheed embarked on a voluntary "Plan for Progress," to "increase minority hiring, promotion and retention," which had been extensively negotiated with the President's Committee on Equal Opportunity. However, the plan was slow moving, premised on the idea that "if an integrated work force with an integrated facility was to become a reality ... progress ... had to be gradual."[40] The plan was signed in a ceremony at the oval office.[41] A month later, the *New York Times* reported that the White House Committee "has made no secret of its intention to use the Lockheed pact as a model in its drive to eliminate employment discrimination" by government contractors."[42]

The NAACP was skeptical of the plan, worried that the company would simply take a "once over lightly" approach. Ruby Hurley, the NAACP regional secretary, observed, "Knowing the attitude of the people down here, we can't be too optimistic."[43] Another NAACP leader, Herbert Hill, was well attuned to the implications of Lockheed's incrementalist approach, telling a reporter, "We reject the idea that it will take years before any tangible results can be expected in getting Negroes into the skilled occupations from which they have been excluded so rigorously by the traditional and institutionalized pattern of discrimination practiced by the company and the union."[44] Rather than taking the criticism seriously, the company president responded that no amount of progress would satisfy the NAACP.[45]

Before the ink was dry on the Lockheed plan, the President's Commission decided to use it as a model for other companies. Within months, eight other major government contractors signed their own Plans for Progress, including General Electric, Boeing, and United Airlines, among others.[46] According to sociologist Frank Dobbin, these plans were all "modeled on Lockheed's, promising strict nondiscrimination policies for hiring and firing, and new recruitment efforts ... including visits to historically black colleges."[47]

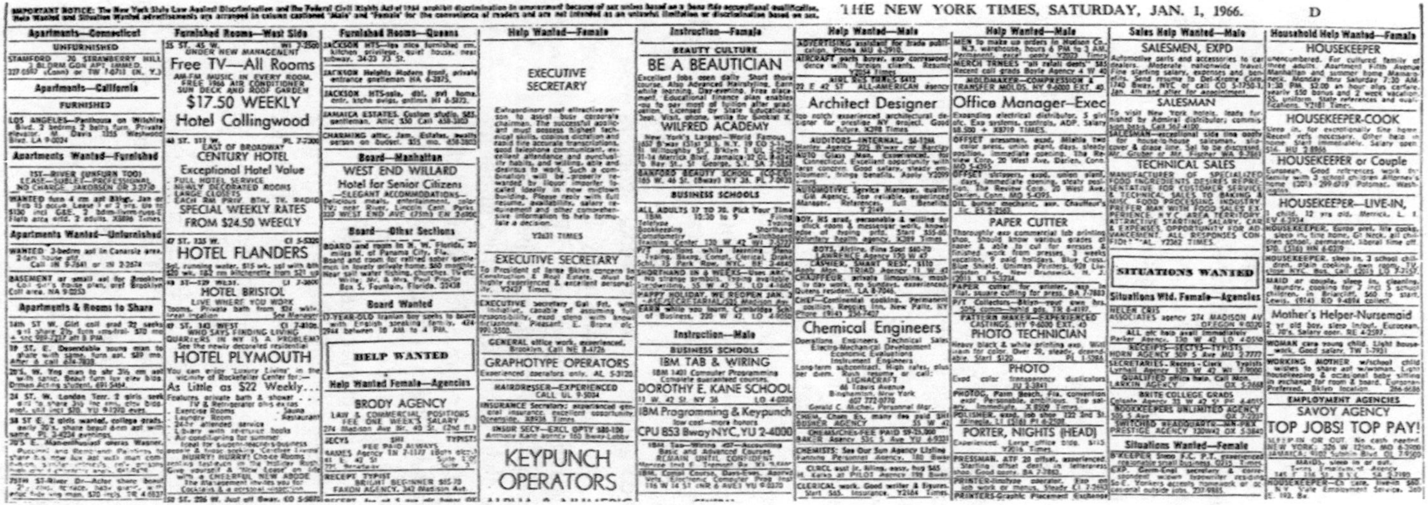

THE NEW YORK TIMES, SATURDAY, JAN. 1, 1966. D

Apartments—Connecticut

Apartments—California

Apartments Wanted—Furnished

Apartments Wanted—Unfurnished

Apartments & Rooms to Share

Furnished Rooms—West Side

Free TV—All Rooms

$17.50 WEEKLY

Hotel Collingwood

CENTURY HOTEL

Exceptional Hotel Value

SPECIAL WEEKLY RATES

FROM $24.50 WEEKLY

HOTEL FLANDERS

HOTEL BRISTOL

HOTEL PLYMOUTH

As Little as $22 Weekly...

Furnished Rooms—Queens

Board—Manhattan

WEST END WILLARD

Hotel for Senior Citizens

Board—Other Sections

Board Wanted

HELP WANTED

Help Wanted Female—Agencies

BRODY AGENCY

Help Wanted—Female

EXECUTIVE SECRETARY

EXECUTIVE SECRETARY

GRAPHOTYPE OPERATORS

KEYPUNCH OPERATORS

Instruction—Female

BEAUTY CULTURE

BE A BEAUTICIAN

WILFRED ACADEMY

BUSINESS SCHOOLS

Instruction—Male

BUSINESS SCHOOLS

IBM TAB & WIRING

DOROTHY E. KANE SCHOOL

IBM Programming & Keypunch

CPU 853 Bway NYC, YU 2-4000

Help Wanted—Male

Architect Designer

Chemical Engineers

Help Wanted—Male

Office Manager—Exec

PAPER CUTTER

PHOTO TECHNICIAN

PHOTO

PORTER, NIGHTS (HEAD)

Sales Help Wanted—Male

SALESMEN, EXPD

SALESMAN

TECHNICAL SALES

SITUATIONS WANTED

Situations Wtd. Female—Agencies

Situations Wanted—Female

Household Help Wanted—Female

HOUSEKEEPER

HOUSEKEEPER-COOK

HOUSEKEEPER or Couple

HOUSEKEEPER—LIVE-IN,

Mother's Helper-Nursemaid

EMPLOYMENT AGENCIES

SAVOY AGENCY

TOP JOBS! TOP PAY!

FIGURE 7. Gender-segregated "help wanted" advertisements published in the *New York Times*, January 1, 1966.

The results of Lockheed's program were mixed. Although its cafeteria had been formally desegregated, the company stripped the area of tables and chairs to avoid "the touchy problem" of people of different races eating together.[48] Likewise, drinking fountains were replaced with paper cups—some sixty-three thousand per day—yet another concession to complaints from white workers about workplace integration.

At the same time, the company also started recruiting at historically Black colleges and high schools and admitting Black workers into its management training programs.[49] The company made some progress in the late 1960s, doubling Black representation in the workforce from 5.7 percent to nearly 10 percent—albeit half the representation the surrounding population demographics would have suggested.[50] Lockheed also promoted many Black workers, though they represented only 2 percent of all workers in supervisory positions.[51] Black workers likewise remained underrepresented among salaried workers, since Lockheed had continued its practice of hiring and promoting white candidates with "no more than a high school degree" into management.[52] Black candidates with similar or superior qualifications were not afforded this streamlined path into salaried and managerial roles.[53]

Between 1965 and 1969, Black workers at Lockheed filed 184 claims with the Equal Employment Opportunity Commission (EEOC).[54] Principal among their complaints was that Black workers were "bird dogged" by supervisors: scrutinized excessively for any perceived failure. Indeed, Lockheed's own records suggested Black workers were terminated at three times their representation in the company.[55] Lockheed aggressively fought the charges and apparently did not fix the problem.[56] In an internal memo, a personnel executive claimed that "not one" of its employment decisions had been "reversed" by the EEOC.[57]

By 1970 Lockheed's employment numbers for Black workers in supervisory, salaried, and clerical jobs were about average compared to other large firms.[58] Even so, in 1970—more than twenty-five years since it had been subject to a nondiscrimination mandate from the federal government—the company was nowhere close to management representation on a level with the general population.

In the intervening period, Lockheed's plan had taken on a life of its own as the Plans for Progress—a network of companies that pledged to undertake their own versions of the program.[59] In 2000, the Department of Labor credited the Plans for Progress as the "current blueprint for affirmative action."[60]

## TITLE VII OF THE CIVIL RIGHTS ACT OF 1964

Following the passage of Title VII, a wide variety of private-sector employers implemented their own watered-down versions of Lockheed's plan. Title VII of the Civil Rights Act was passed as part of a much broader package that protected voting rights and desegregated public accommodations and education. Title VII, which was specific to antidiscrimination in the employment context, was captioned "Equal Employment Opportunity."[61]

Title VII is relatively short. The operative language consists of a few sentences, stating that it is unlawful for an employer "to fail or refuse to hire or to discharge any individual, or otherwise to discriminate against any individual with respect to his compensation, terms, conditions or privileges of employment, because of such individual's race, color, religion, sex, or national origin."[62] The law also prohibits discrimination by unions and retaliation against workers for asserting their rights.[63] Critically, Title VII empowered individuals to bring a private right of action in court. Title VII also created a federal agency, the EEOC, to investigate complaints and conciliate claims.[64]

Like the FLSA, Title VII reflects the social context in which it was passed. The act was a product of the civil rights protest movement led by Dr. Martin Luther King Jr., the NAACP, and nonviolent demonstrators protesting segregation.[65] Until the civil rights movement exploded on the national scene, progress toward antidiscrimination law had been slow and inconsistent. The executive orders previously described were limited to government contractors and federal employment, not private-sector employers.

As of 1964, about half of states had enacted some form of law prohibiting workplace discrimination.[66] Many antidiscrimination laws were introduced in the U.S. House and Senate between 1946 and 1963, but none succeeded other than the Equal Pay Act,[67] which was limited to sex-based wage disparities.[68] It was the nonviolent civil rights activists at lunch counters, on buses, and at schools who led President Kennedy to announce his support for civil rights legislation in 1963.[69]

However, the final shape of the law also reflects the influence of members of Congress who were opposed to the bill or sought to limit its reach. For example, sex discrimination was not part of the draft language for Title VII, and other parts of the Civil Rights Act make no mention of sex. The inclusion of the word "sex" in Title VII came as an amendment by civil rights opponent Congressman Howard Smith of Virginia.

Although the common mythology of the amendment was that Smith introduced the amendment as a joke, its ultimate inclusion would be more accurately attributed to a mix of racism and feminist activism. Smith was persuaded to introduce the amendment by the National Woman's Party (NWP), a feminist organization that predominantly advocated for the interests of white women.[70] The NWP genuinely sought the inclusion of the word "sex" in the bill and persuaded Smith to introduce the amendment to obstruct its progress.[71]

However, Smith's proposed amendment gained political momentum. The handful of female members of Congress argued in support of the amendment. Congresswoman Martha Griffiths made the contradictory argument that adding the word "sex" would protect white women from suffering discrimination relative to Black women, but also ensure that Black women would not be left behind entirely.[72] Griffiths's argument about protecting white women gained the most traction; opponents of the Civil Rights bill seem to have concluded that "if the bill was to pass" they "preferred a bill with a ban on sex discrimination."[73] By the time the law made it to the Senate, the Republican minority leader "gave up" on having the word "sex" removed, "to avoid the wrath of the women."[74]

Business concerns about meddling in internal corporate decision-making are also reflected in the legislative history. The committee report from the House provided that the "internal affairs of employers and labor organizations must not be interfered with except to the limited extent that correction is required in discrimination practices."[75] The statute further provided that applying a "seniority or merit system" would not run afoul of the act absent an "intention to discriminate."[76] Still another amendment provided that the law would not require any employers to "grant preferential treatment to any individual" based on "an imbalance which may exist with respect to the total number or percentage of persons ... in the available workforce"—to address opponents' fear that the law would produce "quota hiring."[77] A late amendment to this section further provided that "the results of any professionally developed ability test" was lawful provided that it was not "designed, intended or used to discriminate."[78] These amendments had the cumulative effect of protecting existing employer practices from scrutiny and limiting the types of reforms they would need to make to comply with the law.

Amendments to the bill also limited the power of the EEOC, the federal agency created to enforce the law. Although the original bill gave the EEOC power to bring lawsuits on behalf of workers, a Senate amendment vested that power in the attorney general out of concern the EEOC would be too powerful.[79] The EEOC's power to bring a "pattern or practice" claim on behalf of employees would be restored in a 1972 amendment to the law.[80]

Title VII would also be phased in slowly. A year after passage, the law would cover only companies with more than one hundred employees. The law would apply to successively smaller employers until the fifth year after passage, at which point any company with twenty-five or more employees would be covered.[81]

The statute's construction around equal opportunity and its tacit endorsement of existing practices (seniority, testing) and prohibitions on alternate approaches (quotas) meant that companies would not be required to dismantle decades of segregation that produced a racial or gender imbalance in various departments. Companies and unions would not have to grant seniority to Black workers previously excluded from unions. Instead, they only had to let them in and start from the ground floor.

It was a model of workplace transformation that, as the statute promised, would provide "equal opportunity" but could not be expected to deliver equality within the workplace in the near term. Indeed, in criticizing Lockheed's plan in 1961, the NAACP correctly identified that an incrementalist approach was no match for the "traditional and institutionalized pattern of discrimination."[82]

## THE LIMITS OF AN EQUAL OPPORTUNITY MODEL

The limits of Title VII's reach were visible in early Supreme Court jurisprudence from the 1970s, despite the court's attempts to construe the statute as broadly as possible. The Supreme Court's first major Title VII ruling, *Griggs v. Duke Power*, is a case in point.

*Griggs* involved a racially segregated power plant in North Carolina. The departments reflected a rigid racial hierarchy and somewhat porous educational hierarchy. The company had two manual labor departments: the "labor" department, which exclusively consisted of Black workers,[83] and the "coal handling" department, which was exclusively white.[84] The company also had favored "indoor" jobs, in the operations, maintenance, and laboratory and test departments.[85] The "indoor" jobs offered the best pay and the most opportunities for advancement. The labor department was the lowest paid, followed by the coal handling department.

94 | The Right to Govern

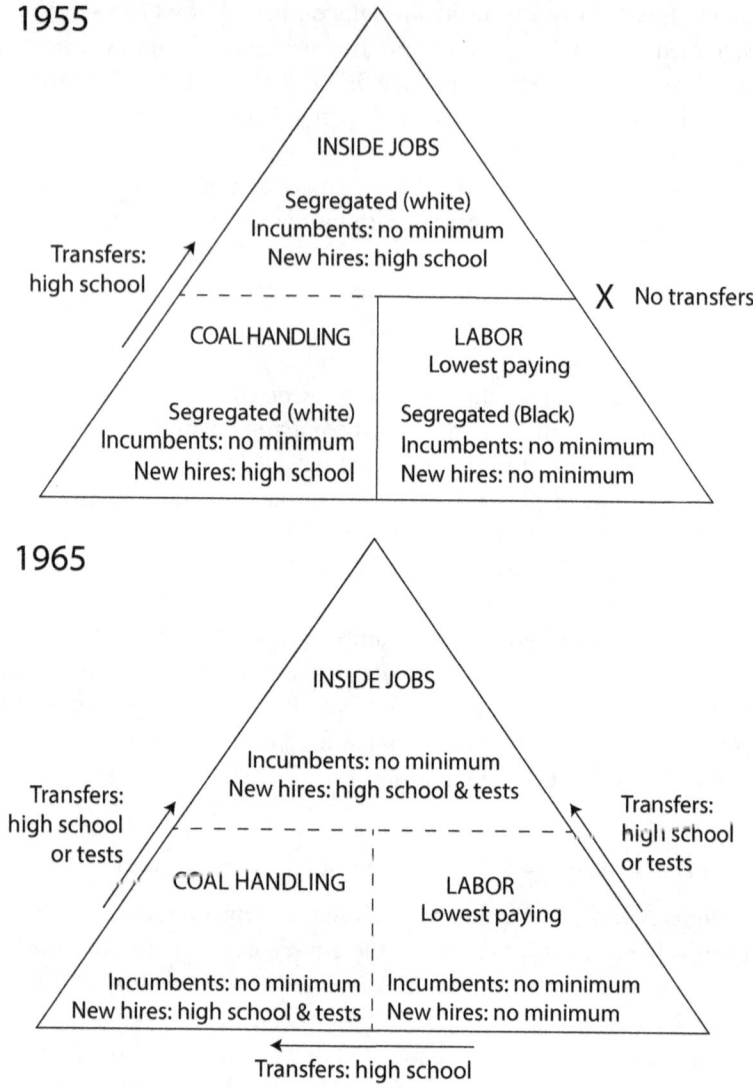

FIGURE 8. Duke Power's hiring and transfer rules in 1955 and 1965.

Around ten years before the effective date of Title VII, Duke Power instituted a high school diploma requirement for all new hires, except in the labor department. However, workers without a high school diploma in other departments could continue working in their jobs, and by all accounts they did so successfully.[86] When white workers in the coal handling department wanted to transfer to an "indoor" department, they successfully lobbied for an alternate to the high school graduation requirement: an aptitude test known as the "Wonderlic test," which measured the "average" attainment of a high school graduate.[87] This included such rarified vocabulary questions as the difference between "adopt" and "adept," "reflect" and "reflex," "pretentions" and "pretensious [sic]," and "large" and "aggrandize."[88]

When Title VII came into effect at Duke Power, the company did not desegregate the labor and coal handling departments, even though both departments appear to have been functionally identical and could have been merged. It also did not automatically promote qualified Black applicants into managerial positions in either department or into jobs at indoor departments. Duke Power also does not appear to have equalized pay rates between the labor and coal handling departments. Indeed, no such measures were even discussed in the subsequent litigation.

As the *Griggs* case illustrates, Title VII did not mandate desegregation or even equal treatment. What it required was equality in "opportunities"—whenever those opportunities happened to be made available. Thus, even assuming Black workers had an "equal opportunity" for transfer between the labor and coal handling department, those transfers would only occur at the rate in which vacancies in the coal handling department were available. In other words, workers who had previously benefited from segregation would be able to maintain those advantages. To comply with Title VII, Duke Power need only stop discriminating in available opportunities going forward.

Even so, Duke Power chose not to implement an easy transfer process that would have begun the slow process of desegregating the labor and coal handling department. Instead, it erected the same barrier for transfers from the labor department to the coal handling department that had previously applied to transfers between coal handling and "indoor" jobs: a high school diploma or a passing score on the Wonderlic test. New hires were subject to an even higher standard: new job applicants had to both have a high school diploma and pass the Wonderlic test.[89]

The government sued Duke Power for its practices, arguing that both the high school graduation requirement and the Wonderlic test appeared to be neutral but had the effect of freezing the status quo in place. And indeed, the combination of the testing requirement for transfers and more stringent rules for new hires kept the company racially segregated until 1966, when the first Black worker succeeded in transferring out of the labor department.[90] Current employees considered the test so difficult that "an overwhelming number" of employees "declined to take it."[91] Only three employees had taken the test—two Black employees and one white employee—and all had failed.[92] The government argued that both the Wonderlic test and the graduation requirement had a disproportionate effect on Black workers as a result of the segregated educational system under Jim Crow laws.[93]

During oral arguments before the Supreme Court, the company's lawyer was asked to justify the company's stringent hiring standards. The lawyer insisted that the standards were necessary to ensure the promotability of workers within the organization. Justice Thurgood Marshall—the Court's first Black justice—found this claim ridiculous, asking why they didn't also impose a PhD requirement on the laborer position,[94] since any employee "might go up to be President too."[95] Justice Marshall noted that the company was not working from a "clean slate" but "kn[ew] fully well that [it] had a prior policy of rigid segregation and exclusion."[96]

In its ruling, the Supreme Court assumed that Title VII did not reach the company's prior practice of segregation, despite its ongoing practices that left the status quo largely in place. The Court would, however, require employers to provide stronger justifications for a seemingly neutral "practic[e], procedur[e] or tes[t]" that "operat[es] to 'freeze' the status quo of prior discriminatory employment practices."[97] The court interpreted Title VII's prohibition on employment decisions "because of" race broadly, to require "the removal of artificial, arbitrary, and unnecessary barriers to employment when the barriers operate invidiously to discriminate on the basis for racial or other impermissible classification."[98]

However, even the Court's sweeping language about "barriers" presumed only a barrier to opportunity. Employers would continue to control the supply of opportunities and the larger organizational structure. Where the most coveted opportunities arose sporadically—particularly hiring into favored positions and promotions—the rate of change within the organization slowed to a trickle.

## THE MCDONNELL DOUGLAS ERA

*Griggs* did not, however, become the defining word in employment discrimination law. Instead, the case became somewhat of an evolutionary dead end. *Griggs* would come to stand for a narrow cause of action known as "disparate impact," through which plaintiffs can use statistics to challenge facially neutral rules with a discriminatory effect. Disparate impact claims are resource intensive to litigate and consequently are relatively rare.[99]

The broad language in *Griggs* about barriers to advancement regardless of intent would be supplanted by a narrower and formalistic approach focused on motive and pretext, articulated in a 1973 case involving a different military contractor, McDonnell Douglas.[100]

*McDonnell Douglas v. Green* involved Percy Green, a St. Louis civil rights activist who had been the lone Black man in a department of one hundred white men working on simulations for NASA's Gemini project at McDonnell Douglas.[101] When the company conducted a layoff in 1964, he was selected for termination.[102] It would have been a good discrimination lawsuit. But Title VII was still in legal purgatory, stalled by a provision in the law that delayed its enforcement.[103]

Without a legal remedy, Green turned to activism. He organized a stall-in, where he and others tied up traffic by parking their cars on the road to the factory. The stall-in lasted about ten minutes, at which point the police towed Green's car.[104] The police arrested Green for obstructing traffic, and he later pled guilty to a minor traffic offense, which carried a $50 fine.[105]

That might have been the end of the story. But in July 1965, when Title VII finally came into effect, McDonnell Douglas advertised for mechanic jobs, work that Green had performed at the company for nine years.[106] Green applied and was rejected the very next day.[107] The company cited his participation in the company protests as the basis for its decision.[108] Green brought a discrimination and retaliation lawsuit under Title VII based on the company's refusal to hire him back.

In *McDonnell Douglas*, the Supreme Court set out a burden-shifting framework for individuals seeking to challenge discriminatory employment decisions.[109] Plaintiffs like Green could establish a prima facie case relatively easily, by showing he was qualified for the job and similarly situated others outside the protected category were treated differently. However, the employer in turn could rebut that case by producing a legitimate nondiscriminatory reason that motivated its decision. The plaintiff would then either have to prove that the employer's decision was motivated by discrimination, or that the reason it had proffered was pretextual.

Unlike *Griggs*, the case would turn on whether the employer was motivated by discrimination, rather than on whether the employer had imposed barriers to advancement that were not job related. Under

FIGURE 9. Poster commemorating Percy Green's activism.

*McDonnell Douglas*, any "legitimate non-discriminatory reason" can serve to rebut a discrimination case.[110] Violating a company policy certainly qualifies as a nondiscriminatory reason,[111] as does insubordination, uncooperative behavior, or poor performance.[112] Even a perceived violation of the company policy—regardless of whether the employee actually violated the policy—is also a valid defense to a discrimination claim.[113] What matters is that the company "held an honest belief" that the employee was a rule breaker.[114]

*McDonnell Douglas* ultimately represents a concession to employer governance. Within the *McDonnell Douglas* framework, the employer retains the discretion to decide the bases it will use to hire, fire, promote, and pay, regardless of merit, regardless of job-relatedness. Unless provably discriminatory, anything goes. Consequently, the *McDonnell Douglas* structure would prove vulnerable to employer compliance strategies that focused more heavily on documentation than on fixing the underlying problem, which are described in greater detail in chapter 7.

The trajectory of Title VII jurisprudence provides a partial explanation for Harry Hudson's experience and the broader statistics at Lockheed. The opportunity-based model illustrated in *Griggs* did not require companies to fix their past practices or make workers whole for past discrimination. Consequently, Lockheed did not attempt to make Hudson whole for the loss of employment opportunities he experienced between 1952 and 1961, when his white contemporaries were placed far above him on the compensation and promotional ladder. Other aspects of Hudson's story may have violated Title VII, particularly the company's refusal to promote him to assistant manager. On the other hand, employers like Lockheed became increasingly sophisticated at using documentation and other HR processes to insulate their decisions from liability. Lockheed touted its aggressive litigation stance in internal communications,[115] suggesting Hudson would have faced a long road had he attempted to sue.

National statistics analyzed in a book by sociologists Kevin Stainback and Donald Tomaskovic-Devey confirm Hudson's experience on a national scale. Using data that companies reported to the EEOC from 1966 to 2005, Stainback and Tomaskovic-Devey found that employment segregation decreased for Black men between 1966 and 1980, after which it leveled off.[116] (They use the term "segregation" not in the sense of a policy of racial and gender separation, but as a numeric measurement of the degree of separation within a workforce by occupation.)[117] During that same time period, white men experienced a substantial decline in labor force representation, as white women joined the workforce, along with Latino and Asian workers.[118] However, white men continued to retain a disproportionate share of the most favored jobs, particularly managerial jobs and skilled trades.[119]

Stainback and Tomaskovic-Devey noticed that both Black men and women, as well as white women, made far greater gains in professional jobs than in managerial jobs, which the authors attributed to the "formal education credentials" associated with the professions.[120] Internal promotions, which are controlled by incumbent workers, tend to favor workers who are similar to those already occupying that position.[121] The researchers concluded that "while white male advantages have been eroded, they remain the norm in nearly all workplaces" and that "white men" continue to be "pushed up in organizational hierarchies."[122]

Stainback and Tomaskovic-Devey also documented intersectional disadvantage for Black women[123]—who experienced additional discrimination as a result of both their race and sex. In the 1970s and 1980s, white women experienced substantial employment gains with the rise of the feminist movement. Black women did not benefit nearly as much from desegregation or the feminist movement.[124] In fact, the data suggested a resegregation of white and Black women between 1970 and 2000. Black women were largely left behind while white women made gains in "traditionally male managerial and professional jobs."[125] By 2000, progress for all women relative to men stopped.[126]

In summary, Title VII's potential to reverse employment discrimination was limited from the start. The blueprint for how employers would be expected to respond to antidiscrimination mandates was established by government contractors, and in particular Lockheed's Plan for Progress. Title VII itself contained a variety of concessions to employer governance, particularly by limiting its scope to employment opportunities, as illustrated by the *Griggs* decision. The *McDonnell Douglas* case would open the door to a new type of employer gamesmanship based on documentation and internal processes that create the illusion of fairness without necessarily addressing the underlying problem. These processes are the subject of chapter 7.

CHAPTER 7

# Human Resources

On June 15, 2020, the Supreme Court issued a landmark opinion, *Bostock v. Clayton County*, declaring that discrimination on the basis of sexual orientation or gender identity qualified as discrimination on the basis of "sex" under Title VII of the Civil Rights Act.[1] It was the most significant expansion of Title VII in decades.

Prior to *Bostock*, LGBT workers faced highly uncertain prospects in court. If a termination was based on gender stereotypes—for example, not conforming to a masculine or feminine ideal—they could potentially rely on Title VII jurisprudence prohibiting stereotype-based decision-making.[2] However, if the termination was based solely on sexual orientation, some courts considered it permissible under Title VII because both men and women would be equally affected by the practice.[3]

Gerald Bostock, a gay man who managed a court-connected child welfare program in Georgia, found himself on the wrong side of this older line of cases. In his complaint, Bostock alleged that his employer initiated an audit into his use of "program funds" four months after joining "a gay recreational softball league."[4] The audit, Bostock alleged, was "a pretext for discrimination against Plaintiff based on his sexual orientation and failure to conform to a gender stereotype."[5] His subsequent termination for "conduct unbecoming a Clayton County Employee" was thus a "pretext for discrimination . . . based on sex and/or sexual orientation."[6]

Bostock's case did not last long at the federal district court, which granted a motion to dismiss, ruling that sexual orientation claims were not actionable under Title VII. His lawyers, Thomas Mew and Edward Buckley, appealed the case to the 11th Circuit, which affirmed the lower court ruling.[7] They appealed to the Supreme Court, which granted certiorari and consolidated Bostock's case with two others brought by workers fired for their LGBT status: Donald Zarda and Aimee Stephens.[8]

Bostock had been litigating for seven years by the time the Supreme Court issued its ruling in 2020. During that period, Zarda and Stephens passed away,[9] leaving Bostock as the only surviving plaintiff.

The day after the ruling, Mew was in a serious car crash involving a driver making an illegal left turn.[10] Mew escaped without serious injury, but his car was totaled.[11] A friend on Facebook suggested he buy a Porsche to celebrate his Supreme Court windfall.[12]

But Mew and Buckley hadn't received a penny in legal fees. The Supreme Court hadn't delivered a judgment for Bostock; it only saved the case from a premature death.[13] Bostock's lawyers still had discovery and a likely motion for summary judgment ahead of them.

Mew bought a pickup truck.[14]

...

This chapter uses facts from the *Bostock* case to illustrate the ways in which employers have adopted defensive systems to protect themselves from Title VII litigation. Gerald Bostock's story also illustrates the strict division of labor between managers and human resources (HR), through which managers retain much of the decision-making authority to hire, fire, and discipline workers. Broadly speaking, the policies and procedures that employers have developed amount to a form of internal governance. Over recent decades, employers have been quite successful at persuading courts to defer to internal governance and managerial discretion.

### THE RISE OF THE HUMAN RESOURCES PLAYBOOK

Sociologist Frank Dobbin traces the modern HR department to its organizational predecessor in the 1940s and 1950s: the labor relations department. Labor relations was predominantly populated by white men who managed the company's relationship with unions.[15] Because union density was relatively high—ranging from 25 to 34 percent of nonfarm labor—labor relations occupied a powerful role within companies.[16]

Failure to properly manage union relations could end in a strike or an unfavorable ruling from a labor arbitrator. However, as union density declined, the labor relations department would eventually be displaced by HR,[17] a profession dominated by white women who specialized in compliance for nonunionized employees.[18]

Sociologists trace the growth of the HR profession to the 1964 passage of Title VII of the Civil Rights Act.[19] Because the law's vague prohibition against "discrimination" provided little guidance on how to comply with the law, HR professionals filled the void by promoting internal antidiscrimination policies and processes for handling employee complaints.[20] According to Dobbin, these policies and processes were a new spin on preexisting labor grievance policies and policies prohibiting "discrimination" against union organizers.[21]

Lauren Edelman's research suggests that federal government agencies were the earliest adopters of antidiscrimination policies and complaint procedures, "followed by colleges, state and local agencies" and federal contractors, beginning in the 1960s.[22] Those practices spread to the private sector in the 1970s and 1980s.[23] Human resources practices also came to include formal job descriptions and performance evaluations, which would be revised to include anti-harassment programs once the Supreme Court first recognized harassment claims under Title VII in 1986.[24]

Human resources processes differ substantially from labor relations systems. The dispute resolution processes available to unionized workers serve as a substantial limit on managerial authority because they are an extension of the rights provided in the NLRA. Labor grievances and arbitration serve to interpret a collective bargaining agreement, which itself was negotiated at arm's length between the union and the company. Collective bargaining agreements can impose both substantive and procedural limits on managerial authority, such as a right to be terminated for cause or on the basis of seniority, rather than at-will. The agreement may also specify the process the employer must follow if it wishes to terminate an employee, or at the very least, offer a worker an opportunity to file a grievance if termination is contrary to the rights specified in the agreement.

By contrast, HR processes are typically drafted exclusively by companies without employee input. Although the policies serve the broader goal of avoiding or reducing lawsuits under Title VII or other civil rights law, they are generally not designed to serve other goals that might be important to employees, such as offering meaningful remedies, punishing wrongdoers, uncovering the truth, or treating workers fairly.[25]

The history of Lockheed Martin, discussed in chapter 6, serves as a case in point. When Lockheed implemented formal performance evaluations, it did not require managers to adopt rigorous, job-related criteria for evaluating worker performance.[26] Instead, the company allowed managers to formalize and document existing criteria for evaluating workers.[27] Formal performance evaluations were an improvement over prior practices insofar as they made performance standards more transparent to workers and forced managers to impose the "same standards" on their direct reports, regardless of race.[28] On the other hand, Lockheed also used the documentation produced by the new performance evaluation system to defend its practice of terminating Black workers at triple the rate of their representation in the workforce.[29] While the Lockheed practices may have initially been devised to reduce discrimination, their eventual function within the workplace would be to document existing practices and defend the company in litigation.[30]

Indeed, after studying HR practices for decades, sociologist Lauren Edelman concluded that they were "symbolic structures," a form of "window-dressing" meant to create the appearance of compliance while doing little to advance the cause of equal employment opportunity.[31] Recent social science research also casts doubt on the efficacy of many common HR practices. In a large-scale study of 708 companies over a fifty-year period, sociologists Alexandra Kalev, Frank Dobbin, and Erin Kelly found that diversity training did not improve the gender or racial diversity of management.[32] Other studies suggest that anti-harassment trainings do not meaningfully alter the attitudes or behavior of participants.[33] Kalev and colleagues also found that formal personnel policies likewise had no positive effects on racial diversity over time and may even have potentially negative effects.[34] The few corporate practices that were associated with improvement in managerial diversity—affirmative action programs and diversity task forces—are the exception rather than the norm in corporate America today.[35]

The poor track record of HR policies and processes speaks to the subordinate role that the HR department plays in corporate organizations.[36] As discussed in greater detail later in this chapter, HR is rarely the ultimate decision-maker in hiring, firing, and promotion decisions. While HR will release a job description and set up an interview, it often is managers that ultimately decide who to hire. Likewise, managers are responsible for completing performance reviews, identifying poor performers, and deciding whether to terminate an employee.[37] While HR may offer guidance or impose certain procedures for managers to follow, management remains the driving force in personnel decisions.

The same is true of internal investigations regarding harassment or discrimination. Although HR conducts the investigation—which may even implicate a particular manager accused of misconduct—it rarely has the authority to determine the discipline or remedy that will result from the investigation. Instead, HR presents its finding to the appropriate level of management, and management will decide whether anyone should be fired, demoted, reprimanded, or sent for further training.

The #MeToo movement, in which masses of women spoke publicly about workplace harassment, helped to reveal the levers of power within organizations.[38] In several high-profile cases, women recounted complaining to HR about the harassment and even participating in an investigation regarding the misconduct.[39] Nevertheless, the men who were the subject of the investigation often retained their positions within the organization and in some cases continued to ascend up the ranks of the organization unimpeded.

While the persistent failure to hold harassers accountable could reflect HR's incentives to protect the organization, it also reflects the department's relative impotence with respect to important personnel decisions. Within organizations, the question of whether to retain a harasser is considered a business decision to be made by management. Likewise, the quick reversal of corporate practices in the wake of #MeToo-related scandals further reflects the division of authority within organizations. The #MeToo movement did not alter the legal risks of a harassment claim or HR's incentives to produce favorable documentation for litigation. Instead, it altered the business costs of inaction by subjecting the company to bad publicity. The business costs of inaction spurred management, and in some cases even boards of directors, to oust bad actors that they otherwise would have retained.

The marginal role that HR often plays in personnel decisions may in part be due to gender-based occupational segregation. Historically, professions dominated by women have tended to be accorded lower status and lower pay than male-dominated ones.[40] Human resources may have suffered a gender-based loss of status when the male-dominated labor department of the 1940s and 1950s gave way to the female-dominated HR profession.[41] HR professionals also started from a weaker position than labor relations because their expertise concerned nonunionized workers with less collective power.

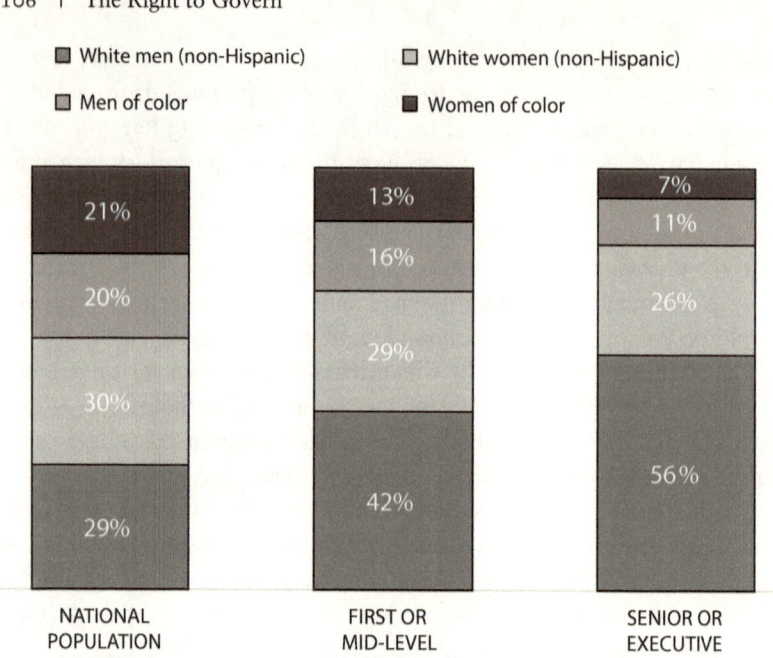

FIGURE 10. Managers by gender and race compared to national population statistics, 2021.

Meanwhile, white men continue to dominate managerial roles.[42] Based on census and EEOC data from 2021, white men are heavily overrepresented in senior and executive roles, occupying some 56 percent of those roles, compared to 29 percent of the population. They are also somewhat overrepresented in first and midlevel management, occupying 42 percent of such positions. Although white women have made substantial progress at moving into first and midlevel management, now occupying a representative share of those positions, they remain underrepresented at the senior and executive levels. People of color, especially women of color, are underrepresented at all levels of management.

The absence of diversity in management is problematic in its own right, partly because it suggests continued discrimination in promotion within organizations and partly due to the everyday power and authority that managers wield over their subordinates, as discussed in chapters 3 and 4. But it is also problematic due to the outsize role that managers play in employment decisions.

## HOW GERALD BOSTOCK LOST HIS JOB

When the Supreme Court decided Bostock's case, the only facts available were those alleged in his complaint. However, once the case was remanded to the trial court, the parties engaged in two more years of discovery and litigation. The facts that emerged were far more complex than those presented before the Supreme Court but nevertheless are representative of the way that employers tend to use internal processes and rules to justify their decision-making.

Gerald Bostock was the chief of the Child Welfare Division at the courthouse in Clayton County, Georgia,[43] about twenty minutes outside of Atlanta. He was responsible for recruiting and managing volunteers for the county's guardian-at-litem program, which represents the interests of children in divorce proceedings.[44] He had two sources of funding to run the program: funds generated from a $500 court fee assessed to parents in a divorce proceeding and those generated by a nonprofit organization, Friends of Clayton County CASA.[45]

Recruiting volunteers was challenging. Sabrina Crawford, a local businesswomen who served as the board chair for Friends of Clayton County, testified that the local area for recruiting volunteers was tapped out, and they were always trying to brainstorm ways to recruit from beyond the county.[46] Bostock began recruiting volunteers and sponsors from within his own networks in Atlanta, inviting them to meet in local restaurants.[47] He told Crawford and other board members that he planned to sponsor his team in the Hotlanta Softball League, which would enable the CASA program to be listed on the team's T-shirts in local competition.[48] They did not object.[49]

During his ten-year tenure with the county, Bostock's identity as a gay man was known to his coworkers and supervisors, including Judge Steven Teske, the chief judge of the Juvenile Court, who oversaw the CASA program.[50] Bostock invited his partner to work functions.[51] Bostock and his partner also socialized occasionally with Teske, who even invited the couple to his daughter's wedding.[52]

Although Bostock received strong performance reviews, his subordinates were not always happy with him and complained of favoritism.[53] A former employee wrote a disgruntled email to Bostock's supervisor alleging that he was using court funds for personal purposes.[54] The supervisor forwarded the complaint to Judge Teske.[55] Teske grew concerned, particularly after hearing from another employee that one of the accounts lacked sufficient funds to purchase volunteer T-shirts.[56]

Teske requested an audit of the two funds at Bostock's disposal.[57] The audit was performed by the county's internal auditors. Unlike HR, the auditors did not concern themselves with personnel matters, and their resulting report focused on the lack of procedures governing the account.[58] The report did not conclude that Bostock had misappropriated funds.[59]

Judge Teske found the report damning. He viewed sponsorship of the softball team to be a form of self-dealing. He also seemed convinced that expenses incurred at restaurants and bars serving a gay clientele were personal in nature.[60] He gave Bostock a series of written "interrogatories"—a type of formal written questioning used in litigation—as a last chance of sorts.[61] Bostock provided detailed answers describing each expense, but Teske was unswayed.[62] He decided to terminate Bostock.[63]

Teske drove to Sabrina Crawford's car dealership to let her know.[64] They sat in her glass-walled office on the showroom floor.[65] She later testified that she was shocked by the news.[66] Crawford asked if Teske had proof that Bostock did anything wrong.[67] Teske insisted he did and started rattling off all the venues where Bostock had spent funds.[68] Crawford responded, "I don't understand why you're saying it was a misuse of money. That's what I understood the money to be for."[69] According to Crawford, Teske slammed his hand down on her desk and said, "But it was at a gay bar."[70]

Remarkably, Teske kept a personal diary during this period, which Bostock's lawyers were able to obtain in discovery.[71] On the day Bostock was fired, Teske wrote that Bostock used funds for "meals with friends (former boyfriends—he is gay) and to sponsor a softball team in a gay softball league in Atlanta."[72] There was, however, no evidence that Bostock had expensed meals with boyfriends or friends, a fact that Teske admitted at his deposition.[73]

Teske called a staff meeting and informed the court employees that Bostock had been fired for mismanaging funds.[74] He seemed intensely worried that the court would suffer bad publicity for Bostock's expenses and gave an interview to a local news reporter, saying "I don't see how you can justify going to Atlanta to recruit volunteers for Clayton County."[75] That night, the local TV station ran a story captioned, "Court Official Fired: Gerald Bostock," alongside a misleading picture resembling a mugshot.[76]

Years later, Teske remained unrepentant, insisting in later news interviews that he supported LGBT rights and did not terminate Bostock for his sexual orientation.[77] In an email to a friend, he wrote "the facts are not on [Bostock's] side," highlighting the fact that Teske had "socialized with Gerald and his partner . . . for many years."[78] The judge wouldn't—or couldn't—acknowledge the possibility that discrimination had crept into his decision-making through the unshakeable assumption that expenses at a gay bar would necessarily be personal, or that sponsoring a gay softball team was self-dealing.[79]

Following discovery, both Bostock and the county filed motions for summary judgment, arguing that the facts were so clear cut that the case did not need to be tried in front of a jury, and the court should instead decide Bostock's Title VII case based on those undisputed facts.

### WINDOW DRESSING FOR COURTS

The events leading up to Bostock's termination are in some respects distinct from the HR processes used by corporate employers. First, Bostock may not have been an at-will employee.[80] Consequently, the county provided an abundance of process before finally terminating him: the audit, as well as Teske's invitation to provide written responses to his questions. In an at-will context, an employer might have conducted a more cursory investigation—or none at all—and terminated Bostock on the mere suspicion of misconduct. Second, Bostock's investigation was conducted by an internal audit department, rather than by HR, and as such as was more focused on financial controls than the more narrow question of whether Bostock had done anything wrong.

Nevertheless, Bostock's story illustrates the role that management typically plays in personnel decisions. Judge Teske, as the overseer of the CASA program, did not conduct the investigation himself; he delegated it to others. However, as management, he retained the decision-making authority to make personnel decisions following the audit. In fact, the auditors testified that they did not make recommendations about personnel matters.[81] In this respect, the audit served a similar function to typical HR processes: to provide documentation for any future legal claims and to distract from the actual decision-making process. Sociologist Lauren Edelman called these sorts of documentary practices "symbolic structures,"[82] because they are a form of corporate virtue signaling, a tempting legal shortcut to proving compliance.

Edelman argued that employers persist in using symbolic structures because courts tend to defer to those structures rather than assess whether harassment or discrimination was present.[83] Her insight is particularly applicable in harassment cases, where courts recognize the *Faragher/Ellerth* defense, set forth in a 1998 Supreme Court ruling.[84] The defense enables employers to avoid liability for a supervisor's harassment if they can show that they took reasonable measures to prevent or address the harassment, and the plaintiff unreasonably failed to make use of the procedures. The rulings meant that even if a plaintiff could prove to a jury that a supervisor created a hostile work environment, the company might avoid liability if the plaintiff didn't use the company's HR complaint process.[85]

The *Faragher/Ellerth* rulings are a concession to an employer's internal governance structures. The rulings rely heavily on older master-servant principles from agency law, holding that the master should not be held liable for a "frolic and detour" by the servant that was beyond the scope of their employment.[86] The Court reasoned that employers should not be held liable in every instance for a supervisor's misconduct, but only if the company had, to one degree or another, been negligent.[87] The Court must then define what qualifies as "reasonable care" for a master.[88] Within a broader frame of governance, that means developing internal governance systems for workers: a policy, a complaint process.[89] Notably, the *Faragher/Ellerth* defense does not require that employers meaningfully discipline or terminate an employee for harassment.[90]

## PINPOINTING THE TRUE DECISION-MAKER

The *Faragher/Ellerth* defense does not apply to discrimination cases, where employers are held strictly liable for discriminatory employment decisions. In discrimination cases, courts also generally do not blindly accept whatever process the employer implemented prior to terminating a given employee. Instead, available forms of proof empower plaintiffs to identify the decision-maker at issue and probe their motives for the decision. These forms of proof can be quite helpful to plaintiffs like Bostock when there is evidence that the decision-maker may have been biased. Master-servant principles nevertheless operate through a handful of doctrines that tip the scales in favor of managerial discretion and authority, as well as preexisting company practices and policies.

In Title VII litigation, the discovery process provides ample opportunity for the plaintiff to identify the ultimate decision-maker in a given employment process. Through depositions and written discovery, plaintiff's counsel can force witnesses and the employer to identify the individual who made the adverse employment decision. In Bostock's case, for example, plaintiff's counsel asked multiple witnesses to identify the decision-maker, and they all pointed to Judge Teske.[91] Teske was also directly questioned on that point and admitted that he made the termination decision.[92]

Once the plaintiff has identified the relevant decision-maker, the plaintiff can marshal whatever direct or circumstantial evidence suggests that the decision-maker was biased. Through *McDonnell Douglas*, plaintiffs could have argued that the reason the company provided was pretextual, perhaps because it was undermined by other evidence.[93] Bostock's lawyers argued that the county's claim that Bostock misused funds was undermined by a variety of available evidence such as the audit itself, which did not state that Bostock had misused funds; by deposition testimony from the auditors to the same effect; and by evidence that Bostock had reported his expenses to relevant superiors.[94]

Plaintiffs in Title VII cases can also rely on other forms of proof to establish that a decision was "because of" discrimination. Following a 1989 case involving a manager at PriceWaterhouse who was denied partnership because she was too "macho," Bostock could have also relied on a gender-stereotyping theory.[95] He might have argued that Judge Teske had a stereotyped view of gay workers, through his assumption that conducting business in a gay-friendly establishment or sponsoring a gay softball team necessarily meant that he was engaged in personal activity. Using a stereotyping framework, Bostock's lawyers could have argued that Teske would not have made the same decision if he had not held such stereotyped views.

Title VII plaintiffs can also rely on "direct" evidence to support discrimination: testimony or documents that directly suggested the decision was tainted by a discriminatory motive. This type of evidence is somewhat rare, as managers are coached by HR and lawyers not to make statements related to an employee's protected category. Bostock's lawyers argued that they had direct evidence of discrimination based on his journal entries and deposition testimony.[96]

In addition, plaintiffs can rely on "mixed motive" forms of proof, arguing that the employer relied on both a discriminatory and a nondiscriminatory reason for the employment decision.[97] In such cases, the employer can assert a limited affirmative defense that the employee would have been terminated regardless, which restricts the damages available.[98] Bostock's lawyers argued in the alternative that Bostock satisfied a mixed-motive framework.[99] Even if a jury believed the county that Bostock had not complied with rules about expense accounts (a nondiscriminatory reason), Bostock's lawyers argued that Judge Teske's assessment of the audit was "infected" by a "sexuality-based bias."[100] The case was unusually well-suited to a mixed motive form of proof because Judge Teske admitted in his deposition that the expenditure of funds at gay-friendly locations by a gay man was a "contributing factor" in Bostock's termination.[101] The county responded, however, that Judge Teske would have terminated Bostock regardless.[102]

Any of the aforementioned methods could be used successfully to prove discrimination.[103] Supreme Court jurisprudence has also grown more flexible in recent years with respect to the ways that plaintiffs can prove a discrimination case.[104] In a religious discrimination case involving a job applicant wearing a hijab, the Supreme Court held that the employer need not have known with certainty that an employee was a member of a protected category, as long as the decision was nevertheless motivated by discrimination.[105] Likewise, in a pregnancy discrimination case, the Court held that plaintiffs can establish a discriminatory motive by showing that a series of policies imposed a significant burden on pregnant women when compared to policies that applied to similarly disabled workers.[106] The *Bostock* decision itself also demonstrated a degree of flexibility on the part of the Supreme Court, by rejecting more technical arguments that LGBT employees of both sexes had been treated similarly and instead ruling that sex had been a "but for" cause of termination.[107] Broadly, the Supreme Court's flexibility about forms of proof in individual discrimination cases is a strongly positive development for workers.

These trends are not necessarily inconsistent with the historical context and trends described in chapter 6. Title VII jurisprudence, as it has developed over time, does not treat employment discrimination as a systemic problem requiring aggressive organizational change. Instead, it treats discrimination as a problem of individual bad actors with bad motives.[108] Because the focus of the inquiry is on the decision-maker rather than the organization, employers have little incentive to adopt practices that are effective at reducing discrimination. Instead, employers invest a lot of resources in creating documentation that presents a narrative of neutral decision-making.

### DEFERENCE TO MANAGERIAL PREROGATIVE

Title VII jurisprudence has adopted a number of subdoctrines that defer to managerial prerogative and employer policy. Although Title VII jurisprudence is quite good at identifying decision-makers, it also has a tendency to grant additional leeway to those decision-makers.

As Sandra Sperino and other legal scholars have documented, Title VII jurisprudence is riven with doctrines that tip the scales in favor of management.[109] There is the "same actor" defense, wherein companies can claim that a manager could not have been biased, because the same manager made both the hiring and firing decisions.[110] The "stray remarks" evidentiary doctrine allows companies to argue that discriminatory comments should be excluded from evidence because they were made outside of the decision-making context, or by non-decision-makers.[111] The "honest belief" doctrine—followed by some lower courts—enables companies to avoid liability on the basis that the decision-maker honestly believed whatever basis they had for terminating the employee, even if that reason is provably false.[112]

Courts also place substantial weight on written employer policies, metrics, or other documentation, particularly if they predate the employment dispute.[113] Employee conduct policies, which specify that certain infractions will lead to termination, go a long way toward protecting companies in mixed-motive cases. Even if discrimination tainted an employment decision, the employer can substantially reduce its damages by presenting a policy suggesting the employee would have been fired for misconduct.

Courts even defer to policies that theoretically might have applied to the plaintiff's case through a doctrine known as the "after-acquired evidence" doctrine. In the course of litigation, if a company uncovers evidence that the employee engaged in some sort of otherwise unknown misconduct during their employment—such as unauthorized photocopying of company documents—it can argue that it would have terminated the employee for that misconduct.[114] Here too, a company policy prohibiting the conduct can serve to substantially reduce the available damages to a plaintiff who has suffered discrimination.

These policies are somewhat distinct from Edelman's concept of "symbolic structures"; the policies are not primarily meant to signal compliance with the law. Rather, the employment policies that courts find so persuasive are governance related. They serve as internal laws within organizations that impose discipline and order, like policies regarding absenteeism, insubordination, or disloyalty. They specify who might be eligible to be employed or promoted or how to select employees for layoff. These policies effectuate the same kind of managerial prerogative described in chapter 2 that courts found so persuasive in the late nineteenth century: the right to terminate a chef who left the stove on in protest or a factory worker who disobeyed instructions about degreasing equipment.

Courts are open about their deference to managerial prerogative. Thousands of federal discrimination cases include language to the effect that courts are not "super-personnel" departments.[115] Many others articulate a related concept that courts should not second guess the business judgments of employers.[116] This stance is not necessarily inconsistent with the purpose of Title VII, as chapter 6 discussed: the legislative history of the act provides that "internal affairs of employers ... must not be interfered with" except as necessary to "correc[t] ... discrimination practices."[117]

Deference to managerial judgment also flows from the at-will presumption, which assumes that any reason at all, arbitrary or not, is an adequate basis to terminate the employment relationship. As Marina Multhaup, an attorney for Workers United, explained, "Lots of times, humans are not perfect and they may have done something that ... would technically grant that reason to the company.... [T]here's never a smoking gun" connecting the employment decision to an unlawful motive. "Companies ... [are] much, much more sophisticated than that."[118]

. . .

Even with a Supreme Court win under his belt, Gerald Bostock's case was not a slam dunk. The legal interpretations of the case were sufficiently disputed that both parties filed a motion for summary judgment.

The district court magistrate denied both motions.[119] Despite Judge Teske's various admissions, the court ruled that a jury "might agree with Judge Teske that plaintiff made these expenditures for his own benefit."[120] As to Bostock's mixed motive claim, the judge likewise concluded that there was a triable factual dispute over whether Judge Teske "would have made the same decision in the absence of the impermissible motivating factor."[121] Having dismissed the summary judgment motions, the case was headed to trial. The parties settled for $825,000.[122]

PART III

# The Duty of Support

CHAPTER 8

# Benefits

My mother, my poor aged mother, go among strangers to toil
for a living! No, a thousand times no! I would rather work
my fingers to the bone, bend over my sewing till the film
of blindness gathered in my eyes; nay even beg from street
to street.
—Elizabeth Keckley, Mary Lincoln's personal couturier,
*Behind the Scenes, or Thirty Years a Slave, and Four Years
in the White House* (1868)

The institution of slavery rested on a variety of falsehoods about white supremacy, violence, and profit. Among them was the false claim that slavery was a reciprocal relationship. As legal historian William Fisher observed, defenders of slavery attempted to "depic[t] . . . Southern society as a whole as patriarchal and humane" through "a stable, familial, and mutually beneficial labor system that contrasts favorably with the . . . tumultuous wage labor system . . . in the industrializing North."[1]

Slavery apologist Thomas Cobb wrote, "The master is the head of his family. Next to his wife and children, he cares for his slaves. He avenges their injuries, protects their persons, provides for their wants, and guides their labors. In return, he is revered and held as protector and master."[2] Similarly, in 1848 a Virginia court insisted that slavery imposed a "constant . . . burthen of care and expenditure" on enslavers, which resulted in "an even balance of profit and loss between [the enslaved] and their former masters."[3]

This claim was exactly backward from a macroeconomic standpoint. Enslaver wealth based on the ownership of enslaved people exceeded $3 billion in 1860, which represented "44 percent of the wealth" in the "South's major cotton-growing states" and nearly 20 percent of the U.S. wealth overall.[4] It represented the daily economic transfer from the enslaved to the enslaver through labor.

As chapter 1 described, that transfer was evident from the value of the cotton that enslaved people harvested without pay, wherein an average

FIGURE 11. Elizabeth Keckley, an enslaved entrepreneur who would later become Mary Lincoln's personal dressmaker.

week of picking would produce around 600 pounds, or $66 in revenue,[5] worth more than $2,000 today in inflation-adjusted dollars.[6] Day by day, enslaved agricultural workers paid the enslaver in labor, while the revenue from that labor was retained exclusively by the enslaver. Cumulatively, the United States produced 2.2 billion pounds of cotton in 1860.[7]

Enslaved people were keenly aware of the economic transfer that their bondage produced. Elizabeth Keckley, an enslaved entrepreneur who would later become Mary Todd Lincoln's personal dressmaker and designer, watched the proceeds from her business venture line the pockets of her enslaver and his extended family. Keckley started her dressmaking business after the enslaver threatened to send Keckley's elderly mother out to work for other families in the community. Keckley was horrified by the threat and proposed instead to bring in revenue through dressmaking. She became quite successful, dressing "the best ladies in St. Louis," and "never lacked for orders."[8]

The enslaver kept the proceeds of Keckley's business, returning nothing to Keckley. In her autobiography, Keckley recalled, "With my needle I kept bread in the mouths of seventeen persons for two years and five months . . . working so hard that others might live in comparative comfort, and move in those circles of society to which their birth gave them entrance."[9] After her enslaver died, his widow extracted a second ransom from Keckley: a self-purchase price of $1,200, then equivalent to the price of the house.[10] Keckley borrowed the funds from her customers and later paid them back as a freedwoman.[11]

### THE DUTY OF SUPPORT

The final part of this book concerns the duty of support. Historically, the concept referred to the idea that the master had a duty to provide for the members of his household, including servants. The duty of support originated in the feudal master-servant system. As discussed in the introduction, the feudal master-servant relationship conferred sovereignty on the head of the household over women, children, servants, and apprentices. The master was also obligated to provide for the basic material needs of those within the household.[12] The duty of support relieved the state of the burden of providing for those individuals and gave the state an incentive to recognize the master-servant relationship. Vagrancy laws, for example, punished those who were not either economically self-sufficient or affiliated with a household, pushing them to submit to servitude while relieving the community of welfare obligations.[13]

In the modern context, I use the term "duty of support" to refer to the employer's role in providing workplace benefits other than a wage, and I argue that it serves a similar function as in prior historical eras: it serves to buttress the master-servant system.

First, the American economic and social welfare system continues to tether basic human necessities to the employment relationship, rather than to the state. As legal scholar Deepa Das Acevedo observed, "the United States funnels an extraordinary range of protections and benefits through work relationships."[14] These include sick leave, vacation pay, family leave, unemployment insurance, retirement savings, and most of all, health care. Indeed, even state-provided welfare programs, such as the Supplemental Nutrition Assistance Program, coerce individuals into employment relationships by imposing work-based eligibility rules.[15]

Second, employers have a remarkable degree of discretion over whether to offer workplace benefits. Beyond unemployment and workers' compensation insurance, many workers find they are not covered by laws mandating workplace benefits or that the law only regulates such benefits if the employer elects to provide them. For example, other than a temporary federal law enacted during the coronavirus pandemic, the United States has no national law mandating sick leave. Likewise, no federal law requires employers to provide vacation pay, and most state laws only apply to vacation if a company chooses to offer it.

The United States is the only industrialized country that does not mandate paid family and medical leave.[16] Under the federal Family Medical Leave Act, leave is only available on an unpaid basis, only for workers at companies with more than fifty people, and only if those individuals have worked for the company for more than one year.[17] Health care, which in other industrialized countries is viewed as a basic human right, is treated in the United States as an employment perk, where coverage for a majority of Americans starts and ends with a particular job.[18]

Third, because employers retain so much power and discretion over workplace benefits, they structure and dispense those benefits to influence employee productivity and decision-making. As discussed in greater detail later in this chapter, American companies have a long history of using benefits to improve employee retention, stave off union organizing, and influence personal choices.

The duty of support helps to explain why master-servant structures have persisted over time. Governments are willing to cede jurisdiction to employers if it also means ceding responsibility and financial obligations. And the duty of support—perhaps even more than other employer claims to authority and control over the workplace—serves as the rhetorical basis for business arguments that employers should be removed from accountability and oversight.

. . .

This chapter recounts how employee benefits came to be associated with employee status, how those benefits are used as a form of control, and their rhetorical function in maintaining the master-servant system. Corporate employers in the late nineteenth and early twentieth centuries experimented with discretionary benefits to alter employee behavior and deter union organizing. While some early industrial welfare programs may have been genuinely motivated by a concern for workers' welfare, what qualified as worker "well-being" was defined within the paternalist preferences and assumptions of management. Many of these corporate motives continue to animate current employee benefit programs. Likewise, much of the law regulating employee benefits continues to treat them as a form of employer largess.

Chapter 9 examines the incentives produced by the master-servant system, in which employment status imposes a variety of legal obligations and costs on employers but also confers substantial power over workers. The chapter focuses on "gig" companies and workers—who have to varying degrees opted out of the master-servant system—to assess the costs and benefits of legal rules defined around employment status. Chapter 10 discusses potential policy reforms, using the Affordable Care Act of 2010 as a case study for possible reforms that benefit workers without further bolstering the master-servant system.

### THE DUTY OF SUPPORT UNDER SLAVERY

Slavery serves to illustrate the true function of the duty of support within the master-servant system. The enslaver's duty to provide basic food and shelter for enslaved people existed primarily as a rhetorical device to defend the institution; it was rarely invoked in legal disputes. On the rare occasion it came up, it largely served as a vehicle to allocate costs between enslavers, third parties, and the state.

The duty of support conferred little to no legal rights upon enslaved people. As legal historian Thomas Morris observed, most slave states did not have laws requiring enslavers to provide basic food and shelter until the 1850s.[19] One rare exception, South Carolina, required enslavers to provide basic food and shelter.[20] However, Morris was only able to locate a single appellate case enforcing the rule over the course of more than one hundred years.[21]

As a practical matter, enslaved people could not assert claims against enslavers because they were barred from testifying in court against white people.[22] Like other legal rights nominally assigned to enslaved people,[23] the duty of support primarily served to allocate costs and liabilities between enslavers and third parties, such as claims for reimbursement by doctors.[24] Enslavers also sued third-party hirers for the injury or death of an enslaved person, claiming the hirer violated an implied contractual duty to "provide for [the enslaved person's] necessary wants."[25]

Enslavers' unchecked and exclusive authority over the subsistence needs of enslaved people allowed them to treat the duty of support as an extension of the right to control, using food to increase productivity or punish noncompliance.[26] Some enslavers offered additional food, such as a bag of sugar, as a prize in contests meant to measure a worker's maximum picking rate.[27] Enslavers also used food and basic necessities to alter productivity over a longer time frame. One Mississippi enslaver set up an annual monetary bonus system based on the behavior, "obedience," and "efficiency" of each individual.[28] Workers would "draw on their accounts" during the year for "extra clothing."[29] Similarly, a Virginia planter used a promised incentive as collective punishment, promising a barrel of corn each year for Christmas but deducting from that collective barrel during the year for any "theft" or "depredation."[30]

Because enslaved people could not rely on enslavers to furnish basic necessities, they often cultivated their own gardens or kept their own livestock.[31] Enslaved women also turned their gardens into entrepreneurial opportunities, selling produce in local markets.[32] Some of these businesses matured into wholesale businesses and commodities brokerages.[33] The most famous of these entrepreneurs, Aletha Turner, sold produce in Washington, D.C., including to President Thomas Jefferson, and used the proceeds to purchase her freedom.[34]

The duty of support was also present in free labor arrangements or quasi-free employment statuses in the nineteenth century, primarily when providing housing or food was central to the labor arrangement or a matter of necessity. In apprenticeships, the master's offer to provide food and shelter to minor apprentices was often a principal motivation for entering into the arrangement. For example, in the 1848 Virginia case *Brewer v. Harris*, the poorhouse contracted out three free Black children—Sally, Joannah, and Milly Harris—as apprentices for "one dollar each, from the age of fourteen to seventeen." In the apprenticeship contract, the tradesperson agreed to teach Milly "the art, trade and mystery of washing and spinning" and to "furnish her with good and wholesome food" during the apprenticeship.[35]

In free labor arrangements, employers also provided food or housing if the work environment lacked basic infrastructure. Early American textile mills were located in rural areas near waterfalls and rivers that powered their machinery. The mills had no choice but to build corporate housing nearby. Starting in the 1820s, mechanized textile factories in Lowell, Massachusetts, employed unmarried women who lived in company-owned housing financed through paycheck deductions.[36] The women were expected to follow "a strict set of moral rules" in the dorms, under the watchful eye of resident widows.[37] Nevertheless, women migrated from family farms to the mills, eager for hourly wages and physical independence from their families.

Company towns, some of which persisted into the twentieth century,[38] were also more physical necessity than corporate largess. Early worksites consisted of logging and mining operations in remote locations,[39] which started out as bare-bones seasonal operations, staffed by young men.[40] Companies sought to reduce turnover by attracting married men and their families with housing and other amenities.[41] Families in company towns rented company-provided housing, attended company churches and schools, and shopped at company stores.[42]

Over time, corporate employers came to realize that housing offered new avenues to exert indirect control and surveillance over workers on and off the clock. As Linda Carlson writes in her history of company towns in the Pacific Northwest, "[T]he most important advantage of company owned housing . . . was the control management wielded, especially over union activities."[43] Company housing served as a bulwark against union organizing through provisions in the lease that declared a strike to be grounds for eviction.[44] Companies also erected fences around corporate housing to keep union organizers out.[45]

Company-sponsored benefits also tend to reflect internal corporate hierarchies as well as broader social stratification and segregation. Corporate housing was also "assigned by professional and marital status as well as by ethnic and racial group."[46] These hierarchies were even reflected in the layout of company towns.[47] In Potlatch, Idaho, managers lived in houses at the top of the hill, above the layer of smoke emitted by the lumber mill.[48] By contrast, "Greek, Italian, and Japanese employees lived farthest down the hill and in the smallest houses."[49] Even

FIGURE 12. "Moving Camp": homes moved by rail, undated, estimated 1910–1920.

cooking classes were sometimes segregated.[50] Similarly, Southern textile and mining companies excluded or segregated Black workers in both the workplace and company-operated schools.[51]

INDUSTRIAL WELFARE CAPITALISM

Industrial employers in urban locations began experimenting with workplace benefits, known as "industrial welfare" programs, in the early twentieth century, portraying such benefits as a form of largess meant to improve the comfort, moral character, and overall well-being of workers.[52] A 1926 survey of the largest American employers found that around 80 percent of companies adopted some form of welfare program.[53] At its peak, writes historian Stuart Brandes, "[w]orkers lived in company houses, were treated by company doctors, attended company schools, played on company teams, purchased company stock, and were represented by company unions."[54] (Today, company unions—which are not truly independent—are illegal under Section 8 of the NLRA.)

An early innovator in this space was the National Cash Register Company (NCR), which introduced welfare programs in the 1890s.[55] The company offered a dizzying array of corporate benefits to its workers. Some were basic by modern standards: chairs, natural light, toilets, and warm drinks.[56] Other aspects of NCR's programs resembled what

FIGURE 13. Calisthenics at the National Cash Register Company, 1903.

we would today associate with high school: cafeterias, gymnasiums, auditoriums, libraries, social clubs, and dances. The company even had an in-house magazine, *Women's Welfare*, written and edited by female employees, meant to spread the gospel of industrial welfare.

Industrial welfare had a strong paternalistic dimension, reflecting managerial beliefs about lifestyle choices deemed conducive to moral development and productive work.[57] Human betterment was the lynchpin connecting welfare programs to productivity. As welfare champion William Tolman argued in 1900, "[T]he individual who improves his own condition cannot fail to be of greater worth to the industry."[58]

However, management did not always have a good grasp of what workers wanted or what might make them more productive.[59] For example, NCR introduced free cafeteria lunches for female workers in hopes of making their afternoons more productive. However, the company appears to have done so without consulting any of the women. Almost no one showed up for lunch. When the company eventually hired a woman named Lena Harvey Tracy to run the industrial welfare program, she explained to the president that workers did not want to be perceived as charity recipients.[60] She rolled out a system in which women could purchase 5 cent lunch tokens, and the cafeteria filled up.

The corporate paternalistic impulse was particularly strong when it came to female workers. Historian Daniel Nelson noted that industrial welfare programs tended to predominate over more Taylorist approaches in companies with "large numbers of female employees."[61] At the time, wage discrimination was legal and presumed a family structure in which white men were breadwinners and white women worked as a matter of preference.[62] Industrial welfare was consistent with this gendered frame. While Taylorism presumed that working men responded to incentives and would increase their productivity for a monetary reward, industrial welfare made corporate expenditures on women's behalf, directing funds toward a more comfortable environment rather than higher pay.

Nevertheless, industrial welfare programs proved to be a rare source of influence for women in the workplace.[63] Corporate "welfare secretaries"— a role performed by both men and women—were an early precursor of what we would today consider HR, acting as "ombudsmen and, in subtle ways, as disciplinarians."[64] They "took over ... personnel functions that foremen had traditionally performed and that personnel departments and labor unions later assumed."[65]

Industrial welfare was also a strategic investment meant to deter workers from unionizing.[66] Although unions were not legally protected at that time, they were a potent economic threat.[67] Unions could disrupt sales by organizing boycotts of the company's products, walking out, striking, or engaging in violence. Companies were spooked by the unpredictable and steep costs that a union might impose.[68]

Industrial welfare sought to mollify workers with better conditions, just as Taylorism promised to deter unionism with incentive pay. And like Taylorism, it was never the perfect antidote. In 1901 NCR locked out its workers rather than recognize or bargain with the union.[69] Lena Harvey Tracy left the company, accepting a much lower-paying job at a church.[70] She may have sensed that enthusiasm for corporate welfare would wane once its success as a union deterrent was no longer guaranteed.

## FORD'S $5 A DAY PROGRAM

NCR's industrial welfare program was structured as a form of largess: the company provided the perks without strings attached. By contrast, the Ford Motor Company offered a different version of industrial welfare, which was more closely tethered to wages. Ford's $5 per day wage program, announced in 1914, imposed a variety of conditions on employee eligibility. Most such conditions were intended to alter employee behavior both inside and outside of the workplace.

Today, Ford's decision to pay its workers $5 a day is often invoked as a principled decision to raise pay so that workers could afford to buy the cars they were building. At the time, paying workers $5 per day was considered an "exorbitant amount for an unskilled factory worker" and was projected to consume about half of the company's $10 million in profits.[71] But it was not a raise. Ford officials referred to it as "a man-to-man, character building proposition."[72] As Stephen Meyer observed, "the essence of the" program "was the use of profits to alter and to control the lives and the behavior of the Ford workers."[73]

To qualify for the premium wage, workers needed to pass a home inspection every six months conducted by the company's Sociological Department. The inspection criteria reflected assimilationist goals for immigrant workers, a desire to keep women in the home, and the enforcement of race-based distinctions. To pass a home inspection, the employee's home needed to be clean; well lit; free of boarders, which was a common practice in immigrant households; and located outside "the congested and slum parts of the city."[74]

Workers also needed to be married. In addition, the wife could not work outside the home or "look haggard from overwork."[75] Other factors that disqualified men from the program included drinking, gambling, and smoking. To qualify, one Turkish worker was forced to give up his religion, style of dress, and language.[76] On another occasion, Ford terminated more than eight hundred Greek and Russian Orthodox workers who celebrated Christmas on a different date than December 25.[77] The company commented that "if these men are to make their home in America they should observe American holidays."[78]

Over time, Ford's investigation department started grading workers—even those who did not qualify for profit sharing—"into four classes: Honor Roll, Class A, Class B, and Class C."[79] Meyer observed that Ford workers suffered the kind of scrutiny and indignity that would today be associated with government welfare recipients: "The Ford investigators were fathers who rewarded and punished the behavior of their wayward working-class children."[80]

Female workers were initially disqualified from the $5 per day wage plan,[81] though they were later included if they had dependents.[82] No such dependent requirement applied to men. Supervisors and executives were exempt from the inspections, which were reserved for "salesman, foremen, clerks, and factory workers."[83] The whole system was designed to foment fear of missing out among eligible workers; those who failed the requirements would be confronted with a paycheck itemizing the profit share they did not receive.[84]

### THE MODERN BENEFIT PLAYBOOK

Several aspects of the employer playbook with respect to industrial welfare remain today.[85] Employers continue to use workplace benefits to resist unionization. In a 2021 campaign against a union vote in a Bessemer, Alabama, warehouse, Amazon urged employees that they could "do it without dues," arguing, "Why pay almost $500 in [union] dues?"[86] when they received a variety of other benefits from Amazon without a union: "We've got you covered with high wages, health care, vision, and dental benefits, as well as a safety committee and an appeals process."[87]

Amazon's anti-union website also advised workers to "get the facts."[88] A union "cannot guarantee better wages and benefits," meaning "you could end up with more, the same . . . or less than what you make today."[89] A union "cannot guarantee you will not lose your job."[90] All "wages, benefits and terms and conditions of employment are on the table," Amazon asserted, suggesting that unionized workers might lose what they already had through the "Amazon Total Rewards Package."[91]

The anti-union campaign was somewhat misleading. Alabama is a right-to-work state, which meant that individual workers were not required to join the union even if a majority of workers voted in favor of the union. Consequently, union dues would not automatically apply to all workers, as Amazon seemed to suggest. The suggestion that workers risked losing their benefits if represented by a union was also questionable, according to labor law scholar Charlotte Garden: Why would a union bargain for an agreement with worse pay and benefits?[92]

Amazon's marketing campaign also implied that its employee benefits were independent of the threat of union organizing. But from a broader historical perspective, workplace benefits exist at least in part because unions exist. Without the threat that workers might join a union, companies would not be so motivated to offer benefits. And as the "do it without dues" motto inadvertently acknowledged, unions do not receive dues for the spillover benefits that the threat of unionization provides to nonunionized workers.

Amazon's marketing and other anti-union campaign strategies worked. The Bessemer warehouse workers voted against the union. Although the union successfully challenged the vote based on Amazon's election tactics, the company won a subsequent election ordered by the NLRB.[93]

BENEFITS WITH STRINGS ATTACHED

Current corporate practices resemble industrial welfare programs in another respect: companies often impose various contingencies on whether and when workers can receive benefits. The most common such contingency is longevity based, wherein a worker must work for a company for a period of time to be eligible for and accrue a particular benefit, such as vacation pay or sick leave.[94] Companies also tend to stretch the accrual of vacation or sick pay over a long period of time, but the accrual rate accelerates over time.[95] Workers with several years of service accrue vacation faster than newly hired workers. Bonuses also tend to be structured to incentivize employee retention, through conditions that require employees to be on the payroll at the end of the year to receive the payment.

These benefit structures are in many cases consistent with existing law. As previously noted, no federal laws mandate sick or vacation leave. Although a minority of states mandate a small amount of sick leave, the law often allows the leave to be earned slowly. For example, New York's sick leave law requires employers to allow employees to accrue one hour of sick leave per thirty hours worked, meaning an employee would need to work full time for about a month and a half to earn a single day of sick leave.[96] These laws also generally permit companies to cap the total amount of sick time an employee can accrue at one week.[97]

Benefit-related laws can also have coverage restrictions, which exclude certain workers or companies from coverage entirely. The Family and Medical Leave Act excludes companies with fewer than fifty employees from coverage.[98] It also excludes workers with less than one year of service, as well as many workers on a part-time schedule.[99] These coverage rules can effectively prevent workers from switching jobs if they are pregnant, experience an ongoing medical condition that periodically requires leave, or provide medical caregiving for a family member. It also places new workers and part-time workers in a precarious situation if they experience an unexpected medical emergency. Unless the employee lives in a state with more generous leave laws, companies can fire workers for taking unauthorized and unprotected leave.

As in decades past, current benefit structures also tend to reflect internal workplace hierarchies. Although Title VII prohibits companies from discriminating against workers on the basis of race, gender, or religion in benefit allocations, they can exclude or limit benefits from workers on other bases, such as whether they are paid on a salaried or hourly basis or whether they work full time. Wal-Mart's "Associate Benefit Book," for example, includes elaborate distinctions based on whether workers are full-time, part-time, temporary, or management.[100]

Brooks Pierce, an economist at the BLS, examined a trove of compensation data in the 1980s and 1990s. Pierce observed that during this period there was an increase in benefits to high-wage workers and large declines in employer benefit outlays for workers in the bottom 10 percent of the compensation distribution.[101] These changes were much larger than already-plummeting wages for that sector of the labor force. For workers in the bottom 10 percent of earners, "nonrequired benefits [were] virtually zero."[102] Pierce concluded that "compensation inequality rose over the past 10–15 years by a greater amount than did wage inequality" and were "large due to declines in health insurance coverage rates."[103]

Today, companies continue to award more generous benefits to the highest earners, as illustrated in table 1. In the private sector, a variety of valuable benefits, including medical care, retirement plans, paid sick leave, and paid holidays, are offered on a nearly universal basis to workers in the top 25 percent of wage earners. By contrast, far fewer workers in the lowest 25 percent of wage earners have access to those benefits. These disparities grow even larger when actual enrollments in those benefits are taken into account.[104] Medical plans often involve some form of contribution, and many uninsured workers report that they declined available coverage because they couldn't afford it.[105] This regressive system for allocating benefits means that the workers who are most vulnerable to serious personal and financial ruin in the event of an emergency have the least access to workplace benefits that might protect them from harm.

Finally, modern workplace benefits can have a paternalistic quality. For example, some of the office perquisites of the prepandemic era, particularly those that tended to proliferate in tech companies like cafeterias, snacks, nap areas, gyms, or laundry service, sought to attend to employees' personal needs so they would stay late in the office. As described in chapter 4, these perquisites were targeted to the needs of salaried workers, paid a fixed amount regardless of the number of hours

TABLE 1.  ACCESS TO WORKPLACE BENEFITS AMONG PRIVATE SECTOR WORKERS (2022)

| Type of Employee Benefit | % of Workers in Bottom Quarter of Wage Earners Offered Benefit | % of Workers in Top Quarter of Wage Earners Offered Benefit |
|---|---|---|
| Medical care | 38 | 94 |
| Retirement plan | 45 | 90 |
| Paid sick leave | 55 | 94 |
| Paid holiday(s) | 59 | 94 |
| Paid family leave | 12 | 40 |

Source: Bureau of Labor Statistics, *Employee Benefits in the United States*, March 2022, https://www.bls.gov/ebs/publications/zip/employee-benefits-in-the-united-states-march-2022.zip.

they work. Consequently, employers had an incentive to cajole them to work longer hours under the guise of making the office more comfortable or convenient. As the president of NCR observed more than a century ago, "There is no charity in anything we do. Isn't it just good business to lose three cents on a girl's lunch and get back five cents' worth of work?"[106]

The most paternalistic dimension of modern employee benefits tends to relate to employee health and wellness. Today's version of "human betterment" is not religious or cultural assimilation but wellness programs meant to reduce health-care costs and absenteeism: fitness programs, gym membership subsidies, counseling programs, and mindfulness seminars. These programs might be welcome to some employees. But wellness programs also send the implicit message that work-related stress is an individual health concern, rather than a problem with the work environment.

Wellness programs administered by health insurance companies can also intrude upon employee privacy and autonomy, in ways reminiscent of Ford's $5 a day program. My own employer offers a health plan with a "health engagement model" that requires participants to complete a lengthy survey about their health behaviors and to commit to engage in various changes to their behavior. Workers who opt out face a higher insurance deductible.

Half of large companies do not stop at a questionnaire and offer biometric screenings for current employees, including measurements like "body mass index, cholesterol, blood pressure, stress and nutrition."[107] Self-insured companies do not even need to conduct such screenings and can make decisions about health-care plans, cost sharing, and wellness programs based on claims data.[108] And because companies are increasingly self-funding health insurance programs—and the ever-escalating cost of such programs—their incentive to exercise even more control over employee wellness will only continue to grow.

CHAPTER 9

# Left Behind

Dominic Oliveira "usually doesn't go anywhere without driving a truck,"[1] so he can make money along the way. "Even missing a single day" of pay "can mess you up big time."[2] And so on October 3, 2018, Oliveira drove a semitruck from Virginia to his own Supreme Court hearing. He blew a tire and missed the oral argument.

Of the nation's 3.5 million truck drivers,[3] 500,000 are independent contractors.[4] Dominic Oliveira was one of them. As a contractor for a company called New Prime, Oliveira had none of the rights and benefits that our legal system attaches to employment status. Instead, he was limited to whatever promises were made in his contract with the company.

Oliveira, a thirty-nine-year-old white man from Massachusetts, found New Prime on the internet after growing frustrated with his job at a moving company. They "lure you in," Oliveira recalled.[5] The company sent him a bus ticket to Springfield, Missouri, and offered to bring him on as a student driver.[6]

As documented in subsequent litigation, drivers like Oliveira formed part of the company's unpaid "apprenticeship" program, in which trainees drive alongside a more senior driver for ten thousand miles.[7] These trainees signed a contract stating that their training program was worth $4,375 and agreed to pay back the "tuition" at a 12.5 percent interest rate if they left the company without completing twelve months of service as employee-drivers or independent contractors.[8]

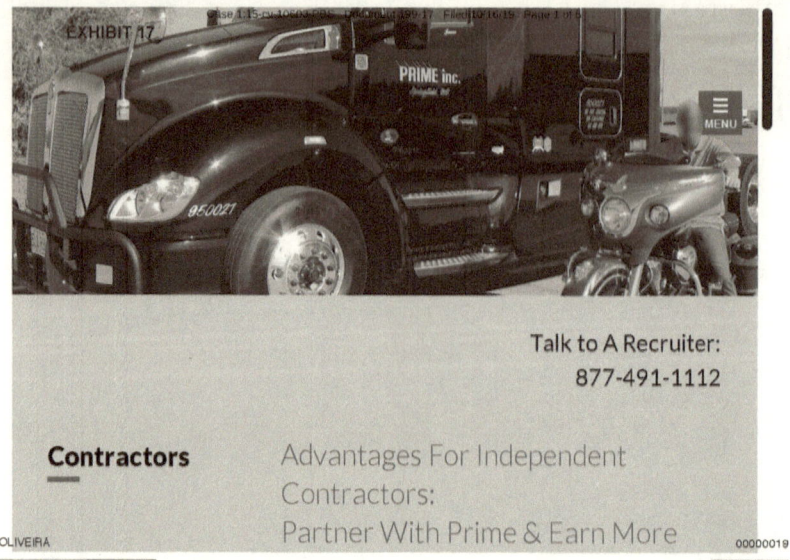

FIGURE 14. Advertisement for independent contractors at New Prime, enclosed as an exhibit in *Oliveira v. New Prime*. The image of the individual appearing in the ad has been blurred.

The "tuition" would be forgiven if the apprentice continued to work for New Prime for a year.[9] Attorney Jennifer Bennett—who argued Oliveira's case before the Supreme Court[10]—compared practices in the trucking industry to indentured servitude, where workers must pay off a debt incurred to the employer through their labor.[11]

Following his completion of the student driver program, New Prime let Oliveira choose whether to work as an employee-driver or a "leased driver" who leased the truck from the company as an independent contractor. But Oliveira recalled that the company presented the contractor option as far more attractive: "[P]art of the thing that you're told but not told" is that "you'll make more money [as a leased driver] than as a company driver."[12] Indeed, an advertisement from the company enticed drivers with the headline, "Lease with Prime: Become an Independent Contractor and Earn More."

Because Oliveira worked as a contractor, New Prime made no effort to pay him in compliance with the wage and hour laws that applied to interstate trucking companies. Oliveira was essentially paid on a piece-rate basis: a specified amount per mile. That rate was subject to various deductions to cover the cost of operations, such as maintenance and fuel, although drivers could opt to pay for those costs out of pocket instead.[13] Oliveira also paid a related corporate entity to lease the truck.[14]

All told, Oliveira was paid an average of $4 an hour to drive for weeks or months at a time.[15] "You would tell them that you want to go home," but "they made it so you would be [losing money] when you got back out, so you couldn't stay home for very long."[16] Oliveira often hauled truckloads of food products that would occasionally get rejected at the delivery site. "Because I didn't have a lot of money," Oliveira recalled, "I would actually eat the rejections."[17] He ate ten boxes of rejected Tyson chicken nuggets by heating them up on the engine.[18]

Oliveira and a class of roughly forty thousand other truck drivers filed a collective-action lawsuit against New Prime, claiming that they were misclassified as contractors and owed unpaid wages.[19] The issue before the court related to an arbitration provision in his independent contractor agreement,[20] which would have precluded him from bringing his claim as a collective action in court. Bennett argued that Oliveira and the other class members could not be forced to file their cases as individual arbitration claims due to an exception for transportation workers in the 1925 Federal Arbitration Act.[21]

Oliveira's case sent Justice Gorsuch on a deep dive into the historical meaning of the phrase "contracts of employment" as of 1925.[22] In the opinion, Gorsuch uses the terms "master" and "servant" interchangeably with "employer" and "employee."[23] As described in the introduction, Gorsuch concludes that the phrase "contracts of employment" in 1925 was not equivalent to employment status. Instead, it "usually meant nothing more than an agreement to perform work,"[24] which might encompass something along the lines of independent contractors.

In the opinion, the Court notes that legal dictionaries, state court rulings, and federal and state statutes at the time did not "distinguish between different kinds of work or workers. All work was treated as employment, whether or not the common law criteria for a master servant relationship happened to be satisfied."[25] Gorsuch also notes that the Federal Arbitration Act later uses the term "workers" instead of a more precise term like "employee" or "servant."[26]

. . .

Chapter 8 examined the respects in which employee benefits tend to enhance employer control while buttressing the master-servant system by relieving the state of welfare obligations. This chapter examines the master-servant system from a different vantage point: that of workers who fall outside the master-servant relationship because they have been treated as independent contractors, whether legally or illegally.

While the rights and benefits of employment status tend to push individual workers toward employment status, those same mandates have the opposite effect on employers. The more rights and benefits accompany employment status, the more costly employment status becomes for companies. This chapter considers why companies gravitate toward hiring independent contractors, with a particular focus on gig economy companies and their gamesmanship with respect to employment law compliance. It also considers the appeal of independent work for workers themselves, both in a modern context and historically, as illustrated by the nineteenth-century ideology of "free labor."

The chapter then returns to the broader question of the persistence of master-servant ideology in American work. While chapter 4 examined the master-servant ideology embedded in managerial practices, this chapter considers the extent to which the pandemic sharpened employee resistance to master-servant ideology.

## THE "FISSURED" WORKPLACE

A 2024 survey of more than six thousand workers observed a notable rise in workers performing independent work over the previous year.[27] The survey estimated that approximately seventy three million workers in the United States perform some sort of independent work occasionally, part time, or full time.[28] Independent workers who participated in the survey overwhelmingly reported that they were "happier working on [their] own."[29] Yet to the extent these individuals work primarily as contractors, rather than supplementing employment income—which appeared to be anywhere from one-third to half of them—they are foregoing all of the benefits and protections of employment law developed over the last one hundred years.[30]

Companies increasingly prefer other forms of work relationships—like independent contractors, suppliers, franchisees, or other arm's-length relationships that take employment liabilities off their books. In an influential 2014 book, economist David Weil described this trend as "fissuring." In *The Fissured Workplace*, Weil argued that large companies were aggressively shedding direct employees through various legal forms.[31] They might franchise individual stores rather than operating them directly, rendering the workers employees of individual franchisees rather than the company itself.[32] Or they might subcontract work to third-party companies on a price basis,[33] and the subcontractor would either fail to comply with applicable law or misclassify workers as contractors.[34] Large companies were the ultimate beneficiaries of this race to the bottom, avoiding the legal liability and financial costs associated with directly employing their own workers.[35]

Oliveira's experience with New Prime is an example of fissuring. The independent contractor arrangement allowed New Prime to shift some of the costs of doing business onto the worker, like the truck, gas, repairs, and insurance. It also shifted training costs onto the worker,[36] and it avoided compliance costs associated with employment status, including minimum wage, workers' compensation coverage, and unemployment insurance. It was such a losing proposition for workers that the arrangement almost seemed like a scam. Not only did New Prime benefit from the freight revenue of Oliveira's work—as an employer would—it also benefited from its other arrangements with Oliveira, such as leasing fees and gas payments.

In a way, New Prime was no longer limited to the trucking business; it was also in the insurance, repair, fueling, and leasing business. Oliveira was both a worker providing services and a customer who purchased insurance, repairs, fuel, and truck leasing.[37] Elements of New Prime's business that previously served as cost centers (trucks, tires, fuel) were now sources of revenue. As legal scholar Jonathan Harris argues, "[F]irms have immunized themselves from liability for otherwise unfair and deceptive acts and practices ... by cloaking their transactions as contractual terms of work."[38] The arrangement also harkens back to company stores in company towns, which employers sometimes used to trap workers in debt.[39] But in other respects, New Prime's arrangement was worse. It would be as if, instead of buying groceries in the company store, workers were buying tools and raw materials for work the following day.

## THE UBER CONTRACTOR

Companies that make up the "gig" economy, such as Uber, Lyft, Door-Dash, and Grubhub, have built their entire business model around fissured employment structures. Other than the computer programmers, marketers, accountants, and other administrators who design and manage the app, gig companies are almost entirely staffed by independent contractors.

"Gig companies," previously dubbed the "sharing economy," first showed up as an organized concept in a 2010 book by Lisa Gansky.[40] Gansky prophesied a bright future in which slack resources—cars, homes, tools, server space—would be rented rather than owned.[41] Gansky's predictions were correct as applied to digital assets such as streaming, software-as-a-service, and cloud storage. They were less correct in the context of physical assets like tools and cars. When it came to the sharing economy, the most valuable "slack" resource turned out to be labor. A car is a slack resource when it's sitting in the driveway. But customers didn't just want the car; they wanted someone to pick them up and drop them off. Sharing requires labor.

Certain aspects of gig work are consistent with the legal test for independent contractor status, outlined in chapter 1. Drivers for Uber, Lyft, DoorDash, or Grubhub drive their own cars and use their own phones to log into the app, whenever and wherever they want. Unlike the hourly workers described in chapter 4, gig workers can turn off the app if customers are scarce or the kids need to be picked up from school. Indeed, worker appetite for gig work can be understood as the extension and natural consequence of uncertain hourly employment in other contexts. Workers unable to undertake a second job because the first job offers unpredictable hours can at least use gig work to fill in the gaps.[42]

While gig workers have control over the decision to turn off an app, that independence dissolves while they are logged in. At that point, gig workers become subject to intense surveillance and an array of metrics. The Uber app, for example, engages in so much data gathering and transmission that a 2015 contract with its drivers advised them to get an unlimited data plan to avoid large overage fees with their cell phone providers.[43] Drivers decline rides at their peril; declining more than three offered rides will log a driver out of the app.[44] Drivers are also expected to accept a ride within fifteen seconds,[45] but—as the Uber contract sets forth–they are advised to "wait at least 10 minutes for a [rider] to show up at the requested pick up location."[46] Drivers are also held to a standard of near-perfection with respect to customer ratings.[47] Yet app companies can change the algorithm that calculates performance standards and compensation for drivers at any time.[48]

Legal scholars have been critical of the gig economy,[49] in part because the entire industry seems like a form of cheating. As taxi spokesman Oleg Uritsky told the *Boston Globe* in 2012, "Uber exploited a loophole in the law. Taxicabs everywhere are heavily, heavily regulated for public safety."⁵⁰ Journalist Matthew Yglesias characterized the entire industry as an "extremely elegant use of technology to, in effect, hack the legal system."⁵¹ Gig companies have a technological advantage over their predecessors, due to location-based smartphone technology. But one of their central competitive advantages is their refusal to pay taxes and licensing fees; contribute to unemployment insurance, workers' compensation, or health insurance; and comply with wage and hour laws.

Uber and Lyft are particularly egregious examples. They refused to reclassify workers as employees despite adverse court rulings and state legislation. Even after a California court ruling and a subsequent statute classified their workers as employees under state law, those companies refused to alter their practices.⁵² The California attorney general eventually sued them for contempt.⁵³ Meanwhile, gig companies introduced a 2020 ballot measure that would cement gig workers as independent contractors, and exclude them from coverage for unemployment insurance, workers' compensation, minimum wage and overtime protections, and the right to unionize.⁵⁴ Instead, the ballot measure provided partial protections for workers, in the form of a wage floor, a healthcare subsidy for purchasing insurance on the Obamacare exchange, and some antidiscrimination protections.⁵⁵

Gig companies spent $200 million promoting the California ballot measure, making the somewhat misleading claim that the ballot measure was meant to protect worker flexibility.⁵⁶ The advertisements suggested that employee status would result in increased corporate control over workers, who would lose the freedom to log in and out of apps whenever they wanted. It's hard to know how much of the claim was a bluff. But if the claims were true, it suggests that these companies are built on little more than regulatory avoidance, rather than on some other form of market innovation.

## OPTING OUT OF THE MASTER-SERVANT SYSTEM

Despite the absence of employment-based protections and benefits, millions of workers have gravitated toward gig work. Legal scholar Veena Dubal spent two years interviewing and observing meetings involving taxi drivers as well as Uber and Lyft drivers.⁵⁷ She emerged with a complex picture of how these workers think about their work. Some workers preferred contractor status, reporting that they liked the "flexibility and/or autonomy."⁵⁸ One driver explained, "I want to be able to go you know, take my daughter fishing on Wednesday in the summer instead of going to work if I want."⁵⁹ Dubal's historical research into similar debates in the 1970s over taxi drivers found that "many immigrant and racial minority drivers, in particular, valued... the structural control and scheduling freedom it permitted" and the associated "entrepreneur identity."⁶⁰

Other gig workers Dubal interviewed would have preferred the benefits and security and employment status.⁶¹ Nevertheless, one leading driver who had advocated for employee status was "plagued by concerns about what working conditions she would have to endure if Uber became her employer."⁶² Rusty, another driver Dubal interviewed, predicted that even if he were reclassified, he could not imagine that Uber would ever "give him basic employee benefits."⁶³ Given everything he knew, Rusty considered contractor status more realistic.⁶⁴

The comparative attractiveness of gig work speaks to the dearth of good alternatives. As Heidi Shierholz, a former chief economist at the U.S. Department of Labor, observed, "[W]hat we've seen over the last four and a half decades is just huge erosion of worker leverage in a way that's led to just incredibly low job quality for huge swaths of our labor market."⁶⁵ Gig workers are not opting out of full-time jobs with benefits, but out of "part time, temporary, poorly paid" work "lacking benefits"—what sociologists call "precarious" work.⁶⁶ Judy Fudge and Rosemary Owens note that precarious work has historically been associated with women, who "predominantly performed precarious work in order to supplement the male wage."⁶⁷ Precarious work has "spread" throughout the labor market since the 1980s, Fudge and Owens argue, even as women continue to perform a disproportionate share of those jobs.⁶⁸

Dubal's interviews suggest that gig workers have a pragmatic view of the costs and benefits of the master-servant system. And they have chosen to either opt out or hedge their bets, combining gig work with other forms of work. For their part, gig companies may be openly flouting employment laws, but in doing so they reveal the weaknesses of a master-servant system that encumbers the employment relationship with many social welfare benefits that should be allocated to the state. In attempting to game the legal tests for employment status, gig companies have also surrendered substantial control over workers, betting that the marginal benefits of day-to-day control are not worth the cost of complying with employment laws and covering employee benefits.

The rise of gig work also parallels other points in history when the ecosystem of employment arrangements was more varied. As Justice Gorsuch observed in the *Oliveira* decision, federal laws in 1925 did not presume a clear demarcation between work performed as a contractor versus an employee.[69] Likewise, as described in chapter 4, early industrial work arrangements contained some of the artisanal structures and rhythms of work, in which artisans directed and paid their own mini-fiefdoms within departments. Similarly, historian Crandall Shifflett's study on company towns in rural Appalachia in the nineteenth and twentieth centuries revealed that rural workers tended to work seasonally in factories and mines, interspersing paid work with rural subsistence living.[70] Historian Juliet Walker also documented a strong tradition of entrepreneurship and self-sufficiency among enslaved Black workers, suggesting that those who were least able to escape the master-servant system were the most determined to find ways to work independently.[71]

## THE FREE LABOR IDEOLOGY

Cultural attitudes toward paid labor have also shifted over time. According to historian Eric Foner, the Republican Party of the 1860s was organized around an ideology of "free labor" in which freedom meant economic independence.[72] The ideology of free labor presumed that wage labor represented a form of dependency on the employer, in the same way reliance on government welfare might be viewed among today's conservatives as a form of dependency. Thus, wage labor was not presumed to be superior to more independent, seasonal, or even subsistence ways of life.

The free labor ideology was in part an abolitionist idea, in which slavery was presented as an affront to free labor.[73] But the ideology also rested on a form of white privilege, in which landownership and economic independence was a reasonable aspiration if not a birthright. In the ideology of free labor, wage labor was an interim status to be tolerated while building savings to buy tribal land seized by the government.[74] "The man who labored for another last year" said Abraham Lincoln, "this year labors for himself, and next year he will hire others to labor for him."[75]

Like all ideologies, the free labor ideology offered a simplified vision that never quite matched the realities of the time. Even in 1860, some 60 percent of the workforce relied in some way on wages.[76] Free labor ideology also overlooked the risks and instability of economic independence,[77] which for many free white workers was closer to subsistence. It also implicitly appealed to white workers' sense of racial superiority. In a postbellum environment in which Black workers joined the ranks of wage laborers, wage labor took on a less elevated status.[78] And as chapter 2 recounted, courts seem to have implicitly adopted this frame, declining to intervene to protect the contract rights of wage laborers in the decades following the Civil War.

The free labor ideology also did not fare well in an increasingly industrialized America, where individuals could not realistically amass the capital necessary to compete on an industrial scale.[79] Even the idea of "freedom of contract"—an outgrowth of the idea of worker independence and self-determination[80]—collided with reality when it came to the high rate of industrial workplace injuries.[81]

### DISRUPTING THE MASTER-SERVANT IDEOLOGY

Both the gig economy and the free labor ideology reveal the extent to which the master-servant system rests on more than just legal doctrine. It also rests on a set of cultural norms and assumptions about employer sovereignty and control over the workplace. The pandemic may have reinvigorated employee resistance toward master-servant ideology. Remote work removed many workers from day-to-day physical control and surveillance and undermined employer claims that in-person work was necessary for business operations. The availability of remote work has become a marker of status in many jobs, making the control inherent in in-person work all the more salient—and oppressive—for everyone else.

The pandemic also undermined the rhetoric of reciprocity that supports the master-servant system, particularly the idea that workers will be "taken care of" in exchange for their labor and loyalty. The physical peril of in-person work escalated dramatically, with few corresponding benefits for frontline workers. Their sense of betrayal was compounded by corporate failure to take even rudimentary precautions to protect workers from infection.

Likewise, working mothers with small and school-age children facing prolonged school shutdowns and little to no childcare access were also betrayed by employers—who had no formal duty to accommodate them beyond providing two weeks of leave under emergency COVID legislation—and by state and local governments that failed to prioritize their needs. Many of these mothers scaled back their career ambitions or dropped out of the workforce entirely: a 2020 survey by McKinsey found that one in three working mothers "considered downshifting their careers or leaving their jobs altogether."[82] As the pandemic dragged on, some 3.5 million working mothers quit, lost their jobs, or went on leave.[83] The pandemic destroyed any illusion that these women may have previously harbored that they were laboring on an equal playing field or that their investment in the workplace would eventually be rewarded.

The pandemic also eroded another cultural assumption underpinning the master-servant system: that customer convenience should always take precedence over the basic needs of workers. This assumption animates a variety of business practices, such as the admonition that the "customer is always right" or store hours that extend late into the night or throughout weekends and holidays. Many of the extreme workplace practices at Amazon warehouses are in service of a minor customer convenience: receiving a package a few hours or days earlier than they otherwise would.

The worker-customer hierarchy in America also has a racialized valence. The racial wealth gap in the United States remains stark: the average white household has an average wealth of $250,000, compared to $27,100 for Black households and $48,700 for Hispanic households.[84] It is thus primarily white Americans who are more frequently in a position to occupy the elevated status of "customer." Although white Americans make up the majority of low-wage workers, Black and Hispanic workers disproportionately occupy lower- and middle-wage jobs.[85] In addition, low-wage jobs are predominantly occupied by women.[86]

The pandemic disrupted the customer-employee hierarchy. First, countless customers were captured behaving badly in viral videos circulated on the internet—whether engaging in racist outbursts, violently threatening workers over masks or other COVID protocols, or throwing tantrums over minor inconveniences. Businesses had to start placing limits on customers if only to protect their reputations as a safe environment for other customers. Though typically filmed by other customers, these videos often portrayed workers in a sympathetic manner, as blameless victims of customer rage. In addition, worker shortages shifted the balance of power between workers and customers. Where frontline workers became so scarce that businesses would need to cut back on opening hours, businesses found that keeping workers happy became more important than satisfying an irrationally angry customer.

More broadly, COVID-related disruptions displaced the centrality of work in American life. Workers who found themselves jobless, working remotely, or working fewer hours due to caregiving found other ways to occupy their time and find meaning in their lives. Even those who worked more than ever began to question whether their sacrifices were proportional to what they were receiving in return. And although the high-status employees who made up the bulk of remote workers already benefited from considerable workplace autonomy, even they may be reluctant to allow work to return to the central place it occupied in their lives prior to the pandemic. Years later, such workers remain resistant to returning to the office full time despite persistent cajoling and threats from management.

The post-COVID version of free labor ideology may consist of questioning whether wage labor and employment relationships ought to be prioritized over other economic and noneconomic arrangements, like independent work, seasonal work, punctuating paid work with caregiving, or shorter workweeks.

In summary, the cultural component of master-servant concepts may be starting to erode, and with it, employee tolerance for abusive employer practices. At the same time, there will be limits to workers' ability to resist employer power and control while living paycheck to paycheck or weathering an economic downturn. Chapter 10 examines the types of legal reform that might meaningfully help to unwind the master-servant system.

. . .

Oliveira eventually left New Prime and drove for other companies as an employee, where he made a good living.[87] He drove throughout the pandemic and remembers delivering oxygen tanks to New York City.[88] If he was driving to a state that was shut down, he arranged for Instacart grocery deliveries at truck stops, where he cooked his own meals in an air fryer.[89]

Oliveira won at the Supreme Court in an 8–0 decision,[90] which enabled his case to proceed at the trial court level. The case settled in 2021 for up to $28 million.[91] As the named plaintiff, Oliveira received $30,000 of that sum.[92] He used it to buy a 2016 Ram Revel pickup, make a down payment on a Harley Davidson, and pay off the camper he was living in "so he would have a place to live that wouldn't be taken from him."[93]

CHAPTER 10

# Policy Interventions

Reforms in the employment realm often produce mixed results for workers over time, partly because employers can successfully blunt the effect of new mandates and identify alternate sources of power over workers, but also because reforms can indirectly fortify the master-servant system. For example, legislation that requires or encourages employers to offer workplace benefits can make it difficult for workers to leave a particular job and privileges employment over more independent forms of work. When the state makes employers responsible for substantial welfare obligations, corporations also have a stronger rhetorical basis for claiming power over the workplace generally and retaining discretion over how benefits are allocated and implemented.

As discussed in chapter 8, employers often distribute workplace benefits in a regressive manner and attach conditions to eligibility that favor corporate interests. And as chapter 9 described, the cumulative effect of legal rules that attach ever more obligations to employment status is a market that rewards companies for misclassifying workers or avoiding benefits-related obligations through part-time or temporary hires, subcontracting, or franchising. Either way, low-wage workers often discover that benefits are inaccessible or unaffordable.

Legislators can also inadvertently limit employee power in the workplace through reforms that presume employee passivity in the workplace and that assign them no role in decision-making. As chapter 1 described, workers' compensation laws offered no-fault compensation to workers but treated workplace safety as a matter of managerial prerogative. Subsequent workplace safety legislation, such as the Occupational Safety and Health Act, likewise treated safety as a matter of expertise, in which an employee's only role is to complain to OSHA and wait for an investigation.

Courts have also served to blunt the transformative potential of employment legislation, as discussed in chapter 3 with respect to state wage and hour law, in chapter 5 with respect to labor law, and in chapters 6 and 7 with respect to antidiscrimination law.

How then might policymakers design and implement workplace reforms without inadvertently fortifying the master-servant system, reducing employee autonomy and decision-making in the workplace, or exacerbating inequality and historical disadvantage?

Beyond the specific workplace improvement the reform is intended to achieve, policymakers should also consider the following factors:

1. whether the reform increases employer discretion and governance over the workplace, for example by indirectly subsidizing employer decision-making, authorizing employers to implement the reform in any manner of their choosing, or deferring to internal employer policies and procedures;
2. whether the reform exacerbates historical disadvantage or inequality between high-wage and low-wage workers;
3. whether the reform privileges employment relationships over other economic relationships or forms of work, such as independent contract work, new business formation, or unpaid caregiving; and
4. the effect of the reform on employee mobility—that is, an employee's practical ability to leave a job, and by extension demand better conditions in a current job.

Notably, reforms that do not fit within the traditional model of employment law can sometimes have the most meaningful impact on employee power and authority in the workplace by making alternative choices available that force employers to respond to employee preferences and concerns. This chapter uses the Affordable Care Act of 2010 (Obamacare) as an example of law reform that made meaningful progress with respect to factors 2, 3, and 4, although recent developments have limited the law's potential positive impact with respect to factor 1.

### OBAMACARE AND THE PROBLEM OF "JOB LOCK"

The United States effectively has two separate health-care systems: a near universal public health-care system for elderly Americans (Medicare),[1] and a byzantine patchwork of public and private insurance for everyone else (Medicaid, the Children's Health Insurance Program, the Veterans Health Administration, and private insurance).[2] For nonelderly Americans, the most common source of health-care coverage is employer-sponsored insurance, which covers 154 million Americans.[3]

Before the 2010 Affordable Care Act, workers with chronic health conditions like diabetes or heart disease—or with family members suffering from a chronic illness—were often stuck in whatever job they had when the health condition first arose. If they were lucky enough to have employer-sponsored health insurance, they risked losing coverage if their employment was terminated. They could attempt to purchase a private health insurance policy, but those policies were expensive; were of varying quality; and often excluded "preexisting" conditions, that is, conditions that predated the purchase of the insurance policy. Even if they started a new job with health benefits, there was no guarantee the new plan would include coverage of the chronic condition.[4]

Economists referred to this phenomenon as "job lock."[5] Job lock was bad for individual workers and for the economy. It discouraged workers from leaving stable jobs to join a riskier enterprise or starting their own business.[6] Jonathan Gruber, an MIT economics professor who served as an adviser in the Obama administration, reported that reversing job lock was "one of the major motivations for health care reform."[7] Austen Goolsbee, another adviser in the Obama administration, observed that "one of the biggest impediments to entrepreneurship has been the fear that you couldn't get health insurance if you did. The [Affordable Care Act] has, potentially, lessened that a great deal."[8]

Obamacare addressed the problem of job lock in multiple respects. First, it prohibited insurers from excluding preexisting conditions and imposed certain minimum standards on health insurance coverage. Second, it created health insurance exchanges that made it easier for individuals to buy insurance in the private market. Third, it offered income-based subsidies that reduced the cost of purchasing insurance on the exchange. Fourth, it expanded Medicaid so that public insurance would be more widely available to low-income Americans.[9]

The law substantially reduced the psychological stakes of losing or switching jobs. Workers could get health insurance on their own if they needed it, sometimes with subsidies. They no longer had to worry about losing coverage for a preexisting condition when they switched insurance. And in states that expanded Medicaid coverage, the working poor could obtain free health insurance through Medicaid even if an employer declined to offer coverage.

Although Obamacare was mostly structured as insurance law reform, the law made substantial progress in reforming the master-servant system, according to the criteria described at the outset of this chapter. In particular, it improved employee mobility by lowering the financial and health stakes associated with leaving a job (factor 4). Obamacare was also significant in reducing the financial and health risks associated with undertaking non-employment-based types of work, like independent contractor work and new business formation, by making affordable insurance available outside an employment relationship (factor 3).

Indeed, venture capitalist Marc Andreessen described Obamacare as "perhaps the single biggest key enabler for the sharing/gig/1099 economy."[10] Tech leaders in the gig economy agreed, somewhat sheepishly, that their workers relied on the health insurance exchanges for coverage.[11] At a private dinner, Uber founder and then-CEO Travis Kalanick described the effect of Obamacare on his business as "huge," claiming that the law "democratiz[ed] . . . those types of benefits" and "allow people to have more flexible ways to make a living. They don't have to be working for The Man."[12]

Obamacare also helped to reduce inequality and historical disadvantage in access to health coverage, both within organizations and at a population level (factor 2). The law contained an employer mandate, which imposed a tax penalty on companies with more than fifty full-time workers for failing to cover at least 95 percent of workers.[13] Although companies can continue to avoid providing coverage to part-time workers—which disproportionately disadvantages low-income workers[14]—the mandate at least forces companies to extend health benefits broadly among full-time workers, rather than limiting the benefit to favored employees. Across the U.S. population, the law increased the number of insured Americans overall and reduced racial and ethnic disparities in health coverage for Latinos and Black Americans, who remain uninsured at higher rates and suffer the associated health disparities and financial losses from lack of coverage.[15]

Obamacare also illustrates the obstacles legislators encounter in trying to move away from existing master-servant structures. President Obama lacked the votes to pass a public insurance option, which made even the reformed health insurance system heavily reliant on corporate decisions to continue to offer health insurance coverage. Had corporate employers chosen to simply cancel their health plans and pay the associated tax penalty—which would have been substantially cheaper than offering health coverage[16]—the law could have resulted in an overall reduction in the number of insured Americans.

In addition, some of the progress that the law achieved has since been reversed by spiraling health-care costs. The original bill included a provision that would have imposed a 40 percent excise tax on expensive "Cadillac" health plans—costing $10,200 per year for individuals or $27,500 for families[17]—but that provision was delayed and later repealed by Congress. Since 2010, health-care costs have risen so dramatically that the average cost of employer-sponsored health insurance in 2024—$8,951 per year for a single worker and $25,572 for family coverage[18]—is approaching what previously would have been considered "Cadillac" territory.[19]

Rising private health-care costs reveal the extent to which the state implicitly subsidizes private spending by employers on health insurance. As political scientist Christopher Howard explains in *The Hidden Welfare State*,[20] the state subsidizes employer-sponsored health insurance through "tax expenditures"—that is, foregone tax revenue through tax breaks.[21] The federal government estimates that it contributes anywhere between $600 and $5,000 per year to the average employee's health insurance coverage as a result of tax breaks.[22] Unlike most direct government outlays, tax expenditures are regressive, meaning the highest income earners benefit the most from tax deduction.[23] Furthermore, tax expenditures put public spending in the hands of private actors. The tax break is as large as the employer's willingness to spend.[24]

Today, the tax expenditure for employer-sponsored health insurance is enormous: projected at $233 billion in 2025, and expected to reach 256 billion by 2028.[25] It is around twice the size of all the subsidies offered on the Obamacare health insurance exchanges.[26] It is "the third largest government expenditure on health care,"[27] exceeded only by government-sponsored health insurance through Medicare and Medicaid.[28] In this sense, Obamacare failed at reducing state reliance on employer-provided benefits and instead subsidizes employer discretion on health spending.

Rising health-care costs counter the productive effects of the Affordable Care Act with respect to the master-servant system. Expensive benefits fuel existing incentives for employers to differentiate between have and have-not employees, through full-time versus part-time status, misclassification of independent contractors, and fissuring strategies. Employers also engage in cost-sharing strategies through high-deductible plans that impose more out-of-pocket costs on workers, which hurts workers who are least able to absorb those costs.[29] Cost sharing can also discourage low-income workers from signing up for insurance when it is offered.

By contrast, the growing tax expenditure disproportionately subsidizes the highest wage earners and deprives public coffers of resources that might otherwise be available to expand public insurance programs or expand subsidies on the health-care exchange. Growing health-care costs also give employers and health insurers more incentive to engage in intensive health surveillance as described in chapter 8.[30]

In summary, Obamacare serves as a useful reference point for thinking about systemic reforms to the master-servant system, particularly because the law was not exclusively targeted at employment relationships. Instead, it served to broaden access to important social welfare benefits beyond the employment relationship, which gave individuals more choice over the types of work they wanted to pursue and reduced the personal risk of leaving a job.

Further reforms to health care—particularly universal health care—would free workers to pursue other forms of work without worrying about health care. Universal health care would also remove health-care-related expenses from employer payrolls and all the distorted incentives that health care imposes with respect to misclassifying contractors and imposing internal barriers to bring workers on full time. Universal health care would also eliminate coverage gaps, reduce the systemic cost of health care, and likely produce better health outcomes overall.[31]

### OTHER TYPES OF REFORM

Some types of law reform—discussed herein—will necessarily be directed at the workplace, as that is the most direct means of altering corporate practices. However, other reforms can alter the balance of power in the workplace by making more options available to individuals regarding the work arrangement they might prefer to pursue.

#### *Untether Other Basic Social Welfare Programs from the Employment Relationship*

Beyond health care, employers should not be relied upon to provide social welfare benefits that are only tenuously related to work itself. Imposing state-like responsibilities on corporate employers bolsters their claim for state-like control and governance over the internal affairs of the workplace. And as discussed in chapter 8, giving employers power over benefits presents an opportunity for them to preferentially allocate those benefits according to their business preferences and internal hierarchies.

Congress and state legislatures have been trending toward legislation that makes social welfare benefits available somewhat more broadly, or at least takes the administration of those benefits out of the hands of employers. For example, the federal COVID stimulus bill extended unemployment insurance to gig workers who lost work or experienced a significant reduction in hours.[32]

California's paid leave program—and other similar state leave laws—are funded through payroll deductions but are administered by the state.[33] As Deborah Widiss observed, state-mandated and -administered leave programs are preferable to voluntary paid leave programs, because they tend to cover a much broader swath of workers, including part-time employees.[34] In California, individuals must have a past work history of contributions to the system to be eligible for leave. However, the system does not require an individual to have worked for a particular employer for a certain period of time to be eligible for leave, unlike the Family and Medical Leave Act. In fact, an individual can be unemployed but looking for work and still be eligible for leave. A setup like this would, for example, enable a pregnant worker to obtain benefits even if she is laid off from her job during the pregnancy.

Paid leave programs should also be coupled with reforms to unpaid leave laws, which tend to make unpaid leave available to workers only if they have lengthy tenure at a particular workplace. In California, for example, employees need to have worked at a company for twelve months and at least 1,250 hours before they are eligible for the unpaid leave.[35] This means that an employee might be eligible for paid leave immediately after starting a new job, but that employee risks being fired if they use the paid leave available to them for reasons other than disability.[36] This restriction produces a form of job lock for expecting parents and punishes unlucky workers who experience a serious medical condition soon after starting a new job.

Leave laws could be further structured to avoid privileging employment over other forms of work by extending their coverage to independent contractors. In this regard, funding leave through payroll taxes is imperfect because it would enable industries that make extensive use of independent contractors to avoid contributions to the program. The tax base for leave programs can, however, be expanded through taxes specific to industries that rely almost exclusively on independent contractors, such as taxes specific to delivery and transportation service that cover taxis, ride sharing, and delivery services.

*Enable Workers to Select or Decline Union Representation At-Will*

As discussed in chapter 2, the at-will presumption confers substantial power and authority on employers by default, by conferring on them the right to terminate the relationship at any time, as well as the right to determine the terms and conditions of that relationship. Unions represent the most potent counterweight to the governance power that the at-will presumption confers on employers by default. However, union representation is not available to workers with the same kind of ease, as discussed in chapter 5.

Labor scholars have observed that a central obstacle to unionization is the barriers to triggering an election, followed by the long delay between when an election is declared and when votes are tallied.[37] Each of these hurdles offers an opportunity for the employer to fire union organizers, hire new employees to dilute the union vote, or lobby employees to vote against the union.[38] Proposed legislation in Congress, such as the Employee Free Choice Act and the PRO Act, would help address those barriers but still impose substantial transaction costs that place unions at a disadvantage relative to employers.[39]

A comparable counterpoint to the at-will presumption could be a legal regime that would enable workers to enter and exit union representation in a frictionless way. Workers could, for example, be offered the opportunity to join a union at the start of their employment and change their minds at any time. If the union has not secured a critical mass of workers within a bargaining unit, members would enjoy certain individual protections.[40] They could request that a union representative assist them in negotiating their individual employment terms, such as their pay, benefits, and vacation. Such representation is not significantly different than what executives already enjoy in the context of their negotiations at the outset of their employment or the kind of bargaining leverage that professional employees enjoy at the start of an employment relationship.

Union members without a critical mass could also be accorded *Weingarten* rights, that is, the right to be represented in disciplinary matters and investigations by a union representative. This would not be a radical shift; the NLRB has extended *Weingarten* rights to nonunionized workers at various points in the past.[41] Union members should also be informed of their right to engage in concerted activity, such as walkouts to protest workplace safety or other conditions of employment—a right that is already available to nonunionized workers but that they tend not to exercise.

Once a critical mass of workers has joined the union, such as a majority of the bargaining unit (as under the current rules), workers could expect to have greater collective rights through the union, such as the right to collectively bargain, access to a formal grievance process, and the right to strike. Those rights would be lost if employees departed the union or selected a different union, until such time as membership surpasses the threshold.

Nonemployees, like gig workers, could also benefit from access to union membership, as several scholars have argued.[42] Independent contractors are not currently covered by the NLRA. Nevertheless, Uber drivers in New York, for example, have organized informally through an organization they call an "Uber Guild," which meets with management to "raise issues of concern."[43] The Freelancer's Union—which advertises its services to "contractors, part-time workers, and temps ... primarily in New York state"—has long served a quasi-union function by helping members purchase insurance and other benefits that would be otherwise unavailable and lobbying the legislature on behalf of members.[44] Jeffrey Hirsch and Joseph Seiner argue that such nontraditional forms of labor representation are beneficial for members, even if "not an equal substitute for unions' advocacy and influence over working conditions."[45]

The City of Seattle attempted to formalize efforts by Uber drivers to organize by passing a municipal ordinance allowing them to unionize.[46] The ordinance was challenged in court by Uber and the Chamber of Commerce, and the dispute was later settled to remove a provision allowing the workers to bargain over pay.[47] Nevertheless, it illustrates the benefits of broader access to union-like representation. Legal scholar Sanjunkta Paul argues that bargaining rights should not be dependent on employee status for companies like Uber, which already operates like a hiring hall by setting market prices for labor.[48] Under such conditions, Paul argues, contractors should be permitted to organize and bargain collectively as a counterweight to that price-setting power.[49]

### Reduce Courts' Reliance on Master-Servant Principles in Harassment and Discrimination Cases

As described throughout this book, courts often implicitly, and occasionally explicitly, adopt master-servant principles, even when interpreting federal or state statutes.

In the Title VII context, courts should stop deferring to internal policies, procedures, and managerial prerogative in determining whether the employer has complied with its legal obligation. As Frank Dobbin argues, much of what we recognize today as equal employment opportunity practices were simply updates of labor relations practices.[50] These practices were not designed to address discrimination; as Lauren Edelman argued, they have served primarily to create the illusion of compliance without any corresponding substance.[51] Although employers made some progress in hiring at the entry level, they were never really forced to reexamine how they defined success on the job, or who should be eligible for promotion and why. The *McDonnell Douglas* structure of proof allowed employers to avoid Title VII liability by documenting whatever legitimate nondiscriminatory reason, however arbitrary, motivated their decision-making.

Legislators could pursue reforms to antidiscrimination law analogous to recent reforms to pay equity laws at the state level. These pay equity reforms preclude employers from relying on the general catch-all defense under the Equal Pay Act, which authorizes pay disparities on "any factor other than sex."[52] Instead, employers may only justify pay disparities based on factors enumerated in the statute. For example, the Oregon Equal Pay Law provides that employers may only base pay decisions on seniority, merit, the quantity or quality of production, location, travel, education, training, or experience, or any combination of those factors, provided they "accoun[t] for the entire compensation differential."[53] Similarly, a California law requires that pay differentials be based on a similar list of enumerated factors or is "job related . . . and consistent with a business necessity."[54]

Similarly, in the context of hiring, firing, and promotions, employers should be held accountable for discriminatory disparities, unless they can show that the disparities can be explained as a result of job performance, formal hiring criteria, conduct rules, or a validated test. As sociologists Stainback and Tomaskovic-Devey suggest, women and people of color have had more success entering professions with formal qualifications, such as a medical or law degree, than roles that use less-formalized criteria and enable entrenched incumbents to maintain the status quo.[55] Further progress in diversifying managerial ranks will require a more rigorous assessment of success in those roles and greater transparency about the evaluation criteria for those moving up the corporate ladder.

In the harassment context, courts should also stop deferring to internal policies and procedures. As discussed in chapter 6 and 7, internal complaint channels for harassment and discrimination create the illusion of providing a meaningful remedy but largely serve to produce documentation that employers can use to defend against any subsequent lawsuits. An employer's superficial efforts to address harassment through a complaint channel that does not provide accountability or a meaningful remedy should not enable the company to avoid liability for harassment that meets the legal standard. Instead, courts should focus their assessment on whether harassment occurred. Legislators could constrain courts by imposing strict liability for harassment, rather than the *Faragher/Ellerth* standard for supervisor harassment and the negligence standard for coworker harassment.[56]

The NLRB could also deter employers from adopting dead-end internal complaint processes through its interpretation of Section 8(a)(2) of the NLRA, which prohibits company unions.[57] The NLRB could treat HR complaint processes that primarily serve the employer's interests as an unfair labor practice equivalent to a company-dominated union. To pass muster, a bona fide internal complaint process should at the very least offer meaningful remedies, including reinstatement, back pay, and other make-whole relief, such as promotion to an employee wrongfully denied a promotion due to discrimination. The process should also afford the opportunity to appeal the final result to a third-party arbitrator. Further, these available remedies should be disclosed to workers in employer policies.

## Promote Employee-Owned Businesses

More than ten million Americans own a portion of the company they work for through employee stock ownership plans (ESOPs),[58] in which the company allocates shares to workers through a retirement fund.[59] A much smaller number of companies are structured as worker-owned cooperatives or purpose trusts operated for the benefit of workers.[60]

Business owners convert to employee ownership for a variety of reasons. The tax code provides substantial tax breaks for setting up employee stock ownership plans and employee cooperatives.[61] Small business owners sometimes convert to employee ownership as a form of succession planning, to avoid having to sell to a competitor when the founder retires.[62] Management will sometimes adopt an employee-owned structure for strategic reasons, such as to resist takeovers or obtain a tax-advantaged loan.[63] In recent years, private equity companies have even gravitated toward partial employee ownership to increase productivity and employee loyalty[64]—and ultimately the resale value of the company.

Studies on employee-owned businesses suggest that they promote employee wealth-building,[65] and that they are less likely to lay off workers during downturns.[66] Some employee-owned business also give workers a formal voice in the management of the business, conferring power on workers that would otherwise only be available through unionization.[67]

Employee stock ownership is not a "panacea."[68] If the stock ownership plan is structured so that the workers' shares vest over time,[69] the vesting schedule can act like golden handcuffs, discouraging workers from quitting until they are fully vested. Employee ownership also makes workers financially vulnerable if the business collapses.[70] Nevertheless, employee ownership through an ESOP often represents retirement assets employees wouldn't otherwise have had—they are generally structured as grants to workers, rather than requiring employees to invest their own money in the business.[71] ESOP ownership also tends to be more equitable than other valuable employee benefits because the tax benefits of ESOP structure are only available if companies extend participation to a substantial portion of "non-highly compensated employees."[72]

Beyond existing tax incentives, Congress and the Department of Labor could further support employee-owned businesses through reforms to ERISA, the federal law that applies to employee retirement plans. Because ERISA imposes complex compliance rules, only relatively large companies have sufficient resources to set up an ESOP, figure out the share valuation, and withstand the risk of litigation over the value of the shares.[73] Reducing the ERISA obligations for small businesses and providing valuation assistance would make ESOPs more feasible for them.[74]

State legislatures can also facilitate employee ownership by making alternate corporate structures available that are compatible with employee ownership, such as Oregon's law creating a form of ownership known as a "purpose trust."[75] As legal scholar Susan Gary explains, purpose trusts are flexible and could be structured for the "purpose" of operating a business that emphasizes employee welfare.[76] They could also be structured to distribute profits to workers through profit sharing or to give workers a say in management.[77] Because purpose trusts are not structured as retirement plans, they also avoid the compliance costs and rules associated with ERISA.

*Implement Reparations for Slavery*

Employment-based remedies like Title VII have helped to reduce workplace discrimination. However, they have not and cannot address the vast transfer of wealth from enslaved people to enslavers through many lifetimes of unpaid labor. Social scientist Thomas Craemer used then-prevailing wage rates to estimate the unpaid wages of enslaved people between 1776 and 1865 and estimated that they would be owed $5.9 trillion in inflation-adjusted dollars.[78]

This staggering figure represents approximately 25 percent of the annual gross domestic product of the United States and exceeds the value of the combined federal relief packages passed during the COVID-19 pandemic. Yet $5.9 trillion is proportional to the wage-related loss when taking into account a lifetime of wages for 3.9 million enslaved people as of 1860 and their enslaved ancestors, who were forced to work from the time they were small children. On a per capita basis, $5.9 trillion in reparations represents approximately $157,700 per individual who identified as Black or African American in the 2006 census.[79] Reparations on that scale would greatly reduce or eliminate the racial wealth gap.[80] Reparations on a smaller scale would still be meaningful.

As a variety of scholars have observed, there is precedent for reparations in the United States, including those paid by the U.S. government to Japanese Americans for internment, the Alaska Native Claims Settlement Act, and the Indian Claims Commission Act of 1946.[81] In the context of slavery, reparations would create a variety of implementation challenges with respect to identifying eligible recipients and how they would be compensated.[82] These challenges should not serve to excuse inaction. As attorney and activist Nkechi Taifa explained, "[W]hy should the government pay reparations now? The answer is succinct: it should be paid because it is owed."[83]

Many scholars favor the approach taken by the proposed House Resolution 40, which would establish a commission to study reparations and make recommendations.[84] Scholars have proposed a variety of forms for reparations, including cash transfers, funding for historically Black colleges and universities,[85] investment in schools in Black communities, "venture capital for black business established in black communities,"[86] increases to social security payments,[87] and community-based land purchase.[88] Scholars William Darity Jr. and A. Kirsten Mullen propose a grant fund "for various asset building projects, including homeownership, additional education, or start-up funds for self-employment, or even vouchers for the purchase of financial assets."[89]

Whatever their form, reparations could serve to help repair the harm of involuntary labor by giving Black descendants more choice regarding how they wish to invest their own labor, such as starting a new business, purchasing an asset that they rent for profit, or even having a greater variety of career options through higher education. A nest egg of assets would make it easier for individuals to leave a job for a new one or step away from the workplace to care for a family member. Reparations would thus satisfy the policy considerations described at the start of this chapter, by addressing historical disadvantage while also improving employee mobility and facilitating other economic relationships or forms of work.

# Conclusion

As of this writing, some five years since the start of the pandemic, the website for the Waterloo Tyson Foods facility still has pictures of workers outfitted for the pandemic, wearing white coats, hardhats, and face masks.[1] A walking tour of the plant shows empty workstations separated by hanging plexiglass.[2]

The pandemic left an uncertain residue on the American workforce. The early promise that it would fundamentally reshape workplace relations dissolved almost as quickly as the phased-out "hero" pay and bonuses for workers at the height of the pandemic.

On the other hand, the persistent shortage of frontline workers would eventually be rewarded as a matter of supply and demand. Between 2019 and 2023, workers in the bottom 10 percent of wage earners saw the highest wage growth among all workers, increasing by 34 percent (12% after adjusting for inflation).[3] Wage growth for low- and middle-income earners stands in stark contrast to earlier decades, in which wage growth was flat or negative on an inflation-adjusted basis.[4] A majority of U.S. states have also increased the minimum wage in recent years, which could help to cement recent trends.[5]

The pandemic did not dislodge the master-servant system, as the Tyson Foods case illustrated. Even beyond the domain of workplace safety described in chapter 1, master-servant concepts are deeply entrenched in legal doctrine, employment practices, and the economic structure of the American social welfare system. As discussed in chapters 2, 3, and 4, master-servant concepts influenced the employment-at-will doctrine and American managerial practices regarding control over pay and working time.

Twentieth-century legislative efforts to address employer power and discretion in the workplace have been meaningful yet limited, as discussed in part II. The NLRA enabled unionized workers to share in workplace governance, but historically low levels of union density mean that few private-sector workers today have the opportunity to bargain with employers on a coequal basis. Likewise, Title VII of the Civil Rights Act has helped to reduce discrimination and harassment in the workplace but serves as only a narrow exception to broader principles of employment-at-will.

As part III of this book argues, the master-servant system remains entrenched because welfare benefits are overwhelmingly tied to employment status. Individual workers are pushed toward employment status to obtain available benefits. However, employers retain substantial discretion over how to award those benefits and tend to award the most generous benefits to the most highly compensated workers. Lower-wage workers tend to be offered only those limited benefits required by law or are misclassified as contractors to avoid employment-related costs entirely.

The government plays an ambivalent role in this system. It legislates and regulates employer conduct and adjudicates disputes involving alleged violations of that legislation. But it too is dependent upon employers to provide basic welfare benefits and tends to defer to employer power and discretion as a result.

Legislative gridlock at the federal level has meant that few work-related laws have passed in recent decades. Instead, states have proven to be the sources of the most legislative innovation during that period. These legislative efforts have included improvements in sick leave laws and expansions of paid leave programs. Federal regulators have also attempted to fill the gap where possible, as illustrated by the Federal Trade Commission's stalled 2024 rule banning noncompete agreements.

Recent social movements have had both legislative and social impacts. Following the #MeToo movement, states passed hundreds of laws, including laws relating to pay equity, expansions of harassment law, and increasing transparency.[6] The Black Lives Matter movement also spurred progress with respect to racial equity, including increased attention to educating the public about historical sources of injustice. Some states and municipalities have explored providing reparations for slavery, segregation, or housing discrimination.

And as chapters 2 and 3 illustrated, managerial practices and social and cultural influences also have a substantial impact on the workplace, separate and apart from the law. While social and cultural influences can be a source of oppression, they can also be a source of progress. Both Black Lives Matter and the #MeToo movement imposed social pressures on employers in ways that led them to adopt fairer internal practices. The #MeToo movement made employers more inclined to hold harassers accountable for wrongdoing and to revisit questions of gender equity in the workplace. Black Lives Matter likewise led many employers to revisit their hiring and promotion practices and to hire officers of diversity. While some of these interventions have a performative quality, others may improve equity over time.[7]

As discussed in chapter 9, more subtle cultural shifts may also have implications for the workplace. The promising trend toward union organizing may signal greater worker resistance to managerial prerogative. Polling in recent years suggesting high levels of public support for unions may likewise signal a shift in public attitudes.

COVID also rearranged public attitudes toward work and pressures on frontline workers. Many office workers continue to prefer hybrid work arrangements over fully in-person work, and physical distance from the workplace offers some degree of freedom from physical control and surveillance, even if it tends to blur the boundary between work and home. Like the great depression, COVID may have fundamentally rewired our collective psychology to resist the "hustle" culture of 24/7 work.

COVID also unmasked some of the cruelty and exploitation inherent in the American labor system, embodied in the stark contrast of essential workers exposed to a novel virus while customers demanded multiple modifications to their oatmilk latte through the drive-through microphone. As Starbucks worker Jessica Jaszewski explained, "[I]t's the culture that has been created at this company [that] really engenders a feeling by customers that they can do no wrong . . . you can yell at the barista and throw your drink at them" and the barista is "just going to get on their knees and beg for forgiveness."[8] That dynamic, Jaszewski said, "convinced me that [unionizing] was going to be worth it, no matter how long it took or how hard it was."[9]

Social stigmatization of the "Karen" caricature—an entitled, and sometimes racist, white woman with a default tendency to escalate complaints—suggests that the cultural assumption of customer supremacy may be eroding. To the extent that American culture moves away from one in which customer convenience is prioritized over all over values, it may have a positive effect on dignity of and respect for workers.

As chapter 10 described, unraveling the most oppressive aspects of the master-servant system would be a complex and challenging process, given its stubborn persistence over time. A more equitable system would be one that lowers the stakes of employment in general, and in which unexpected job loss does not pose the risk of catastrophic medical debt. As the Affordable Care Act illustrates, reducing job lock can be a boon for innovation, entrepreneurship, and ultimately community building. Workers can more readily step away from traditional jobs to form new businesses, provide caregiving, switch to burgeoning start-ups with more uncertain prospects, or return to school.

In addition, hourly employees deserve some autonomy, control, and freedom from surveillance in their work, not unlike the kind of autonomy that many salaried workers have come to expect. Courts, for their part, should stop treating employers as a mini-sovereign and instead assess the cases before them on the merits, whether the dispute involves a breach of contract or a discrimination claim. Finally, the United States should begin to repay the debt owed to Black Americans for the wage theft of slavery.

No master should be the seat of government.

# Epilogue

In May 2025, the Iowa Supreme Court ruled that the lower court properly dismissed claims against Tyson Foods for gross negligence and fraud. However, it allowed the estates of deceased workers to proceed in their claims against individual corporate executives and managers. The litigation continues.

. . .

Maetta Vance no longer works at Ball State University.

. . .

Ian Meagher lives in Portland, Oregon. They still work for Starbucks. Meagher has been involved in multiple organizing campaigns and was nominated to serve as a bargaining representative for the union in upcoming negotiations.

Meagher owns "probably like seven" Starbucks United T-shirts, including a hoodie.

. . .

Jessica Jaszewski moved to Chicago to pursue her dream of working in the theater industry. She is an assistant house manager for Broadway in Chicago.

. . .

Gerald Bostock became internationally famous as the lead plaintiff in *Bostock v. Clayton County*. He has given "something like 100 or 120 interviews" to the press about his experience.[1] He currently works as a counselor at a mental health facility in Clayton County, Georgia.

The Clayton County Court Appointed Special Advocates website still features a picture of Bostock from 2010, posing with other staff members in matching red polo shirts.[2] Attorney Edward Buckley, who represented Bostock in litigation, passed away in 2025.

. . .

In 2019 Dominic Oliveira received the "Change Maker Award" from Public Justice.

In 2022 Oliveira was in a serious motorcycle accident and was unable to work for more than a year. He went back to work before he was fully recovered to maintain his health insurance. He now drives shorter routes and is worried about keeping up with the debt he incurred during the recovery from his injury.

Friends in law school tell Oliveira that he is "in LexisNexis." They ask him if he knows what that is. Yes, he does.

# Acknowledgments

Thank you to Kevin, Holly, George, Stu, Ben, Bethany, mom, dad, and Hillie.

I am grateful to everyone who agreed to be interviewed in this book, including those who were not quoted in the final manuscript or did not wish to be quoted on the record.

I am also grateful to Maura Roessner and Sam Warren at UC Press; Bryan Keogh at The Conversation; Sharon Langworthy for copyediting; the two anonymous reviewers who provided detailed feedback; and research assistants Charity Martinez, Matthew McMillen, Elizabeth Clark, Georgia Zacest, Sam Haimowitz, Seth Jaksha, Tim Smith, Hayley Cloyd, Colin Messke, and Romeo Adams-Patterson.

The University of Oregon Law School provided research support and the sabbatical support to make this project possible, with further support from the James O. and Alfred T. Goodwin Senior Fellowship.

I am grateful to the many scholars who provided support and feedback through the many years it took to finish this book, including but not limited to Michael Z. Green, Jamillah Williams, Jennifer Reynolds, Erik Girvan, Michael Musheno, Richard Brooks, Joseph Slater, Juliet E.K. Walker, Randall Patton, David Oppenheimer, Ariana Levinson, Rachel Arnow-Richman, Sachin Pandya, Joe Seiner, Rebecca Zietlow, Charlotte Garden, Sam Estreicher, Michael Harper, Susan Carle, Lea VanderVelde, Richard B. Freeman, Brantly Callaway, William J. Collins, Catherine Fisk, Elizabeth S. Anderson, Jonathan Harris, Antonio Rodrigues de Freitas Jr., Adriana Calvo, Angela Morrison, Stephanie Bornstein, Blair Bullock, Laurie Hauber, Marcy Karin, Jean-Christian Vinel, Angela Addae, Susan Gary, Anthony Hunt, Megan Austin, Jesse Abdenour, Alix Devendra, and faculty at the University of Oregon History Department.

# Notes

INTRODUCTION

1. This account is based on Maetta Vance's deposition testimony, as well as statements of fact in the various court decisions. However, because the Vance case was decided on summary judgment, the procedural posture requires the court to construe all facts in Ms. Vance's favor. The trial court nevertheless liberally cites evidence submitted by Ball State. *See* Vance v. Ball State University, Case No. 1:06-cv-1452 (S.D. Ind. 2007), Deposition of Maetta Vance (May 21, 2007) 51, 94 (on file with author); Vance v. Ball State, 133 S.Ct. 2434, 2449 (2013); Vance v. Ball State, 646 F.3d 461 (7th Cir. 2011); Vance v. Ball State University, Entry on Pending Motions, Case No. 1:06-cv-1452 (S.D. Ind. 2007), 2008 WL 4247836. I was unable to obtain copies of the other depositions from the court reporter. In a 2021 interview, Ball State's lawyer, Scott Shockley, recalled that Vance's testimony was "largely accurate." Interview with Scott Shockley, March 2, 2021 (on file with author). Shockley noted that at times Vance's testimony was somewhat imprecise about the exact chronology of events. However, Shockley did not doubt the credibility of her deposition testimony, except regarding one allegation about Davis, which Vance had omitted from an earlier NAACP complaint.

2. Vance v. Ball State, 646 F.3d at 465. The trial court refers to this incident as occurring in "1999 or 2001." Vance v. Ball State University, 2008 WL 4247836, *21 note 5. Vance's 2007 deposition includes a correction stating that Davis hit her in 1999, not 2001. Vance Deposition at 131.

3. Vance Deposition at 38–39.

4. Vance Deposition at 40.

5. Vance Deposition at 39.

6. *Vance*, Entry on Pending Motions, Case No. 1:06-cv-1452 (S.D. Ind. 2007), 2008 WL 4247836, *21 note 5.

7. *Vance*, 646 F.3d at 466.
8. *Vance*, 133 S.Ct. 2434, 2449 (2013).
9. *Vance*, 646 F.3d at 466.
10. *Vance*, 646 F.3d at 466.
11. *Vance*, 646 F.3d at 466.
12. *Vance*, 2008 WL 4247836, *4.
13. *Vance*, 2008 WL 4247836, *22.
14. *Vance*, 2008 WL 4247836, *3.
15. *Vance*, 2008 WL 4247836, *4.
16. *Vance*, 2008 WL 4247836, *5.
17. *Vance*, 2008 WL 4247836, *5.
18. *Vance*, 2008 WL 4247836 *8.
19. *Vance*, 2008 WL 4247836 *8.
20. Vance Deposition at 159 (Exhibit C).
21. *Vance*, 2008 WL 4247836, *12.
22. *Vance*, 2008 WL 4247836, *16.
23. *Vance*, 646 F.3d at 473.
24. Interview with Daniel Ortiz, March 12, 2021 (on file with author).
25. The case had become so abstract that the U.S. government inexplicably intervened at the Supreme Court, only to argue that it was not taking a position. Sri Srinivasan, who argued the case on behalf of the U.S. government and is now a federal judge, declined an interview request.
26. *Vance*, Oral Argument, U.S. Supreme Court (November 26, 2012), 4.
27. *Vance*, Oral Argument, 4.
28. *Vance*, Oral Argument, 4–5.
29. *Vance*, Oral Argument, 4.
30. *Vance*, 133 S.Ct. at 428.
31. Joanna L. Grossman, "The First Bite Is Free: Employer Liability for Sexual Harassment," *Pittsburgh Law Review* 61 (2000): 733.
32. Faragher v. Boca Raton, 524 U.S. 775, 807 (1998). The affirmative defense is not available if the company took a tangible employment action against the plaintiff, such as a firing or demotion.
33. Faragher v. Boca Raton, 524 U.S. at 807 (1998).
34. Philosopher Elizabeth S. Anderson characterizes the modern workplace as a "dictatorship" in which "bosses govern in ways that are largely unaccountable to those who are governed." Elizabeth S. Anderson, *Private Government: How Employers Rule Our Lives (and Why We Don't Talk About It)* (Princeton University Press, 2017), xxii.
35. David Sherwyn et al., "Don't Train Your Employees and Cancel Your '1-800' Harassment Hotline: An Empirical Examination and Correction of the Flaws in the Affirmative Defense to Sexual Harassment Charges," *Fordham Law Review* 69 (2001): 1272; Elizabeth Tippett, "The Legal Implications of the MeToo Movement," *Minnesota Law Review* 103 (2018): 241; Lauren B. Edelman, *Working Law: Courts, Corporations, and Symbolic Civil Rights* (Chicago: University of Chicago Press, 2016), 173–74, 184–88; Susan Bisom-Rapp, "Fixing Watches with Sledgehammers: The Questionable Embrace of Employee

Sexual Harassment Training by the Legal Profession," *Thomas Jefferson Law Review* 24 (2002): 145.

36. Karen Orren, *Belated Feudalism: Labor, the Law, and Liberal Development in the United States* (Cambridge University, 1991), 102. Referring to feudal labor relations, explaining that "jurisdiction was an attribute of the master's property in the servant, just as was the claim over the servant's labor. Concretely, the workplace, and the persons and property that composed it, was a jurisdiction."

37. Faragher v. Boca Raton, 524 U.S. 775 (1998).

38. Nationwide Mut. Ins. Co. v. Darden, 503 U.S. 318, 323–24 (1992). *See also* discussion in chapter 1.

39. Clackamas Gastroenterology P.C. v. Wells, 538 U.S. 440, 448 (2003).

40. New Prime, Inc. v. Oliveira, 139 S.Ct. 532, 541 (2019).

41. *Oliveira*, 139 S.Ct. at 541. The Court borrows the phrase "historical baggage" from a law review article by Richard Carlson. Richard Carlson, "Why the Law Still Can't Tell an Employee When It Sees One and How It Ought to Stop Trying," *Berkeley Journal of Employment & Labor Law* 22 (2001): 309. Carlson writes that the term "servant" "connoted a feudal relationship of domination and dependence that was offensive to the American culture. Thus, some courts confined the meaning of 'servant' to household servants."

42. The Dutra Group v. Batterton, 139 S.Ct. 2275 (2019).

43. Southwest Airlines v. Saxon, 142 S.Ct. 1783, 1788 (2022).

44. Bryan A. Garner, *Black's Law Dictionary*, 11th ed. (Thomson Reuters, 2019).

45. The Restatement was announced in 2002 and published in 2015. Matthew Finkin characterized the Restatement as a "project to restate the law of employment: not all of the law . . . but only the corner occupied by the common law, of contract and tort, and not even all of that." Matthew Finkin, "Shoring Up the Citadel (At-Will Employment)," *Hofstra Labor and Employment Law Journal* 24, no. 1 (2006): 1.

46. "This Restatement generally uses the terms 'employer' and 'employee,' rather than the terms 'master' and 'servant'. . . . It reflects a change in common usage and the terminology of modern decisions—one more appropriate in a society where most individuals provide services to for-profit, nonprofit, or government enterprises, rather than to individuals and their families." *Restatement of Employment Law* (American Law Institute, 2015).

47. *See* Horace G. Wood, *A Treatise on the Law of Master and Servant: Covering the Relation, Duties and Liabilities of Employers and Employees* (J. D. Parsons Jr., 1877), 215. Lea VanderVelde traces American master-servant law to the influence of William Blackstone's *Commentaries on the Laws of England*, which "provided the received common law in the United States" and "organized the legal rules into a system of formal inequality that subordinated servant to master." Lea VanderVelde, "Anti-Republican Origins of the At-Will Doctrine," *American Journal of Legal History* 60 (December 2020): 401. However, as Jean-Christian Vinel observes, the terms "employer" and "employee" have been used "since the middle of the nineteenth century," though at the time "judges . . . were

confounded by [their] meaning." Jean-Christian Vinel, *The Employee: A Political History* (University of Pennsylvania Press, 2013), 13, 26.

48. Wood, *Treatise on the Law of Master and Servant*.

49. C. B. Labatt, *Commentaries on the Law of Master and Servant: Including the Modern Laws on Workmen's Compensation, Arbitration, Employers' Liability Etc. Etc.* (The Lawyers Cooperative, 1913); Ernest Huffcut, *The Law of Agency: Including the Law of Principal and Agent and the Law of Master and Servant* (Little, Brown, 1901); Charles Manley Smith, *A Treatise on the Law of Master and Servant: Including Therein Masters and Workmen in Every Description of Trade and Occupation* (T. & J. W. Johnson, 1852). Cf. Vinel, *Employee*, 17. Vinel recounts debates about the meaning of "employee" in the late nineteenth century and whether it referred to a broader class of worker than the term "servant," and identified the first court ruling defining the term "employés" as "those in regular and continual service." Vinel, *Employee*, 18.

50. Orren, *Belated Feudalism*, 68. Political scientist Karen Orren characterizes the master-servant relationship as a "feudal" idea, arguing that "there was, in actuality, an unbroken line stretching from labor regulation in Tudor England ... to labor regulation in Gilded Age America." Orren, *Belated Feudalism*, 15. See Robert J. Steinfeld, *The Invention of Free Labor: The Employment Relation in English and American Law and Culture, 1350–1870* (University of North Carolina Press, 1991), 57.

51. Steinfeld, *Invention of Free Labor*, 57. Orren, *Belated Feudalism*, 71–74. Describing the feudal labor order.

52. Steinfeld, *Invention of Free Labor*, 58.

53. "[T]he term [servant] did not signify wage worker[s] generally but only a wage worker who resided with a master and who served him for a term, generally a year. ... Some of them, such as servants in housewifery, performed domestic chores, but others performed a broad range of manual labor ... [such as] agricultural laborers ... [or] unskilled workers in the crafts." Steinfeld, *Invention of Free Labor*, 19, 56.

54. Steinfeld, *Invention of Free Labor*, 55.

55. Steinfeld, *Invention of Free Labor*, 27, 33, 67.

56. Steinfeld, *Invention of Free Labor*, 59.

57. Marc Linder, *The Employment Relationship in Anglo-American Law: A Historical Perspective* (Greenwood Press, 1989), 46–47.

58. Steinfeld, *Invention of Free Labor*, 56; Linder, *Employment Relationship*, 56–57. Poor laws in the late 1600s permitted individuals to move to a new locality only if they entered into and performed service for one year. James Schmidt, *Free to Work: Labor Law, Emancipation, and Reconstruction, 1815–1880* (University of Georgia Press, 1998), 63–65. Describing poor laws in colonial America and subsequent state reforms in the nineteenth century that relieved community welfare obligations through workhouses for the poor or by "hiring out, binding out, or auctioning off adults charged with vagrancy."

59. Steinfeld, *Invention of Free Labor*, 56. See also Orren, *Belated Feudalism*, 4, 8; and Linder, *Employment Relationship*, 46.

60. Linder, *Employment Relationship*, 45; Steinfeld, *Invention of Free Labor*, 22–24; Orren, *Belated Feudalism*, 102–3.

61. Orren, *Belated Feudalism*, 4. *See also* Anderson, *Private Government*, xxii.

62. Christopher Tomlins, *Law, Labor, and Ideology in the Early American Republic* (Cambridge University Press, 1993), 232; Schmidt, *Free to Work*, 8–10; Lea VanderVelde, "The Last Legally Beaten Servant in America: From Compulsion to Coercion in the American Workplace," *Seattle University Law Review* 39, no. 3 (2016): 785; Lea VanderVelde, "The Labor Vision of the Thirteenth Amendment," *University of Pennsylvania Law Review* 138, no. 2 (1989): 488. *See also* Christopher Tomlins, "Law and Power in the Employment Relationship," in *Labor Law in America*, ed. Christopher Tomlins and Andrew King (Johns Hopkins Press, 1992), 77. Discussing master-servant law in colonial America.

63. "In classical contract theory, then, the wife was the analog of the servant, and marriage was the analog of the wage relationship." Amy Dru Stanley, *From Bondage to Contract: Wage Labor, Marriage, and the Market in the Age of Slave Emancipation* (Cambridge University Press, 1998), 10.

64. Catherine Fisk, "Removing the 'Fuel of Interest' from the 'Fire of Genius: Law and the Employee-Inventor, 1830–1930," *University of Chicago Law Review* 65 (1998) 1163; Catherine Fisk, "Working Knowledge: Trade Secrets, Restrictive Covenants in Employment, and the Rise of Corporate Intellectual Property, 1800–1920," *Hastings Law Journal* 52 (2001): 447.

65. Vinel, *Employee*, 13, 26.

66. *See, for example,* Matthew Finkin, "Disloyalty! Does Jefferson Standard Stalk Still?," *Berkeley Journal of Employment & Labor Law* 28 (2007): 548; Ken Matheny and Marion Crain, "Disloyal Workers and the 'Un-American' Labor Law," *North Carolina Law Review* 82 (2004): 1711–12; Julia Tomassetti, "From Hierarchies to Markets: Fedex Drivers and the Work Contract as Institutional Marker," *Lewis & Clark Law Review* 19 (2015): 1101; Timothy Glynn, "The Limited Viability of Negligent Supervision, Retention and Intentional Infliction of Emotional Distress Claims in Employment Discrimination Cases in Minnesota," *William Mitchell Law Review* 24 (1998): 588; Charles A. Sullivan, "Mastering the Faithless Servant? Reconciling Employment Law, Contract Law, and Fiduciary Duty," *Wisconsin Law Review* 2011 (2011): 793; Martha Chamallas, "Two Very Different Stories: Vicarious Liability Under Tort and Title VII Law," *Ohio State Law Journal* 75 (2014): 1333; Matthew Bodie, "Employment as Fiduciary Relationship," *Georgetown Law Journal* 105 (2017): 823; Carlson, "Why the Law Still Can't Tell an Employee," 302.

67. James Atleson, *Values and Assumptions in American Labor Law* (University of of Massachusetts Press 1983).

68. Atleson, *Values and Assumptions*, 10. *See also* Evelyn Nakano Glenn, *Unequal Freedom: How Race and Gender Shaped American Citizenship and Labor* (Harvard University Press, 2002), 16. Observing that with respect to "race and gender, . . . power is lodged in taken-for-granted assumptions and practices."

69. There are several reasons this latter question has been relatively underexplored. Prior to the Civil War, certain legal technicalities made slavery distinct from other areas of master-servant law. American jurists inherited the centuries-old master-servant law from Britain, particularly as summarized in Blackstone's

*Commentaries on the Laws of England*. See Lea VanderVelde, *Modern Employment Law: In Time and Place* (West Academic Publishing, 2022), 17. Blackstone's eighteenth-century summary of master-servant law distinguished slavery from servitude because slavery was prohibited under English law. *See* William Blackstone, *Commentaries on the Laws of England* (Project Gutenberg Ebook, 2009), 411, https://www.gutenberg.org/files/30802/30802-h/30802-h.htm. Thus, historically precise discussions of antebellum master-servant law likewise do not necessarily assume that enslaved people fell within the broader category of "servant." In addition, the law of slavery was genuinely distinct from other employment-related laws because it treated people as chattel property. Finally, the abolition of slavery following the Civil War marked a drastic break in American law, rendering modern connections to antebellum law somewhat tenuous.

70. *See, for example*, Caitlin Rosenthal, *Accounting for Slavery: Masters and Management* (Harvard University Press, 2018), 99; Edward E. Baptist, *The Half Has Never Been Told: Slavery and the Making of American Capitalism* (Basic Books, 2016), 140; Ariela Gross, *Double Character: Slavery and Mastery in the Antebellum Southern Courtroom* (Princeton University Press, 2001):74; Sven Beckert and Seth Rockman, *Slavery's Capitalism*, ed. Sven Beckert and Seth Robinson (University of Pennsylvania Press, 2016), 3, 5; Mark Tushnet, *The American Law of Slavery: 1810–1860: Considerations of Humanity and Interest* (Princeton University Press, 1981), 183–85; Paul Finkleman, "Slaves as Fellow Servants: Ideology, Law, and Industrialization," *American Journal of Legal History* 31 (1987): 280–81; Ronald Lewis, *Coal, Iron, and Slaves: Industrial Slavery in Maryland and Virginia, 1715–1865* (Geenwood Press, 1979): 82; Mary Turner, introduction to *From Chattel Slaves to Wage Slaves: The Dynamics of Labor Bargaining in the Americas*, ed. Mary Turner (Indiana University Press, 1995), 1–2.

71. Thomas D. Morris, *Southern Slavery and the Law, 1619–1860* (UNC Press 1996), 13; William Fisher III, "Ideology and Imagery in the Law of Slavery," in *Slavery and the Law*, ed. Paul Finkelman (Rowman & Littlefield, 1997), 45; Elizabeth Tippett, "Enslaved Agents," *Arizona Law Review* 63 (2021): n232–33.

72. Dylan Penningroth, "Race in Contract Law," *University of Pennsylvania Law Review* 170 (2022): 1216–17. Noting that "many of the concepts and doctrines that underpinned slavery were tangled with other areas of law . . . especially 'master-servant' law (what would eventually become employment law)."

73. Lea VanderVelde argues that Blackstone's discussion of slavery in the *Commentaries*—notwithstanding the British prohibition on slavery—rendered slavery the conceptual "foundation" for the hierarchical master-servant order, in which enslaved people served as the "base of absolute subjugation." *Modern Employment Law*, 20. *See also* Joseph Slater, "Jeffrey Kahana, the Unfolding of American Labor Law: Judges, Workers, and Public Policy Across Two Political Generations, 1790–1850," *New York University Journal of Law & Liberty* 10, no. 1 (2016): 418.

74. VanderVelde, "Labor Vision of the Thirteenth Amendment," 488. Noting that "the law defined the status of lower laborers in opposition to slavery." *See also* VanderVelde, *Modern Employment Law*, 20. *See also* Slater, "Jeffrey Kahana," 418. Critiquing labor history that failed to take slavery into account.

75. Nell Irvin Painter, *Southern History Across the Color Line* (University of North Carolina Press, 2002), 21.

76. U.S. Bureau of Labor Statistics, "Union Members–2024" January 28, 2025, https://www.bls.gov/news.release/union2.nro.htm.

77. Title VII of the Civil Rights Act of 1964, Pub. L. No. 88-352, § 703 (1964); 42 U.S.C.A. § 2000e-2.

78. Edelman, *Working Law*, 101.

79. Deepa Das Acevedo, "Unbundling Freedom in the Sharing Economy," *Southern California Law Review* 91 (2018): 799.

80. Evelyn Nakano Glenn, "From Servitude to Service Work: Historical Continuities in the Racial Division of Paid Reproductive Labor," *Signs* 18 (1992): 2–3. Noting that racial theories "focus[ing] exclusively on the paid labor market" tend to "take for granted or ignore women's unpaid household labor." Inés Valdez notes the "entanglement between white enfranchisement and the exclusion of nonwhite migrants, and how racialized foreigners were recruited to 'solve' problems of labor control raised by the partial emancipation of Black slaves." *Democracy and Empire: Labor, Nature and the Reproduction of Capitalism* (Cambridge University Press, 2023), 19. *See also* Glenn, *Unequal Freedom*, 144–235. Discussing the role of Mexican laborers in the Southwest and Japanese laborers in Hawaii. Tanya Katerí Hernández, *Multiracials and Civil Rights: Mixed-Race Stories of Discrimination* (New York University Press, 2018), 19. Observing a gap between legal theory regarding multiracial identity and the actual experience and treatment of multiracial plaintiffs in litigation, much of which involved anti-Black bias.

## CHAPTER 1. PHYSICAL CONTROL

1. Tyson Foods and its counsel did not respond to interview requests. "About Us," Tyson Foods Investor Relations, https://ir.tyson.com/about-tyson/about-us/default.aspx.

2. Tyson Foods, Form 10-K, Securities and Exchange Commission, September 28, 2019, https://www.sec.gov/ix?doc=/Archives/edgar/data/0000100493/000010049319000118/tsn201910kq4.htm. Referencing "chicken further-processing operations" in China.

3. Wilson v. Tyson Foods In. et al., First Amended Petition and Demand for Jury Trial, Case No. LACV145094, Iowa District Court for Black Hawk County (April 20, 2023): 10.

4. "Memorandum," Select Subcommittee on the Coronavirus Crisis, United States House of Representatives (October 27, 2021), 9 (quoting TYSON-SSCC-00000026, https://coronavirus.house.gov/sites/democrats.coronavirus.house.gov/files/TYSON-SSCC-00000026.pdf, obtained via the Wayback Machine).

5. Interview with Tony Thompson, April 17, 2024 (on file with author); Michael Grabell and Bernice Yeung, "As COVID-19 Ravaged This Iowa City, Officials Discovered Meatpacking Executives Were the Ones in Charge," *ProPublica*, December 21, 2020, https://features.propublica.org/waterloo-meatpacking/as-covid-19-ravaged-this-iowa-city-officials-discovered-meatpacking-executives-were-the-ones-in-charge/.

6. Interview with Tony Thompson; Grabell and Yeung, "COVID-19 Ravaged."
7. Interview with Tony Thompson.
8. Interview with Tony Thompson.
9. Interview with Tony Thompson; Grabell and Yeung, "COVID-19 Ravaged."
10. Interview with Tony Thompson.
11. Interview with Tony Thompson.
12. Interview with Tony Thompson; Grabell and Yeung, "COVID-19 Ravaged."
13. Interview with Tony Thompson; Grabell and Yeung, "COVID-19 Ravaged."
14. Interview with Tony Thompson.
15. Interview with Tony Thompson.
16. Grabell and Yeung, "COVID-19 Ravaged."
17. Interview with Mel Orchard, May 2, 2023 (on file with author).
18. Wilson v. Tyson, *First Amended Petition*, 31.
19. Ryan Foley, "Tyson Fires 7 at Iowa Pork Plant After COVID Betting Inquiry," Associated Press, December 16, 2020, https://apnews.com/article/iowa-lawsuits-coronavirus-pandemic-lakes-meat-processing-af173a053c5ac8b31e2bd4cb6e8ab83f.
20. "Memorandum," Select Subcommittee on the Coronavirus Crisis, 8.
21. Grabell and Yeung, "COVID-19 Ravaged."
22. Descriptions of Ms. Joseph are based on Grabell and Yeung, "COVID-19 Ravaged." Counsel for the surviving relatives of Tyson workers did not make them available for an interview, and I did not attempt to contact them directly, in deference to principles of legal ethics.
23. "Obituary of José Luis Ayala," *Laredo Morning Times*, May 27, 2020, https://obituaries.lmtonline.com/obituary/jose-ayala-1083907657/; Julia Wallace, "Laredo Man's Death in Iowa Due to COVID Makes Waves Locally After His Story Goes Viral," *Laredo Morning Times*, June 15, 2020, https://www.lmtonline.com/local/article/Jose-Ayala-remembered-15340526.php.
24. Wallace, "Laredo Man's Death."
25. Wallace, "Laredo Man's Death."
26. Wallace, "Laredo Man's Death."
27. Wallace, "Laredo Man's Death."
28. Wallace, "Laredo Man's Death."
29. Wallace, "Laredo Man's Death."
30. Wilson v. Tyson, *First Amended Petition*.
31. Some whistleblower laws are available to nonemployees, such as the False Claims Act.
32. Legislators can also extend protections under a given law to independent contractors, although they rarely do so.
33. Nationwide Mut. Ins. Co. v. Darden, 503 U.S. 318, 323–24 (1992).
34. Darden v. Nationwide, 796 F.2d 701 (4th Cir. 1986).
35. Darden v. Nationwide, 969 F.2d 76, n.1 (4th Cir. 1992).
36. *Nationwide*, 503 U.S. at 323. The common law control test has been subject to substantial criticism by employment law scholars. *See, for example,* V. B. Duval, "Wage Slave or Entrepreneur? Contesting the Dualism of Legal

Worker Identities," *California Law Review* 105 (2017): 65. Keith Cunningham-Parmeter, "From Amazon to Uber: Defining Employment in the Modern Economy," *Boston University Law Review* 96 (2016): 1691, 1705. Critiquing courts for "unnecessarily confin[ing] the concept" of control and offering a more rigorous definition of control based on "the subjects, direction, and obligations of control." Matthew T. Bodie, "Participation as a Theory of Employment," *Notre Dame Law Review* 89 (2013): 665. Arguing that the control test for employee status should be replaced with a test focused on whether "employees are participants in a common economic enterprise organized into a business entity." Katherine V. W. Stone, "Legal Protections for Atypical Employees: Employment Law for Workers Without Workplaces and Employees Without Employers," *Berkeley Journal of Employment and Labor Law* 27 (2006): 282.

37. *Nationwide*, 503 U.S. at 324. Quoting Community for Creative Non-Violence v. Reid, 490 U.S. 730, 751 (1989).

38. The test also considers the tax treatment, "whether the hiring party is in business," and "the provision of employee benefits." *Nationwide*, 503 U.S. at 324.

39. "[T]he concept of control has served as the unifying idea behind the use of 'employee' and 'employment' in different contexts." Bodie, "Participation as a Theory of Employment," 662. Cf. Duval, "Wage Slave or Entrepreneur?," 67. Concluding that the "the two-category division of workers in U.S. employment and labor laws is much more recent than commonly understood."

40. Sec'y of Lab. v. Lauritzen, 835 F.2d 1529, 1534–35 (7th Cir. 1987). Applying economic realities test. Anna Deknatel and Lauren Hoff-Downing, "ABC on the Books and in the Courts: An Analysis of Recent Independent Contractor and Misclassification Statutes," *University of Pennsylvania Journal of Law and Social Change* 18, no. 1 (2015)," 68. Describing "ABC" test adopted in a minority of states. Duval, "Wage Slave or Entrepreneur?," 72. Summarizing applicable legal tests. Bodie, "Participation as a Theory of Employment," 675–91. Describing control test, and alternate tests, including the economic realities test and the entrepreneurial opportunities test. *Restatement of Employment Law* § 1.01 (American Law Institute, 2015).

41. Nationwide Mut. Ins. Co. v. Darden, 503 U.S. 318 (1992). "The common law 'control test' comes out of the original conceptions of master and servant from pre-industrial English law." Bodie, "Participation as a Theory of Employment," 662.

42. Jean-Christian Vinel, *The Employee: A Political History* (University of Pennsylvania Press, 2013), 26.

43. Joseph Seiner, "Workplace Power," *Boston College Law Review* 65 (2024): 82–83. Using abusive employer responses to COVID-19 to illustrate excessive employer power over workers.

44. Following the practice of modern historians, I use the term "enslaver" rather than the term "slaveholder" to refer to individuals that owned enslaved people.

45. Sir William Blackstone, *Commentaries on the Laws of England*, 1st ed. (Clarendon Press, 1765–1769), vol. 1, chap. 14, 410–20, https://avalon.law.yale.edu/subject_menus/blackstone.asp; Robert Steinfeld, *The Invention of Free*

*Labor: The Employment Relation in English and American Law and Culture, 1350–1870* (University of North Carolina Press, 1991), 45. Summarizing early modern English law.

46. "Assault [is] an attempt or offer to beat another, without touching him: as if one lifts up his cane, or his fist, in a threatening manner at another. . . . Battery [is] the unlawful beating of another. The least touching of another's person willfully, or in anger, is a battery. . . . But battery is, in some cases, justifiable or lawful; as where one who hath authority, a parent or master, gives moderate correction to his child, his scholar or his apprentice." Blackstone, *Commentaries*, vol. 3, 120. Lea VanderVelde, "The Last Legally Beaten Servant in America: From Compulsion to Coercion in the American Workplace," *Seattle University Law Review* 39 (2016): 730.

47. See Blackstone, *Commentaries*, vol. 3, 120.

48. Steinfeld, *Invention of Free Labor,* 59; Blackstone, *Commentaries*, vol. 3, 120.

49. Steinfeld, *Invention of Free Labor*, 26.

50. Steinfeld, *Invention of Free Labor*, 26.

51. Steinfeld, *Invention of Free Labor*, 31.

52. "American law was composed in unequal parts of vaguely and inaccurately remembered fragments of common law, local law and Mosaic law." Kermit Hall, William Wiecek, and Paul Finkelman, *American Legal History: Cases and Materials* (Oxford University Press, 1991), 23. Jeffrey Steven Kahana, *The Unfolding of American Labor Law: Judges, Workers and Public Policy Across Two Political Generations, 1790–1850* (LFB Scholarly Publishing, 2014), 36, 41, 52. Noting that some scholars "distanced American law from the English common law."

53. Steinfeld, *Invention of Free Labor*, 31, 152.

54. Steinfeld, *Invention of Free Labor*, 152; Jonathan A. Bush, "Take This Job and Shove It: The Rise of Free Labor," *Michigan Law Review* 91 (1993): 1402–3. Discussing Steinfeld's work. "[A]s property rights in labor declined, jurists and others believed the free laborers could not be subjected to physical punishment." James Schmidt, *Free to Work: Labor Law, Emancipation, and Reconstruction, 1815–1880* (Athens: University of Georgia Press, 1998), 8. "Workplace corporal punishment was initially the undisputed province of masters." But the most extreme form of corporal punishment—whipping—"fell out of favor" for white workers decades before the Civil War. VanderVelde, "Last Legally Beaten Servant," 732, 733. "[E]ven accepting the fact that the law did not sanction the physical discipline of adult workers who were not slaves, it still appears that the law of master-servant effectively gave a great deal of control to employers." Joseph Slater, "Jeffrey Kahana, the Unfolding of American Labor Law: Judges, Workers, and Public Policy Across Two Political Generations, 1790–1850," *New York University Journal of Law and Liberty* 10, no. 1 (2016): 418.

55. Vandervelde, "Last Legally Beaten Servant," 758, Milburne v. Byrne, 1 Cranch C.C. 239 (D.C. Cir. Ct. 1805).

56. Vandervelde, "Last Legally Beaten Servant," 764. Commonwealth v. Baird, 1 Ash. 268 (1828), in John W. Ashmead, *Reports of Cases Adjudged in the Courts of Common Pleas, Quarter Sessions, Oyer and Terminer, and*

*Orphans' Court, of the First Judicial District of Pennsylvania* (J. Towar & D.M. Hogan, 1831), 237. Citing Commonwealth v. Baird as decided in 1828. George Warton Pepper & William Draper Lewis, *Pepper and Lewis' New Digest: A Digest of the Laws of Pennsylvania from 1700 to 1894* (T. & J.W. Johnson, 1896), 153.

57. Nell Irvin Painter, *Southern History Across the Color Line* (University of North Carolina Press, 2002), 6.

58. State v. Will, 18 N.C. 154, 165 (1834).

59. Thomas D. Morris, *Southern Slavery and the Law, 1619–1860* (University of North Carolina Press 1996), 172. Jenny Bourne Wahl, "Legal Constraints on Slave Masters: The Problem of Social Cost," *American Journal of Legal History* 41 (1997): 6. Arguing that "[a]lthough a few states permitted killing of one's slaves, most stopped far short, particularly after the turbulent 1830s. North Carolina, Virginia, Mississippi, and Alabama were willing to convict masters who murdered their own slaves, with a North Carolina court sentencing the master to death in one case."

60. Dred Scott v. Sandford, 60 U.S. 393, 411 (1857).

61. *Dred Scott*, 60 U.S. at 431, 452.

62. *Dred Scott*, 60 U.S. at 411.

63. *Dred Scott*, 60 U.S. at 411.

64. *Dred Scott*, 60 U.S. at 411.

65. "And if the Constitution recognises the right of property of the master in a slave, and makes no distinction between that description of property and other property owned by a citizen, no tribunal, acting under the authority of the United States . . . has a right to draw such a distinction or deny to it the benefit of the provisions and guarantees which have been provided for the protection of private property against the encroachments of the Government." *Dred Scott*, 60 U.S. at 451–52. "A slave society, Tushnet pointed out, was based on devolution of authority to the masters on the plantation." Morris, *Southern Slavery and the Law*, 13.

66. Referencing the "line of division which the Constitution has drawn between the citizen race, who formed and held the Government, and the African race, which they held in subjugation and slavery and governed at their own pleasure." *Dred Scott*, 60 U.S. at 411, 420.

67. "The only two provisions [of the Constitution] which point to them and include [African Americans] treat them as property and make it the duty of the Government to protect [their status as property]. . . . The Government of the United States had no right to interfere for any other purpose but that of protecting the rights of the [slave] owner, leaving it altogether with the States to deal with this race." *Dred Scott*, 60 U.S. at 425–26.

68. E. N. Elliott, *Cotton Is King and Pro-Slavery Arguments* (Pritchard, Abbott & Loomis, 1860), n6, https://archive.org/details/cottoniskingprosooelli/page/n5. See Morris, *Southern Slavery and the Law*, 62, quoting Elliott. Elliott, *Cotton Is King*, vii.

69. Caitlin Rosenthal, *Accounting for Slavery: Masters and Management* (Harvard University Press, 2018), 99.

70. The State v. John Mann, 2 Dev. 263, 267 (N.C. 1829).

71. Frederick Douglass, *Narrative of the Life of Frederick Douglass, an American Slave* (Project Gutenberg Literary Archive Foundation, 1845), 8.
72. Douglass, *Narrative of the Life*, 8.
73. Gross, *Double Character: Slavery and Mastery in the Antebellum Southern Courtroom* (Princeton University Press, 2001), 110.
74. William Fisher III, "Ideology and Imagery in the Law of Slavery," in *Slavery and the Law*, ed. Paul Finkelman (Rowman & Littlefield, 1997), 45.
75. Gross, *Double Character*, 106.
76. Edward Baptist, *The Half Has Never Been Told: Slavery and the Making of American Capitalism* (Basic Books, 2014), 140.
77. Baptist, *Half Has Never Been Told*, 133.
78. Baptist, "Toward a Political Economy of Slave Labor," in *Slavery's Capitalism*, ed. Sven Beckert and Seth Robinson (University of Pennsylvania Press, 2016), 50.
79. Baptist, *Half Has Never Been Told*, 139.
80. Baptist, *Half Has Never Been Told*, 139.
81. Baptist, "Toward a Political Economy," 51; Rosenthal, *Accounting for Slavery*, 72.
82. Baptist, *Half Has Never Been Told*, 130, 128.
83. Baptist, *Half Has Never Been Told*, 127; Rosenthal, *Accounting for Slavery*, 102–3. Arguing that yield increases reflected both coercive practices and experimentation in cotton varieties.
84. Rosenthal, *Accounting for Slavery*, 101. See Baptist, *Half Has Never Been Told*, 133.
85. Baptist, "Toward a Political Economy," 35.
86. Caitlin Rosenthal, "Slavery's Scientific Management: Masters and Managers," in *Slavery's Capitalism*, ed. Sven Beckert and Seth Robinson (University of Pennsylvania Press, 2016), 70.
87. "They meted out lashes in precise relation to picking, whipping slaves as many strokes as the number of pounds they fell short of during their daily or weekly tasks." Rosenthal, *Accounting for Slavery*, 97.
88. Mary Turner, introduction to *From Chattel Slaves to Wage Slaves: The Dynamics of Labor Bargaining in the Americas*, ed. Mary Turner (Indiana University Press, 1995), 1–2.
89. Rosenthal, *Accounting for Slavery*, 98.
90. Rosenthal, *Accounting for Slavery*, 98, quoting Frederick L. Olmstead, *The Cotton Kingdom*, (Mason Brothers, 1861), 1:128.
91. "Historians have, for example, provided ample documentation demonstrating that slaves were sometimes able to control and define the pace of their labor and thus, in a very practical sense, regulate the rate of their work. But such efforts were not without their dangers. 'For killing time' in this way, recalled a former slave. . . . Starvation was another punishment." Mark Smith, *Mastered by the Clock: Time, Slavery, and Freedom in the American South* (University of North Carolina Press, 1997), 143.
92. Smith, *Mastered by the Clock*, 143.
93. Rosenthal, *Accounting for Slavery*, 92–94.

94. "Like progress reports tacked to the walls of modern corporations, these constant notations made the data of plantation operations daily visible." Rosenthal, *Accounting for Slavery*, 100.

95. Rosenthal, *Accounting for Slavery*, 2.

96. Rosenthal, *Accounting for Slavery*, 2; Rosenthal, "Slavery's Scientific Management," 75.

97. According to historian Nell Irvin Painter, "In 1880 about one-half the United States work force was in agriculture. By 1920, only a little more than a quarter remained on the land" and some 40 percent of the labor force worked in industry. Nell Irvin Painter, *Standing at Armageddon: The United States 1877–1919* (W. W. Norton, 1987), xxxiv; Ruth Schwartz Cowan, *A Social History of American Technology* (Oxford University Press, 1978), 178. See Eric Foner, *Free Soil, Free Labor, Free Men: The Ideology of the Republican Party Before the Civil War* (Oxford University Press, 1995), 32. In 1860, 60 percent of the American labor force consisted of wage laborers.

98. John Fabian Witt, *The Accidental Republic: Crippled Workingmen, Destitute Widows, and the Remaking of American Law* (Harvard University Press, 2004), 2.

99. Witt, *Accidental Republic*, 26–27.

100. "According to an 1865 census of occupations in the South, there were only 20,000 skilled white craftsmen and tradesmen, compared to 100,000 skilled blacks, most of whom were former slaves." This skill gap between African American and white tradespeople would lead Southern legislatures to enact various protectionist measures intended to disadvantage Black tradespeople and businesses following emancipation. Juliet Walker, *History of Black Businesses in America: Capitalism, Race, Entrepreneurship*, 2nd ed. (University of North Carolina Press, 2009), 150–51.

101. John Hope Franklin, *Reconstruction After the Civil War* (University of Chicago Press, 1994), 178. See also Inés Valdez, *Democracy and Empire: Labor, Nature and the Reproduction of Capitalism* (Cambridge University Press, 2023), 69. Noting that "while ethnic whites in the United States were allowed to fill low skilled positions in factories that incorporated new machinery, nonwhite workers were confined to strenuous bodily work in the fields, mining, or railway construction, pointing to the stricter labor segregation and exclusions affecting these groups."

102. Witt, *Accidental Republic*, 30.

103. Witt, *Accidental Republic*, 65. Even ordinary negligence rules seemed unfair when workers were injured for reasons unrelated to negligence, yet due to the dangerous nature of the job. See also Emily Spieler, "(Re)Assessing the Grand Bargain: Compensation for Work Injuries in the United States, 1900–2017," *Rutgers Law Review* 69 (2017): 915. Noting the "unholy trinity" of tort doctrines: "the assumption of risk doctrine, the fellow servant rule, and the doctrine of contributory negligence." Stephen Fessenden, "Present Status of Employers' Liability in the United States," *Bulletin of the Department of Labor* 31 (1900): 1157–61. Cf. Shawn Evert Kantor and Price V. Fishback, "Nonfatal Accident Compensation and the Common Law at the Turn of the Century," *Journal of Law, Economics, & Organization* 11 (1995): 406, 429–30. Study on

historical accident payments, finding that common law defenses affected settlements but that other factors, such as severity of injury, also seemed to matter.

104. Farwell v. Boston and Worcester Rail Road Corp., 4 Metcalf 49, 57 (Mass. 1842). "The notion that accidents in the workplace were caused by the negligence of the employees was the favorite refuge of scoundrel employers." Witt, *Accidental Republic*, 31, 33. See Christopher Tomlins, *Law, Labor, and Ideology in the Early American Republic* (Cambridge University Press, 1993), 359–63; Mark Tushnet, *The American Law of Slavery: 1810–1860: Considerations of Humanity and Interest* (Princeton University Press, 1981), 183–85; Paul Finkelman, "Slaves as Fellow Servants: Ideology, Law, and Industrialization," *American Journal of Legal History* 31 (1987): 279.

105. *Farwell*, 4 Metcalf at 57.

106. *Farwell*, 4 Metcalf at 59.

107. Witt, *Accidental Republic*, 13; Foner, *Free Soil, Free Labor, Free Men*, 16–18. See chapter 9 for a further discussion of the ideology of free labor.

108. Witt, *Accidental Republic*, 30.

109. Witt, *Accidental Republic*, 30.

110. Witt, *Accidental Republic*, 27, 30.

111. Witt, *Accidental Republic*, 79.

112. *See* discussion in chapter 8.

113. Witt, *Accidental Republic*, 4.

114. Today, scholars refer to this trade-off as the "grand bargain" of workers' compensation—though legal historian Witt argues that it's not historically correct. Employers, he notes, strongly opposed the increased insurance costs a mandate would impose. And in the everyday workings of the modern workers' compensation system, there is no bargaining involved. Workers must accept workers' compensation over a lawsuit, regardless of their preferences. Witt, *Accidental Republic*, 129, 147. Prince v. Fishback and Shawn Everett Kantor, "The Adoption of Workers' Compensation in the United States 1900–1930," *Journal of Law & Economics* 41 (1998): 307.

115. Charles W. McCurdy, "The Roots of Liberty of Contract Reconsidered: Major Premises in the Law of Employment, 1867–1937" *Yearbook: Supreme Court Historical Society* 1984 (1984): 20, 26. The new laws offered the further benefit of being structured as "insurance," thus avoiding the constitutional attack that doomed many wage and hour laws of the era. *See* discussion in chapter 3.

116. Witt, *Accidental Republic*, 127.

117. Witt, *Accidental Republic*, 145.

118. Witt, *Accidental Republic*, 133. It was called "workmens'" compensation for a reason—it paid widowers a much lower rate than widows, if anything.

119. Witt, *Accidental Republic*, 41, quoting U.S. Industrial Commission, *Report of the Industrial Commission on the Relations and Conditions of Capital and Labor* (U.S. Government Printing Office, 1901), 14:163.

120. Witt, *Accidental Republic*, 41, quoting U.S. Industrial Commission, *Report*.

121. Witt quotes Hourwich in his analysis, primarily to illustrate the challenge that industrial accidents presented to the then-prevailing ideology of workers as free agents.

122. *See* Paul Finkleman, "Slaves as Fellow Servants: Ideology, Law, and Industrialization," *American Journal of Legal History* 31 (1987): 280–81; Ariela Gross, "Slavery, Antislavery, and the Coming of the Civil War," in *The Cambridge History of Law in America*, vol. 2, ed. Michael Grossberg and Christopher Tomlins (Cambridge University Press, 2007), 23.

123. Finkleman, "Slaves as Fellow Servants," 269, 280–81; Elizabeth Tippett, "Enslaved Agents," *Arizona Law Review* 63, no. 4 (2021): n232–33.

124. Tushnet, *American Law of Slavery*, 183–85 (see ch. 1, n79). Unlike tort claims brought by injured white workers, disputes between the enslaver and the hirer often involved contract disputes over whether the dangerous work had been authorized by the enslaver.

125. Tushnet, *American Law of Slavery*, 183–85.

126. Scudder v. Woodbridge, 1 Ga. 195, 199 (Ga. 1846).

127. *Scudder*, 1 Ga. at 199; Andrew Fede, "Legitimized Violent Slave Abuse in the American South, 1619–1865: A Case Study in Six Southern States," *American Journal of Legal History* 29 (1985): 95–96; Tushnet, *American Law of Slavery*, 183–85.

128. Witt, *Accidental Republic*, 187.

129. Witt made a similar observation in his book on the history of workers' compensation, noting that "increased work safety in the decades after 1910, in turn, was driven by the expansion and consolidation of managerial bureaucracies." Witt, *Accidental Republic*, 188.

130. 29 U.S.C. § 651 *et seq.*

131. 29 C.F.R. § 1910 Subpart D; 29 C.F.R. § 1910.141(c)(1)(i).

132. 29 C.F.R. § 1910.101 *et seq.*; 29 C.F.R. § 1910.95.

133. Workers can only bring a private right of action if their employer retaliates against them. 29 C.F.R. § 1977.9.

134. 29 C.F.R. 1977.12(B); see Whirlpool Corp. v. Marshall, Sec'y of Lab., 445 U.S. 1 (1980).

135. 29 C.F.R. 1977.12(B); see *Marshall, Sec'y of Lab.*, 445 U.S. 1.

136. NLRB v. Wash. Aluminum Co., 370 U.S. 9 (1962).

137. *Wash. Aluminum Co.*, 370 U.S. at 11; "Death on the Job: The Toll of Neglect," *ALF-CIO*, April 2019, https://aflcio.org/sites/default/files/2019-05/DOTJ2019Fnb_1.pdf.

138. Ryan Foley, "Iowa Finds No Violations at Tyson Plant with Deadly Outbreak," Associated Press, June 23, 2020, https://apnews.com/article/336ad340b0a01f9ab870aef1a32785f2.

139. Buljic et al v. Tyson Foods et al; Fernandez et al. v. Tyson Foods et al., Ruling on Motion to Dismiss, Case No. LACV140822, Iowa District Court for Black Hawk County (January 20, 2023).

## CHAPTER 2. TERMINATION

1. Interview with Stephen Murphy, December 16, 2020 (on file with author).
2. Guz v. Bechtel Nat'l, Inc., 63 Cal. Rptr. 2d 572, 573–74 (1997).
3. *Guz*, 63 Cal. Rptr. 2d at 573.

4. Interview with Paul Cane and Paul Grossman, December 7, 2020 (on file with author).

5. Interview with Paul Cane and Paul Grossman.

6. "An employment, having no specified term, may be terminated at the will of either party on notice to the other." Cal. Lab. Code § 2922 (West 1971).

7. Pugh v. See's Candies, Inc., 116 Cal. App. 3d 311 (1981); Foley v. Interactive Data Corp., 47 Cal. 3d 654, 680 (1988). Quoting *Pugh* for the proposition that various types of evidence might overcome the at-will presumption, such as "personnel policies or practices . . . longevity of service, actions or communications by the employer reflecting assurances of continued employment."

8. Guz v. Bechtel, 100 Cal. Rptr. 2d 352, 371–72 (2000).

9. *Guz*, 100 Cal. Rptr. 2d at 359, 362.

10. Interview with Paul Cane and Paul Grossman.

11. "[I]n actions for . . . damages for breach of contract . . . an issue of fact must be tried by a jury." Cal. Code of Civ. Proc. § 592 (West 1872).

12. Interview with Paul Cane and Paul Grossman.

13. Deborah A. Ballam, "Exploding the Original Myth Regarding Employment-at-Will: The True Origins of the Doctrine," *Berkeley Journal of Employment and Labor Law* 17, no. 1 (1996): 97; Deborah A. Ballam, "The Development of the Employment at Will Rule Revisited: A Challenge to Its Origins as Based in the Development of Advanced Capitalism," *Hofstra Labor & Employment Law Journal* 13, no. 1 (1995): 87; Deborah A. Ballam, "The Traditional View on the Origins of the Employment-at-Will Doctrine: Myth or Reality?" *American Business Law Journal* 33, no. 1 (1995): 47. Ballam argues that the relative dearth of free laborers in the United States gave agricultural day laborers leverage against potential employers. These workers preferred short-term contracts over the one-year renewable contract that represented the dominant arrangement in Britain.

14. James D. Schmidt, *Free to Work: Labor Law, Emancipation, and Reconstruction 1815–1880* (University of Georgia Press, 1999), 33.

15. Steinfeld quotes a letter from a disgruntled employer dismayed to find competitors greeting servants at the docks and declaring that they were "free as birds," with no obligation to work off their travel costs. Robert Steinfeld, *The Invention of Free Labor: The Employment Relation in English and American Law and Culture, 1350–1870* (University of North Carolina Press, 1991), 165.

16. Steinfeld, *Invention of Free Labor*, 139–40; Phoebe v. Jay, 1 Ill. 268 (1828). Upholding a forty-year-long indenture contract involving a Black woman, because the contract predated the state's prohibition on involuntary servitude.

17. Evelyn Nakano Glenn, *Unequal Freedom: How Race and Gender Shaped American Citizenship and Labor* (Harvard University Press, 2002), 68.

18. Steinfeld, *Invention of Free Labor*, 25, 28, 162.

19. The "voluntary" component of apprenticeship arrangements did not apply to coercive apprenticeships in California in the 1850s and 1860s, which authorized "white petitioners to take custody and bind [Native American] minors . . . to periods of indenture." Glenn, *Unequal Freedom*, 68.

20. *See, for example,* Evans v. Gregory, 15 B. Mon. 317 (Ky. 1855). Referring to a "reversionary interest" in an escaped slave; Worthington v. Crabtree, 1 Met. 478, 480 (Ky. 1858), excerpted in Helen T. Catterall, ed., *Judicial Cases Concerning American Slavery and the Negro,* vol. 1, *Cases from the Courts of England, Virginia, West Virginia, and Kentucky,* ed. (Carnegie Institution of Washington, 1926), 437. Referring to a life estate interest in an enslaved man. Connor v. Trawick, 37 Ala. 289 (1861), excerpted in Helen T. Catterall, ed., *Judicial Cases Concerning American Slavery and the Negro,* vol. 3, *Cases from the Courts of Georgia, Florida, Alabama, Mississippi, and Louisiana* (Carnegie Institution of Washington, 1932), 249. Defendant "conveyed a slave to each of his three grandchildren, reserving the use for himself for life, and appointing a trustee to manage them after his death." Mercer v. Byrd, 4 Jones Eq. 358 (N.C. 1859), excerpted in Helen T. Catterall, ed., *Judicial Cases Concerning American Slavery and the Negro,* vol. 2, *Cases from the Courts of North Carolina, South Carolina, and Tennessee* (Carnegie Institution of Washington, 1929), 229. Referring to a life tenancy in an enslaved person; "the plaintiffs alleged ... that their father had a life estate in two slaves." Coffey v. Wilkerson, 1 Met. 101, 103 (Ky. 1858), excerpted in Catterall, *Judicial Cases,* vol. 1, 434; "one hundred and twenty slaves, were divided between the widow and children," Mobley v. Cureton, 2 S.C. 140, 141 (1870), excerpted in Catterall, *Judicial Cases,* vol. 2, 476. Doubrere v. Grillier's Syndic, 2 Mart (n.s.) 171, 182 (La. 1824). Enslaved man, who had paid all but $100 of self-purchase seized by enslaver's debtors and confined to jail. Tucker v. Sweney, Rand Sir. J. 39 (Va. 1730), excerpted in Catterall, *Judicial Cases,* vol. 1, 83–84. Enslaved people "are looked upon as part of [decedent's] Estate, and are liable to be taken for his Debts." "[T]he law has protected slaves from ... sale, where there is a sufficiency of other personal estate to pay debts ... but this qualified exemption does not change their nature [as chattels]." Walden v. Payne, 2 Wash. 1 (Va. 1794), excerpted in Catterall, *Judicial Cases,* vol. 1, 103. Fitzhugh v. Fitzhugh, 6 B. Mon. 4, 6 (Ky. 1845), excerpted in Catterall, *Judicial Cases,* vol. 1, 371. Directing an enslaved person to be "sold in satisfaction of the debt." Farr v. Sims, Rich. Cas. 122, 139 (S.C. 1832), excerpted in Catterall, *Judicial Cases,* vol. 2, 348. Conveyance of enslaved woman to family member declared "void against subsequent creditors." Bogard v. Gardley, 4 S. & M. 302, 310 (Miss. 1845), excerpted in Catterall, *Judicial Cases,* vol. 3, 302. Norris v. Wait, 2 Rich. 148, 149 (S.C. 1845), excerpted in Catterall, *Judicial Cases,* vol. 2, 396-97. Referring to enslaved people being transported across state lines "by the creditors and sold by the sheriff." Gaulden v. McPhaul, 4 La. Ann. 79, 81–82 (La. 1849), excerpted in Catterall, *Judicial Cases,* vol. 3, 595–96. Referring to an enslaver's incentive to instruct a slave to run off "to save his property from the grasp of a determined ... creditor" and reciting a rule in Louisiana that slaves can only be seized by creditors after the debtor defaults.

21. Ballam, "Exploding the Original Myth," 108.

22. VanderVelde writes that the treatises of the time suggest that "different workplace settings invented work rules to suit the circumstances without a uniform default rule" to apply across all types of work, where trade-based customs reflected the typical "beginnings, middles, and endings" of employment.

VanderVelde, "Anti-Republican Origins," 425. See also Lea VanderVelde, "Servitude & Captivity in the Common Law of Master-Servant: Judicial Interpretation of the Thirteenth Amendment's Labor Vision Immediately After Its Enactment," *William & Mary Bill of Rights Journal* 27 no. 4 (2019): 1084; Jay Feinman, "The Development of the Employment at Will Rule," *American Journal of Legal History* 20, no. 2 (1976): 130.

23. Schmidt, *Free to Work*, 5. "[I]f his dismissal be unjust, the master can not, by his wrongful discharge, prevent the servant from recovering a compensation for his services. Thus the law carefully protects the rights of both master and servant." Libhart v. Wood, 1 Watts & Serg. 265, 267 (Pa. 1841). Arguing that rule providing for forfeiture in the event of premature resignation was "reciprocal, for if the employer turn off the servant before the expiration of the time agreed upon, without any just cause, the latter may recover the full amount agreed upon, as if he had worked out his whole time." Badgley v. Heald, 9 Ill. 64, 67 (1847).

24. Horace G. Wood, *A Treatise on the Law of Master and Servant: Covering the Relation, Duties and Liabilities of Employers and Employees* (John D. Parsons, 1877), 278–79. Asserting that the majority rule is that, "under an entire contract" an employee who "abandons the service" "can recover nothing for the services already performed." James Fox, "The Law of Many Faces: Antebellum Contract Law Background of Reconstruction-Era Freedom of Contract," *American Journal of Legal History* 49, no. 1 (2007): 61, 89–91. Describing conflicting lines of jurisprudence, some of which allowed workers to recover for work already performed, even if they left prematurely, while others denied recovery. In the early decades of the nineteenth century, courts often treated employment contracts as "contracts of the entirety," an all-or-nothing conception of employment performance, in which workers were either owed all of the wages under a contract or none of the wages. "It was an entire contract, and the performance of it was a condition precedent to the plaintiff's right of recovery." Mullen v. Gilkinson, 19 Vt. 503 (1847). "In all these cases, and in others which might be cited, the agreement was held to be entire, and not severable, even though there was a rate per month specified in the contract for compensation for the labor to be performed." Larkin v. Buck, 11 Ohio St. 561, 568 (1860). Providing, "But if the dismissal be unjust, and without cause, the master cannot, by his wrongful discharge, prevent the servant from receiving compensation, not only for services rendered, but also the wages he would have earned had the contract continued in full force." Singer v. M'Cormick, 4 Watts & Serg. 265, 267 (Pa. 1842). However, "by the 1830s [the doctrine of contract of the] entirety faced a growing challenge from a different construction of free labor based on the concept of *quantum merit*" under which workers who quit could recover wages for the work performed. Schmidt, *Free to Work*, 15. See also Ballam, "Exploding the Original Myth," 103.

25. However, former employers sometimes used "enticement" or other common law claims against rival employers who lured workers away during their contract term. *See* Catherine Fisk, *Working Knowledge: Employee Innovation and the Rise of Corporate Intellectual Property, 1800–1930* (University of North Carolina Press, 2009), 26; VanderVelde, "Last Legally Beaten Servant,"

734n28; Fox, "Law of Many Faces," 95–96. Enticement "was a cause of action available in the United State only against indentured servants and apprentices." *See also* Stephen Plass, "Dualism and Overlooked Class Consciousness in American Labor Laws," *Housing Law Review* 37, no. 3 (2000): 823, 837n64, 840, 840n75; Karen Orren, *Belated Feudalism: Labor, the Law, and Liberal Development in the United States* (Cambridge University Press, 1991), 104.

26. *Shaver*, 58 Mich. at 655.
27. Wood, *Law of Master and Servant*, 227.
28. Paul v. School Dist. No. 2 in Hartland, 28 Vt. 575 (1856).
29. *Hartland*, 28 Vt. at 580.
30. *Hartland*, 28 Vt. at 580.
31. *Hartland*, 28 Vt. at 582.
32. *See, for example,* Jones v. Graham & Morton Transp. Co., 51 Mich. 539 (1883); Jaffray v. King, 34 Md. 217, 222 (1871); *Singer*, 4 Watts & Serg. 265; Adams' Express Co. v. Trego, 35 Md. 47 (1872); Shaver v. Ingham, 58 Mich. 649 (1886); Weaver v. Halsey, 1 Ill. App. 558 (1878); Wright v. Falkner, 37 Ala. 274, 275–76 (1861). *See also* Wood, *Law of Master and Servant*, 209–34. Describing the bases upon which an employment contract can be terminated.
33. Wood, *Law of Master and Servant*, 212.
34. Wood, *Law of Master and Servant*, 215.
35. Disloyalty tended to be viewed in terms of tangible harms. Theft of a customer's property, for example, would be clearly terminable. However, workers could successfully challenge termination decisions based on more abstract transgressions or intangible economic harms. *See, for example*, Bradford v. Pearson, 12 Mo. 71, 72 (1848); Fisk, *Working Knowledge*, 35. Antebellum courts focused on protecting the physical property rather than the idea. Wood, *Law of Master and Servant*, 212; Shattuck v. Nellis, 44 Vt. 262 (1872).
36. VanderVelde writes, "[t]he law defined the status of lower laborers in opposition to slavery. . . . [L]aborers may have had little real autonomy from their employers, but they could pride themselves on the differences between their status and that of slaves." Lea VanderVelde, "The Labor Vision of the Thirteenth Amendment," *University of Pennsylvania Law Review* 138, no. 2 (1989): 442. "No matter how much American convention exempts whites from paying any costs for the enslavement of blacks, the implications of slavery did not stop at the color line; rather, slavery's theory and praxis permeated the whole of slave-holding society." Nell Irvin Painter, *Southern History Across the Color Line* (University of North Carolina Press, 2002), 18. "A better explanation for the new freedom of colonial wage laborers relates to the spread of slave labor. . . . It was also harder to coerce white laborers because the ideological foundations of slavery became exclusively racial; by definition white labor was free, though the precise definition of freedom had yet to be developed." Jonathan A. Bush, "'Take This Job and Shove It': The Rise of Free Labor," *Michigan Law Review* 91, no. 6 (1993): 1399–1400.
37. Orlando Patterson, *Slavery and Social Death* (Harvard University Press, 1982), ix.
38. For example, Horace Wood noted that "obscene and blasphemous language" was terminable if used in front of children or a master of "refined tastes and keep moral sensibilities" but not if the master commonly indulged in such

language himself. Wood, *Law of Master and Servant*, 211. Terminable offenses included hiring someone else to do your job, "refusing to work at harvesting, unless the master would furnish him with beer" or getting in a "quarre[l] with another clerk in the presence of customers and dr[awing] a revolver." Wood, *Law of Master and Servant*, 215, 221–22.

39. "Most southern prewar labor contract law was dominated by one particular type of litigation, that between planters and overseers." Schmidt, *Free to Work*, 45.

40. Teri A. McMurtry-Chubb, *Race Unequals: Overseer Contracts, White Masculinities, and the Formation of Managerial Identity in the Plantation Economy* (Lexington Books, 2021), xiv–xv.

41. McMurtry-Chubb, *Race Unequals*, 45–46; Schmidt, *Free to Work*, 45.

42. *See, for example*, Prichard v. Martin, 27 Miss. 305, 309 (Miss. Err. & App. 1854). Involving an overseer, with the following jury instructions: "If the jury believe from the evidence that [the employer] discharged the plaintiff without sufficient cause, they will find for the plaintiff, and the measure of damages will be the injury sustained by the plaintiff."

43. Martin v. Everett, 11 Ala. 375, 376 (1847).

44. The court reasoned that, just as "a single act of intemperance would be considered as forgiven" if the drunken worker is allowed to return the next day, so should violence be deemed excused by continued employment. *Everett*, 11 Ala. at 377.

45. For example, an 1853 Tennessee case involved an overseer who was described by one witness as "uncontrollable . . . very cruel to slaves, but was industrious, and attended closely to business." Jones v. Jones, 32 Tenn. 605, 606 (1853). Although the trial court declared the termination justifiable, the jury sided with the overseer and awarded him an entire year's worth of wages. *Jones*, 32 Tenn. at 610. Similarly, in an 1841 Missouri case, an enslaver fired an overseer for beating an enslaved person to death with a handspike. Posey v. Garth, 7 Mo. 94, 95–6 (1841). The enslaver refused to pay any wages. The overseer sued, recovered a portion of his unpaid wages at the trial court, and appealed the case to recover wages for the entire duration of the contract. Although the Missouri Supreme Court refused to award damages for the entire contract, it left the lower court's partial award untouched. *Posey*, 7 Mo. at 98.

46. In *Jones*, the appellate court reversed the verdict, concluding that the jury had erred in failing to set off the overseer's substitute wages. *Jones*, 32 Tenn. at 611. *Posey*, 7 Mo. at 98.

47. See discussion in Elizabeth Tippett, "Enslaved Agents: Business Transactions Negotiated by Slaves in the Antebellum South," *Arizona Law Review* 63, no. 4 (2021): 925, 937.

48. See James Pope, "The Workers' Freedom of Association Under the Thirteenth Amendment," *The Promises of Liberty*, ed. Alexander Tsesis (Columbia University Press, 2010) 139, 147–48. Pope notes that labor leaders and activists in the early twentieth century believed that the Thirteenth Amendment should protect far more than simply the right to quit. However, this interpretation of the Thirteenth Amendment was rejected by the Supreme Court in its famous ruling in the Slaughter-House Cases, 83 U.S. 36, 72 (1873).

49. Andrew Morriss characterizes the Horace Wood theory as a "myth." Andrew Morriss, "Exploding Myths: An Empirical and Economic Reassessment of the Rise of Employment At-Will," *Missouri Law Review* 59, no. 1 (Winter 1994): 681. Morriss further notes that only about nine states cited Wood's treatise in adopting the rule, and many courts cited no authority at all. Morriss, "Exploding Myths," 697.

50. Wood, *Law of Master and Servant*, 272.

51. Ballam, "Exploding the Original," 97; Ballam, "Employment at Will Rule Revisited," 87; Ballam, "Origins of the Employment-at-Will Doctrine," 47.

52. Schmidt, *Free to Work*, 33.

53. "Most hirings in New England textile firms were not contracts at all. . . . Rather, operatives submitted to work . . . under a long list of regulations." Schmidt, *Free to Work*, 33.

54. VanderVelde, "Last Legally Beaten Servant in America," 785. *See also* VanderVelde, "Labor Vision," 488. Describing various efforts by Southern planters attempting to reassert control over emancipated Black workers.

55. VanderVelde, "Last Legally Beaten Servant," 784.

56. VanderVelde, "Anti-Republican Origins," 438. Jay Feinman also pins the at-will doctrine on industrialization and class conflict, arguing that Gilded Age courts aligned themselves with capitalists and used the at-will doctrine to oppress middle-class workers—like salesmen, cashiers, and managers—terminated over contracts for term. Feinman, "Development of Employment at Will Rule," 131–33. *See also* Orren, *Belated Feudalism*, 173–74.

57. Morriss, "Exploding Myths," 736. Morriss also points to a more mundane culprit: state codification efforts, through which states memorialized existing common law by statute. Morriss, "Exploding Myths," 697. This account is consistent with Ballam's claim that the at-will doctrine formed part of the common law background, even if it was not formalized until a later date.

58. For example, Horace Wood's 1877 treatise—famous for its recitation of the at-will presumption—devoted scores of pages to the complexities of then-prevailing employment contract law. Wood, *Law of Master and Servant*, 215.

59. *Graham & Morton*, 51 Mich. at 539.

60. *Graham & Morton*, 51 Mich. at 541. See also *Shaver*, 58 Mich. at 649. Finding in favor of worker unjustly terminated for absenteeism, holding, "We are not prepared to hold that, even in what is known as menial service, every act of disobedience may be lawfully punished by the penalty of dismissal."

61. *Shaver*, 58 Mich. at 654.

62. Matthews v. Park Bros. & Co., 146 Pa. 384, 391 (1892).

63. *Matthews*, 146 Pa. at 391.

64. *Matthews*, 146 Pa. at 391.

65. Courts and juries also protected a range of disloyal and insubordinate conduct among middle-class workers like clerks and sales agents. Employees terminated for disobeying orders they considered unreasonable could expect to be able to present their side of the story to a jury, as in the case of an overseer who successfully challenged his termination after ignoring an enslaver's order to remove some cotton. *See, for example, Prichard*, 27 Miss. at 311. Affirming jury verdict in favor of overseer terminated for "countermanding his employer's

orders in relation to the removal of . . . cotton." Wood observed that minor acts of disobedience or insolence would not necessarily be terminable: "[T]he mere fact that he has been guilty of improper or unbecoming conduct, or that he has, in some slight matters, been guilty of a violation of his master's orders, will not warrant his discharge." Wood, *Law of Master and Servant*, 220.

66. Koll v. Bush, 6 Colo. App. 294 (1895).
67. *Koll*, 6 Colo. App. at 299.
68. *Koll*, 6 Colo. App. at 299.
69. *Koll*, 6 Colo. App. at 295.
70. *Koll*, 6 Colo. App. at 300.
71. "The rule of obedience was qualified by the idea that the orders of the master must be lawful and reasonable." Orren, *Belated Feudalism*, 96.
72. *Koll*, 6 Colo. App. at 300.
73. *Koll*, 6 Colo. App. at 301.
74. *Graham & Morton*, 51 Mich. at 541.
75. *Koll*, 6 Colo. App. at 299.
76. Carson v. W. Branch Hosiery Co., 15 Pa. Super. 476, 481 (1900). Andrew Morriss identified 1891 as the year Pennsylvania adopted the at-will rule, based on Henry v. Pittsburgh, etc. R.R., 21 A 157, 157 (Pa 1891). Morriss, "Exploding Myths," 700. Morriss's methodology identified the earliest case to adopt the at-will rule. This method would not fully capture legal developments if the adoption of the at-will presumption was an intermittent process, or if courts applied the in-between approach for a period of time. Morriss notes that the Pennsylvania Supreme Court did not weigh in on the question until 1909. Morriss at 772.
77. Peniston v. John Y. Huber Co., 196 Pa. 580, 585 (1900).
78. *Peniston*, 196 Pa. at 585.
79. O'Neil v. Schneller, 63 Pa. Super. 196, 200 (1916). "If plaintiff's conduct was such as to indicate that his interests were hostile to those of his master, it was the right of the master to discharge him before any injury was in fact done." Miller v. Jones, 178 Iowa 168 (1916).
80. Legal historian Jay Feinman argued that the at-will doctrine served to oppress the middle class, since many of the plaintiffs bringing breach of contract claims were "middle-level employees" like clerks and sales agents. Feinman, "Employment at Will Rule," 127. However, many of the workers who sued their employers in earlier decades were also clerks, managers, and sales agents. *Singer*, 4 Watts & Serg. at 4833 (clerk); Waugh v. Shunk, 188 Pa. 95 (1852) ("manager in the erection of a blast furnace"); Jaffrey v. King, 34 Md. 217 (1871) (salesman); *Shattuck*, 44 Vt. at 262 (clerk); *Trego*, 35 Md. at 47 (assistant superintendent); Dieringer v. Meyer, 42 Wis. 311 (1877) (salesperson); *Weaver*, 1 Ill. App. at 56 (hired hand).
81. Christopher Tomlins charts a shift during the first half of the nineteenth century toward "interpreting an ever-widening sphere of employment relations as master-servant relations." In particular, "employment became a much less heterogenous relationship than it had been throughout the colonial era, acquiring a uniform definition and set of characteristics as a single universal and impersonal relation founded on wage labor." Christopher Tomlins, "Law and Power in the

Employment Relationship," in *Labor Law in America*, ed. Christopher Tomlins and Andrew King (Johns Hopkins University Press, 1992), 74, 77.

82. At the time, complex industrial operations and capitalism were also considered the antidote to slavery, which was considered preindustrial, inefficient, and backwards. Eric Foner, *Free Soil, Free Labor, Free Men: The Ideology of the Republican Party Before the Civil War* (Oxford University Press, 1995), 40–46.

83. Plessy v. Ferguson, 163 U.S. 537, 551 (1896); Henry Louis Gates Jr., *Stony the Road: Reconstruction, White Supremacy, and the Rise of Jim Crow* (Penguin Press, 2019), 34–35.

84. *See, for example,* Susan Carle, *Defining the Struggle: National Organizing for Racial Justice, 1880–1915* (Oxford University Press, 2013), 2–3.

85. Amy Dru Stanley, *From Bondage to Contract: Wage Labor, Marriage, and the Market in the Age of Slave Emancipation* (Cambridge University Press, 1998), 60.

86. Morriss, "Exploding Myths," 695, 752. And as James Schmidt persuasively documented, courts gradually soured on calculating the damages associated with premature termination and resignation, preferring to simply award wages as of the termination date in either case. Schmidt, *Free to Work*, 15, 195–96, 201–3. Richard Epstein offers a similar argument in his defense of the employment-at-will doctrine: "There is one last way in which the contract at will has an enormous advantage over its rivals. It is very cheap to administer. Any effort to use a for-cause rule will in principle allow all, or at least a substantial fraction of, dismissals to generate litigation." Epstein, "Contract at Will," 970.

87. Morriss, "Exploding Myths," 699.

88. Morriss, "Exploding Myths," 688.

89. Mont. Code Ann. §§ 39-2-901to -915 (2021). Rachel Arnow-Richman and J. H. Verkerke, "Deconstructing Employment Contract Law," *Florida Law Review* 75 (2023): 906, 908. Characterizing the at-will presumption as "remarkably resilient," and "akin to a substantive rule."

90. *Guz*, 100 Cal. Rptr. 2d at 369.

91. *Guz*, 100 Cal Rptr. 2d at fn 8, quoting Samuel Williston, *Williston on Contracts*, 3rd ed. (Baker, Voorhis and Co., 1957), 134.

92. *Guz*, 100 Cal Rptr. 2d at fn 8, quoting Williston, *Contracts*, 134.

93. *Guz*, 100 Cal. Rptr. 2d at 376.

94. *Guz*, 100 Cal. Rptr. 2d at 373.

95. Murphy reported the settlement was "decent." Interview with Stephen Murphy.

96. Interview with Paul Cane and Paul Grossman.

97. Based on the author's search for the term "at-will" on Westlaw for all state and federal employment cases, sorted by "most cited." According to Westlaw, *Guz v. Bechtel* was cited 25,771 times as of April 2025.

CHAPTER 3. PAY

1. Richard Gillespie, *Manufacturing Knowledge: A History of the Hawthorn Experiments* (Cambridge University Press, 1991), 39.

2. Gillespie, *Manufacturing Knowledge*, 42.

3. Gillespie, *Manufacturing Knowledge*, 51. Cynthia Estlund, *Working Together: How Workplace Bonds Strengthen a Diverse* Democracy (Oxford University Press, 2003), 43. Characterizing the Hawthorne experiments as part of the "human relations school of management," which "reflected in part a strategy of union substitution and avoidance."

4. Gillespie, *Manufacturing Knowledge*, 42.

5. The researchers concluded that "the effects of increased supervision and the psychological factors incident to test conditions are of a much larger degree of magnitude than the increases which might possibly be ascribed to illumination." Gillespie, *Manufacturing Knowledge*, 43.

6. As described in greater detail below, some states attempted to pass wage and hour laws, but such laws were vulnerable to being declared unconstitutional under freedom of contract principles.

7. Fred W. Taylor, "A Piece Rate System," *Economic Studies* 1, no. 2 (1896): 96.

8. See Josephine Goldmark, *Fatigue and Efficiency* (Charities Publication Committee, 1912), 60. Describing the use of piece-rate pay in the garment industry and canneries. Gerald Zahavi, *Workers, Managers, and Welfare Capitalism* (University of Illinois Press, 1988), 82–84.

9. Describing the "putting-out system" of production, which "endured not only into the nineteenth century . . . it persists still" in the form of "cloud sourced" gig economy work. Matthew Finkin, "Beclouded Work, Beclouded Workers in Historical Perspective," 37 *Comparative Labor Law & Policy Journal* 37, no. 3 (2016): 603, 605–7, 615. Marc Linder, *The Employment Relationship in Anglo-American Law: A Historical Perspective* (Greenwood Press, 1989), 7–8.

10. See Kati L. Griffith, "The Fair Labor Standards Act at 80: Everything Old is New Again," *Cornell L. Rev.* 104, no. 3 (2019): 574. Describing "industrial homework" as "clothing or other types of assembly work performed at home," which mostly "involved big businesses subcontracting with small contractors . . . who then contracted with homeworkers." This, the author points out, is an early example of Weil's fissuring concept.

11. Irving Richter, "Four Years of the Fair Labor Standards Act of 1938: Some Problems of Enforcement," *Journal of Political Economy* 51, no. 2 (1943): 102.

12. Gillespie, *Manufacturing Knowledge*, 60.

13. Gillespie, *Manufacturing Knowledge*, 60.

14. James Atleson, *Values and Assumptions in American Labor Law* (University of Massachusetts Press, 1983), 65.

15. Gillespie, *Manufacturing Knowledge*, 63.

16. Gillespie, *Manufacturing Knowledge*, 64.

17. As one woman explained in a 1905 edition of *Women's Welfare* magazine, this social assumption belied a starker reality: "The majority of the girls are working because they must work. Many are orphans. Many are helping to support large families. Some are working to save money to attend college or to take up some special work." A. B. B., "How Some Women Spend the Weekly Wage," *Women's Welfare Magazine* January 1905, 152.

18. Taylor, "Piece Rate System," 90. *See also* Daniel Nelson, *Fredrick W. Taylor and the Rise of Scientific Management* (University of Wisconsin Press, 1980), 8. Manufacturers "closely watched the payroll and [were] tempted to interfere whenever piece-workers' incomes exceeded the day work rate." "As employees increased production to take advantage of piece-work rates, the rates were routinely cut back, a process recognized even by employers." Atleson, *Values and Assumptions*, 65.

19. Taylor, "Piece Rate System," 91.
20. Taylor, "Piece Rate System," 90.
21. Taylor, "Piece Rate System," 90.
22. Nelson, *Rise of Scientific Management*, 57, 53, 199.
23. Nelson, *Rise of Scientific Management*, 200.
24. Taylor, "Piece Rate System," 92.
25. John Fabian Witt, *The Accidental Republic: Crippled Workingmen, Destitute Widows, and the Remaking of American Law* (Harvard University Press, 2004), 109.
26. Braceville Coal Co. v. People, 147 Ill. 66 (1893).
27. Ritchie v. People, 155 Ill. 98 (1895).
28. Low v. Rees Printing Co., 59 N.W. 362 (Neb. 1894).
29. Commonwealth v. Perry, 155 Mass. 117 (MA 1891)
30. *Perry*, 155 Mass. at 122; *Braceville*, 147 Ill. at 72; *Rees Printing*, 59 N.W. at 364; *Ritchie*, 155 Ill. at 107.
31. *Ritchie*, 155 Ill at 104.
32. *Rees Printing*, 59 N.W. at 367.
33. "The right to contract necessarily includes the right to fix the price at which labor shall be performed, and the mode and time of payment." *Rees Printing*, 59 N.W. at 367.
34. *Perry*, 155 Mass. at 122.
35. *Perry*, 155 Mass. at 122.
36. Lochner v. New York, 198 U.S. 45, 53 (1905). *Lochner* was so reviled among legal scholars and jurists in subsequent decades that it forms part of the "anticanon": a case that "embodies a set of propositions that all legitimate constitutional decision must be prepared to refute." Jamal Greene, "The Anticanon," *Harvard Law Review* 125, no. 2 (2011): 380. Other cases in this ignominious group include *Dred Scott*, *Plessy v. Ferguson*, and *Korematsu*.
37. David Bernstein, "Lochner v. New York: A Centennial Retrospective," *Washington University Law Quarterly* 83, no. 5 (2005): 1476–79.
38. *Lochner*, 198 U.S. at 53.
39. *Lochner*, 198 U.S. at 53.
40. *Lochner*, 198 U.S. at 54. "The act is not, within any fair meaning of the term, a health law, but is an illegal interference with the rights of individuals ... to make contracts regarding labor upon such terms as they may think best." *Lochner*, 198 U.S. at 61. Rebecca Zietlow, *Enforcing Equality: Congress, the Constitution and the Protection of Individual Rights* (New York University Press, 2006), 68. Moreover, the judicial claim of equality in bargaining power between workers was more fantasy than reality, as historian Amy Dru Stanley observed. Amy Dru Stanley, *From Bondage to Contract: Wage Labor, Marriage,*

*and the Market in the Age of Slave Emancipation* (Cambridge University Press, 1998), 9–13. Or as philosopher Elizabeth Anderson put it, "[I]f one looks at the actual conditions experienced in the workers' fulfilling the contract, the workers stand in a relation of profound subordination to their employer." Elizabeth Anderson, *Private Government: How Employers Rule Our Lives (and Why We Don't Talk About It)* (Princeton University Press, 2019), 35.

41. *Lochner*, 198 U.S. at 62.
42. Karen Orren, *Belated Feudalism: Labor, the Law, and Liberal Development in the United States* (Cambridge University Press, 1991), 112.
43. Orren, *Belated Feudalism*, 113–14.
44. *Lochner*, 198 U.S. at 64. Following *Lochner*, the Supreme Court continued to declare efforts to regulate employment law unconstitutional. In *Adair v. United States*, for example, Justice Harlan wrote that "any legislation that disturbs that equality [between employer and employee] is an arbitrary interference with the liberty of contract, which no government can legally justify in a free land." Adair v. United States, 208 U.S. 161, 175 (1908). Jean-Christian Vinel, *The Employee: A Political History* (University of Pennsylvania, 2013), 42.
45. Charles McCurdy argued that judicial scrutiny of employment legislation proceeded from "two unarticulated assumptions": that "contracts of employment were somehow special and therefore distinguishable for commercial contracts" and that "alleged disparities of bargaining power between workers and employers did not provide a legitimate basis for exercises of police power." Charles W. McCurdy, "The Roots of Liberty of Contract Reconsidered: Major Premises in the Law of Employment, 1867–1937," *Yearbook: Supreme Court Historical Society* 1984 (1984): 24. Lawrence Friedman, *A History of American Law* (Simon & Schuster, 1973), 521. Cf. William E. Nelson, "The Impact of the Antislavery Movement upon Styles of Judicial Reasoning in Nineteenth Century America," *Harvard Law Review* 87, no. 3 (1974): 537. Arguing that Supreme Court's assertions about freedom of contract were grounded in abolitionist thought, which devoted considerable "attention [to] property and contract rights."
46. McCurdy, "Roots of Liberty," 21, 26. "Vestiges of master/servant doctrine helped to underpin workplace discipline and legitimate supervisory prerogative." Rebecca Zietlow, *The Forgotten Emancipator: James Mitchell Ashley and the Ideological Origins of Reconstruction* (Cambridge University Press 2018), 49.
47. Plessy v. Ferguson, 163 U.S. 537, 545 (1896). Rejecting a freedom of contract argument in upholding segregation law.
48. Hammer v. Dagenhart, 247 U.S. 251, 272 (1918).
49. United States Constitution, Art. 1 § 8.
50. Hammer v. Dagenhart, 247 U.S. at 272. *See also* Schechter Poultry Corp et al. v. United States, 295 U.S. 495, 543 (1935). In *Schecter Poultry*, the Court ruled that an industry code regulating the poultry industry exceeded the scope of the commerce clause. Although the chickens crossed state lines, the workers did not.
51. Hammer v. Dagenhart, 247 U.S. 251, 272 (1918).
52. Frances Perkins, *The Roosevelt I Knew* (The Viking Press, 1946), 208.

53. Perkins, *Roosevelt*, 208–9. Kate Andrias, "An American Approach to Social Democracy: The Forgotten Promise of the Fair Labor Standards Act," *Yale Law Journal* 128, no. 3 (2019): 656.

54. A.L.A. Schechter Poultry Corp. et al. v. United States, 295 U.S. 495, 543 (1935).

55. Suzanne Mettler, "Federalism, Gender, & the Fair Labor Standards Act of 1938," *Polity* 26, no. 4 (1994): 638, 640.

56. Mettler, "Standards Act," 640.

57. Oswalt Garrison Villard, "Issues and Men: And a Woman—Frances Perkins," *Nation*, March 8, 1933, 253.

58. Melvyn Dubofsky, *The State and Labor in Modern America* (University of North Carolina Press, 1994), 108.

59. Dubofsky, *State and Labor*, 108.

60. Perkins, *Roosevelt*, 248. "Administration officials were reined in not by the Constitution itself, but rather by their uncertainty about the permanence of the Supreme Court's recent conversion on New Deal policies." Mettler, "Federalism, Gender," 643. See also John S. Forsythe, "Legislative History of the Fair Labor Standards Act," *Law and Contemporary Problems* 6, no. 3 (1939): 467. At the hearings on the draft FLSA, the assistant attorney general "took great pains in demonstrating the bill was not 'another NRA' and . . . demonstrated the constitutional bases upon which the various sections would be supported."

61. Mettler, "Federalism, Gender," 646; Mutari, "Brothers & Breadwinners," 144.

62. Perkins, *Roosevelt*, 254.

63. Perkins, *Roosevelt*, 255.

64. West Coast Hotel Co. v. Parrish, 300 U.S. 379, 391 (1937). "[M]any historians subscribe to the contemporary view of Roberts' vote, that a 'switch in time saved nine.'" Jonathan Grossman, "Fair Labor Standards Act of 1938: Maximum Struggle for a Minimum Wage," *Monthly Labor Review* 101, no. 6 (1978): 24. Roosevelt did not see it that way. He unsuccessfully continued to press the bill, which lost its momentum after the Supreme Court's shift. William Leuchtenburg, *The Supreme Court Reborn: The Constitutional Revolution in the Age of Roosevelt* (Oxford University Press, 1995), 153.

65. Leuchtenburg, *Supreme Court Reborn*, 165. *See also* Laura Kalman, "The Constitution, the Supreme Court, and the New Deal," *American Historical Review* 110 (2005): 1054–55. Summarizing the scholarly debate over whether politics influenced Justice Robert's vote in *West Coast Hotel*. Barry Cushman, "Some Varieties and Vicissitudes of Lochnerism," *Boston University Law Review* 85 (2005): 982–83. Cushman criticized other scholars for their "fetishistic focus on 1937 and on *West Coast Hotel* in particular," though conceded the more narrow point that the 1937 decisions "signaled the close of an era" that placed "constitutional obstacles to progressive labor legislation."

66. 29 U.S.C. § 201 *et seq*. The law does not include an automatic adjustment for inflation, instead forcing Congress to pass new legislation anytime it wants to raise the minimum wage.

67. Grossman, "Fair Labor," 29. "While the bill became bogged down amidst conflicts in the ranks of organized labor, southern forces intent on preserving

the region's low-wage scale mobilized against the pending legislation." Mettler, "Federalism, Gender," 650.

68. Paul Douglas and Joseph Hackman, "The Fair Labor Standards Act of 1938 I," *Political Science Quarterly* 53, no. 4 (1938): 491.

69. Perkins, *Roosevelt*, 259.

70. 29 U.S.C. § 207.

71. Perkins characterized home work as "another method of evading the provisions of wage and hour legislation." Griffith, "Standards Act at 80," 576. Based on her review of the legislative history of the FLSA, Kati Griffith concluded that legislators were well aware of the ways in which employers might attempt to circumvent the law, including through mechanisms that we would today call "fissuring." Griffith, "Standards Act at 80," 576–79. The FLSA decimated the home work industry. Richter, "Four Years," 103.

72. *See* chapter 9 for a discussion of piece-rate pay for independent contractors. *See also* Secretary of Labor v. Lauritzen, 835 F.2d 1529 (7th Cir., 1987), involving agricultural workers who had been paid on a piece-rate basis.

73. United States v. Darby, 312 U.S. 100 (1941).

74. A relatively major amendment occurred with the passage of the Portal-to-Portal Act, discussed in chapter 4. 29 U.S.C. §§ 251-252. The law was amended in 1966 to cover agricultural employees. Pub. L. No. 89-601 (Sept. 23, 1966); Mettler, "Federalism, Gender," 653. The law was also amended in 1974 to cover domestic workers. Pub. L. No. 93-259 (April 8, 1974); Mettler, "Federalism, Gender," 653.

75. Ellen Mutari, "Brothers and Breadwinners: Legislating Living Wages in the Fair Labor Standards Act of 1938," *Review of Social Economy* 62, no. 2 (2004): 133. *See also* Deborah Malamud, "Engineering the Middle Classes: Class Line-Drawing in New Deal Hours Legislation," *Michigan Law Review* 96, no. 8 (1998): 2214. Assessing the way the overtime exemptions constructed class through white collar exemptions. See also Judy Fudge and Rosemary Owens, introduction to *Precarious Work, Women and the New Economy: The Challenge to Legal Norms*, edited by Judy Fudge and Rosemary Owens (Hart Publishing, 2006): 3–4. Arguing that "the industrial model of employment" since World War II "was premised upon a gendered division of labour in which men had the primary responsibility for paid employment and women were primarily concerned with unpaid care work." Evelyn Nakano Glenn, *Unequal Freedom: How Race and Gender Shaped American Citizenship and Labor* (Harvard University Press, 2002), 154. Noting that "separate wage scales were established for Anglo male, Anglo female, Mexican male, and Mexican female jobs."

76. The law cemented "prevailing distinctions" regarding wage earning of the era "between white male breadwinners, income poolers in African American families ... and white women as temporary or supplemental earners." Mutari, "Brothers and Breadwinners," 131.

77. Agricultural workers and domestic workers—as well as independent contractors—were similarly excluded from the National Labor Relations Act. Andrias, "American Approach," 637. "It was in the quiet drafting of the bill by the Roosevelt officials that the majority of low-paid women workers and blacks ... were exempted from coverage." Mettler, "Federalism, Gender," 643. "The limited

coverage of the legislation meant that most female-dominated industries and the two key industries employing African American men and women (agriculture and domestic labor) were excluded from the federal minimum wage standard." Mutari, "Brothers and Breadwinners," 133. Vinel, *Employee*, 59. Discussing the race-related implications of the exclusion and noting the efforts of Black advocacy organizations to introduce an amendment to the Wagner Act that would protect Black workers (59–60).

78. Juan Perea, "The Echoes of Slavery: Recognizing the Racist Origins of the Agricultural and Domestic Worker Exclusion from the National Labor Relations Act," *Ohio State Law Journal* 72, no. 1 (2011): 96. "[A]lthough it was ostensibly a gender-neutral piece of legislation, the FLSA was constructed to foster appropriate gender and racial-ethnic relations." Mutari, "Brothers and Breadwinners," 132.

79. Marc Linder, "Farm Workers and the Fair Labor Standards Act: Racial Discrimination in the New Deal," *Texas Law Review* 65, no. 7 (1987): 1336, 1351; Ira Katznelson, Kim Geiger, and Daniel Kryder, "Limiting Liberalism: The Southern Veto in Congress, 1933–1950," *Political Science Quarterly* 108 no 2. (1993): 297.

80. Linder, "Farm Workers," 1374. A senator from South Carolina also claimed that the FLSA sought to deprive the South of the "splendid gifts of God."

81. "Black employment in the South was disproportionately concentrated in unskilled agricultural and domestic labor." Linder, "Farm Workers," 1343.

82. Linder, "Farm Workers," 1343; Perea, "Echoes of Slavery," 100.

83. "By the late 1920s Chicanos and Mexicanos made up three-quarters of farm labor in California." Glenn, *Unequal Freedom*, 152.

84. Linder, "Farm Workers," 1373, quoting Roosevelt. "During the New Deal Era, Southern Democrats dominated Congress. . . . President Roosevelt simply would not embrace civil rights or egalitarian measures because they endangered the coalition necessary to enact his legislative agenda." Perea, "Echoes of Slavery," 102–3.

85. P.L. 89-601 (Sept. 23, 1966); "Fact Sheet #12: Agricultural Employers Under the Fair Labor Standards Act," U.S. Department of Labor, Wage and Hour Division, January 2020, https://www.dol.gov/agencies/whd/fact-sheets/12-flsa-agriculture.

86. Women—and especially Black women—represented the bulk of domestic workers at the time. Pamela N. Williams, "Historical Overview of the Fair Labor Standards Act," *Florida Coastal Law Review* 10 (2009): 677. "In 1936 most domestic service workers were African American. Now there is still a disproportionate number of minorities who work in domestic jobs, but there are more people of other cultures, including people of Central American, Caribbean, and Mexican descent." Williams, "Historical Overview," 678. Evelyn Nakano Glenn notes that in 1930, "25.4 percent of nonagricultural Japanese American women workers were listed as servants." Glenn, "From Servitude to Service Work: Historical Continuities in the Racial Division of Paid Reproductive Labor, *Signs* 18 (1992): 9. Glenn observes that many Japanese women returned to domestic service upon their release from World War II internment camps. Many detainees lost their homes and other assets as a result of internment, yet

were required to have a job and address to be released from the camps. Domestic service provided both. Glenn, "Servitude to Service Work," 13–14.

87. "When concerns arose among southerners that FLSA would mandate that housewives, 'pay your negro girl eleven dollars a week,' Roosevelt was clear: 'No law ever suggested intended a minimum wages and hours bill to apply to domestic help.'" Mettler, "Federalism, Gender," 647.

88. Premilla Nadasen, "Citizenship Rights, Domestic Work, and the Fair Labor Standards Act," *Journal of Policy History* 24, no. 1 (2012): 82.

89. Discussing debates from the 1970s, "by relegating the rights of domestic workers to 'women's sphere,' male politicians employed a rhetorical strategy that absolved them of any responsibility for the legal rights of domestic workers." Nadasen, "Citizenship Rights," 81. Perea, "Echoes of Slavery," 117.

90. Patricia Mulkeen, "Private Household Workers and the Fair Labor Standards Act," *Connecticut Law Review* 5, no. 4 (1973): 625–26. Quoting S. Rep. No. 842, 92d Cong., 2d Sess. 5, 98 (1972).

91. Nadasen, "Citizenship Rights," 82. Quoting Peter Brennan, U.S. Senate, *Hearings Before the Subcommittee on Labor of the Committee on Labor and Public Welfare*, June 1973, 330–31.

92. Perkins was pressed on a minimum wage that applied equally to men and women in hearings on the legislation. She responded that "wages were economic factors and that pay should be the same for the same work no matter who does it." Grossman, "Fair Labor," 29 (see n66). *See also* Mettler, "Federalism, Gender," 649. "[M]en's unions feared the law would supplant collective bargaining and thus act to weaken unions"; "Equal wages, even at the minima, was a difficult concept for many at the hearings— both members of Congress and those who testified— to absorb." Mutari, "Brothers and Breadwinners," 145.

93. "The Southerners favored language which would . . . set lower rates in regions where the prevailing pattern was below the national standard. . . . [B]ut the Southerners ultimately yielded." Perkins, *Roosevelt*, 264. "Southern manufacturers, dependent on a large, cheap supply of black labor, argued for an explicit racial differential." Perea, "Echoes of Slavery," 105. The NRA included a separate wage rate in the South. Perea, "Echoes of Slavery," 106. *See also* Mettler, "Federalism, Gender," 644.

94. *See* chapters 6 and 7 for a discussion of antidiscrimination law, which subsequently prohibited such practices.

95. 29 U.S.C. § 213.

96. 29 C.F.R. 541.0 *et seq.*

97. Judge Gerald Rosen et al., "Coverage and Exemptions—In General," in *Rutter Group Practice Guide: Federal Employment Litigation* (Thompson Reuters, 2024), Chp. 6-B, §§ 6:150–6:332. Summarizing particularities of exemptions, as developed in federal case law, and citing relevant case law.

98. 29 C.F.R. § 541.602.

99. Regan Rowan, "Solving the Bluish Collar Problem: An Analysis of the DOL's Modernization of the Exemptions to the Fair Labor Standards Act," *University of Pennsylvania Journal of Labor and Employment Law* 7, no. 1 (Fall 2004), 124.

100. Malamud, "Engineering the Middle Classes," 2289; Rowan, "Bluish Collar Problem," 124.

101. 29 C.F.R. 541.3 (the white collar exemptions "do not apply to manual laborers or other 'blue collar' workers who perform work involving repetitive operations with their hands, physical skill and energy" "no matter how highly paid they might be"); William Whittaker, "The Fair Labor Standards Act: A Historical Sketch of the Overtime Pay Requirements of Section 13(a)(1)," *CRS Report for Congress* 9 (May 9, 2005).

102. Sociologists Robert Lynd and Helen Lynd characterized the difference in 1925 as between the "working class" and the "business class"—which ran the gamut from "cashier to the factory owner and professional man." Malamud, "Engineering the Middle Classes," 2227. Quoting Robert Lynd and Helen Lynd's "Middletown" studies.

103. Malamud, "Engineering the Middle Classes," 2288. Vinel, *Employee*, 97–98. Noting the practice of paying managers on a salary basis at the Packard Motor Company.

104. Malamud, "Engineering the Middle Classes," 2224.

105. Stuart Chinn, *Recalibrating Reform: The Limits of Political Change* (Cambridge University Press, 2014), 4. Arguing that progressive legislative achievements, like the NLRA, are followed by periods of retrenchment that "demonstrate the stubborn resilience of older ideas, principles, and institutions that carried elements of the old order into the new."

106. "President Roosevelt and congressional leaders tailored New Deal legislation to southern preferences." Ira Katznelson, Kim Geiger, and Daniel Kryder, "Limiting Liberalism: The Southern Veto in Congress, 1933–1950," *Political Science Quarterly* 108, no 2 (1993): 297.

107. Karen Orren characterized the court system as the bad actor responsible for perpetuating feudal master-servant principles, while the legislature represented the democratic will of the people. For this reason, Orren ended her historical analysis at the New Deal, on the basis that the master-servant system had finally been disrupted through legislation. Orren, *Belated Feudalism*, 215

108. *See* Chinn, *Recalibrating Reform*, 17–18. Arguing that legislative achievements tend to be followed by a period of "recalibration" because they tend to "set forth principles in broad, open-ended, and universalistic terms" which (1) raise "uncertainties about the scope of . . . reforms"; (2) tend to "disrupt, impinge on, and affect" entrenched interests and "governing arrangements"; and (3) often fail to anticipate or address the "problems of recalibration" in the legislation itself.

109. Lauren Edelman, *Working Law: Courts, Corporations, and Symbolic Civil Rights* (University of Chicago Press, 2016), 221–22; Frank Dobbin and Erin Kelly, "How to Stop Harassment: Professional Construction of Legal Compliance in Organization," *American Journal of Sociology* 112 (2007): 4.

CHAPTER 4. TIME MANAGEMENT

1. Vance v. Ball State University, Case No. 1:06-cv-1452 (S.D. Ind. 2007), Deposition of Maetta Vance (May 21, 2007) 7.

2. Meritor Sav. Bank, FSB v. Vinson et al., 477 U.S. 57, 60 (1986).

3. *Meritor Sav. Bank*, 477 U.S. at 67.

4. *See generally Meritor Sav. Bank*, 477 U.S. at 57. *See also* Angela Onwuachi-Willig, "What About #UsToo? The Invisibility of Race in the #MeToo Movement," *Yale Law Journal Forum* 128 (2018): 107; Jamillah Bowman Williams, "Maximizing #MeToo: Intersectionality & the Movement," *Boston College Law Review* 62 (2021): 1826–32. Noting the respects in which courts have failed to "take into account the complexities of intersectional identities, where gender and racial subordination may be compounded to create particular vulnerabilities to harassment".

5. Vance Deposition, 131.

6. Faragher v. City of Boca Raton, 524 U.S. 799 (1998); Burlington Indus., Inc. v. Ellerth, 524 U.S. 742 (1998).

7. *Faragher*, 524 U.S. at 799.

8. *Faragher*, 524 U.S. at 808.

9. *Vance*, Oral Argument, U.S. Supreme Court (November 26, 2012), 4.

10. Vance v. Ball State Univ., 570 U.S. 421, 431 (2013).

11. *Meritor Sav. Bank*, FSB v. Vinson et al., 477 U.S. at 77.

12. Edward Baptist, "Toward a Political Economy of Slave Labor," in *Slavery's Capitalism*, ed. Sven Beckert and Seth Robinson (University of Pennsylvania Press, 2016), 34; Caitlin Rosenthal, "Slavery's Scientific Management," in *Slavery's Capitalism*, ed. Sven Beckert and Seth Robinson (University of Pennsylvania Press, 2016), 70.

13. Brandeis, who represented shipping companies in opposing the fee hike, was so incensed by the railroads' actions that he argued the case *pro bono*. Robert Kanigel, *The One Best Way: Frederick Winslow Taylor and the Enigma of Efficiency* (MIT Press, 2005), 430.

14. "Battle over Figures in the Rate Inquiry," *New York Times*, September 9, 1910, https://www.nytimes.com/1910/09/09/archives/battle-over-figures-in-the-rate-inquiry-admission-made-that.html; "Roads Could Save $1,000,000 a Day," *New York Times*, November 22, 1910. https://www.nytimes.com/1910/11/22/archives/roads-could-save-1000000-a-day-brandels-says-scientific-management.html.

15. Kanigel, *One Best Way*, 430.

16. John Fabian Witt, *The Accidental Republic: Crippled Workingmen, Destitute Widows, and the Remaking of American Law* (Harvard University Press, 2004), 89, 104–5; Sanford Jacoby, *Employing Bureaucracy: Managers, Unions, and the Transformation of Work in the 20th Century*, rev. ed. (Lawrence Erlbaum Associates Publishers, 2004), 25.

17. Ruth Schwartz Cowan, *A Social History of Technology* (Oxford University Press, 1997), 140–45.

18. Wharton Business School, the "first collegiate business school" in the country, was founded in 1881. Harvard's MBA program was established in 1908.

19. Witt, *Accidental Republic*, 108. Taylor's time-based approach was not the only one of that era—in part III I discuss how managers used workplace benefits to shape employee behavior.

20. Caitlyn Rosenthal, *Accounting for Slavery: Masters and Management* (Harvard University Press, 2018), 98.

21. "Taylor's contributions were the substitution of a stopwatch for the foreman's conventional timepiece, and, more significantly, the division of the work into basic steps or elements, each of which he timed separately." Daniel Nelson, *Frederick Taylor and the Rise Scientific Management* (University of Wisconsin Press, 1980), 41.

22. Frederick Winslow Taylor, "A Piece Rate System," *Economic Studies*, 1(2) (1896): 100.

23. Rosenthal, "Slavery's Scientific Management," 70.

24. Baptist, "Political Economy," 320n64. *See also* Mark M. Smith, *Mastered by the Clock: Time, Slavery and Freedom in the American South* (University of North Carolina Press, 1997), 97. Noting references to clock time in 1830s advertisements and articles directed at enslavers, such as one that referenced enslaved workers who could pick a bale of cotton in 6.5 minutes. Similarly, an 1829 illustration of a Black overseer shows a watch chain hanging from his suit jacket, suggesting that clock time governed the work. Smith, *Mastered by the Clock*, 145.

25. Baptist, "Political Economy," 51 (quoting Brown, *Slave Life in Georgia*).

26. Time-based management was not exclusively an American phenomenon. Even further back in time, "the earliest British factory managers . . . timed their workers but did so out of a profound distrust." Smith, *Mastered by the Clock*, 6.

27. Smith, *Mastered by the Clock*, 119.

28. Although Taylor did not himself testify, he sent Brandeis his various writings, and his business "disciples" testified in his stead. Kanigel, *One Best Way*, 433.

29. "The language planters use to describe their efforts to improve labor productivity bears a striking resemblance to the late nineteenth-century language of scientific management." Rosenthal, "Slavery's Scientific Management," 77. "[I]t seems that eighteenth and nineteenth-century industrial capitalists occasionally shared enslavers' fundamental view of workers as inherently slothful and reluctant to labor unless forced to." Smith, *Mastered by the Clock*, 7.

30. "Roads Could Save."

31. Kanigel, *One Best Way*, 434.

32. Witt, *Accidental Republic*, 101, 103.

33. Nelson, *Frederick Taylor*, 52.

34. Nelson, *Frederick Taylor*, 56, 65.

35. Nelson, *Frederick Taylor*, 57, 69, 86.

36. Frederick Winslow Taylor, *The Principles of Scientific Management* (New York: Harper & Bros., 1911).

37. Charles Were and Richard Hodgetts, "Frederick Taylor's 1899 Pig Iron Observations: Examining Fact, Fiction, and Lessons for the New Millennium," *Academy of Management Journal* 43, no. 6 (2000): 1288.

38. Were and Hodgetts, "Taylor's 1899 Pig Iron Observations," 1288.

39. Josephine Clara Goldmark, *Fatigue and Efficiency: A Study in Industry* (Russell Sage Foundation, 1912), 9. Goldmark served as the chairwoman for the Committee on the Legal Defense of Labor Laws of the National Consumers' League. Goldmark, *Fatigue and Efficiency*, vii.

40. Goldmark, *Fatigue and Efficiency*, 10.

41. Goldmark, *Fatigue and Efficiency*, 54.

42. Goldmark, *Fatigue and Efficiency*, 45–47.

43. Witt, *Accidental Republic*, 109.

44. Deborah Malamud, "Engineering the Middle Classes: Class Line-Drawing in New Deal Hours Legislation," *Michigan Law Review* 96 (1998): 2288.

45. Anderson v. Mt. Clemens Pottery Co., 328 U.S. 680, 691 (1946).

46. Edward Lamb, *No Lamb for Slaughter* (Harcourt, Brace & World, 1963), 70.

47. In the three years since the FLSA had been passed, Lamb had already handled more than three hundred minimum wage and overtime cases. Lamb, *No Lamb for Slaughter*, 72.

48. Lamb, *No Lamb for Slaughter*, 74.

49. On October 30, 1894, Daniel Cooper patented his invention, a "workman's time recorded" (https://patents.google.com/patent/US528223A/en). The original punch clock contained a giant stamp on a wheel that moved according to the dial of the clock itself, which included tiny stamps from 1 to 59; in other words, precise enough to record time by the minute. At the end of the week, a single card would itemize a worker's clock in and clock out times for the entire week, so that—in Cooper's words—"the amount of wages due him at the end of this time could be readily computed."

50. Instead, as of 1941, some three years after the FLSA went into effect, the company continued to pay its workers on a piece-rate basis. Although the FLSA did not prohibit piece-rate pay, employers would almost certainly need to make after-the-fact adjustments to employee paychecks to comply with the FLSA mandates.

51. Lamb, *No Lamb for Slaughter*, 74.

52. Lamb, *No Lamb for Slaughter*, 73.

53. Anderson et al. v. Mt. Clemens Pottery Co., 69 F. Supp. 710, 712 (E.D. Mich. 1947).

54. Lamb, *No Lamb for Slaughter*, 75.

55. 56 minutes x 5 days x 50 weeks (assuming 2 weeks off), is 14,000 minutes, divided by 60 is approximately 230 hours.

56. Lamb, *No Lamb for Slaughter*, 72.

57. Lamb, *No Lamb for Slaughter*, 78.

58. *Mt. Clemens*, 328 U.S. at 691.

59. *Mt. Clemens*, 328 U.S. at 691.

60. *Mt. Clemens*, 328 U.S. at at 692–93.

61. "In the six months following this Court's decision in *Anderson*, unions and employees filed more than 1,500 lawsuits under the FLSA [seeking] $6 billion in backpay and liquidated damages." Integrity Staffing Sols., Inc. v. Busk, 574 U.S. 27, 31–32 (2014).

62. Lamb, *No Lamb for Slaughter*, 83.

63. Lamb, *No Lamb for Slaughter*, 83.

64. Lamb, *No Lamb for Slaughter*, 85. As Lamb observed, "the government's position now was actually more antilabor than that of the pottery company itself."

65. Lamb, *No Lamb for Slaughter*, 85. The preamble to the Portal to Portal Act (1947) states that existing interpretations of the FLSA would "bring about the financial ruin of many employers and seriously impair the capital resources

of many others, thereby resulting in the reduction of industrial operations." 29 U.S.C. § 251.

66. Lamb, *No Lamb for Slaughter*, 86.
67. Portal-to-Portal Act of 1947; *Integrity Staffing*, 574 U.S. at 33.
68. Masaaki Imai, *Kaizen (Ky'zen), the Key to Japan's Competitive Success* (Random House, 1986).
69. Imai, *Kaizen* (1986), xxix, 5, 23.
70. Imai, *Kaizen* (1986), 25–26.
71. Imai, *Kaizen* (1986), 83; Masaaki Imai, *Gemba Kaizen: A Commonsense Low-Cost Approach to Management* (McGraw-Hill, 1997), xxvi–ii. Using the Japanese terminology.
72. Imai, *Gemba Kaizen*, 23, 80.
73. Imai, *Gemba Kaizen*, 14, 46, 77.
74. Kanigel writes that the postwar Japanese revolution in production had "been cleared by an earlier generation of American management leaders." Kanigel, *One Best Way*, 492.
75. Kanigel, *One Best Way*, 492.
76. Imai, *Gemba Kaizen*, 26–27, 29, 34.
77. "[T]he 'quality circle' idea was imported from Japan to . . . improv[e] . . . the firm's production quality and efficiency." Paul Weiler, *Governing the Workplace* (Harvard University Press, 1990), 31.
78. Satoshi Sasaki, "The Introduction of Scientific Management by the Mitsubishi Electric Engineering Co. and the Formation of an Organised Scientific Management Movement in Japan in the 1920s and 1930s," *Business History* 34, no. 2 (1992): 12–27.
79. Sasaki, "Scientific Management," 17.
80. Sasaki, "Scientific Management," 14–15.
81. Sasaki, "Scientific Management," 18–19.
82. Sasaki, "Scientific Management," 19.
83. Imai, *Kaizen*, xxix, 5, 23.
84. Udit Madan, "Amazon Is Increasing the Average Total Compensation Package for Fulfillment and Transportation Employees in the US to over $29 per Hour," Amazon, September 18, 2024, https://www.aboutamazon.com/news/workplace/amazon-wage-increase-new-benefits-for-hourly-us-employees.
85. Christopher Mims, "The Way Amazon Uses Tech to Squeeze Performance Out of Workers Deserves Its Own Name: Bezosism," *Wall St. Journal*, September 11, 2021.
86. Mims, "Way Amazon Uses Tech." Citing a statement from an Amazon spokesperson. Emily Guendelsberger, *On the Clock: What Low-Wage Work Did to Me and How It Drives America Insane* (Little, Brown, 2019), 90. Noting that the rate was set at ninety per hour on a particular day she was working.
87. Gillespie, *Manufacturing Knowledge*, 60.
88. Gillespie, *Manufacturing Knowledge*, 60. See also Mims, "Way Amazon Uses Tech." Comparing Amazon's practices to Taylorism.
89. Jodi Kantor, Karen Weise, and Grace Ashford, "Inside Amazon's Employment Machine," *New York Times*, June 15, 2021, https://www.nytimes.com/interactive/2021/06/15/us/amazon-workers.html.

90. Kantor et al., "Amazon's Employment Machine."

91. Alan Boyle, "Amazon Wins a Pair of Patents for Wireless Wristbands That Track Warehouse Workers," *GeekWire*, January 30, 2018, https://www.geekwire.com/2018/amazon-wins-patents-wireless-wristbands-track-warehouse-workers/.

92. "[H]aptic feedback can be delivered to the worker to alert the worker to a possible incorrect item placement or retrieval." U.S. Patent No. 9,881,276, "Ultrasonic Bracelet and Receiver for Detecting Position in 2d Plane," January 30, 2018, https://patents.justia.com/patent/9881277.

93. Ceylan Yeginsu, "If Workers Slack Off, the Wristband Will Know," *New York Times*, February 1, 2018, https://www.nytimes.com/2018/02/01/technology/amazon-wristband-tracking-privacy.html; Olivia Solon, "Amazon Patents Wristband That Tracks Warehouse Workers' Movements," *Guardian*, January 31, 2018, https://www.theguardian.com/technology/2018/jan/31/amazon-warehouse-wristband-tracking.

94. According to his LinkedIn profile, the inventor, Jonathan Evan Cohn, worked at Amazon Go as a "Senior Technical Program Manager" when the patent was approved. https://www.linkedin.com/in/jonathan-e-cohn.

95. Boyle, "Amazon Wins Patents."

96. Kantor et al., "Amazon's Employment Machine."

97. Kantor et al., "Amazon's Employment Machine."

98. Interview with Tony Thompson, April 19, 2024 (on file with author).

99. Interview with Jessica Jaszewski, March 19, 2024 (on file with author). Counsel for Starbucks declined to be interviewed.

100. Charlotte Alexander and Anna Haley-Lock, "Underwork, Work Hour Insecurity, and a New Approach to Wage and Hour Regulation," *Industrial Relations: Journal of Economy & Society* 54 (2015): 696, 699.

101. Elizabeth Tippett and Charlotte Alexander, "The Problem with Employee Scheduling Software," Oregon Law Lab, April 10, 2019, YouTube, 7:47, https://youtu.be/8ikGVBSLKHc.

102. "Reporting Time Pay: A Key Solution to Curb Unpredictable and Unstable Scheduling Practices," National Women's Law Center, January 2015, https://nwlc.org/wp-content/uploads/2015/08/reporting_time_pay_fact_sheet_jan_2015.pdf. At least eight states and the District of Columbia have passed "reporting time" pay laws. *See also* California Industrial Welfare Commission Wage Order 1-15 § 4. Requiring companies to pay a "split shift" premium.

103. Jodi Kantor, "Working Anything but 9 to 5," *New York Times*, August 13, 2014, https://www.nytimes.com/interactive/2014/08/13/us/starbucks-workers-scheduling-hours.html; Noam Scheiber, "Starbucks Falls Short After Pledging Better Labor Practices," *Seattle Times*, September 23, 2015, https://www.seattletimes.com/business/starbucks-falls-short-after-pledging-better-labor-practices-2/. Some stores were still using "clopenings" as of 2015.

104. Elizabeth Tippett, "How Employers Profit from Digital Wage Theft Under the FLSA," *American Business Law Journal* 55, no. 2 (2018): 316 (citing Pl.'s Mot. For Class Certification, at 8); Doyel v. McDonalds Corp., No. 4:08-CV-1198, 2010 WL 3199685, at *1 (E.D. Mo. Aug. 12, 2010).

105. Plaintiff's Motion and Memorandum for Class Certification, Doyel, 2010 WL 3199685, at 22.

106. Plaintiff's Motion and Memorandum for Class Certification, Doyel, 2010 WL 3199685, at 21. Tippett "Digital Wage Theft," 377–78. *See also* Leah F. Vosko et al., "The Compliance Model of Employment Standards Enforcement: An Evidence-Based Assessment of Its Efficacy in Instances of Wage Theft," *Industrial Relations Journal* 48 (2017): 265–66.

107. Tippett "Digital Wage Theft," 374–75.

108. Tippett "Digital Wage Theft," 46 (discussing Castle v. Wells Fargo Fin., Inc., No. C 06-4347SI, 2008 WL 495705, at *1 (N.D. Cal. 2008)).

109. See discussion in chapter 10.

110. Internal Revenue Service, "Identifying Full-Time Employees," January 22, 2021, https://www.irs.gov/affordable-care-act/employers/identifying-full-time-employees.

111. *Mt. Clemens Pottery Co.*, 328 U.S. at 683.

112. *Integrity Staffing*, 574 U.S. at 27.

113. *Integrity Staffing*, 574 U.S. at 36.

114. *Integrity Staffing*, 574 U.S. at 36.

115. For "white collar" workers, that means supervisory work, or nonmanual administrative work with substantial discretion and independent judgment, or professional work marked by a prolonged period of study. This, as Deborah Malamud noted, was likely a class distinction at the time that has since been cemented into law. Malamud, "Engineering the Middle Classes," 2227.

116. 29 C.F.R. § 541.602.

117. Jodi Kantor and David Streitfeld, "Inside Amazon: Wrestling Big Ideas in a Bruising Workplace," *New York Times,* August 15, 2015.

118. Kantor & Streitfeld, "Inside Amazon."

119. 29 U.S.C. 8 § 207; H.R. 676, 75th Cong. (June 25, 1938). In the words of Frances Perkins, FDR's secretary of labor, "any employer in the land can legally and automatically ask his employees to work as many hours beyond 40 as he cares to without asking permission of the Government so long as he pays the overtime rate of time and one-half." Marc Linder, *Moments Are the Elements of Profit: Overtime and the Deregulation of Working Hours Under the Fair Labor Standards Act* (Fǎnpìhuà Press, 2000), 36.

120. "The overtime pay provisions of the FLSA were designed to advance three main policy goals: a shorter workweek, compensation for overworked employees, and work spreading." Regan Rowan, "Solving the Bluish Collar Problem: An Analysis of the DOL's Modernization of the Exemptions to the Fair Labor Standards Act," *University of Pennsylvania Journal of Labor & Employment Law* 7, no. 1 (2004): 123. According to a 1912 government study of the iron and steel industry, 42 percent of workers worked more than seventy-two hours a week—more than twelve hours a day. Goldmark, *Fatigue and Efficiency,* 4. Citing Charles Patrick Neill, *Report on Conditions of Employment in the Iron and Steel Industry in the United States, Summary of the Wages and Hours of Labor* (Government Printing Office, 1912), 36, 57.

121. "[T]he recent growth in annual-earnings inequality is primarily due to growing inequality in hourly wage rates." Gary Burtless, "The Contribution of Employment and Hours Changes to Family Income Inequality," *American Economic Review* 83, no. 2 (1993): 133. Daniele Checci et al., "Are Changes in the Dispersion of Hours Worked a Cause of Increased Earnings Inequality?," *IZA Journal of European Labor Studies* 5, no. 15 (2016): 3. Estimating that two-thirds of income inequality in the United States is attributable to wage rates rather than the distribution of hours.

122. Hours inequality between high-wage and low-wage workers is also attributable to periods of unemployment by workers near the bottom of the income distribution. *See* Burtless, "Income and Earnings," 134. Jonathan Heathcote et al., "Unequal We Stand: An Empirical Analysis of Economic Inequality in the United States 1967–2006," *Review of Economic Dynamics* 13, no. 1 (January 2010): 16.

123. Daniel Markovits, *The Meritocracy Trap* (Penguin Books, 2019), 292.

124. Markovits, *Meritocracy Trap*, 292.

## CHAPTER 5. UNIONS

1. Starbucks did not make its attorneys available for an interview.
2. Amelia Lucas, "Here's a Map of Starbucks Stores That Vote to Unionize," CNBC, December 9, 2022, https://www.cnbc.com/2022/12/09/map-of-starbucks-stores-that-voted-to-unionize.html.
3. Interview with Jessica Jaszewski and Ian Meagher, March 19, 2024 (on file with author).
4. Interview with Jessica Jaszewski and Ian Meagher.
5. Interview with Jessica Jaszewski and Ian Meagher.
6. Lucas, "Here's a Map."
7. Interview with Marina Multhaup, January 8, 2024.
8. Starbucks and Workers United, Order, April 27, 2022, Case No. 19-RC-289815 ("Starbucks ALJ Decision").
9. Starbucks ALJ Decision, 9–10. The administrative law judge ruled that the meetings themselves were lawful and that it was permissible to warn workers they might lose a direct relationship with management. However, Starbucks engaged in unlawful labor practices when asserting that managers would no longer be able to assist workers, and that they would no longer be able to borrow workers from other stores. ALJ Decision, 21–26.
10. Starbucks ALJ Decision, 10. The ALJ ultimately ruled that Starbucks had a right to make such statements under prevailing labor law. Starbucks ALJ Decision, 22.
11. Starbucks ALJ Decision, 12.
12. Starbucks ALJ Decision, 14.
13. Starbucks ALJ Decision, 13.
14. Starbucks ALJ Decision, 13–17, 19.
15. Starbucks ALJ Decision, 16. See also "Employee Rights Notice Posting," National Labor Relations Board, accessed April 24, 2025, https://www.nlrb.gov/news-publications/publications/employee-rights-notice-posting.

16. Starbucks ALJ Decision, 16.
17. Starbucks ALJ Decision, 16.
18. Robert Steinfeld, *The Invention of Free Labor: The Employment Relation in English and American Law and Culture, 1350–1870* (University of North Carolina Press, 1991), 57–58.
19. Frederick Douglass, *Narrative of the Life of Frederick Douglass, An American Slave* (Antislavery Office, 1845; W. W. Norton, 2017), 17.
20. State v. Mann, 13 N.C. 263, 267 (1829).
21. Elizabeth Anderson, *Private Government: How Employers Rule Our Lives (and Why We Don't Talk About It)* (Princeton University Press, 2017), xxii. In the context of her dictatorship framework, Anderson acknowledges that workers can and do leave jobs. But in leaving for another job, she argues, an employee merely trades one dictatorship for another. *See also* Christopher Tomlins, "Law and Power in the Employment Relationship," in *Labor Law in America*, ed. Christopher Tomlins and Andrew King (Johns Hopkins University Press, 1992), 73. Describing a shift in the nineteenth century toward viewing "the decision to enter employment . . . [as] a decision to become subject to the employer's power" where "government was devolved upon the employer[.]" Karen Orren, *Belated Feudalism: Labor, the Law, and Liberal Development in the United States* (Cambridge University Press, 1991), 112. Characterizing judicial sympathy toward master-servant principles as a preservation of the "labor remnant of feudal governance against legislative encroachment." "Employers are still willing to use their unprecedented power to exploit workers both physically and emotionally." Joseph Seiner, "Workplace Power," *Boston College Law Review* 65 (2024): 77.
22. 29 U.S.C. § 151-169.
23. Title VII of the Civil Rights Act of 1964, 42 U.S.C. § 2000e *et seq*; The Equal Pay Act of 1963, 29 U.S.C. § 206(d); Age Discrimination in Employment Act, 29 U.S.C. § 621 *et seq.*; The Americans with Disabilities Act, 42 U.S.C. §12111 *et seq.* But see Joseph Slater, "The 'American Rule' That Swallows the Exceptions," *Employee Rights and Employment Policy Journal* 11 (2007): 54. Arguing that the at-will rule "is crippling the effectiveness of the two most important exceptions to that doctrine, Title VII of the Civil Rights Act of 1964 and the National Labor Relations Act." Cynthia Estlund observes that "workplace relations are often undemocratic, unfree, and permeated by elements of economic coercion and power." *Working Together: How Workplace Bonds Strengthen a Diverse* Democracy (Oxford University Press 2003), 125.
24. Bureau of Labor Statistics, "Union Members—2024," January 28, 2025, https://www.bls.gov/news.release/pdf/union2.pdf.
25. James Atleson, *Values and Assumptions in American Labor Law* (University of Massachusetts Press, 1983), 51. *See also* Stuart Chinn, *Recalibrating Reform: The Limits of Political Change* (Cambridge University Press, 2014), 4, 14. Noting the central role of the Supreme Court in "delimiting" the reach of landmark legislation, including the NLRA.
26. See, for example, Nell Irvin Painter, *Standing at Armageddon: The United States 1877–1919* (W. W. Norton 1989), 30, 41. Knights of Labor started out as a secret society of tailors. "[W]ith the exception of the United Mine

Workers, most nineteenth century unions were trade unions, organizing only skilled members or particular trades." Ruth Schwartz Cowan, *A Social History of Technology*, (Oxford University Press, 1997), 179–81. "[B]y the second half of the nineteenth century ... local organizations of skilled workers began to federate in national trade unions." Christopher Tomlins, *The State and the Unions: Labor Relations, Law, and the Organized Labor Movement in America, 1880–1960* (Cambridge University Press, 1985), 10.

27. See discussion in chapter 2.

28. "According to an 1865 census of occupations in the South, there were only 20,000 skilled white craftsmen and tradesmen, compared to 100,000 skilled blacks, most of whom were former slaves." Juliet E. K. Walker, *History of Black Business in America: Capitalism, Race, Entrepreneurship* (Macmillan Library Reference USA, 1998), 150–51.

29. Walker, *History of Black Business*, 65.

30. Blache v. Loreins, 13 La. Hist. Q. 361 (La. 1778), excerpted in Helen T. Catterall, ed., *Judicial Cases Concerning American Slavery and the Negro*, vol. 3, *Cases from the Courts of Georgia, Florida, Alabama, Mississippi, and Louisiana* (Carnegie Institution of Washington, 1932), 400. Referring to an enslaved man who "kn[ew] the trade of a brick mason." Elena v. Desprez, 14 La. Hist. Q. 619 (La. 1780), excerpted in Helen T. Catterall, ed., *Judicial Cases*, vol. 3 (Carnegie Institution of Washington, 1932), 444. Involving a master carpenter. Hamilton v. M'Carty, 1 Dev. and Bat. 226 (N.C. 1835), excerpted in Catterall, *Judicial Cases Concerning American Slavery and the Negro*, vol. 2 (Carnegie Institution of Washington, 1929), 71. Enslaved man hired out to learn "art and trade of boot and shoe making"; Clancy v. Overman, 1 Dev. and Bat. 402 (N.C. 1835), excerpted in Catterall, *Judicial Cases*, vol. 2, 74. Involving a coachmaker. Bell v. Walker, 3 Jones N.C. 320 (N.C. 1856), excerpted in Catterall, *Judicial Cases*, vol. 2, 197. Involving ship carpenter's and caulker's trade. Webb v. Bellinger, 2 Desaussure 482 (S.C. 1807), excerpted in Catterall, *Judicial Cases*, vol. 2, 290. Referring to "two drivers ... sixteen tradesmen, fifteen sawyers." Wright v. Wright, 2 Little 8 (Ky. 1822), excerpted in Catterall, *Judicial Cases*, vol. 1, 302. Referring to a blacksmith.

31. Ronald Lewis, *Coal, Iron and Slaves: Industrial Slavery in Maryland and Virginia, 1715–1865* (Greenwood Press, 1979).

32. Lewis, *Coal, Iron and Slaves*, 32.

33. Lewis, *Coal, Iron and Slaves*, 32.

34. Tomlins, *State and the Unions*, 17.

35. *See* discussion in chapter 4.

36. Cowan, *Social History of Technology*, 179. "Industrialization tended to reduce even the skilled laborer to the status of a semiskilled or even unskilled worker." John Hope Franklin, *Reconstruction After the Civil War* (University of Chicago Press, 1994), 174.

37. Karen Orren makes an even stronger claim: that "the American labor movement was the agent of one such transition [toward liberalism] from the regulation of employment by the law of master and servant to the regime of collective bargaining." Orren, *Belated Feudalism*, 19, 122.

38. Union organizing had some protection during World War I under the War Labor Board, and also under the National Recovery Administration, which provided for the right to organize, collective bargaining, and prohibition on employer interference in union organizing and bargaining. Atleson, *Values and Assumptions*, 36.

39. Tomlins, *State and the Unions*, 33. In the early nineteenth century, unions contended with criminal conspiracy charges, alleging that they restrained trade, used strikes "to extort large sums of money," or oppressed and coerced their masters and other workers. Tomlins, *State and the Unions*, 37–39. Jeffrey Steven Kahana argues that hostility toward unions in the early republic stemmed from a larger political hostility toward "a state within a state," wherein unions represented a threatening "private power that existed separate from the fount of state authority." *The Unfolding of American Labor Law: Judges, Workers and Public Policy Across Two Political Generations 1790–1850* (LFB Scholarly Publishing, 2014), 96, 115. In 1840 a Massachusetts court partially lifted the criminal veil over union activity, holding that unions were not inherently illegal if they did not have an illegal purpose. Com. v. John Hunt, 45 Mass. 111, 119 (1842); Tomlins, *State and the Unions*, 46. As unions became more powerful and centralized in the late nineteenth century, they once again ended up on the wrong end of criminal conspiracy charges for engaging in "boycott[s], unfair lists, most forms of picketing." Tomlins, *State and the Unions*, 48.

40. Indeed, Tomlins argued that the AFL was more powerful prior to the passage of the NLRA because the union was not subject to government rules about elections, bargaining units, and collective bargaining. Instead, the AFL operated according to customs and practices it had developed over time. *State and the Unions*, 144–47. Melvyn Dubofsky offers a different perspective, arguing that the NLRA represented "perhaps the most radical piece of New Deal legislation" because it "codified all existing federal legislation which guaranteed workers the right to form unions of their own choosing." *The State and Labor in Modern America* (University of North Carolina Press, 1994), 129.

41. As Karen Orren observed, "judges were doing just what they said they were doing, to wit, protecting the employment contract from outside intrusion." *Belated Feudalism*, 127.

42. Tomlins, *State and the Unions*, 50; Victoria Hattam, *Labor Visions and State Power* (Princeton University Press, 1993), 70.

43. Tomlins, *State and the Unions*, 50; Hattam, *Labor Visions*, 161.

44. Orren, *Belated Feudalism*, 123, 134. Victoria Hattam, "Courts and the Question of Class," in *Labor Law in America*, ed. Christopher Tomlins and Andrew King (Johns Hopkins University Press, 1992), 56–57. Discussing conspiracy charges. Amy Dru Stanley, *From Bondage to Contract: Wage Labor, Marriage, and the Market in the Age of Slave Emancipation* (Cambridge University Press, 1998), 83.

45. Legal historian Christopher Tomlins described these cases as "the tip of an iceberg of judicial antipathy reaching far back into the nineteenth century." Companies were then, as today, fiercely resistant to this challenge to their authority; in 1902, the president of the Reading Railroad, George Baer, declared,

"'There cannot be two masters in the management of business.'" Tomlins, *State and the Unions*, 30, 12. Indeed, Victoria Hattam argues that "the dominance of the courts in regulating industrial conflict" was a primary reason unions abandoned a political approach to labor reform, in contrast to other industrialized countries. *Labor Visions*, 21, 73.

46. Plessy v. Ferguson, 163 U.S. 537, 545 (1896).

47. James Pope, "The Workers' Freedom of Association Under the Thirteenth Amendment," *The Promises of Liberty*, ed. Alexander Tsesis (Columbia University Press, 2010), 138.

48. According to historian John Hope Franklin, Black workers had little hope of securing coveted industrial jobs, forcing them to work in service sector jobs. *Reconstruction After the Civil War*, 178. *See also* Steelworkers v. Weber, 443 U.S. 193, n.1 (1979). Aggregating case law, stating "judicial findings of exclusion from craft unions on racial grounds are so numerous as to make such exclusion a proper subject for judicial notice."

49. David Augustus Straker, *New South Investigated* (Ferguson Printing, 1888; Arno Press 1973), 97, quoted in Susan Carle, *Defining the Struggle: National Organizing for Racial Justice, 1880–1915* (Oxford University Press, 2013), 320. Straker also noted the prevalence of race-based wage discrimination: "It is not an unusual thing to see a white and a black mechanic, who although doing the same work, yet receive different wages. Discrimination is introduced even into the precincts of the schoolhouse. A first-class colored teacher never receives the equal salary as a first class white teacher." *New South Investigated*, 96, quoted in Carle, *Defining the Struggle*, 66–67.

50. Carle, *Defining the Struggle*, 346–47, n81.

51. Carle, *Defining the Struggle*, 89.

52. Susan Kleinberg, "The Systematic Study of Urban Women," in *Class, Sex, and the Woman Worker*, ed. Milton Cantor and Bruce Laurie (Greenwood Press, 1977), 24; Carol Groneman, "She Earns as a Child: She Pays as a Man," in *Class, Sex, and the Woman Worker*, ed. Cantor and Laurie, 85. In the early twentieth century, some women gained access to better paying industrial jobs, clerical work, and teaching jobs, albeit at a lower rate than men. Kleinberg, "Systematic Study of Urban Women," 24. However, Black women were largely excluded from this even limited progress. As of 1930, 90 percent of employed Black women worked in farm or domestic labor. Rosalyn Terborg-Penn, "Survival Strategies Among African-American Workers," in *Women, Work and Protest: A Century of US Women's Labor History*, 2nd ed., ed. Ruth Milkman (Routledge, 2013), 141.

53. Kleinberg, "Systematic Study of Urban Women," 29.

54. Kleinberg, "Systematic Study of Urban Women," 29. "Through the nineteenth and early twentieth centuries, work, especially for married women, indicated inadequate income from other sources." Terborg-Penn, *Survival Strategies*, 148. Black women were paid less than white women in the garment industry. Carol Groneman, "She Earns as a Child," 85. Study suggesting that 44 percent of Irish women in a section of New York in the mid-nineteenth century were employed outside the home. Evelyn Nakano Glenn, "From Servitude to Service Work: Historical Continuities in the Racial Division of Paid Reproductive Labor," *Signs* 18 (1992): 4–5.

55. Kleinberg, "Systematic Study of Urban Women," 27. A similar study from 1911 found that Black men were paid less than European immigrants, and Black women had higher labor force participation rates. Miriam Cohen, "Italian-American Women in New York City," in *Class, Sex, and the Woman Worker*, ed. Cantor and Laurie, 123.

56. Vicki Ruiz, *Cannery Women, Cannery Lives* (University of New Mexico Press, 1987), 15. The same study found that child labor contributed 35 percent of the household income.

57. Alice Kessler-Harris, "Organizing the Unorganizable: Three Jewish Women and Their Union," *Class, Sex, and the Woman Worker*, ed. Cantor and Laurie, 144; Alice Kessler-Harris, "Where Are All the Organized Women Workers?," *Feminist Studies* 3, nos. 1/2 (1975): 92. Union density among women in industrial occupations varied from 1.5 percent to 6.6 percent between 1900 and 1920.

58. Elizabeth Jameson, "Imperfect Unions," in *Class, Sex, and the Woman Worker*, ed. Cantor and Laurie, 182. "The common fear prevailed that women took men's jobs and depressed wages." Kessler-Harris, "Organized Women Workers," 95.

59. Kessler-Harris, "Organized Women Workers," 95, 96.

60. Kessler-Harris, "Organized Women Workers," 96.

61. Kessler-Harris, "Organized Women Workers," 99. "Prior to 1873, only two among the thirty-plus national unions then in existence admitted women to membership." Martha May, "Bread Before Roses," in *Women, Work and Protest: A Century of US Women's Labor History*, 2nd ed., ed. Ruth Milkman (Routledge, 2013), 6.

62. Kessler Harris, "Organized Women Workers," 99.

63. Elizabeth Jameson, "Imperfect Unions," 182. Noting that "several hundred" women in retail, laundry, cooking, and typography positions in a mining town were union members. Kessler-Harris, "Organized Women Workers," 95.

64. Kessler-Harris, "Organized Women Workers," 97; May, "Bread Before Roses," 9.

65. Kessler-Harris, "Organized Women Workers," 98. Referencing male leadership of unions in industries dominated by women, such as the garment industry. Ruth Milkman, "Two Worlds of Unionism: Women and the New Labor Movement," in *The Sex of Class: Women Transforming American Labor*, ed. Sue Cobble (Cornell University Press, 2011), 66. A rare exception was the short-lived United Cannery, Agricultural, Packing, and Allied Workers of America, in which Mexicana and Mexican American women played a central role, as documented by Vicki Ruiz in *Cannery Women, Cannery Lives*, 83, 87, 92.

66. "During a cap-makers' strike, for example, married men got strike benefits amounting to $6.00 per week, but women, even those who supported widowed mothers and young siblings, got nothing." Alice Kessler-Harris, "Organizing the Unorganizable," 149. Kessler-Harris also offered historical examples of women's involvement in militant labor actions in the late nineteenth century and early twentieth century. "Organized Women Workers," 93–94.

67. Kessler Harris, "Organized Women Workers," 99.

68. In that same report, the Bureau of Labor Statistics concluded that "the leadership of most unions did not reflect the sexual composition of the

organizations' membership." Bureau of Labor Statistics, *Directory of National Unions and Employee Associations, 1975*, U.S. Department of Labor, 1977, 66, http://fraser.stlouisfed.org.

69. Tomlins, *State and the Unions*, 33.

70. National Labor Relations Act (NLRA), 29 U.S.C. §§ 151–69.

71. NLRA, Section 7, 13.

72. The duty of fair representation doctrine was to some extent an attempt to address discrimination by unions. The duty prohibits unions from "conduct toward a member of the collective bargaining unit that [is] arbitrary, discriminatory or in bad faith." Vaca v. Sipes, 386 U.S. 171, 190 (1967). It did not, however, require unions to admit workers regardless of race. Charlotte Garden and Nancy Leong, "'So Closely Intertwined': Labor and Racial Solidarity," *George Washington Law Review* 81 (2013): 1135, 1163.

73. Dubofsky, *State and Labor*, 130.

74. Tomlins, *State and the Unions*, 148.

75. Tomlins, *State and the Unions*, 252.

76. *See* discussion in chapter 8.

77. Jake Rosenfeld and Patrick Denice, "What Do Government Unions Do? Public Sector Unions and Nonunion Wages, 1977–2015," *Social Science Research* 78 (2019): 43. Summarizing the literature.

78. Abood v. Detroit Bd. of Ed., 431 U.S. 209, 222 (1977). Discussing the problem of free riders. *See also* Janus v. American Federation of States, 138 S.Ct. 2448 (2018).

79. Atleson, *Values and Assumptions*, 51. *See also* Chinn, *Recalibrating Reform*, 4, 14.

80. Atleson, *Values and Assumptions* 21–28; Pope, "Workers' Freedom of Association," 149. Pope also attributes the decline of unions in part to the "permanent replacement rule."

81. Atleson, *Values and Assumptions*, 6, 23. Discussing N.L.R.B. v. Mackay Radio & Telegraph Co. (1938).

82. Atleson notes that the right to hire permanent replacements erodes union power in another respect: the replacements are allowed to vote in any later attempt to decertify the union, making it more likely the union will lose its right of representation going forward. Atleson, *Values and Assumptions*, 27.

83. Atleson, *Values and Assumptions*, 33.

84. Elk Lumber Co., 91 NLRB 333 (1950); Atleson, *Values and Assumptions*, 50–51.

85. Atleson, *Values and Assumptions*, 51.

86. "The traditional judicial deference given to productivity, hierarchical control, and continued production has thus remained significant after, as well as before, the NLRA." Atleson, *Values and Assumptions*, 9, 33.

87. Atleson, *Values and Assumptions*, 59.

88. Atleson, *Values and Assumptions*, 59.

89. Atleson, *Values and Assumptions*, 102.

90. Atleson, *Values and Assumptions*, 102. In a more recent example, *Glacier Northwest v. Intern. Brotherhood of Teamsters Local 174*, the Supreme Court ruled that workers going on strike are required to take "reasonable precautions

to protect" the employer's property, and that failure to do so could make the union liable under state tort law. 143 S.Ct. 1404, 1415 (2023).

91. Based on Tomlins's report of 3.7 million union members and a nonfarm labor force of 32.15 million workers, estimated in Stanley Lebergott, "Labor Force, Employment, and Unemployment, 1929–39: Estimating Methods," Bureau of Labor Statistics, July 1948, https://www.bls.gov/opub/mlr/1948/article/labor-force-employment-and-unemployment-1929-39-estimating-methods.htm.

92. Paul Weiler, *Governing the Workplace: The Future of Labor and Employment* (Harvard University Press, 1990), 6.

93. Weiler, *Governing the Workplace*, 6. See, for example, Pamela N. Williams, "Historical Overview of the Fair Labor Standards Act," *Florida Coastal Law Review* 10 (2009): 675. Noting the role of the National Women's Trade Union League in organizing women between the 1900s and 1930 and that "male labor unions disapproved of the attention and offered limited support."

94. Michael Goldfield, *The Decline of Organized Labor in the United States* (University of Chicago Press, 1987), 134–36; Milkman, "Two Worlds," 66. Referencing the historical tendency among male union leadership to "believe that women were 'unorganizable.'"

95. Goldfield, *Decline of Organized Labor*, 134–36; Milkman, "Two Worlds," 77.

96. Milkman, "Two Worlds," 68–69.

97. Milkman, "Two Worlds," 78.

98. Garden and Leong, "'So Closely Intertwined,'" 1172.

99. Erin Hatton, *The Temp Economy: From Kelly Girls to Permatemps in Postwar America* (Temple University Press, 2011), 52. Summarizing these macroeconomic pressures.

100. Weiler, *Governing the Workplace*, 106. Francis Thomas Coleman Jr., *The Deunionizing Handbook*, 2nd ed. (Federal Publications, 1987). Attributing deunionization to "the changing nature of the workforce from blue collar to white collar." Goldfield, *Decline of Organized Labor*, 19, 109. Noting that unionization also "weaken[ed] even in those areas of traditional strength."

101. Weiler, *Governing the Workplace*, 107.

102. See, for example, Richard Freeman, "Contraction and Expansion: The Divergence of Private Sector and Public Sector Unionism in the United States," *Journal of Economic Perspectives* 2, no. 2 (1988): 70.

103. Figure 6 attempts to roughly estimate membership in employee associations between 1956 and 1966, using the proportional membership in employee organizations versus unions recorded between 1968 and 1978.

104. Joseph Slater, *Public Workers: Government Employee Unions, the Law and the State, 1900–1962* (ILR Press, 2004), 72, 92.

105. Slater, *Public Workers*, 71.

106. Prior to 1968, the BLS apparently did not gather data on membership in "employee associations"—which are similar and to some extent indistinguishable from unions—and only collected data on membership in national, rather than local unions. Bureau of Labor Statistics, *Directory of National Unions and Employee Associations, 1975*, iii, 66. Consequently, the often-quoted statistic that unionization nearly tripled from 10–12 percent in the 1950s to over

35 percent in the early 1970s almost certainly underestimates union membership in the 1950s and early 1960s. Richard B. Freeman, "Unionism Comes to the Public Sector," National Bureau of Economic Research, Working Paper No. 1452, 1984, 6, 7, https://www.nber.org/papers/w1452. *See, for example,* Goldfield, *Decline of Organized Labor,* 15; Freeman, "Contraction and Expansion," 63. I am grateful to Joseph Slater for sharing his insights on the history of employee associations and discussing the gaps in the BLS data.

107. Slater, *Public Workers,* 158–59, 184. Economists examining state variation in labor law protections for public-sector workers concluded that favorable labor laws were attributable to much higher rates of unionization. Freeman, *Unionism Comes to the Public Sector,* 3, 11, 68, 78. See also Henry S. Farber, "Union Membership in the United States: The Divergence Between the Public and Private Sectors," Working Paper 503, Princeton University, September 2005, 1, 14–15, 20.

108. Executive Order 10988 (1962); Slater, *Public Workers,* 190.

109. *See, for example,* Janus v. American Federation of State, County and Municipal Employees, 138 S.Ct. 2448 (2018).

110. The 2018 Janus decision, which prohibited public-sector unions from collecting dues from nonmembers on First Amendment grounds, does not yet appear to have had a substantial impact on public-sector union density. 138 S.Ct. at 2478.

111. Freeman, "Contraction and Expansion," 80. Citing various studies reaching the same conclusion as his own.

112. Freeman, "Contraction and Expansion," 80.

113. *See generally* Coleman, *Deunionizing Handbook,* n98. Offering advice to companies on how to decertify a union. Joel Rogers, *Institutional Aspects of Postwar U.S. Union Decline,* ed. Christopher Tomlins and Andrew King (Johns Hopkins University Press, 1992), 293; Freeman, "Contraction and Expansion," 80–81.

114. National Labor Relations Act §§ 7–8.

115. Freeman, "Contraction and Expansion," 79, 85; Farber, "Union Membership in the United States," 11, 12.

116. Starbucks ALJ Decision, 9–10.

117. Kate Gibson, "Starbucks and Workers United Agree to Resume Contract Negotiations," *CBS News,* February 27, 2024, https://www.cbsnews.com/news/starbucks-workers-united-union-nlrb/.

118. Starbucks Corp., NLRB Case No. 19-CA-322644 (filed 07/27/2023).

119. Gibson, "Starbucks and Workers United."

## CHAPTER 6. EQUAL OPPORTUNITY

1. Harry Hudson, *Working for Equality,* ed. Randall L. Patton (University of Georgia Press, 2015).

2. Hudson, *Working for Equality,* 38.

3. Randall Patton, *Lockheed, Atlanta, and the Struggle for Racial Integration* (University of Georgia Press, 2019), 62.

4. Patton, *Lockheed, Atlanta, and the Struggle,* 80.

5. Hudson, *Working for Equality*, 38.
6. Patton, *Lockheed, Atlanta, and the Struggle*, 62.
7. Patton, *Lockheed, Atlanta, and the Struggle*, 43. The inspector eventually had a crisis of conscience and recanted.
8. Patton, *Lockheed, Atlanta, and the Struggle*, 80.
9. Patton, *Lockheed, Atlanta, and the Struggle*, 55.
10. Patton, *Lockheed, Atlanta, and the Struggle*, 37.
11. Patton, *Lockheed, Atlanta, and the Struggle*, 73.
12. Hudson, *Working for Equality*, 103.
13. Patton, *Lockheed, Atlanta, and the Struggle*, 95.
14. Hudson, *Working for Equality*, 140, 171. Hudson received a minor promotion to "semi-senior buyer" sometime between 1968 and 1969. After eight years in purchasing, Hudson requested and received a promotion to "senior buyer." He would not be promoted beyond that position.
15. Hudson, *Working for Equality*, 103.
16. See discussion regarding Executive Order 11246 in note 22.
17. Patton, *Lockheed, Atlanta, and the Struggle*, 88, 94–95.
18. Frank Dobbin, *Inventing Equal Opportunity* (Princeton University Press, 2009), 15, 46–47.
19. Exec. Order 8022; Exec Order 9346; U.S. Equal Employment Opportunity Commission, *Legislative History of Titles VII and XI of Civil Rights Act of 1964* (U.S. Governmentt Printing Office, 1968), 2.
20. U.S. Equal Employment Opportunity Commission, *Legislative History*, 3.
21. Exec. Order No. 10308; Exec. Order 10479. "The PCGC, like its predecessors under Franklin Delano Roosevelt and Harry S. Truman, had no real enforcement power and had no objective standards or criteria by which to gauge compliance." Patton, *Lockheed, Atlanta, and the Struggle*, 58.
22. U.S. Equal Employment Opportunity Commission, *Legislative History*, 3; Dobbin, *Inventing Equal Opportunity*, 32–33. Lyndon Johnson's Executive Order 11246, established a federal agency, the Office of Federal Contract Compliance, to hold companies accountable for implementing their affirmative action plans. Executive Order 11246 was subsequently amended but remained in effect until rescinded by President Donald Trump in January 2025.
23. Patton, *Lockheed, Atlanta, and the Struggle*, 58.
24. Patton, *Lockheed, Atlanta, and the Struggle*, 70.
25. Patton, *Lockheed, Atlanta, and the Struggle*, 70.
26. Patton, *Lockheed, Atlanta, and the Struggle*, 75.
27. A. H. Raskin, "Negro Makes Job Gain in South Under Initial Drive and Lockheed," *New York Times*, June 18, 1961. The NAACP had also recently sued the company and the union for discrimination. Any Black worker applying to the company in 1961 would need to compete with thousands of predominantly white workers who had recently been laid off and had rights to reemployment under a collective bargaining agreement with the International Association of Machinists. And although the previously race-based unions had been merged, Black workers insisted on keeping their union representative, fearful that their interests and votes would be diluted. Patton, *Lockheed, Atlanta, and the Struggle*, 65. Offering a slightly different account.

28. Patton, *Lockheed, Atlanta, and the Struggle*, 58.
29. Dobbin, *Inventing Equal Opportunity*, 58.
30. Dobbin, *Inventing Equal Opportunity*, 57.
31. Peter Braestrup, "NAACP Fights Big Jet Contract," *New York Times*, April 7, 1961.
32. Patton, *Lockheed, Atlanta, and the Struggle*, 80. When Lockheed management invited a few Black supervisors and a mathematician to one of its monthly executive dinner meetings in 1961, it was the first time a Black person had "attended such a meeting and exchanged ideas with the company's top executives." Raskin, "Negro Makes Job Gain in South."
33. Braestrup, "NAACP Fights Big Jet Contract"; Patton, *Lockheed, Atlanta, and the Struggle*, 78.
34. Braestrup, "NAACP Fights Big Jet Contract."
35. Braestrup, "NAACP Fights Big Jet Contract."
36. Patton, *Lockheed, Atlanta, and the Struggle*, 2.
37. Patton, *Lockheed, Atlanta, and the Struggle*, 88.
38. Kevin Stainback and Donald Tomaskovic-Devey, *Documenting Desegregation: Racial and Gender Segregation in Private-Sector Employment Since the Civil Rights Act* (Russell Sage Foundation, 2012), 60.
39. See Classified advertisements, *New York Times*, January 1, 1966, 35(D), https://timesmachine.nytimes.com/timesmachine/1966/01/01/issue.html.
40. Patton, *Lockheed, Atlanta, and the Struggle*, 83. Quoting Eugene Mattison, the director of industrial relations at the Marietta plant.
41. Patton, *Lockheed, Atlanta, and the Struggle*, 89.
42. Raskin, "Job Gain in South."
43. Raskin, "Job Gain in South," 50. Quoting Harley.
44. Raskin, "Job Gain in South," 50.
45. Raskin, "Job Gain in South," 50.
46. Dobbin, *Inventing Equal Opportunity*, 46.
47. Dobbin, *Inventing Equal Opportunity*, 46.
48. Raskin, "Job Gain in South."
49. Raskin, "Job Gain in South." Even then, the response from Black applicants was initially tepid given Lockheed's track record. At a large Black high school in Atlanta, only one student filled out an application and took the qualifying test from the company, and only after a personal appeal by a representative from the Urban League.
50. Patton, *Lockheed, Atlanta, and the Struggle*, 108.
51. Patton, *Lockheed, Atlanta, and the Struggle*, 108, 166.
52. Patton, *Lockheed, Atlanta, and the Struggle*, 113, 123.
53. Patton, *Lockheed, Atlanta, and the Struggle*, 122.
54. Patton, *Lockheed, Atlanta, and the Struggle*, 107.
55. Patton, *Lockheed, Atlanta, and the Struggle*, 107.
56. Patton, *Lockheed, Atlanta, and the Struggle*, 107.
57. Patton, *Lockheed, Atlanta, and the Struggle*, 107, 109.
58. Patton, *Lockheed, Atlanta, and the Struggle*, 166.
59. Dobbin, *Inventing Equal Opportunity*, 78.

60. Dobbin, *Inventing Equal Opportunity*, 78. Quoting the Department of Labor in 2000, stating that the "current blueprint for affirmative action" had its "origins in Plans for Progress."

61. Pub. L. No. 88-253, 78 Stat. 241, Section 701, codified at 42 U.S.C. § 2000e.

62. 42 U.S.C. § 2000e-2 (Section 703).

63. 42 U.S.C. § 2000e-3 (Section 704).

64. Title VII of the Civil Rights Act of 1964, Pub. L. No. 88-352, § 706 (1964); 42 U.S.C.A. § 2000-e (et. seq).

65. David Oppenheimer, "The Story of Green v. McDonnell Douglas," in *Employment Discrimination Stories*, ed. Joel W. Friedman (West Academic, 2006); Francis Vaas, "Title VII: Legislative History," *Boston College Industrial and Commercial Law Review* 7 (1966): 432. *See also* Rebecca Zietlow, *Enforcing Equality: Congress, the Constitution and the Protection of Individual Rights* (New York University Press, 2006), 99. Noting the contributions of "civil rights activists dating back to the New Deal Era" including Black World War II veterans whose "jobs were taken away by returning white soldiers."

66. EEOC, *Legislative History*, 5–6.

67. EEOC, *Legislative History*, 6–7; Vaas, "Title VII," 431; Zietlow, *Enforcing Equality*, 103.

68. Public Law 88-38, codified at 29 U.S.C. § 206(d).

69. Oppenheimer, "Story of Green v. McDonnell Douglas," 20.

70. Robert Bird, "More Than a Congressional Joke: A Fresh Look at the Legislative History of Sex Discrimination of the 1964 Civil Rights Act," *William and Mary Journal of Women and Law* 3 (1997): 148.

71. Bird, "More Than a Congressional Joke," 149–50.

72. Bird, "More Than a Congressional Joke," 156.

73. Bird, "More Than a Congressional Joke," 158.

74. Bird, "More Than a Congressional Joke," 160.

75. Additional views on H.R. 7152, Pub. L. No. 88-352, 1964 U.S.C.C.A.N (2516) 29.

76. Title VII of the Civil Rights Act of 1964 § 703(h).

77. EEOC, *Legislative History*, 3, 7.

78. Title VII, § 703(h).

79. Vaas, "Title VII," 452.

80. Equal Employment Opportunity Act of 1972, Pub. L. No. 92-261 (1972).

81. Today, the law covers employers with fifteen or more workers. Title VII, § 701(b).

82. Raskin, "Negro Makes Job Gain in South."

83. Transcript of Oral Argument at 6, Griggs v. Duke Power, 401 U.S. 424 (1970). The labor department also had a white foreman.

84. Transcript of Oral Argument at 6 *Griggs*, 401 U.S. 424.

85. Transcript of Oral Argument at 8, *Griggs*, 401 U.S. 424.

86. Transcript of Oral Argument at 8, *Griggs*, 401 U.S. 424. Non–high school graduates were promoted at the same rate as high school graduates. Transcript of Oral Argument at 13, *Griggs*, 401 U.S. 424. About one-third of the workers at the plant had no high school diploma.

87. Transcript of Oral Argument at 7, *Griggs*, 401 U.S. 424.
88. Transcript of Oral Argument at 14, *Griggs*, 401 U.S. 424.
89. Transcript of Oral Argument at 20, *Griggs*, 401 U.S. 424.
90. Transcript of Oral Argument at 7, *Griggs*, 401 U.S. 424.
91. Transcript of Oral Argument at 10, *Griggs*, 401 U.S. 424.
92. Transcript of Oral Argument at 10, *Griggs*, 401 U.S. 424.
93. Transcript of Oral Argument at 16, *Griggs*, 401 U.S. 424.
94. Transcript of Oral Argument at 35, *Griggs*, 401 U.S. 424.
95. Transcript of Oral Argument at 35, *Griggs*, 401 U.S. 424.
96. Transcript of Oral Argument at 36, *Griggs*, 401 U.S. 424. It is not certain that Justice Marshall was leading this particular colloquy, as the old transcripts do not identify a particular justice. However, one of the counsel's answers in this series of questions addresses Justice Marshall by name, suggesting the colloquy came from him.
97. Griggs v. Duke Power, 401 U.S. 424, 430 (1971). The court reached this conclusion despite the language in the statute providing that "professionally developed ability test[s]" were permissible unless "designed intended or used" to discriminate. Title VII of the Civil Rights Act § 703(h).
98. *Griggs*, 401 U.S. at 431.
99. See Elizabeth Tippett, "Robbing a Barren Vault: The Implications of Dukes v. Wal-Mart for Cases Challenging Subjective Employment Practices," *Hofstra Labor and Employment Law Journal* 29 (Spring 2012): 453.
100. Sandra Sperino writes that "the McDonnell Douglas framework is now the most widely used method for establishing circumstantial evidence of discrimination in Title VII cases." Sperino, "Flying Without a Statutory Basis: Why McDonnell Douglas Is Not Justified by Any Statutory Construction Methodology," *Houston Law Review* 43, no. 3 (2006):756. Katie Eyer notes that "McDonnell Douglas is the thirteenth most cited Supreme Court case of all time—cited 58,073 times in subsequent cases" compared to only 3,400 citations for *Griggs*. Eyer "The Return of the Technical McDonnell Douglas Paradigm," *Washington Law Review* 94 (2019): 975; Charles Sullivan, "Circling Back to the Obvious: The Convergence of Traditional and Reverse Discrimination in Title VII Proof," *William & Mary Law Review* 46 (2004): 1034.
101. Transcript of Oral Argument at 20, McDonnell Douglas Corp v. Percy Green, 411 U.S. 792 (1973) (No. 72-490); Transcript of Oral Argument at 5, *McDonnell Douglas*, 411 U.S. 792.
102. Transcript of Oral Argument at 5, *McDonnell Douglas*, 411 U.S. 792.
103. Title VII of the Civil Rights Act of 1964 § 716.
104. Oppenheimer, "Story of Green v. McDonnell Douglas," 24.
105. Oppenheimer, "Story of Green v. McDonnell Douglas," 24.
106. Transcript of Oral Argument at 3, *McDonnell Douglas*, 411 U.S, 792.
107. Oppenheimer, "Story of Green v. McDonnell Douglas," 25.
108. *McDonnell Douglas*, 411 U.S. at 796.
109. *McDonnell Douglas*, 411 U.S. at 802–5.
110. *McDonnell Douglas*, 411 U.S. at 803.
111. McKennon v. Nashville Banner Publ'g, Co., 115 S.Ct. 879, 886 (1995). Limiting available damages if employer discovers policy violation after employee

has already been terminated. Diaz v. Eagle Produce P'ship, 521 F.3d 1201, 1206, 1208 (9th Cir. 2008). Employee properly terminated for operating a check cashing business for coworkers, which represented a "repeated violation of rules established in the Company Handbook." "[V]iolation of company policy [a] legitimate reason[s] for termination." Kiel v. Select Artificials, Inc., 169 F.3d 1131, 1135 (8th Cir. 1999). Smith v. Papp Clinic, P.A., 808 F.2d 1450, 1453 (11th Cir. 1987). Employee terminated for closing a lab thirty minutes early—in violation of company policy—when she had become drowsy because of medication and after consulting others, holding that jury instructions in related Section 1981 case properly stated that "if the employer fired an employee because it honestly believed that the employee had violated a company policy, even if it was mistaken in such belief, the discharge is not 'because of race.'"

112. Employer "offered a clear-cut, legitimate, nondiscriminatory reason for terminating Putman—he refused to obey a direct order of his supervisor after being warned in the Last Chance Agreement that such insubordination would result in his discharge." Putman v. Unity Health Sys., 348 F.3d 732, 737 (8th Cir. 2003). "Our cases have repeatedly held that insubordination and violation of company policy are legitimate reasons for termination." Kiel, 169 F.3d at 1135. Matima v. Celli, 228 F.3d 68, 79 (2nd Cir. 2000). Companies can terminate workers who complain about retaliation if termination is motivated by a desire to "preserve a workplace environment that is governed by rules, subject to a chain of command, free of commotion, and conducive to the work of the enterprise." Hochstadt v. Worcester Found. for Experimental Biology, 545 F.2d 222, 230 (1st Cir., 1976). Even when an employee complains about discrimination, "an employer remains entitled to loyalty and cooperativeness from employees." "Legitimate, nondiscriminatory reasons for the action taken by the employer may include, but are not limited to, insubordination on the part of the employee claiming discrimination." Hood v. Diamond Prods., Inc., 74 Ohio St.3d 298, 302 (1996). Fane v. Locke Reynolds, LLP, 480 F.3d 534, 541 (7th Cir. 2007). Affirming summary judgment against employee terminated for "rude behavior, insubordination, and not recognizing her own inappropriate behavior."

113. Sybrandt v. Home Depot, U.S.A., Inc., 560 F.3d 553, 559 (6th Cir. 2009). Summary judgment properly granted when "there is no genuine issue of material fact as to whether Home Depot held an honest belief that Sybradt had violated company policy."

114. *Sybrandt*, 560 F.3d at 559.

115. Patton, *Lockheed, Atlanta, and the Struggle*, 107, 109.

116. Stainback and Tomaskovic-Devey, *Documenting Desegregation*, 31.

117. Stainback and Tomaskovic-Devey, *Documenting Desegregation*, 30. Cf. Cynthia Estlund, *Working Together: How Workplace Bonds Strengthen a Diverse* Democracy (Oxford University Press, 2003), 126–27, 132–33. Arguing that workplaces are more integrated than other institutions and voluntary associations and an important source of cross-racial interaction.

118. Stainback and Tomaskovic-Devey, *Documenting Desegregation*, 31.

119. Stainback and Tomaskovic-Devey, *Documenting Desegregation*, 35.

120. Stainback and Tomaskovic-Devey, *Documenting Desegregation*, 36.

121. "Internal labor markets have been found to heighten both gender and ethnic inequality. Because internal labor markets allow the current labor force to make promotion decisions, this is not surprising." Stainback and Tomaskovic-Devey, *Documenting Desegregation*, 285.

122. Stainback and Tomaskovic-Devey, *Documenting Desegregation*, xxii.

123. Kimberle Crenshaw, "Mapping the Margins: Intersectionality, Identity Policies, and Violence Against Women of Color," *Stanford Law Review* 43 (1991): 1241.

124. Stainback and Tomaskovic-Devey, *Documenting Desegregation*, 31.

125. Stainback and Tomaskovic-Devey, *Documenting Desegregation*, 147, 168.

126. Stainback and Tomaskovic-Devey, *Documenting Desegregation*, 168.

## CHAPTER 7. HUMAN RESOURCES

1. Bostock v. Clayton County Bd. of Comm'rs, 140 S.Ct. 1731, 1742 (2020).

2. Price Waterhouse v. Hopkins, 490 U.S. 228 (1989); Glenn v. Brumby, 663 F.3d 1312 (11th Cir. 2011).

3. Evans v. Georgia Regional Hospital, 850 F.3d 1248, 1255 (11th Cir. 2017); Blum v. Gulf Oil Corp, 597 F.2d 936, 938 (5th Cir. 1979).

4. *Second Amended Complaint* at ¶¶ 17–18, Bostock v. Clayton Cnty. (N.D.Ga. 2016) (No. 1:16-CV-1460) 2016 WL 11586428 at *4–*5.

5. *Bostock, Second Amended Complaint* ¶ 20.

6. *Bostock, Second Amended Complaint* ¶ 23.

7. *Bostock*, 723 F. App'x 964, 964–65 (11th Cir. 2018) (per curiam).

8. *Bostock*, 140 S.Ct. at 1738.

9. *Bostock*, 140 S.Ct. at 1738.

10. Interview with Thomas Mew, July 18, 2023 (on file with author). Mr. Bostock was also represented by Edward Buckley.

11. Interview with Thomas Mew.

12. Interview with Thomas Mew.

13. Bostock v. Clayton County Bd. of Comm'rs, Case No. 1:16-CV-1460 (N.D. Ga. 2017), Order, July 20, 2017, 2017 WL 4456898, Bostock v. Clayton Cty. Bd. of Comm'rs, 723 F. App'x 964, 964–65 (11th Cir. 2018); *Bostock*, 140 S.Ct. at 1754; Bostock v. Clayton Cty. Bd. of Comm'rs, 819 Fed.Appx. 891 (11th Cir. 2020).

14. Interview with Thomas Mew.

15. Frank Dobbin. *Inventing Equal Opportunity* (Princeton University Press, 2009) 9, 44.

16. See chapter 5; Dobbin, *Inventing Equal Opportunity*, 107, figure 5.

17. Dobbin, *Inventing Equal Opportunity*, 76, 84, 201.

18. Dobbin, *Inventing Equal Opportunity*, 9, 168–69.

19. Lauren Edelman, *Working Law: Courts, Corporations, and Symbolic Civil Rights* (University of Chicago Press, 2016), 221–22; Frank Dobbin and Erin Kelly, "How to Stop Harassment: Professional Construction of Legal Compliance in Organization," *American Journal of Sociology* 112 (2007): 4.

20. Edelman, *Working Law*, 221–22; Dobbin and Kelly, "How to Stop Harassment," 4.

21. Dobbin, *Inventing Equal Opportunity*, 105–6.

22. Edelman, *Working Law*, 113–14.

23. Edelman, *Working Law*, 115, 117; Dobbin, *Inventing Equal Opportunity*, 95.

24. Dobbin, *Inventing Equal Opportunity*, 114–16, 121–22.

25. Laura Beth Nielson and Robert Nelson argue that internal complaint processes can serve as "evidence against the inference of discrimination, by redefining possible incidents of discrimination as 'misunderstandings'" and "may operate to deflect employees from pursuing their claims as a matter of rights." "Rights Realized—An Empirical Analysis of Employment Discrimination Litigation as a Claiming System," *Wisconsin Law Review* 2005, no. 2 (2005): 686.

26. Randall Patton, *Lockheed, Atlanta and the Struggle for Racial Integration* (University of Georgia, 2019), 114–18.

27. Randall Patton, *Lockheed*, 118.

28. Patton, *Lockheed*, 109. Quoting a Lockheed training manual.

29. Patton, *Lockheed*, 107, 184.

30. "In the 1970s, personnel managers realized that such reviews offered a way to respond to the federal government's equal employment imperative and insulate firms from lawsuits, as the use of standardized evaluations could provide proof that decisions had not been made for discriminatory reasons." Patton, *Lockheed*, 115–16.

31. Lauren Edelman, "Judicial Deference in the Modern State," in *The Legal Process and the Promise of Justice: Studies Inspired by the Work of Malcolm Feeley*, ed. Rosann Greenspan et al. (Cambridge University Press, 2019), 196, 201; Edelman, *Working Law*, 32.

32. Alexandra Kalev, Frank Dobbin, and Erin Kelly, "Best Practices or Best Guesses? Assessing the Efficacy of Corporate Affirmative Action and Diversity Policies," *American Sociological Review* 71 (2006): 603. See also Frank Dobbin and Alexandra Kalev, "Why Diversity Programs Fail," *Harvard Business Review* (July–August 2016): 4. Noting that "the positive effects of diversity training rarely last beyond a day or two, and a number of studies suggest that it can activate bias or spark a backlash."

33. Elizabeth Tippett, "Harassment Training: A Content Analysis," *Berkeley Journal of Employment & Labor Law* 39 (2018): 481, 494. Summarizing empirical evidence. Vicki Magley et al., "Changing Sexual Harassment Within Organizations via Training Interventions: Suggestions and Empirical Data," in *The Fulfilling Workplace: The Organization's Role in Achieving Individual and Organizational Health*, ed. Ronald Burke and Cary Cooper (Routledge 2013), 229; Equal Employment Opportunity Commission (EEOC), *Select Task Force on the Study of Harassment in the Workplace*, 2016, https://www.eeoc.gov/eeoc/task_force/harassment/report.cfm; and Frank Dobbin and Alexandra Kalev, "The Promise and Peril of Sexual Harassment Programs," *Proceedings of the National Academy of Sciences* 116, no. 25 (June 2019): 12258.

34. Alexandra Kalev, Frank Dobbin, and Erin Kelly, "Best Practices or Best Guesses? Assessing the Efficacy of Corporate Affirmative Action and Diversity Policies," *American Sociological Review* 71 (2006): 603.

35. Affirmative action programs tend to be confined to government contractors legally required to adopt such programs, and less than one quarter of mid-to-large employers had diversity staff or a task force. Kalev et al., "Best Practices or Best Guesses?," 603; Frank Dobbin et al., "You Can't Always Get What You Need: Organizational Determinants of Diversity Programs," *American Sociological Review* 76, no. 2 (2011): 392.

36. In the 1980s Jacoby observed that HR served as a "business partner" to management, which left "line managers free to do a mediocre job of managing employees. . . . The attitude of many line managers was 'Don't call us; we'll call you' and the phone never rang." Sanford Jacoby, *Employing Bureaucracy: Managers, Unions, and the Transformation of Work in the 20th Century*, rev. ed. (Lawrence Erlbaum Associates, 2004), 264.

37. Legal scholar Natasha Martin argues that supervisors are not solely responsible for employment decisions, noting that peers, subordinates, and even customers will contribute to performance reviews in workplaces that follow "360-degree reviews." "Immunity for Hire: How the Same-Actor Doctrine Sustains Discrimination in the Contemporary Workplace," *Connecticut Law Review* 40 (2008): 1144.

38. Activist Tarana Burke founded the movement in 2006, which exploded in 2017 following public revelations against mogul Harvey Weinstein and a viral tweet by actress Alyssa Milano.

39. Elizabeth Tippett, "The Legal Implications of the #MeToo Movement," *Minnesota Law Review* 103, no. 1 (November 2018): 232–36; Noam Scheiber and Julie Cresswell, "Sexual Harassment Cases Show the Ineffectiveness of Going to H.R.," *New York Times*, December 12, 2017, https://www.nytimes.com/2017/12/12/business/sexual-harassment-human-resources.html; Tovia Smith, "When It Comes to Sexual Harassment Claims, Whose Side Is HR Really On?," *NPR*, November 15, 2017, https://www.npr.org/2017/11/15/564032999/when-it-comes-to-sexual-harassment-claims-whose-side-is-hr-really-on.

40. Vicki Lovell et al., "More Than Raising the Floor: The Persistence of Gender Inequalities in the Low-Wage Labor Market," in *The Sex of Class: Women Transforming American Labor*, ed. Dorothy Sue Cobble (Cornell University Press, 2011).

41. Dobbin, *Inventing Equal Opportunity*, 44; 9, 168–69.

42. Kevin Stainback and Donald Tomaskovic-Devey, *Documenting Desegregation: Racial and Gender Segregation in Private-Sector Employment Since the Civil Rights Act* (Russell Sage Foundation, 2012), 35.

43. Bostock v. Clayton County Bd. of Comm'rs, Final Report and Recommendation, Case No. 1:16-CV-1460 (N.D. Ga, 2022) (Document 166), June 7, 2022, *5.

44. *Bostock*, Final Report and Recommendation, *5, 9–10.

45. *Bostock*, Final Report and Recommendation, *8–11.

46. Bostock v. Clayton County Bd. of Comm'rs, Deposition of Sabrina Crawford (Document 142-9), 28, Case No. 1:16-cv-1460 (March 21, 2022).

47. *Bostock*, Crawford Deposition, 27, 156–57; Bostock v. Clayton County Bd. of Comm'rs, Deposition of Gerald Bostock (Document 142-1), 172, Case No. 1:16-cv-1460 (March 21, 2022).

48. *Bostock*, Bostock Deposition, 210–15. Bostock informed Crawford and the board about his decision to sponsor the softball team. *Bostock*, Crawford Deposition, 28.
49. *Bostock*, Crawford Deposition, 27–29; Bostock Deposition, 110, 112.
50. *Bostock*, Teske Deposition, 275, 277 (Document 142-3).
51. *Bostock*, Final Report and Recommendation, 6.
52. *Bostock*, Final Report and Recommendation, 7.
53. *Bostock*, Teske Deposition, 160, 201; *Bostock*, Slay Deposition, 153, Exh. 17 (Document 142-4).
54. *Bostock*, John Johnson III Deposition (Document 142-6), 41–42, Case No. 1:16-cv-1460 (March 21, 2022); Bostock v. Clayton County Bd. of Comm'rs, Deposition of Colin Slay (Document 142-4), 69, Plaintiff's Exhibit 19, Case No. 1:16-cv-1460 (March 21, 2022).
55. *Bostock*, Johnson Deposition, 43.
56. *Bostock*, Teske Deposition, 201.
57. *Bostock*, Johnson Deposition, 186–87; *Bostock*, Teske Deposition, 162–64.
58. *Bostock*, Merritt Deposition, 3436, 100, Plaintiff's Exhibit 10; *Bostock*, Teske Deposition, 255–56.
59. *Bostock*, Merritt Deposition, 61, 123, Plaintiff's Exhibit 10; *Bostock*, Crawford Deposition, 85.
60. *Bostock*, Moore Deposition, 44–45; *Bostock*, Teske Deposition, 169, 171–72, 177–78.
61. *Bostock*, Johnson Deposition, 141.
62. *Bostock*, Johnson Deposition, 141, 251, 253; *Bostock*, Teske Deposition, 238.
63. *Bostock*, Teske Deposition, 44–45.
64. *Bostock*, Crawford Deposition, 39; *Bostock*, Teske Deposition, 59–60.
65. *Bostock*, Crawford Deposition, 85.
66. *Bostock*, Crawford Deposition, 40.
67. *Bostock*, Crawford Deposition, 40.
68. *Bostock*, Crawford Deposition, 43; *Bostock*, Teske Deposition, 72.
69. *Bostock*, Crawford Deposition, 43.
70. *Bostock*, Crawford Deposition, 43, 45–46. In his deposition, Teske denied slamming his hand on the desk or making "reference [to] the gay bar in that meeting." *Bostock*, Teske Deposition, 73.
71. *Bostock*, Teske Deposition, 145.
72. Bostock v. Clayton County Bd. of Comm'rs, Memorandum of Law in Support of Plaintiff's Motion for Summary Judgment (Document 127-1), 8–9, Case No. 1:16-cv-1460 (March 21, 2022).
73. *Bostock*, Plaintiff's Motion for Summary Judgment (Document 127-1), 9; *Bostock*, Teske Deposition, 175.
74. *Bostock*, Teske Deposition, 68, 101–2.
75. *Bostock*, Teske Deposition, 108–12.
76. Teske testified that the television news story was broadcast on Bostock's termination date. *Bostock*, Teske Deposition, 68–69, 107.
77. *Bostock*, Teske Deposition, 284, Plaintiff's Exh. 38; Bill Torpy, "The 'Villain' in Gay Workers Rights Case Has Plenty to Say," *Atlanta Journal Constitution*, June 17, 2020.

78. *Bostock*, Teske Deposition, 121, Plaintiff's Exhibit 46.

79. *Bostock*, Teske Deposition, 177–78, 181–82.

80. Bostock's termination letter cites specific Clayton County Civil Service Rules that he was alleged to have violated, which may suggest the county believed it needed to have a basis for the termination. Deposition of Colin Slay, 153, Exhibit 17 (Document 142-4).

81. *Bostock*, Merritt Deposition, 35, 36 ("But once we do our audit, it's very rare that we know what happens to the person."); *Bostock*, Moore Deposition, 8. One auditor testified that she was "sort of" surprised when Bostock was terminated because her concerns related primarily to "the accounting procedures." *Bostock*, Moore Deposition, 84.

82. Edelman, *Working Law*, 43.

83. Edelman, *Working Law*, 173. *See also* Doron Dorfman, "Suspicious Species," *University of Illinois Law Review* 2021 (2021): 1402. Applying Edelman's theory to the service dog context.

84. Faragher v. City of Boca Raton, 524 U.S. 775 (1998), Burlington Indus., Inc. v. Ellerth, 524 U.S. 742 (1998).

85. The defense does not apply if the employee suffered a tangible employment action, like a termination, a demotion, pay reduction, or the loss of a promotion. *Faragher*, 524 U.S. at 808.

86. *Faragher*, 524 U.S. at 793–94.

87. *Faragher*, 524 U.S. at 798–801, 807.

88. *Faragher*, 524 U.S. at 805.

89. *Faragher*, 524 U.S. at 807.

90. Tippett, "Legal Implications of the #MeToo Movement," 249–51.

91. *Bostock*, Teske Deposition, 42–43.

92. *Bostock*, Teske Deposition, 42–43.

93. McDonnell Douglas Corp. v. Green, 411 U.S. 792, 802 (1973); Texas Department of Community Affairs v. Burdine, 450 U.S. 248 (1981); St. Mary's Honor Center v. Hicks, 509 U.S. 510 (1981); Reeves v. Sanderson Plumbing Prod., Inc., 530 U.S. 133, 153–54 (2000).

94. *Bostock*, "Plaintiff's Response in Opposition to Defendant's Motion for Summary Judgment," 9-20 (Document 157) Case 1:16-cv-01460.

95. Price Waterhouse v. Hopkins, 490 U.S. 228, 235 (1989); Stephanie Bornstein, "Unifying Antidiscrimination Law Through Stereotype Theory," *Lewis & Clark Law Review* 20 (2016): 937.

96. *Bostock*, Memorandum of Law in Support of Plaintiff's Motion for Summary Judgment, 13–16 (Document 127-1), (March 21, 2022), Case No. 1:16-cv-01460; Bostock, *Final Report and Recommendation*, 52–53.

97. Desert Palace, Inc. v. Costa, 539 U.S. 90 (2003); Susan Bison-Rapp, "Of Motives and Maleness: A Critical View of Mixed Motive Doctrine in Title VII Sex Discrimination Cases," *Utah Law Review* 1995, no. 4 (1995): 1039.

98. Desert Palace, 539 U.S. 94–95.

99. Bostock, *Memorandum in Support of Plaintiff's Motion for Summary Judgment*, 22; Bostock, *Final Report and Recommendation*, 45.

100. Bostock, *Memorandum in Support of Plaintiff's Motion for Summary Judgment*, 23.

101. Bostock, *Final Report and Recommendation*, 39.
102. Bostock, *Final Report and Recommendation*, 48.
103. Katie Eyer has criticized lower courts for shoehorning cases into a *McDonnell Douglas* theory, denying plaintiffs opportunities to apply other forms of proof or directly prove that a decision was "because of" the plaintiff's protected category. "The Return of the Technical McDonnell Douglas Paradigm," *Washington Law Review* 94, no. 3 (2019): 981. Sperino further notes that "hybrid" claims that "draw from one or more of the current types of discrimination" can also be disadvantaged by existing forms of proof. Sperino, "Rethinking Discrimination Law," *Michigan Law Review* 110, no. 1 (2011): 90.
104. In a 2012 law review article, Lisa Durham Taylor noted the "real possibility of a pro-employee bent on the current Roberts Court." "The Pro-Employee Bent of the Roberts Court," *Tennessee Law Review* 79, no. 4 (Summer 2012): 803.
105. EEOC v. Abercrombie & Fitch Stores, Inc. 575 U.S. 768 (2015).
106. Young v. United Parcel Service, Inc., 575 U.S. 206 (2015); Bornstein, "Unifying Antidiscrimination Law," 948.
107. Terrence Cain, "Cause for Concern or Cause for Celebration? Did Bostock v. Clayton County Establish a New Mixed Motive Theory for Title VII Cases and Make It Easier for Plaintiffs to Prove Discrimination Claims?," *Seattle University Law Review* 45, no. 2 (Winter 2022): 517–19, 521.
108. Sperino, "Rethinking Discrimination Law," 95; Eyer, "Technical McDonnell Douglas," 979.
109. Sandra Sperino, "Disbelief Doctrines," *Berkeley Journal of Employment & Labor Law* 39, no. 1 (2018): 231; Eyer, "Return of Technical *McDonnell Douglas*," 978–79; Sandra Sperino and Suja Thomas, *Unequal: How America's Courts Undermine Discrimination Law* (Oxford University Press, 2017), 60, 66, 69, 73.
110. Proud v. Stone, 945 F.3d 796, 798 (4th Cir. 1991). Natasha Martin argues that the same-actor concept gained "a cult-like following by other circuits and their lower courts." "Immunity for Hire," 1127. Indeed, Quintanilla and Kaiser documented increased judicial reliance on the same-actor doctrine between 1990 and 2013. Victor Quintanilla and Cheryl Kaiser, "The Same-Actor inference of Nondiscrimination: Moral Credentialing and the Psychological and Legal Licensing of Bias," *California Law Review* 104 (2016): 43. See also Anna Laurie Bryant and Richard Bales, "Using the Same Act 'Inference' in Employment Discrimination Cases," *Utah Law Review* 1999 (1999): 255, 262; Sperino, "Disbelief Doctrines," 236; Eyer, :Return of Technical McDonnell Douglas," 979.
111. Kerri Lynn Stone, "Taking in Strays: A Critique of the Stray Comment Doctrine in Employment Discrimination Law," *Missouri Law Review* 77 (2012): 149; Sperino, "Disbelief Doctrines," 233; Sandra Sperino, "Evidentiary Inequality," *Boston University Law Review* 101 (2021): 2115; Jessica Clarke, "Explicit Bias," *Northwestern University Law Review* 113 (2018): 542. Bornstein notes that "application of the stray remarks doctrine has not been consistent, and a number of courts have signaled its lessening value." "Unifying Antidiscrimination Law," 957.

112. Sperino, "Disbelief Doctrines," 238; Sperino, "Evidentiary Inequality," 2115. Kearney characterized the doctrine as having been "dismantle[d]" after the Seventh Circuit declined to apply it. Robert Kearney, "Death of a Rule," *UC Davis Business Law Journal* 16 (2015): 4, 24.

113. "Judges . . . regularly admit employer evidence derived from a variety of documents, including past performance reviews." Sperino, "Evidentiary Inequality," 2107, 2134–35. In addition, "employers are allowed to introduce almost any kind of past misconduct, even if it is not the same conduct that the employer is using to support its reason for taking negative action against the plaintiff." "Evidentiary Inequality," 2147.

114. McKennon v. Nashville Banner Publishing Co., 513 U.S. 352, 360 (1995); Anne McGinley, "Reinventing Reality: The Impermissible Intrusion of After-Acquired Evidence in Title VII Litigation," *Connecticut Law Review* 26 (1993): 175–76. "This doctrine incentivizes employers to look for past employee misconduct, even if the misconduct would otherwise have remained undiscovered without the litigation." Sperino, "Evidentiary Inequality," 2148.

115. *See, for example*, Verniero v. Air Force Academy School Dist No. 20, 705 F.3d 388, 391 (10th Cir. 1983). Charles Sullivan noted in 2004 that "literally hundreds of cases recite some version of the slogan that courts do not sit as 'super-personnel departments" while others provide jury instructions not to "second-guess the employer." "Circling Back," 1116. In a 2017 book, Sperino and Thomas characterized the number of cases relying on the "super-personnel" concept to "thousands." A 2024 Westlaw search of federal cases for the keywords "super-personnel," "discrimination," and "Title VII" produced more than 5,000 cases. *See also* Sperino, "Disbelief Doctrines," 242; Eyer, "Return to Technical McDonnell Douglas," 980; Sperino and Thomas, *Unequal*, 78.

116. *Verniero*, 705 F.3d at 391; Sullivan, "Circling Back," 1116. "In the employment discrimination context, deference to employers' business judgment is salient." Martin, "Immunity for Hire," 1127.

117. Additional views on H.R. 7152, Pub. L. No. 88-352, 1964 U.S.C.C.A.N (2516) 29. *But see* Steelworkers v. Weber, 443 U.S. 193, 207 (1979). Quoting the reference to managerial prerogative in the legislative record to uphold an aggressive affirmative action plan bargained between the union and the employer.

118. Interview with Marina Multhaup, January 8, 2024 (on file with author).

119. Bostock, *Final Report and Recommendation*, 1.

120. Bostock, *Final Report and Recommendation*, 54.

121. Bostock, *Final Report and Recommendation* 56.

122. Associated Press, "Man Who Won Gay Rights Case at Supreme Court Agrees to Settlement," *NBC News*, November 7, 2022, https://apnews.com/article/us-supreme-court-lawsuits-discrimination-georgia-atlanta-dff346f4d8720a32773b07df27bc4206.

## CHAPTER 8. BENEFITS

1. William Fisher III, "Ideology and Imagery in the Law of Slavery," in *Slavery and the Law*, ed. Paul Finkelman (Madison House, 1997), 52; Eugene Genovese, *Roll, Jordan, Roll: The World the Slaves Made* (Vintage Books, 1976), 45.

Over time, historians have become increasingly skeptical toward the Southern claim of reciprocity. In the 1970s historian Eugene Genovese characterized slavery as based on "mutual obligations—duties, responsibilities, and ultimately even rights," which served to "morally justify a system of exploitation." Mark Tushnet, *The American Law of Slavery: 1810–1860* (Princeton University Press, 1981), 183–85. In the 1980s legal historian Mark Tushnet characterized slavery as a "totalistic relationship" that the South defined in opposition to the bourgeois capitalism in the North; cf. Ariela Gross, *Double Character: Slavery and Mastery in the Antebellum Southern Courtroom* (Princeton University Press, 2000), 101. More recently, historians such as Ariela Gross, Caitlin Rosenthal, and Edward Baptist have challenged conceptions of slavery as a precapitalist, relational system and have instead highlighted the capitalist dimension of slavery. See chapter 1, citations in notes 76–90.

2. Thomas R. R. Cobb, *Inquiry into Law of Negro Slavery in the United States of America: To Which Is Prefixed an Historical Sketch of Slavery* (Applewood Books, 1858), ccxvii–ccxviii.

3. Peter v. Hargrave, 46 Va. 12, 22 (5 Gratt) (S.C. Appeals, VA 1848).

4. Edward Baptist, *The Half Has Never Been Told: Slavery and the Making of American Capitalism* (Basic Books, 2014), 245, 246; Thomas D. Russell, "Slave Auctions on the Courthouse Steps: Court Sales of Slaves in Antebellum South Carolina," in *Slavery and the Law*, ed. Paul Finkelman (Madison House, 1997), 339.

5. James L. Watkins, *Production and Price of Cotton for One Hundred Years*, Miscellaneous Series, Bulletin No. 9 (U.S. Department of Agriculture Division of Statistics, 1895).

6. Baptist's calculations suggest enslaved workers picked an average of more than one hundred pounds of cotton per day in 1860. Baptist, *Half Has Never Been Told*, 127. In 1860 cotton prices in New York averaged 11 cents per pound. Watkins, "Production and Price of Cotton," 10. If we assume six days of picking in a week, that would represent more than six hundred pounds of cotton, or $66 worth of revenue in a week, equivalent to about $2,000 today. The U.S. Bureau of Labor Statistics CPI inflation calculator only dates back to 1913, but based on its inflation calculator, $66 would be about $2,100 in 2025 dollars. Bureau of Labor Statistics, "CPI Inflation Calculator," accessed April 28, 2025, https://www.bls.gov/data/inflation_calculator.htm?source=syndication.

7. Watkins, *Production and Price of Cotton*, 10. Watkins's figures showed production for the period from September 1860 to August 1861 of 4.86 million bales of hay, and the net weight of hay bales at 461 pounds, equivalent to 2.2 billion pounds. Baptist likewise cites a national cotton production figure of "almost 2 billion pounds" for 1859. *Half Has Never Been Told*, 386.

8. Keckley, *Behind the Scenes*, 20.

9. Keckley, *Behind the Scenes*, 45.

10. Juliet E. K. Walker, *History of Black Business in America: Capitalism, Race, Entrepreneurship* (University of North Carolina Press, 1998), 69; Keckley, *Behind the Scenes*, 22. The price was for both Keckley's freedom and that of her son. Judith Thurman, "Eye of the Needle," *New Yorker* 49 (March 29, 2021).

11. Keckley reported that the loans were repaid in a "short time" and did not specify the duration of the repayment. *Behind the Scenes*, 28.

12. Robert Steinfeld, *The Invention of Free Labor: The Employment Relation in English and American Law and Culture, 1350–1870* (University of North Carolina Press, 1991), 56–57.

13. Steinfeld, *Invention of Free Labor*, 36, 63; James Schmidt, *Free to Work: Labor Law, Emancipation and Reconstruction 1815–1880* (University of Georgia Press, 1998), 66.

14. Deepa Das Acevedo, "Unbundling Freedom in the Sharing Economy," *Southern California Law Review* 91 (2018): 799. "Employee status and the distinctions it requires are important today mainly because of modern social welfare legislation." Richard Carlson, "Why the Law Still Can't Tell an Employee When It Sees One and How It Ought to Stop Trying," *Berkeley Journal of Employment and Labor Law* 22 (2001): 301.

15. U.S. Department of Agriculture, Food and Nutrition Service, "SNAP Work Requirements," https://www.fns.usda.gov/snap/work-requirements. Erin Hatton, *Coerced: Work Under Threat of Punishment* (University of California Press, 2020), 47–51. Discussing workfare.

16. Gretchen Livingston and Deja Thomas, "Among 41 Countries, Only U.S. Lacks Paid Parental Leave," Pew Research Center, December 16, 2019, https://www.pewresearch.org/fact-tank/2019/12/16/u-s-lacks-mandated-paid-parental-leave/.

17. The Family and Medical Leave Act, Public Law 103-3, Section 101(2),(4).

18. Katherine Keisler-Starkey and Lisa Bunch, "Health Insurance Coverage in the United States: 2021," United States Census Bureau, September 13, 2022, https://www.census.gov/library/publications/2022/demo/p60-278.html.

19. Thomas D. Morris, *Southern Slavery and the Law 1619–1860* (University of North Carolina Press, 1996), 195; Judith Kellere Schafer, "'Details Are of a Most Revolting Character': Cruelty to Slaves as Seen in Appeals to the Supreme Court of Louisiana," in *Slavery and the Law*, ed. Paul Finkelman (Madison House, 1997), 241.

20. South Carolina Slave Code (1740), quoted in Kermit Hall, William Wiecek, and Paul Finkelman, *American Legal History: Cases and Materials* (Oxford University Press, 1991), 36.

21. Morris, *Southern Slavery and the Law*, 195; State v. Bowen, 34 S.C.L. 573 (1849).

22. Regarding the prohibition on testimony against white people, see Morris, *Southern Slavery and the Law*, 193; Fisher, "Ideology and Imagery in the Law of Slavery," 55; Schafer, "'Details Are of a Most Revolting Character,'" 247; Gross, *Double Character*, 68–69. Ariela Gross noted that courts sometimes found their way around the testimony ban where convenient—for example, by allowing white witnesses to refer to statements made by enslaved people. South Carolina offered an additional escape route for enslavers, who could defend the case by signing an "oath" that they had provided adequate support, absent "positive proof" to the contrary. South Carolina Slave Code § 38 (1740), quoted in Hall, Wiecek, and Finkelman, *American Legal History*, 40. Cf. State v. Morris no. 1293, 4 La. Ann. 177 (1849), quoted in Schafer, "'Details Are of a Most Revolting Character,'" 286. Oath does not serve as conclusive proof of innocence in case involving brutal murder of enslaved person.

23. Jenny Bourne Wahl, "Legal Constraints on Slave Masters: The Problem of Social Cost," *American Journal of Legal History* 41 (1997): 5. Economist Jenny Bourne Wahl argued that legal restrictions on "slaveholder cruelty" were an attempt to limit social costs that cruel slaveowners imposed on other white people in the community. Historian Ariela Gross also noted that poor treatment was often at issue in breach of warranty cases between buyers and sellers, in which one or the other party attributed a "defective" slave to poor living conditions. Gross, *Double Character*, 100.

24. Fairchild v. Bell, 2 Brev. 129 (S.C. 1807). Claim by bystander physician for cost of caring for an enslaved woman who was in chains, "almost naked, shockingly beaten." Dunbar v. Williams, 10 Johns. 249 (N.Y. 1813). *See* Livingston v. Dugan, 20 Mo. 102 (Mo. 1854). Claim to recover "money paid for medical attendance upon a slave." Emanuel v. Norcum, 7 How. Miss. 150, 154 (Miss. 1843). Estate administrator required to "procur[e] medicines and medical aid." Bomford v. Grimes, 17 Ark. 567 (Ark. 1856). Recovery of medical expenses from enslaver's estate. *See* Mitchell v. Talapaloosa County, 30 Ala. 130, 131 (Al. 1857). Claim by state to recoup expenses of medical care for imprisoned enslaved person from enslaver's estate, noting the master "cannot absolve himself . . . to provide for his necessary wants in sickness, whilst confined under a criminal charge." Morgan v. Mitchell, 3 Mart. N.S. 576 (La. 479). Sheriff claims reimbursement from enslaver for "clothing, sustenance, and medical aid" of imprisoned slaves.

25. Hogan v. Carr, 6 Ala. 471, 472 (Al. 1844). Echols v. Dodd, 20 Tex. 190, 194 (Text. 1857). Enslaved person beaten to death while leased to work at a sawmill, slaveowner sued. Trotter v. McCall, 4 Cushm. 410, 413 (Miss. High Ct. of Errors & App. 1853). Beardslee v. Perry, 14 Mo. 88 (Mo. 1851). Alleging that hirer "took such bad and negligent care of him. . . . [S]aid slave became totally lost to them." Carney v. Walden, 16 B. Mon. 388 (Ky. 1855). Claim by enslaver against hirer for "death of the slave by inhuman treatment."

26. Caitlin Rosenthal, "Slavery's Scientific Management: Masters and Managers," in *Slavery's Capitalism*, ed. Sven Beckert and Seth Rockman (University of Pennsylvania, 2016), 79.

27. Rosenthal, "Slavery's Scientific Management," 70.

28. Rosenthal, "Slavery's Scientific Management," 72.

29. Rosenthal, "Slavery's Scientific Management," 72.

30. Rosenthal, "Slavery's Scientific Management," 73–74.

31. Edward Baptist, "Toward a Political Economy of Slave Labor," in *Slavery's Capitalism*, ed. Sven Beckert and Seth Rockman (University of Pennsylvania, 2016), 38. *See* Mark M. Smith, *Mastered by the Clock: Time, Slavery and Freedom in the American South* (University of North Carolina Press, 1997), 123; Baptist, "Toward a Political Economy of Slave Labor," 38.

32. Walker, *History of Black Business in America*, 69.

33. Walker, *History of Black Business in America*, 69.

34. Walker, *History of Black Business in America*, 69.

35. Brewer v. Harris, 5 Gratt. 285, 286 (S.C. of Appeal, VA, Oct. 1848).

36. Ruth Schwartz Cowan, *A Social History of Technology* (Oxford University Press, 1997), 87.

37. Cowan, *Social History of Technology*, 87.

38. Daniel Nelson, *Frederick W. Taylor and the Rise of Scientific Management* (University of Wisconsin Press, 1980), 4. "[T]he building of coal towns began in the 1880s, peaked in the 1920s, and virtually ended with the coming of the Great Depression." Crandall Shifflett, *Coal Towns: Life, Work, and Culture in Company Towns of Southern Appalachia 1880–1960* (University of Tennessee Press, 1991), 32. Andrew Herod, "Social Engineering Through Spatial Engineering," in *Company Towns in the Americas: Landscape, Power, and Working-Class Communities*, ed. Oliver Dininus and Angela Vergara (University of Georgia Press, 2011), 33.

39. Stuart Brandes, *American Welfare Capitalism: 1880–1940* (University of Chicago Press,1970), 43.

40. Shifflett *Coal Towns*, 35; Linda Carlson, *Company Towns of the Pacific Northwest* (University of Washington Press, 2003), 9.

41. Carlson, *Company Towns*, 11. Brandes, *American Welfare Capitalism*, 44. Company-provided housing, according to historian Stuart Brandes, was a means of attracting "superior" workers in tight labor markets through reduced rent. Brandes, *American Welfare Capitalism*, 45.Company stores with inflated prices and easy credit subsidized corporate losses on housing. See Carlson, *Company Towns*, 27. Sanford Jacoby, *Modern Manors: Welfare Capitalism Since the New Deal* (Princeton University Press, 1997), 14.

42. Cowan, *Social History of Technology*, 85.

43. Carlson, *Company Towns*, 27.

44. Brandes, *American Welfare Capitalism*, 48. See Carlson, *Company Towns*, 11.

45. Brandes, *American Welfare Capitalism*, 50. See Christopher W. Post, "The Making of the Federal Company Town," in *Company Towns in the Americas: Landscape, Power, and Working-Class Communities*, ed. Oliver Dininus and Angela Vergara (University of Georgia Press, 2011), 124; Herod, "Social Engineering," 28. Andrew Herod noted that fencing "allows those in charge to regulate spaces more easily by controlling what and who enters and exists them."

46. Carlson, *Company Towns*, 29.

47. Geographer Andrew Herod argues that the physical layout and arrangement of company towns reflect the embedded power structures: "Build environments reflect accumulative conditions at the time they were initially constructed" and thus "have the effect of ossifying in the landscape the social relations extant at the time of their creation." Herod, "Social Engineering," 29.

48. Carlson, *Company Towns*, 29.

49. Carlson, *Company Towns*, 29.

50. Brandes, *American Welfare Capitalism*, 56.

51. Brandes, *American Welfare Capitalism*, 56.

52. *See* Nelson, *Rise of Scientific Management*, 16. Quoting the National Civic Federation, defining "welfare work" as "special considerations for physical comfort whoever labor is performed; opportunities for recreation; educational advantages; and the providing of suitable sanitary homes, . . . plans for saving and lending money, and provisions of insurance and pensions."

53. Brandes, *American Welfare Capitalism*, 28; Gerald Zahavi, *Workers, Managers, and Welfare Capitalism* (University of Illinois Press, 1988), 37.

54. Brandes, *American Welfare Capitalism*, 28.

55. Nelson, *Rise of Scientific Management*, 17. Historian Daniel Nelson attributes welfare capitalism to William Tolman and his book, published in 1900: William Tolman, *Industrial Betterment* (Social Service Press, 1900), 3. However, Tolman's book described various corporate initiatives already underway, drawing most of his examples from the National Cash Register Company. See Lena Harvey Tracy, *How My Heart Sang: The Story of Pioneer Industrial Welfare Work* (Richard R. Smith, 1950), 139. NCR's programs began in 1894. Samuel Crowther, *John H. Patterson: Pioneer in Industrial Welfare* (Garden City Publishing, 1924), 190, 196–197; Stanley Allyn, *My Half Century with NCR* (McGraw-Hill, 1967), 33.

56. Allyn, *My Half Century with NCR*, 34.

57. Jacoby, *Modern Manors*, 15.

58. Tolman, *Industrial Betterment*, 4.

59. Herod, "Social Engineering," 33.

60. Tracy, *How My Heart Sang*, 144.

61. Nelson, *Rise of Scientific Management*, 16–17.

62. See discussion in chapter 5.

63. Sanford Jacoby. *Employing Bureaucracy: Managers, Unions, and the Transformation of Work in the 20th Century*, rev. ed. (Lawrence Erlbaum Associates, 2004), 47, 58.

64. Martha Banta, *Taylored Lives* (University of Chicago Press, 1993), 113. Following Tracy's departure, NCR would become an early innovator in routinized personnel practices. In the early 1900s the company "creat[ed] a centralized system of hiring and firing" and "codifying rules and grievance procedures." Jacoby, *Employing Bureaucracy*, 68.

65. Nelson, *Rise of Scientific Management*, 19. Jacoby, *Employing Bureaucracy*, 68. Noting that Lena Harvey Tracy "had little say in employment matters and exercised no control over the company's foremen."

66. "The anti-union overtones of welfare were clear and definite. . . . [T]he spurt in welfare programs during the 1920s was in part a response to the gains made by organized labor during World War I. Another indicator is the fact that welfare work was often directed at skilled employees—those who seemed most susceptible to the troublesome pleas of union organizers." Brandes, *American Welfare Capitalism*, 32. Tracy, *How My Heart Sang*, 138. Prior to instituting the welfare programs, the NCR factory had been "set afire three times," and "there had been a succession of strikes and lockouts."

67. See chapter 5.

68. Unions represented conflict between worker and employer, argues labor historian Jean-Christien Vinel in *The Employee: A Political History* (University of Pennsylvania Press, 2013). Industrial welfare was more consistent with an alternate labor ideology that Vinel characterizes as "an American social order premised on a harmony of interests" where "the relationship between 'employer an employee' was mutually beneficial." Vinel, *Employee*, 26-27.

69. Tracy, *How My Heart Sang*, 163.

70. Nelson claims that Tracy was "dismissed" by the president. Nelson, *Rise of Scientific Management*, 18. However, in her autobiography Tracy claims that

NCR offered to cover her living expenses during the lockout, but she declined the offer and moved in with her brother, later accepting employment with a church. Tracy, *How My Heart Sang*, 169, 171.

71. Stephen Meyer III, *The Five Dollar Day: Labor Management and Social Control in the Ford Motor Company, 1908–1921* (State University of New York Press, 1981), 109. The $5 per day wage was worth about $136 in today's dollars, or $17 an hour for an eight-hour day.

72. Meyer, *Five Dollar Day*, 114.

73. Meyer, *Five Dollar Day*, 111.

74. Brandes, *American Welfare Capitalism*, 88–89.

75. Meyer, *Five Dollar Day*, 133, 141.

76. Meyer, *Five Dollar Day*, 155.

77. Meyer, *Five Dollar Day*, 156.

78. Meyer, *Five Dollar Day*, 156.

79. Meyer, *Five Dollar Day*, 145.

80. Meyer, *Five Dollar Day*, 147.

81. Brandes, *American Welfare Capitalism*, 89.

82. No such dependent requirement applied to men. Meyer, *Five Dollar Day*, 117.

83. Meyer, *Five Dollar Day*, 116.

84. Meyer, *Five Dollar Day*, 113.

85. Jacoby, *Modern Manors*, 5. Arguing that welfare capitalism "did not die in the 1930s but instead went underground . . . where it would reshape itself."

86. Wayback Machine, "Do It Without Dues," captured January 27, 2021, https://web.archive.org/web/20210329213754/https://www.doitwithoutdues.com.

87. Wayback Machine, "Do It Without Dues." The text associated with the asterisk said, "applies to regular full time employees."

88. Wayback Machine, "Do It Without Dues."

89. Wayback Machine, "10 Union Facts & FAQs," https://web.archive.org/web/20210225195546/https://www.doitwithoutdues.com/joining-a-union, captured Feb. 25, 2021.

90. Wayback Machine, "10 Union Facts & FAQs."

91. Wayback Machine, "What Really Happens in a Union Negotiation?," https://web.archive.org/web/20210225195552/https://www.doitwithoutdues.com/union-negotiations, captured February 25, 2021.

92. Interview with Charlotte Garden, May 6, 2021 (on file with author).

93. Scheiber, "Union Vote at Amazon Warehouse."

94. Jacoby, *Modern Manors*, 24. Observing that "benefit plans" in the 1920s "contained various incentives to increase employee stability and loyalty" through eligibility conditions based on tenure.

95. Bureau of Labor Statistics, "Employee Benefits Survey: Paid Sick Leave, Paid Vacation, and Consolidated Leave Plan Provisions in the United States, December 2022," April 2023, https://www.bls.gov/ebs/notices/2023/paid-sick-leave-paid-vacation-and-consolidated-leave-plan-provisions-in-the-united-states-december-2022.htm.

96. N.Y. Labor Law § 196.

97. See "The State of Paid Sick Time in the U.S. in 2023," The American Progress Institute, January 5, 2023, https://www.americanprogress.org/article/the-state-of-paid-sick-time-in-the-u-s-in-2023/.

98. The Family and Medical Leave Act ("FMLA"), Public Law 103-3, Section 101(4).

99. FMLA, § 101(2).

100. "Walmart 2023 Associate Benefits Book: Summary Plan Descriptions," Walmart, May 1, 2023, https://one.walmart.com/content/uswire/en_us/me/link-page/benefitsbook.html.

101. Brooks Pierce, "Compensation Inequality," *Quarterly Journal of Economics* 116, no. 4 (2001): 1493.

102. ("Nonrequired benefits are virtually zero in the lowest decile." Pierce, "Compensation Inequality," 1500).

103. Pierce, "Compensation Inequality," 1520. *See also* Mindy Marks, "Minimum Wages, Employer-Provided Health Insurance, and the Non-Discrimination Law," *Industrial Relations* 50 (2011): 241, 260. Low-wage workers are disproportionately likely to lose their employer-sponsored health insurance following an increase in the minimum wage.

104. Data from the Bureau of Labor Statistics indicate that only 60 percent of workers in the lowest quartile of wage earners sign up for medical benefits when they are offered, compared to 85 percent of those in the highest quartile. For retirement benefits, only 52 percent of low-wage earners enrolled in the benefit when offered, compared to 89 percent for the highest earners. Bureau of Labor Statistics, "March 2022 Employee Benefits in the United States," data file, accessed April 28, 2025, https://www.bls.gov/ebs/publications/zip/employee-benefits-in-the-united-states-march-2022.zip.

105. Jennifer Tolbert and Patrick Drake, "Key Facts About the Uninsured Population," Kaiser Family Foundation, December 19, 2022, https://www.kff.org/uninsured/issue-brief/key-facts-about-the-uninsured-population/.

106. Crowther, *John H. Patterson*, 206.

107. "Employer Health Benefits, 2020 Annual Survey," Kaiser Family Foundation, 2020, 12, https://www.kff.org/health-costs/report/2020-employer-health-benefits-survey/.

108. Steven Goldberg, Maren Fragala, and Jay Wohlgemuth, "Self-Insured Employer Health Benefits Strategy Established a Negative Cost Trend While Improving Performance," *Population Health Management* 22 (2019): 548. "Employer Health Benefits, 2020 Annual Survey," 163. Self-insured firms will fund their own health-care plans and then will sometimes cap their liability through stoploss insurance coverage. *See* "Employer Health Benefits, 2020 Annual Survey," 170.

## CHAPTER 9. LEFT BEHIND

1. Interview with Dominic Oliveira, March 15, 2024 (on file with author). One of Oliveira's lawyers, Hillary Schwab, recalled that during the six years she

represented him and his fellow plaintiffs in litigation, they rarely met in person because he was "always driving." Interview with Hillary Schwab, January 21, 2021 (on file with author). Attorney Theodore Boutros, who argued the case on behalf of New Prime, was also interviewed in connection with this book project. We spoke generally about the legal principles at issue in the case but not the specific factual allegations regarding New Prime's drivers. The author's attempts to contact the company's media relations team regarding the specific statements in this chapter received no response.

2. Interview with Oliveira.

3. Jennifer Cheeseman Day and Andrew W. Hait, "America Keeps on Truckin': Number of Truckers at All-Time High," *United States Census Bureau*, June 6, 2019, https://www.census.gov/library/stories/2019/06/america-keeps-on-trucking.html.

4. Brief for Petitioner at *28, New Prime, Inc. v. Oliveira, Case No. 17-340, Supreme Court of the United States, filed May 14, 2018.

5. Interview with Dominic Oliveira.

6. Interview with Dominic Oliveira.

7. During the apprenticeship, they would not be paid beyond $200 a week for food (which they would later have to repay through a paycheck deduction). Brief for Respondent at 6. Oliveira v. New Prime, Inc., 857 F.3d 7 (1st Cir. 2017). Appeals court ruling. Defendant New Prime, Inc.'s Opposition to Plaintiff's Motion for Collective Action Certification Pursuant to 29 U.S.C. § 216(B) and Class Certification on Missouri State Law Claims pursuant to Fed. R. Civ. P. 23, (Exhibit A), Oliveira v. New Prime Inc. (No. 1:15-cv-10603-PBS) (D. Mass. 2019), Filed November 6, 2019 (Document 206-1).

8. Plaintiff's Motion for Collective Action Certification, Oliveira v. New Prime, Docket No. 1:15-cv-10603 (filed Oct. 16, 2019) (D.Mass. 2019), Exhibit 11 ("Training Program Contract"); Defendant's Opposition to Plaintiff's Motion for Collective Action Certification at Exhibit A. Testimony by New Prime representative that "a driver needs to complete the one full year or the full amount is due." Exhibit to Plaintiff's Motion for Certification (Document 199-1).

9. Motion for Collective Action Certification at *6.

10. Although Jennifer Bennett of Public Justice P.C. represented Oliveira at oral argument, he was primarily represented by Hillary Schwab at Fair Work P.C. in Boston and Andrew Schmidt at Andrew Schmidt Law PLLC at other stages in the litigation.

11. Interview with Jennifer Bennett, September 1, 2021 (on file with author).

12. Interview with Dominic Oliveira.

13. Brief for Respondent in Opposition to Cert. at *4, Oliveira v. New Prime.

14. Plaintiff's Motion for Collective Action Certification, Oliveira v. New Prime (No. 1:15-cv-10603) (D. Mass. 2015), 4, Exhibits 5, 19, 20 (hereinafter "Motion for Collective Action Certification"). The plaintiffs alleged that "the individuals who own Prime also own several related companies, including ... Success Leasing," the entity that leased a truck to Oliveira and others. Oliveira then leased the truck back to New Prime in a separate contract.

15. Oliveira v. New Prime, Memorandum & Order, 141 F.Supp.3d 125, 128 (D.Mass. 2015).

16. Interview with Dominic Oliveira.
17. Interview with Dominic Oliveira.
18. Interview with Dominic Oliveira.
19. Oliveira v. New Prime Inc., "Plaintiffs' Corrected Assented-to Motion for Preliminary Settlement Approval," Case No. 1:15-cv-10603 (July 23, 2020), 2020 WL 10572981.
20. Arbitration is a private dispute resolution process in which a third-party arbitrator, rather than a judge, decides the case. Arbitration cases are not filed in court. Many arbitration provisions include a class and collective action waiver, which prevents workers from filing any joint claims in arbitration or in court. This forces workers to bring claims on an individual basis.
21. New Prime v. Oliveira, 139 S.Ct. 532 (2019).
22. At issue were a few words in the 1925 Federal Arbitration Act, which rendered any agreement to arbitrate enforceable according to its terms. The statute included an exclusion for any "contracts of employment of seamen, railroad employees, or any other class of workers engaged in foreign or interstate commerce." 9 U.S.C. § 1. If Oliveira's contract would have been considered a "contract of employment" as a "worker engaged in . . . interstate commerce" as those terms were understood in 1925, he and his fellow drivers would not be forced to arbitrate.
23. New Prime v. Oliveira, 139 S.Ct. 532, 539 (2019).
24. *Oliveira*, 139 S. Ct at 539.
25. *Oliveira*, 139 S. Ct at 539–40; *see* Amici Curiae Supporting Respondent, New Prime Inc. v. Oliveira, 139 S. Ct 532 (July 25, 2018).
26. *Oliveira*, 139 S. Ct at 541.
27. MBO Partners, "The Independent by Choice Movement: Authentic and Intentional, State of Independence in America 2024," accessed March 10, 2025, https://www.mbopartners.com/state-of-independence/.
28. MBO Partners, "Independent by Choice Movement."
29. MBO Partners, "Independent by Choice Movement."." Rani Molla, "More Americans Are Taking Jobs Without Employer Benefits Like Health Care or Paid Vacation," *Vox*, September 3, 2021. "According to survey-based research, the majority of drivers for labor platforms Uber and Lyft . . . [prefer] independent contractor status." Veena Dubal, "An Uber Ambivalence," in *Beyond the Algorithm: Qualitative Insights for Gig Work Regulation*, ed. Deepa Das Acevado (Cambridge University Press, 2020), 35. Dubal, "An Uber Ambivalence," 45. Qualitative research conducted by Duval suggested that roughly half of the 214 drivers she surveyed preferred employee status.
30. MBO Partners, "Independent by Choice Movement"; Dubal, "Uber Ambivalence," 45. Dubal's study of 214 Uber drivers suggested that 58 percent "worked as a ride-hail driver as their only job," while others combined it with other work.
31. David Weil, *The Fissured Workplace: Why Work Became So Bad for So Many and What Can be Done to Improve It* (Harvard University Press, 2017): 3–4.
32. Weil, *Fissured Workplace*, 122–58.
33. Weil, *Fissured Workplace*, 99–121.

34. Although subcontractors can be sued, they tend to be undercapitalized, making it difficult to collect on legal judgments.

35. Weil, *Fissured Workplace*, 10. *See also* Erin Hatton, *The Temp Economy: From Kelly Girls to Permatemps in Postwar America* (Temple University Press, 2011), 2. Arguing that "the temp industry provides American employers with convenient, reliable tools to turn 'good' jobs into 'bad' ones (and bad jobs into worse ones)."

36. Jonathan F. Harris, "Consumer Law as Work Law," *California Law Review* 112 (2024): 105, 112–13.

37. Harris, "Consumer Law," 104. Attorney Hillary Schwab reported that in some of her cases involving the trucking industry, they have proceeded under "alternate theories," arguing that company practices constituted consumer protection violations if workers were properly classified as independent contractors, and wage and hour violations if the workers were misclassified. Interview with Hillary Schwab.

38. Harris, "Consumer Law," 103.

39. Harris, "Consumer Law," 107.

40. Lisa Gansky, *The Mesh: Why the Future of Business Is Sharing* (Portfolio Penguin, 2010).

41. Gansky, *Mesh*, 15–18.

42. Ruth Berins Collier, Veena Dubal, and Christopher Carter, "The Regulation of Labor Platforms: The Politics of the Uber Economy," *Berkeley Roundtable on the International Economy*, March 1, 2017, 4, https://brie.berkeley.edu/publications/regulation-labor-platforms-politics-uber-economy.

43. Rasier, LLC, "Technology Services Agreement," 2015, https://www.documentcloud.org/documents/2645988-RASIER-Technology-Services-Agreement-December-10.

44. Julia Tomassetti, "Algorithmic Management," in *Beyond the Algorithm: Qualitative Insights for Gig Work Regulation*, ed. Deepa Das Acevado (Cambridge University Press, 2020), 139.

45. Tomassetti, "Algorithmic Management," 139.

46. See Mohamed v. Uber Techs., 115 F. Supp. 3d 1024 (N.D. Cal. 2015); Rasier, LLC, "Technology Services Agreement."

47. Elizabeth Tippett, "Employee Classification," in *Cambridge Handbook on Regulating the Sharing Economy*, ed. Nestor Davidson, Michele Finck, and John Infranca (Cambridge University Press, 2018).

48. Rebecca Smith and Maya Pinto, "Rewriting the Rules," in *Beyond the Algorithm: Qualitative Insights for Gig Work Regulation*, ed. Deepa Das Acevado (Cambridge University Press, 2020), 192.

49. See Charlotte Alexander and Elizabeth Tippett, "The Hacking of Employment Law," *Missouri Law Review* 82 (2017): 980–81; Noah D. Zatz, "Does Work Have a Future If the Labor Market Does Not?," 91 *Chicago-Kent Law Review* 91 (2016): 1086; Veena Dubal, "Wage Slave or Entrepreneur? Contesting the Dualism of Legal Worker Identities," *California Law Review* 101 (2017): 65; Keith Cunningham-Parmeter, "From Amazon to Uber: Defining Employment in the Modern Economy," *Boston University Law Review* 96 (2016): 1684; Valerio De Stefano, "The Rise of the 'Just-in-Time Workforce':

On-Demand Work, Crowdwork, and Labor Protection in the 'Gig-Economy,'" *Comparative Labor Law and Policy Journal* 37 (2016): 481; Charlotte Garden, "Disrupting Work Law: Arbitration in the Gig Economy," *University of Chicago Legal Forum* 205 (2017): 206; Benjamin Means and Joseph A. Seiner, "Navigating the Uber Economy," *University of California Davis Law Review* 49 (2016): 1529–30; Brishen Rogers, "Employment Rights in the Platform Economy: Getting Back to Basics," *Harvard Law and Policy Review* 10 (2016): 480; Miriam A. Cherry, "Beyond Misclassification: The Digital Transformation of Work," *Comparative Labor Law and Policy Journal* 37 (2016): 597.

50. Michael B. Farrell, "Cab Drivers Irate as Ban Against Livery App Reversed," *Boston Globe*, August 17, 2012, https://www.boston.com/news/technology/2012/08/17/cab-drivers-irate-as-ban-against-livery-app-reversed/.

51. See Matthew Yglesias, "When Is a Taxi Not a Taxi?," *Slate*, December 15, 2011, https://slate.com/technology/2011/12/uber-car-service-exposing-the-idiocy-of-american-city-taxi-regulations.html; Alexander and Tippett, "Hacking of Employment Law," 977–82. Discussing the concept of a "regulatory hack."

52. Smith and Pinto, "Rewriting the Rules," 204; Deepa Das Acevedo, "The Rise and Scope of Gig Work Regulation," in *Beyond the Algorithm: Qualitative Insights for Gig Work Regulation*, ed. Deepa Das Acevado (Cambridge University Press, 2020); California Assembly Bill 5; Dynamex Operations W. v. Superior Court, 416 P.3d 1 (Cal. 2018).

53. State of California v. Uber Tecs., Inc., Lyft Inc., (No. CGC-20-584402) Complaint for Injunctive Relief, Restitution, and Penalties (May 5, 2020).

54. California Proposition 22.

55. California Proposition 22.

56. Miriam Cherry, "Dispatch—United States: 'Proposition 22: A Vote on Gig Worker Status in California,'" *Comparative Labor Law and Policy Journal* (forthcoming): *6.

57. Dubal, "Wage Slave," 68.

58. Dubal, "Uber Ambivalence," 46.

59. Dubal, "Uber Ambivalence," 35.

60. Dubal, "Uber Ambivalence," 41.

61. Dubal, "Uber Ambivalence," 45.

62. Dubal, "Uber Ambivalence," 48.

63. Dubal, "Uber Ambivalence," 49.

64. Dubal, "Uber Ambivalence," 49.

65. Molla, "More Americans Are Taking Jobs."

66. Judy Fudge and Rosemary Owens, introduction to *Precarious Work, Women and the New Economy: The Challenge to Legal Norms*, ed. Judy Fudge and Rosemary Owens (Hart Publishing, 2006): 12.

67. Fudge and Owens, introduction, 12.

68. Fudge and Owens, introduction, 12.

69. *Oliveira*, 139 S.Ct. at 539.

70. "[T]he first generation of mine labor was noted for its tendency to farm in the spring, summer, and fall and mine coal in the winter." Crandall Shiflett, *Coal Towns: Life, Work, and Culture in Company Towns of Southern Appalachia, 1880–1960* (University of Tennessee Press, 1994), 9.

71. Juliet E. K. Walker, *History of Black Business in America: Capitalism, Race, Entrepreneurship*, 1st ed. (University of North Carolina Press, 1998).

72. Eric Foner, *Free Soil, Free Labor, Free Men: The Ideology of the Republican Party Before the Civil War* (Oxford University Press, 1995), 16–18; Jean-Christian Vinel, *The Employee: A Political History* (University of Pennsylvania, 2013), 28. Discussing free labor ideology in the late nineteenth century.

73. See Rebecca Zietlow, *The Forgotten Emancipator: James Mitchell Ashley and the Ideological Origins of Reconstruction* (Cambridge University Press 2018), 44–45.

74. D. A. Ballam, "Exploding the Original Myth Regarding Employment-at-Will: The True Origins of the Doctrine," *Berkeley Journal of Employment and Labor Law* 17 (1996): 99.

75. Foner, *Free Soil, Free Labor*, 77.

76. Foner, *Free Soil, Free Labor*, 32.

77. Foner, *Free Soil, Free Labor*, xxiv.

78. Foner, *Free Soil, Free Labor*, xix.

79. Foner, *Free Soil, Free Labor*, 13, 31.

80. The "ideology of free contract ... represented employment as a relationship whose design was arrived at in a process of mutual bargaining sufficiently free of power disparities that the employee might reasonably be held responsible for the consequences of her own decision to enter." Christopher Tomlins, "Law and Power in the Employment Relationship," in *Labor Law in America*, ed. Christopher Tomlins and Andrew King (Johns Hopkins University Press, 1992), 88.

81. John Fabian Witt, *The Accidental Republic: Crippled Workingmen, Destitute Widows, and the Remaking of American Law* (Harvard University Press, 2004), 5.

82. McKinsey & Company, "For Mothers in the Workplace, a Year (and Counting) Like No Other," May 5, 2021, https://www.mckinsey.com/featured-insights/diversity-and-inclusion/for-mothers-in-the-workplace-a-year-and-counting-like-no-other.

83. Misty L. Heggeness, Jason Fields, Yazmin A. García Trejo, and Anthony Schulzetenberg, "Tracking Job Losses for Mothers of School-Age Children During a Health Crisis," U.S. Census Bureau, *Moms, Work and the Pandemic* (blog), March 3, 2021, https://www.census.gov/library/stories/2021/03/moms-work-and-the-pandemic.html.

84. Pew Research Center, "Wealth Gaps Across Racial and Ethnic Groups," December 4, 2023, https://www.pewresearch.org/race-ethnicity/2023/12/04/wealth-gaps-across-racial-and-ethnic-groups/.

85. *See* Vicky Lovell et al., "More Than Raising the Floor: The Persistence of Gender Inequalities in the Low-Wage Labor Market," in *The Sex of Class: Women Transforming American Labor* ed. Dorothy Sue Cobble (Cornell University Press, 2011), 42.

86. Lovell et al., "More than Raising the Floor," 42.

87. Interview with Dominic Oliveira.

88. Interview with Dominic Oliveira.

89. Interview with Dominic Oliveira.

90. Kavanaugh's confirmation hearings were ongoing during the Supreme Court hearing for Oliveira's case, so only eight justices presided over the case.

91. Oliveira v. New Prime Inc., Plaintiffs' Corrected Assented-to Motion for Preliminary Settlement Approval, Case No. 1:15-cv-10603 (July 23, 2020) (D.Mass. 2020), 2020 WL 10572981. The actual amount of the settlement will depend on the number of class members who file a claim.

92. Final Settlement Approval Order and Separate and Final Judgment, Oliveira v. New Prime, (No. 1:15-cv-10603-PBS), January 26, 2021 (Document 289).

93. Interview with Dominic Oliveira.

## CHAPTER 10. POLICY INTERVENTIONS

1. "Program Statistics," Centers for Medicare and Medicaid Services, accessed February 28, 2022, https://www.cms.gov/Research-Statistics-Data-and-Systems/Statistics-Trends-and-Reports/CMSProgramStatistics/.

2. "February 2023 Medicaid & CHIP Enrollment Data Highlights," Medicaid.gov, accessed June 8, 2023, https://www.medicaid.gov/medicaid/program-information/medicaid-and-chip-enrollment-data/report-highlights/index.html; "Trends in the U.S. Uninsured Population, 2010–2020," Assistant Secretary for Planning and Evaluation, February 11, 2021, https://aspe.hhs.gov/system/files/pdf/265041/trends-in-the-us-uninsured.pdf; "New HHS Data Show More Americans Than Ever Have Health Coverage Through the Affordable Care Act," Health and Human Services, June 5, 2021, https://www.cms.gov/newsroom/press-releases/new-hhs-data-show-more-americans-ever-have-health-coverage-through-affordable-care-act .

3. "Employer Health Benefits, 2020 Annual Survey," Kaiser Family Foundation, October 8, 2020, 6, https://www.kff.org/health-costs/report/2020-employer-health-benefits-survey/.

4. *See also* "Despite the protection of HIPAA for pre-existing conditions, an employee who has insurance with a certain level of coverage for a specific condition . . . may nevertheless lose that level of coverage . . . because the new employers' health plan does not cover that condition." "Tax Expenditures for Health Care," Joint Committee on Taxation, July 31, 2008, 11, https://www.finance.senate.gov/imo/media/doc/073108ektest.pdf. Economists also documented the obvious phenomenon that losing a job was associated with losing health insurance. Melissa Thomasson, "The Importance of Group Coverage: How Tax Policy Shaped U.S. Health Insurance," NBER Working Paper Series, 7543, 2003, 3. Citing Jonathan Gruber and Brigitte C. Madrian, "Employment Separation and Health Insurance Coverage." *Journal of Public Economics* 66 (1997): 349–82.

5. "Present Law and Analysis," Joint Committee on Taxation, March 6, 2006, JCX-12-06, 17.

6. "Tax Expenditures for Health Care," 11, 12.

7. Evan McMorris-Santoro and Johana Bhuiyan, "How Obamacare Drives the Sharing Economy," *BuzzfeedNews*, October 14, 2014, https://www.buzzfeednews.com/article/evanmcsan/how-obamacare-drives-the-sharing-economy.

8. McMorris-Santoro and Bhuiyan, "How Obamacare Drives."

9. The Medicaid expansion required states to opt in, and some states declined to do so. *See* "Status of State Medicaid Expansion Decisions: Interactive Map," Kaiser Family Foundation, May 24, 2023, https://www.kff.org/medicaid/issue-brief/status-of-state-medicaid-expansion-decisions-interactive-map/.

10. McMorris-Santoro and Johana Bhuiyan, "How Obamacare Drives."

11. McMorris-Santoro and Johana Bhuiyan, "How Obamacare Drives."

12. Johana Bhuiyan and Ben Smith, "Uber CEO: Obamacare Has Been 'Huge' for Business," *BuzzfeedNews*, November 15, 2014, https://www.buzzfeednews.com/article/johanabhuiyan/ubercare.

13. "Employer Shared Responsibility Provisions," Internal Revenue Service, accessed February 28, 2022, https://www.irs.gov/affordable-care-act/employers/employer-shared-responsibility-provisions. The first thirty workers were excluded from the penalty.

14. See chapter 8, table 1.

15. Thomas Buchmueller et al., "Effect of the Affordable Care Act on Racial and Ethnic Disparities in Health Insurance Coverage," *American Journal of Public Health* (August 2016): 1416–21.

16. The tax penalty was set at $2,000 per employee. Jonathan Gruber, "The Impacts of the Affordable Care Act: How Reasonable Are the Projections?," NBER Working Paper 17168 June 2011, 15; "Employer Health Benefits, 2020 Annual Survey."

17. "Present Law and Analysis," 21.

18. Kaiser Family Foundation, "2024 Employer Health Benefits Survey," October 9, 2024, https://www.kff.org/report-section/ehbs-2024-section-1-cost-of-health-insurance/.

19. The tax would have imposed a 40 percent excise tax on expensive health plans that cost $10,200 for individuals or $27,500 for families. "Present Law and Analysis," 21.

20. Christopher Howard, *The Hidden Welfare State* (Princeton University Press, 1997).

21. Most tax experts consider tax breaks to be equivalent to direct government spending. "[M]any people are unfamiliar with the term tax expenditures and are unaware of their magnitude.... [I]t may seem strange to equate the failure to collect taxes with government spending, yet most public finance experts consider tax expenditures to be conceptually equivalent to direct spending". Howard, *Hidden Welfare State*, 3. In this view, spending a dollar is equivalent to failing to collect a tax dollar that otherwise would have been owed. It's an "expenditure" in the sense that the government "spent" tax dollars by leaving them in private hands to use for the purpose designated in the tax code.

22. "Tax Expenditures for Health Care," 5.

23. Tax expenditures are regressive, meaning they disproportionately benefit the richest Americans, since they are in higher tax brackets. Leonard Burman, Christopher Geissler, and Eric Toder, "How Big are Total Individual Income Tax Expenditures, and Who Benefits from Them?," *American Economic Review* 98, no. 2 (2008): 83. "[T]he argument that the exclusion . . . for employer-provided health care is unfair because it is regressive is somewhat incomplete, in that the asserted unfairness of the exclusion follows directly from the tax rate structure

being progressive." "Tax Expenditures for Health Care," 14. "[R]elative to a flat credit, a deduction for health insurance expenditures is regressive, providing the largest tax break for the most well off employed person." Jonathan Gruber and Michael Lettau, "How Elastic Is the Firms' Demand for Health Insurance?," *Journal of Public Economics* 88 (2004): 1274. An assessment by the Joint Committee on Taxation found that the tax exclusion for health care saved those in lower-income brackets between $600 and $3,000 per year, while those earning $100,000 or more saved between $4,000 and $5,000. "Tax Expenditures for Health Care," 5. Another study estimated that the health-care-related tax expenditures represented 0.5 percent of after-tax income for the bottom quintile of workers, 3.8 percent for middle-income workers, and 4.7 percent for the top earners. Burman et al., "How Big Are . . . Expenditures," 82.

24. As the Joint Committee on Taxation noted in a 2006 report to the Senate, there is "no limit on amount excludable" from taxes on "contributions to health plan for the taxpayer, spouse and dependents." "Present Law and Analysis," 3.

25. *Estimates of Federal Tax Expenditures for Fiscal Years 2024–2028*, December 11, 2024, Joint Committee on Taxation, 31, https://www.jct.gov/getattachment/765709fb-9a4b-430a-8f9e-4d342ec97f7e/x-48-24.pdf. "The exclusion for employer-provided health care . . . has consistently been one of the three largest tax expenditure items/". "Present Law and Analysis," 10.

26. "Tax Expenditures . . . 2020–2024," 33.

27. Jonathan Gruber, "The Tax Exclusion for Employer-Sponsored Health Insurance," 64, no. 2 *National Tax Journal* (2011): 511.

28. "Details About Baseline Projections for Selected Programs: Medicare," Congressional Budget Office, March 2020) https://www.cbo.gov/data/baseline-projections-selected-programs#10; "Details About Baseline Projections for Selected Programs: Medicaid," Congressional Budget Office, March 2020, https://www.cbo.gov/data/baseline-projections-selected-programs#10.

29. "Employer Health Benefits, 2020 Annual Survey," 9.

30. "Key Facts About the Uninsured Population," Kaiser Family Foundation, December 19, 2022, https://www.kff.org/uninsured/issue-brief/key-facts-about-the-uninsured-population/; Irene Papanicolas, Liana Woskie, and Ashish Jha, "Health Care Spending in the United States and Other High-Income Countries," *Journal of the American Medical Association* 319, no. 10 (2018): 1024, 1025, 1028.

31. The fractured American health-care system imposes the greatest cost of any industrialized nation yet produces worse health outcomes than its industrialized peers, particularly for people of color and low-income Americans. Vickie Shavers and Brenda Shavers, "Racism and Health Inequity Among Americans," *Journal of the American Medical Association* 98, no. 3 (2006): 386.

32. U.S. Department of Labor, "Unemployment Insurance Relief During COVID-19 Outbreak," https://www.dol.gov/coronavirus/unemployment-insurance; Pub. L. No. 116-136, 116th Congress ("CARES Act") § 2102(a)(3)(a)(ii)(II).

33. See discussion in Deborah A. Widiss, "Privatizing Family Leave Policy: Assessing the New Opt-in Insurance Model," *Seton Hall Law Review* 53, no. 5 (2023): 1543–76.

34. Widiss, "Privatizing Family Leave Policy."

35. Cal. Govt Code § 12945.2.

36. Pregnancy Discrimination Act, 42 U.S.C. § 2000(e)(k); Pregnant Workers Fairness Act, H.R. 1065 (17th Congress, 2021–2022).

37. *See, for example*, Paul Weiler, "Promises to Keep: Securing Workers' Rights to Self-Organization Under the NLRA," *Harvard Law Review*. 96 (1983): 1769; Cynthia Estlund, *Regoverning the Workplace: From Self-Regulation to Co-Regulation* (Yale University Press, 2010), 32.

38. See discussion in chapter 5.

39. Protecting the Right to Organize Act, H.R. 842. Bill shortening time period for holding elections, extending NLRA coverage to independent contractors, and other reforms. Employee Free Choice Act of 2016, H.R. 5000. Bill would have replaced elections with a card check program.

40. Jeffrey Hirsch and Joseph Seiner describe a similar informal setup at Volkswagon known as a "community engagement program," in which "groups that VW has certified as representing 15 percent or 30 percent of employees" meet with the company to discuss "workplace issues" such as shift assignments and compensation for temporary employees. "A Modern Union for the Modern Economy," *Fordham Law Review* 86, no. 4 (2018): 1754–55. These groups may later obtain "minority union" status, whereby they can "represen[t] and negotiat[e] contracts" for member employees. "Modern Union," 1755. Hirsch and Seiner note, however, that "union-lite" arrangements are legally fraught under existing law, because employee participation groups risk running afoul of the NLRA's prohibition on "company unions." "Modern Union," 1759. *See also* Joseph Seiner, "Workplace Power," *Boston College Law Review* 65 (2024):94.

41. Michael Harper, Samuel Estreicher, and Joan Flynn, *Labor Law: Cases Materials and Problems*, 6th ed. (Wolters Kluwer, 2007), 246–47.

42. *See* Charlotte Garden, "The Seattle Solution: Collective Bargaining by For-Hire Drivers & Prospects for Pro-Labor Federalism," *Harvard Law & Policy Review Online* 12 (2017): 4; Sanjukta Paul, "Uber as For-Profit Hiring Hall: A Price-Fixing Paradox and its Implications," *Berkeley Journal of Employment & Labor Law* 34, no. 2 (2017): 236. Paul argues that Uber drivers should be able to organize because Uber could be considered to engage in a form of price-fixing with respect to labor. Ruth Berins Collier, Veena Dubal, and Christopher Carter, "The Regulation of Labor Platforms: The Politics of the Uber Economy," *Berkeley Roundtable on the International Economy*, March 1, 2017, 15–16, https://brie.berkeley.edu/publications/regulation-labor-platforms-politics-uber-economy; Elizabeth J. Kennedy, "Employed by an Algorithm: Labor Rights in the On-Demand Economy," *Seattle University Law Review* 40, no. 3 (2017): 1000–1001.

43. Hirsch and Seiner, "Modern Union," 1750.

44. Hirsch and Seiner, "Modern Union," 1746.

45. Hirsch and Seiner, "Modern Union," 1765.

46. *See* Garden, "Seattle Solution," 2.

47. Heidi Groover, "Lengthy Legal Fight over Seattle's Uber Union Comes to an End," *Seattle Times*, April 13, 2020, https://www.seattletimes.com/seattle-news/transportation/lengthy-legal-fight-over-seattles-uber-unionization-law-comes-to-an-end/.

48. Paul, "Uber as Hiring Hall," 233.
49. Paul, "Uber as Hiring Hall," 261.
50. Frank Dobbin, *Inventing Equal Opportunity* (Princeton University Prees, 2009): 42.
51. Lauren Edelman, *Working Law: Courts, Corporations, and Symbolic Civil Rights* (University of Chicago Press, 2016), 173–74, 186–88.
52. 29 U.SC. § 201.
53. Or. Rev. Stat. § 652.220.
54. Cal. SB-358.
55. Kevin Stainback and Donald Tomaskovic-Devey, *Documenting Desegregation: Racial and Gender Segregation in Private-Sector Employment Since the Civil Rights Act* (Russell Sage Foundation, 2012): 36.
56. Joanna L. Grossman, "The First Bite Is Free: Employer Liability for Sexual Harassment," *Pittsburgh Law Review* 61 (2000): 733.
57. National Labor Relations Act, § 8(a)(2).
58. National Center for Employee Ownership, "A Statistical Snapshot of ESOPs: Company and Participant Numbers, and Industry Distribution," accessed April 29, 2025, https://www.esop.org/infographics/statistical-snapshot-esops.php. *See also* Douglas Kruse et al., "Shared Capitalism in the U.S. Economy: Prevalence, Characteristics, and Employee Views of Financial Participation in Enterprises," NBER Working Paper Series, 2008, http://nber.org/papers/w14225. Estimating that "about 5% of employees are part of ESOPs." This figure does not include employees who receive equity through stock options. For a detailed account of employee equity through stock options, see Joseph Blasi et al., *In the Company of Owners: The Truth About Stock Options (and Why Every Employee Should Have Them)* (Basic Books, 2003), 79–87. Kruse et al.'s 2008 analysis of all forms of employee stock ownership found that "roughly one-fifth of employees report owning some company stock." "Shared Capitalism," 12.
59. *See* Steven Arsenault, "Fiduciary Duties of ESOP Trustees Under ERISA in Tender Offers: The Impact of Herman v. NationsBank Trust Company and a Proposal for Reform," *University of Pennsylvania Journal of Labor and Employment Law* 3, no. 1 (Fall 2000): 91. Employee cooperatives are distinct from employee stock ownership plans: "[I]n a true worker co-op, each worker has one share of ownership and one vote, creating property ownership and formal decision-making power for all." Ariana Levinson, "Union Co-ops and the Revival of Labor Law," *Cardozo Journal of Conflict Resolution* 19, no. 3 (Spring 2018): 457. Ariana Levinson and Chad Eisenback, "Cooperative Ownership and the Fair Labor Standards Act," *Michigan State Law Review* 2021, no.1 (2021): 85.
60. Levinson, "Union Co-ops," 457; Susan Gary, "The Oregon Stewardship Trust: A New Type of Purpose Trust That Enables Steward-Ownership of a Business," *University of Cincinnati Law Review* 88, no. 3 (2020): 725, 728–29.
61. Internal Revenue Code §§ 404(a)(9) (employee stock ownership plan), § 404(k) (employee stock ownership plan), § 1042 (employee cooperatives and employee stock ownership plan), and § 415(c)(6) (employee stock ownership plan); 29 U.S.C. Subchapter T ("cooperatives and their patrons"). Lee T. Polk, "Miscellaneous Fiduciary Issues—ESOPs," *ERISA Practice and Litigation* 1 (August 2023 update): § 3:43. Citing applicable provisions of the tax code.

62. Michael Murphy, "The ESOP at Thirty: A Democratic Perspective," *Willamette Law Review* 41 (2005): 665.

63. Polk, "ESOPs," § 3:43; Arsenault, "Fiduciary Duties of ESOP Trustees," 88, 92–94; Henry C. Blackiston III et al., "ESOPs: What They Are and How They Work," *Business Lawyer (ABA)* 45, no. 1 (1989–1990): 88.

64. Hamza Shad et al., "Ownership Trends in Private Equity: 2024," *Carta*, September 10, 2024, https://carta.com/data/ownership-trends-private-equity-2024/; Ernest O'Boyle, "Employee Ownership and Firm Performance: A Meta-analysis," *Human Resource Management Journal*, no. 26 (2016): 439. Meta-analysis from multiple countries finding a small increase in firm performance based on employee ownership. Sarah Jenkins and Wil Chivers, "Can Cooperatives/Employee-Owned Businesses Improve 'Bad' Jobs? Evaluating Job Quality in Three Low-Paid Sectors," *British Journal of Industrial Relations* 60 (2022): 512.

65. Nancy Wiefek and Nathan Nicholson, "S Corporation ESOPs and Retirement Security," National Center for Employee Ownership, December 2018, https://www.nceo.org/assets/pdf/articles/NCEO-S-ESOPs-Retirement-Dec-2018.pdf; Steven Freeman, "Effects of ESOP Adoption and Employee Ownership: Thirty Years of Research and Experience," University of Pennsylvania Organizational Dynamics Working Papers, January 4, 2007, 6.

66. National Center for Employee Ownership, "Research on Employee Ownership," accessed April 29, 2025, https://www.nceo.org/employee-ownership-data/academic-research. Co-ops can also be a vehicle for employees to purchase a company or branch from owners intending to dissolve the company or shutter the location. Levinson, "Union Co-ops," 459.

67. John Logue and Jacquelyn Yates, *The Real World of Employee Ownership* (ILR Press, 2001), 72–73. Employee ownership does not preclude unionization, although as Ariana Levinson observes, it does raise some challenges in the context of employee co-ops. Levinson, "Union Co-ops," 468.

68. Daniel Souleles, "Another Workplace Is Possible: Learning to Own and Changing Subjectivities in American Employee Owned Companies," *Critique of Anthropology* 40, no. 1 (2020): 30, 32.

69. The tax code imposes a five- or seven-year limit on vesting schedules, depending on the percentage vested each year. 29 U.S.C. § 411(a)(2); Blackiston et al., "ESOPs," 89.

70. Murphy, "ESOP at Thirty," 663. Noting that ESOPs are not diversified investments. But see Wiefek and Nicholson, "ESOPs and Retirement Security," 4. Study of ESOPs finding that almost all of the ESOP companies surveyed had "at least one other retirement plan in addition to the ESOP."

71. Wiefek and Nicholson, "ESOPs and Retirement Security," 4. Evidence that ESOP employees have far more retirement savings overall than comparators. Freeman, "Effects of ESOP Adoption," 6. Review of literature suggests "that company stock appears to come on top of, and not in place of, other compensation."

72. Internal Revenue Code, § 401(a)(4). Blackiston et al., "ESOPs," 88–89.

73. Polk, "ESOPs," § 3:43. Observing that "[b]ecause lawsuits can be initiated by private parties as well as the government, the risk of a titanic legal

battle in corporate transactions involving ESOPs is ever present." Herman v. NationsBank Trust Co., 126 F.3d at 1361. Summarizing ERISA fiduciary rules in the context of an ESOP.

74. In 2024 the Department of Labor launched an "Employee Ownership Initiative," which will "provide education, outreach, and training" as well as technical assistance regarding employee ownership. Anca Voinea, "US Department of Labor Launches Employee Ownership Initiative," *Co-op News*, September 6, 2024, https://www.thenews.coop/us-department-of-labour-launches-employee-ownership-initiative/.

75. Oregon amended its trust law in 2019 to create an exception to the rule against perpetuities for purpose trusts. Or. Rev. Stat. §130.193. Susan Gary explains that purpose trusts authorize "the people actively involved in a business control[ling] the business," management is permitted to "focus on the business's purposes and not just business," and "returns are . . . shared by stakeholders." Gary, "Oregon Stewardship Trust," 707. The state of Colorado has an Employee Ownership Office, which provides "training, support, education, and consulting for businesses considering employee ownership structures." See Colorado Office of Economic Development & International Trade, "Colorado Employee Ownership Office," accessed April 29, 2025, https://oedit.colorado.gov/colorado-employee-ownership-office ().

76. Susan Gary, "The Changing Landscape of Business Succession: How and Why Purpose Trusts Matter," *Ohio State Business Law Journal* 18 (2023): 48.

77. Gary, "Changing Landscape," 48.

78. Thomas Craemer, "Estimating Slavery Reparations: Present Value Comparisons of Historical Multigenerational Reparations Policies," *Social Science Quarterly* 96 (2015): 649.

79. Craemer, "Estimating Slavery Reparations," 649.

80. The size of the racial wealth gap as of 2016 varies greatly depending on whether median household net worth versus average net worth is used for the calculation. The racial gap according to median household net worth is $154,000, compared to $791,700 based on average net worth, because the average figure for white households is heavily "influenced by very rich families." Kriston McIntosh, Emily Moss, Ryan Nunn, and Jay Shambaugh, "Examining the Black-White Wealth Gap," Brookings, February 27, 2020, https://www.brookings.edu/blog/up-front/2020/02/27/examining-the-black-white-wealth-gap/.

81. Eric Posner and Adrian Vermeule, "Reparations for Slavery and Other Historical Injustices," *Columbia Law Review* 103, no. 3 (2003): 695–96; Alfred Brophy, "Reconsidering Reparations," *Indiana Law Journal* 81, nbo. 3 (2006): 816.

82. William Darity Jr. and Dania Frank, "Political Economy of Ending Racism," in *Redress for Historical Injustices in the United States: On Reparations for Slavery, Jim Crow, and their Legacies*, ed. Michael T. Martin amd Marilyn Yaquinto (Duke University Press, 2007), 252. Darity and Frank recommend making eligibility for reparations contingent upon (1) "provid[ing] reasonable documentation that they had at least one ancestor who was enslaved in the United States, and (2) . . . demonstrat[ing] that at least ten years prior to the onset of the reparations program they self-identified as black, African American,

colored, or Negro on a legal document." Nkechi Taifa, "Let's Talk About Reparations," *Columbia Journal of Race & Law* 10, no. 1 (2020): 31. Taifa argues that tracing ancestry back to enslavement is too difficult, given the absence of genealogical records. "[W]hile most lawsuits demand a one-to-one connection between wrongdoer and beneficiary, we rarely see such a close connection in legislation." Brophy, "Reconsidering Reparations," 834–35.

83. Taifa, "Let's Talk About Reparations," 29.

84. H.R. 40 (117th Congress, 1st Session); Michael Blevins, "Restorative Justice, Slavery and the American Soul, a Policy-Oriented Intercultural Human Rights Approach to the Question of Reparations," *Thurgood Marshall Law Review* 31 (2006): 305; Taifa, "Let's Talk About Reparations," 30.

85. Mechele Dickerson, "Designing Slavery Reparations: Lessons from Complex Litigation," *Texas Law Review* 98 (2020): 1276.

86. Roy L. Brooks, "Racial Reconciliation Through Black Reparations," 63 *Howard L. J.* (2010): 359.

87. Dickerson, "Designing Slavery Reparations," 1281.

88. *Repair: Redeeming the Promise of Abolition* (Haymarket Books, 2019), 131.

89. William Darity Jr. and Kirsten Mullen, *From Here to Equality: Reparations for Black Americans in the Twenty-First Century* (University of North Carolina Press, 2020), 264–65. *See also* Roy L. Brooks, "Racial Reconciliation Through Black Reparations," *Howard Law Journal* 63, no. 3 (Spring 2020): 358. Advocating that reparations should be used for homeownership, investment property, or education.

## CONCLUSION

1. Tyson Foods, "Here at Waterloo, We're Taking Extra Steps to Help Keep You Safe," accessed March 14, 2025, https://www.tysonfoods.com/waterloo; "Beating COVID-19 Together," accessed April 18, 2025, https://www.tysonfoods.com/news/viewpoints/fighting-covid-19-together.

2. Tyson Foods, "Waterloo Fresh Meats Facility," accessed April 18, 2025, https://www.tysonfoods.com/waterloo.

3. Elise Gould and Katherine DeCourcy, "Fastest Wage Growth over the Last Four Years Among Historically Disadvantaged Groups," March 21, 2024, https://www.epi.org/publication/swa-wages-2023/.

4. Gould and DeCourcy, "Fastest Wage Growth."

5. Gould and DeCourcy, "Fastest Wage Growth."

6. Jamillah Bowman Williams, Elizabeth C. Tippett, and Anu Ramdin, "Mind the Gap(s): Mitigating Harassment in a Post #MeToo Workplace," *University of Southern California Law Review* (forthcoming).

7. *See* Jamillah Bowman Williams, Elizabeth C. Tippett, and Anu Ramdin, "Legislative Approaches to Social Change During #MeToo" (unpublished manuscript, on file with author).

8. Interview with Jessica Jaszewski, March 19, 2024 (on file with author).

9. Interview with Jessica Jaszewski.

EPILOGUE

1. Interview with Thomas Mew, July 18, 2023 (on file with author).
2. Clayton County CASA, "Older Events," accessed April 30, 2025, https://claytoncasa.com/events/past-events/.

# Bibliography

A. B. B. "How Some Women Spend the Weekly Wage." *Women's Welfare Magazine*, January 1905.

Alexander, Charlotte, and Anna Haley-Lock. "Underwork, Work Hour Insecurity, and a New Approach to Wage and Hour Regulation." *Industrial Relations* 54, no. 4 (October 2015): 695–716.

Alexander, Charlotte, and Elizabeth Tippett. "The Hacking of Employment Law." *Missouri Law Review* 82, no. 4 (Fall 2017): 973–1022.

Allyn, Stanley. *My Half Century with NCR*. New York: McGraw-Hill, 1967.

Anderson, Elizabeth. *Private Government: How Employers Rule Our Lives (and Why We Don't Talk About It)*. Princeton, NJ: Princeton University Press, 2017.

Andrias, Kate. "An American Approach to Social Democracy: The Forgotten Promise of the Fair Labor Standards Act." *Yale Law Journal* 128, no. 3 (January 2019): 616–709.

Arnow-Richman, Rachel, and J. H. Verkerke. "Deconstructing Employment Contract Law." *Florida Law Review* 75 (2023): 897–970.

Arsenault, Steven. "Fiduciary Duties of ESOP Trustees Under ERISA in Tender Offers: The Impact of Herman v. NationsBank Trust Company and a Proposal for Reform." *University of Pennsylvania Journal of Labor and Employment Law* 3, no. 1 (Fall 2000): 87–112.

Ashmead, John W. *Reports of Cases Adjudged in the Courts of Common Pleas, Quarter Sessions, Oyer and Terminer, and Orphans' Court, of the First Judicial District of Pennsylvania*. Philadelphia: J. Towar & D. M. Hogan, 1831.

Associated Press. "Man Who Won Gay Rights Case at Supreme Court Agrees to Settlement." *NBC News*, November 7, 2022. https://apnews.com/article/us-supreme-court-lawsuits-discrimination-georgia-atlanta-dff346f4d8720a32773b07df27bc4206.

Atleson, James. *Values and Assumptions in American Labor Law*. Amherst: University of Massachusetts Press, 1983.

Ballam, Deborah A. "The Development of the Employment at Will Rule Revisited: A Challenge to Its Origins as Based in the Development of Advanced Capitalism." *Hofstra Labor Law Journal* 13, no. 1 (Fall 1995): 75–108.

———. "Exploding the Original Myth Regarding Employment-at-Will: The True Origins of the Doctrine." *Berkeley Journal of Employment and Labor Law* 17, no. 1 (1996): 91–130.

———. "The Traditional View on the Origins of the Employment-at-Will Doctrine: Myth or Reality?" *American Business Law Journal* 33, no. 1 (Fall 1995): 1–50.

Banta, Martha. *Taylored Lives*. Chicago: University of Chicago Press, 1993.

Baptist, Edward. "Toward a Political Economy of Slave Labor: Hands, Whipping Machines, and Modern Power." In *Slavery's Capitalism*, edited by Sven Beckert and Seth Rockman, 32–61. Philadelphia: University of Pennsylvania Press, 2016.

Baptist, Edward. *The Half Has Never Been Told: Slavery and the Making of American Capitalism*. New York: Basic Books, 2014.

Beckert, Sven, and Seth Rockman. *Slavery's Capitalism*. Edited by Sven Beckert and Seth Robinson. Philadelphia: University of Pennsylvania Press, 2016.

Beiner, Theresa. "The Misuse of Summary Judgment in Hostile Environment Cases." *Wake Forest Law Review* 34, no. 1 (1999): 71–134.

Bell, Derrick. "White Superiority in America: Its Legal Legacy, Its Economic Costs." *Villanova Law Review* 33, no. 5 (September 1988): 767–80.

Bernstein, David. "Lochner v. New York: A Centennial Retrospective." *Washington University Law Quarterly* 83, no. 5 (2005): 1469–1528.

Bhuiyan, Johana, and Ben Smith. "Uber CEO: Obamacare Has Been 'Huge' for Business." *BuzzfeedNews*, November 15, 2014. https://www.buzzfeednews.com/article/johanabhuiyan/ubercare.

Binus, Josh. "Moving Camp." Oregon History Project. 2003. https://www.oregonhistoryproject.org/articles/historical-records/moving-camp/.

Bird, Robert. "More Than a Congressional Joke: A Fresh Look at the Legislative History of Sex Discrimination of the 1964 Civil Rights Act." *William and Mary Journal of Women and Law* 3, no. 1 (April 1997): 137–61.

Bisom-Rapp, Susan. "Fixing Watches with Sledgehammers: The Questionable Embrace of Employee Sexual Harassment Training by the Legal Profession." *Thomas Jefferson Law Review* 24, no. 2 (Spring 2002): 125–48.

———. "Of Motives and Maleness: A Critical View of Mixed Motive Doctrine in Title VII Sex Discrimination Cases." *Utah Law Review* 1995, no. 4 (1995): 1029–96.

Blackiston, Henry, III, et al. "ESOPs: What They Are and How They Work." *Business Lawyer (ABA)* 45, no. 1 (1989–1990): 85–144.

Blackstone, William. *Commentaries on the Laws of England*. 1st ed. Oxford: Clarendon Press, 1765–1769. https://avalon.law.yale.edu/subject_menus/blackstone.asp.

———. *Commentaries on the Laws of England*. 4th ed. San Francisco: Bancroft-Whitney, 1916.

———. *Commentaries on the Laws of England*. Project Gutenberg, 2009. https://www.gutenberg.org/files/30802/30802-h/30802-h.htm.

Blasi, Joseph, et al. *In the Company of Owners: The Truth About Stock Options (and Why Every Employee Should Have Them)*. New York: Basic Books, 2003.

Blevins, Michael. "Restorative Justice, Slavery and the American Soul, a Policy-Oriented Intercultural Human Rights Approach to the Question of Reparations." *Thurgood Marshall Law Review* 31, no. 2 (Spring 2006): 253–322.

Bodie, Matthew. "Employment as Fiduciary Relationship." *Georgetown Law Journal* 105 (2017): 819–70.

———. "Participation as a Theory of Employment." *Notre Dame Law Review* 89, no. 2 (2013): 661–91.

Bornstein, Stephanie. "Unifying Antidiscrimination Law Through Stereotype Theory." *Lewis & Clark Law Review* 20 (2016): 919–80.

Boyle, Alan. "Amazon Wins a Pair of Patents for Wireless Wristbands That Track Warehouse Workers." *GeekWire*, January 30, 2018. https://www.geekwire.com/2018/amazon-wins-patents-wireless-wristbands-track-warehouse-workers/.

Braestrup, Peter. "NAACP Fights Big Jet Contract." *New York Times*, April 7, 1961.

Brandes, Stuart. *American Welfare Capitalism: 1880–1940*. Chicago: University of Chicago Press, 1970.

Brooks, Roy L. "Racial Reconciliation Through Black Reparations." *Howard Law Journal* 63, no. 3 (Spring 2020): 349–62.

Brophy, Alfred. "Reconsidering Reparations." *Indiana Law Journal* 81, no. 3 (Summer 2006): 811–50.

Bryant, Anna Laurie, and Richard Bales. "Using the Same Actor 'Inference' in Employment Discrimination Cases." *Utah Law Review* 1999 (1999): 255–84.

Buchmueller, Thomas, Zachary M. Levinson, Helen G. Levy, and Barbara L. Wolfe. "Effect of the Affordable Care Act on Racial and Ethnic Disparities in Health Insurance Coverage." *American Journal of Public Health* 106, no. 8 (August 2016): 1416–21.

Bureau of Labor Statistics. "CPI Inflation Calculator." Accessed April 28, 2025. https://www.bls.gov/data/inflation_calculator.htm?source=syndication.

———. *Directory of National Unions and Employee Associations, 1975*. U.S. Department of Labor, 1977. http://fraser.stlouisfed.org.

———. *Directory of National Unions and Employee Associations, 1979*. U.S. Department of Labor, September 1980. http://fraser.stlouisfed.org.

———. *Employee Benefits in the United States*. March 2022. https://www.bls.gov/ebs/publications/zip/employee-benefits-in-the-united-states-march-2022.zip.

———. "Employee Benefits Survey: Paid Sick Leave, Paid Vacation, and Consolidated Leave Plan Provisions in the United States, December 2022." April 2023. https://www.bls.gov/ebs/notices/2023/paid-sick-leave-paid-vacation-and-consolidated-leave-plan-provisions-in-the-united-states-december-2022.htm.

———. "Employment, Hours, and Earnings from the Current Economic Statistics Survey (Industry: Government)." Data Viewer, Series ID CES9000000001. Accessed April 29, 2025. https://beta.bls.gov/dataViewer/view/timeseries/CES9000000001.

———. "March 2022 Employee Benefits in the United States." Data file. Accessed April 29, 2025. https://www.bls.gov/ebs/publications/zip/employee-benefits-in-the-united-states-march-2022.zip.

———. "Union Affiliation Data from the Current Population Survey." Data Viewer, Series ID LUU0204899600. https://beta.bls.gov/dataViewer/view/timeseries/LUU0204899600.

———. "Union Affiliation Data from the Current Population Survey." Data Viewer, Series ID LUU0204922700. https://beta.bls.gov/dataViewer/view/timeseries/LUU0204922700.

———. "Union Members Summary." January 23, 2024. https://www.bls.gov/news.release/union2.nr0.htm.

———. "Union Members—2024." January 28, 2025. https://www.bls.gov/news.release/pdf/union2.pdf.

Burman, Leonard, Christopher Geissler, and Eric Toder. "How Big Are Total Individual Income Tax Expenditures, and Who Benefits from Them?" *American Economic Review* 98, no. 2 (May 2008): 79–83.

Burtless, Gary. "The Contribution of Employment and Hours Changes to Family Income Inequality." *American Economic Review* 83, no. 2 (1993): 131–35.

Bush, Jonathan A. "Take This Job and Shove It: The Rise of Free Labor." *Michigan Law Review* 91, no. 6 (May 1993): 1382–1413.

Callaway, Brantly, and William J. Collins. "Unions, Workers and Wages at the Peak of the American Labor Movement." NBER Working Paper Series, Working Paper 23516. 2017. http://www.nber.org/papers/w23516.

Carle, Susan. *Defining the Struggle: National Organizing for Racial Justice, 1880–1915*. Oxford: Oxford University Press, 2013.

Carlson, Linda. *Company Towns of the Pacific Northwest*. Seattle: University of Washington Press, 2003.

Carlson, Richard. "Why the Law Still Can't Tell an Employee When It Sees One and How It Ought to Stop Trying." *Berkeley Journal of Employment and Labor Law* 22, no. 2 (2001): 295–368.

Carpenter, Dale. "Bumping the Status Quo: Actual Relief for Actual Victims Under Title VII." *University of Chicago Law Review* 58, no. 2 (April 1991): 703–32.

Catterall, Helen T., ed. *Judicial Cases Concerning American Slavery and the Negro*. Vol. 3, *Cases from the Courts of Georgia, Florida, Alabama, Mississippi, and Louisiana*. Washington, DC.: Carnegie Institution of Washington, 1932.

Chamallas, Martha. "Two Very Different Stories: Vicarious Liability Under Tort and Title VII Law." *Ohio State Law Journal* 75 (2014): 1315–44.

Checci, Daniele, Cecilia Garcia-Penalosa, and Lara Vivian. "Are Changes in the Dispersion of Hours Worked a Cause of Increased Earnings Inequality?" *IZA Journal of European Labor Studies* 5, no. 15 (2016): 1–34.

Cherry, Miriam. "Beyond Misclassification: The Digital Transformation of Work." *Comparative Labor Law and Policy Journal* 37, no. 3 (Spring 2016): 577–602.

———. "Dispatch—United States: 'Proposition 22; A Vote on Gig Worker Status in California.'" *Comparative Labor Law and Policy Journal*. Forthcoming.

Chew, Pat, and Robert E. Kelley. "Unwrapping Racial Harassment Law." *Berkeley Journal of Employment and Labor Law* 27, no. 1 (2006): 49–110.

Chinn, Stuart. *Recalibrating Reform: The Limits of Political Change*. Cambridge: Cambridge University Press, 2014.

Clarke, Jessica. "Explicit Bias." *Northwestern University Law Review* 113 (2018): 505–86.

Cobb, Thomas R. R. *Inquiry into Law of Negro Slavery in the United States of America: To Which Is Prefixed an Historical Sketch of Slavery*. Philadelphia: T & J.W. Johnson, 1858.

Cohen, Miriam. "Italian-American Women in New York City." In *Class, Sex, and the Woman Worker*, edited by Milton Cantor & Bruce Laurie, 123. Westport, CT: Greenwood Press, 1977.

Coleman, Francis Thomas, Jr. *The Deunionizing Handbook*. 2nd ed. Washington, DC: Federal Publications, 1987.

Collier, Ruth Berins, Veena Dubal, and Christopher Carter. "The Regulation of Labor Platforms: The Politics of the Uber Economy." *Berkeley Roundtable on the International Economy* (March 1, 2017): 1–42. https://brie.berkeley.edu/publications/regulation-labor-platforms-politics-uber-economy.

Colorado Office of Economic Development & International Trade. "Colorado Employee Ownership Office." Accessed April 29, 2025. https://oedit.colorado.gov/colorado-employee-ownership-office.

Congressional Budget Office. "Details About Baseline Projections for Selected Programs: Medicaid." March 2020. https://www.cbo.gov/data/baseline-projections-selected-programs#10.

Cooper, D. M. "Workman's Time Recorder." US Patent 528,223. Filed May 14, 1894, and issued October 30, 1894.

Cowan, Ruth Schwartz. *A Social History of Technology*. Oxford: Oxford University Press, 1997.

Craemer, Thomas. "Estimating Slavery Reparations: Present Value Comparisons of Historical Multigenerational Reparations Policies." *Social Science Quarterly* 96, no. 2 (June 2015): 639–55.

Crenshaw, Kimberlé. "Demarginalizing the Intersection of Race and Sex: A Black Feminist Critique of Antidiscrimination Doctrine, Feminist Theory and Antiracist Politics." *University of Chicago Legal Forum* 1989 (1989): 139–68.

———. "Mapping the Margins: Intersectionality, Identity Policies, and Violence Against Women of Color." *Stanford Law Review* 43, no. 6 (July 1991): 1241–1300.

Crowther, Samuel. *John H. Patterson: Pioneer in Industrial Welfare*. New York: Garden City Publishing, 1924.

Cunningham-Parmeter, Keith. "From Amazon to Uber: Defining Employment in the Modern Economy." *Boston University Law Review* 96, no. 5 (October 2016): 1673–1728.

Cushman, Barry. "Some Varieties and Vicissitudes of Lochnerism." *Boston University Law Review* 85 (2005): 881–998.

"Confidence in Institutions." Gallup. Accessed April 29, 2025. https://news.gallup.com/poll/1597/confidence-institutions.aspx.

D'Angelo-Corker, Kristy. "Severe or Pervasive Should Not Mean Impossible and Unattainable: Why the 'Severe or Pervasive' Standard for a Claim of Sexual Harassment and Discrimination Should Be Replaced with a Less Stringent and More Current Standard." *Hofstra Law Review* 50, no. 1 (Fall 2021): 1–50.

Darity, William, Jr., and Dania Frank. "Political Economy of Ending Racism and the World Conference Against Racism." In *Redress for Historical Injustices in the United States: On Reparations for Slavery, Jim Crow, and their Legacies*, edited by Michael T. Martin and Marilyn Yaquinto, 249–54. Durham, NC: Duke University Press, 2007.

Darity, William, Jr., and Kirsten Mullen. *From Here to Equality: Reparations for Black Americans in the Twenty-First Century*. Chapel Hill: University of North Carolina Press, 2020.

Das Acevedo, Deepa. "The Rise and Scope of Gig Work Regulation." In *Beyond the Algorithm: Qualitative Insights for Gig Work Regulation*, edited by Deepa Das Acevado, 15–32. Cambridge: Cambridge University Press, 2020.

———. "Unbundling Freedom in the Sharing Economy." *Southern California Law Review* 91, no. 5 (July 2018): 793–838.

Day, Jennifer Cheesman, and Andrew W. Hait. "America Keeps on Truckin': Number of Truckers at All-Time High." United States Census Bureau. June 6, 2019. https://www.census.gov/library/stories/2019/06/america-keeps-on-trucking.html.

de la Fuente, Alejandro, and Ariela Gross. "Comparative Studies of Law, Slavery and Race in the Americas." *Annual Review of Law and Social Science* 6 (2010): 469–85.

De Stefano, Valerio. "The Rise of the 'Just-in-Time Workforce': On-Demand Work, Crowdwork, and Labor Protection in the 'Gig-Economy.'" *Comparative Labor Law and Policy Journal* 37, no. 3 (Spring 2016): 471–504.

Deknatel, Anna, and Lauren Hoff-Downing. "ABC on the Books and in the Courts: An Analysis of Recent Independent Contractor and Misclassification Statutes." *University of Pennsylvania Journal of Law and Social Change* 18, no. 1 (2015): 53–104.

"Details About Baseline Projections for Selected Programs: Medicaid." Congressional Budget Office. March 2020. https://www.cbo.gov/data/baseline-projections-selected-programs#10.

"Details About Baseline Projections for Selected Programs: Medicare." Congressional Budget Office. March 2020. https://www.cbo.gov/data/baseline-projections-selected-programs#10.

Dickerson, Mechele. "Designing Slavery Reparations: Lessons from Complex Litigation." *Texas Law Review* 98, no. 7 (June 2020): 1255–82.

Dinius, Oliver, and Angela Vergara. *Company Towns in the Americas*. Athens: University of Georgia Press, 2011.

Dobbin, Frank. *Inventing Equal Opportunity*. Princeton, NJ: Princeton University Press, 2009.

Dobbin, Frank, and Alexandra Kalev. "The Promise and Peril of Sexual Harassment Programs." *Proceedings of the National Academy of Sciences* 116, no. 25 (June 2019): 12255–60.

———. "Why Diversity Programs Fail." *Harvard Business Review* (July–August 2016). https://hbr.org/2016/07/why-diversity-programs-fail.

Dobbin, Frank, and Erin Kelly. "How to Stop Harassment: Professional Construction of Legal Compliance in Organization." *American Journal of Sociology* 112, no. 4 (January 2007): 1203–43.

Dobbin, Frank, et al. "You Can't Always Get What You Need: Organizational Determinants of Diversity Programs." *American Sociological Review* 76, no. 2 (2011): 386–411.

Dorfman, Doron. "Suspicious Species." *University of Illinois Law Review* 2021 (2021): 1363–1416.

Douglas, Paul, and Joseph Hackman. "The Fair Labor Standards Act of 1938 I." *Political Science Quarterly* 53, no. 4 (December 1938): 491–515.

Douglass, Frederick. *Narrative of the Life of Frederick Douglass, an American Slave.* New York: W. W. Norton, 2017. First published 1845 by Antislavery Office (Boston).

Douglass, Frederick. *Narrative of the Life of Frederick Douglass, An American Slave.* Project Gutenberg Literary Archive Foundation, 1845.

Dubal, Veena. "An Uber Ambivalence." In *Beyond the Algorithm: Qualitative Insights for Gig Work Regulation*, edited by Deepa Das Acevado, 33–56. Cambridge: Cambridge University Press, 2020.

———. "Wage Slave or Entrepreneur? Contesting the Dualism of Legal Worker Identities." *California Law Review* 105, no. 1 (February 2017): 65–123.

Dubofsky, Melvyn. *The State and Labor in Modern America.* Chapel Hill: University of North Carolina Press, 1994.

*Economist.* "America Is a Health-Care Outlier in the Developed World." April 26, 2018. https://www.economist.com/special-report/2018/04/26/america-is-a-health-care-outlier-in-the-developed-world.

Edelman, Lauren. "Judicial Deference in the Modern State." In *The Legal Process and the Promise of Justice: Studies Inspired by the Work of Malcolm Feeley.* New York: Cambridge University Press, 2019.

———. *Working Law: Courts, Corporations, and Symbolic Civil Rights.* Chicago: University of Chicago Press, 2016.

Elliott, E. N. *Cotton Is King and Pro-Slavery Arguments.* Augusta: Pritchard, Abbott & Loomis, 1860. https://archive.org/details/cottoniskingprosooelli/page/n5.

"Employee Rights Notice Posting." National Labor Relations Board. Accessed April 29, 2025. https://www.nlrb.gov/news-publications/publications/employee-rights-notice-posting.

"Employer Health Benefits, 2020 Annual Survey." Kaiser Family Foundation. 2020. https://www.kff.org/health-costs/report/2020-employer-health-benefits-survey/.

"Employer Shared Responsibility Provisions." Internal Revenue Service. Accessed February 28, 2022. https://www.irs.gov/affordable-care-act/employers/employer-shared-responsibility-provisions.

Epstein, Richard. "In Defense of the Contract at Will." *University of Chicago Law Review* 51, no. 4 (Fall 1984): 947–82.

Equal Employment Opportunity Commission (EEOC). *Select Task Force on the Study of Harassment in the Workplace*. 2016. https://www.eeoc.gov/eeoc/task_force/harassment/report.cfm.

"Estimates of Federal Tax Expenditures for Fiscal Years 2024–2028." Joint Committee on Taxation. December 11, 2024. https://www.jct.gov/getattachment/765709fb-9a4b-430a-8f9e-4d342ec97f7e/x-48-24.pdf.

Estlund, Cynthia. *Regoverning the Workplace: From Self-Regulation to Co-Regulation*. New Haven, CT: Yale University Press, 2010.

———. *Working Together: How Workplace Bonds Strengthen a Diverse Democracy*. Oxford: Oxford University Press, 2003.

Eyer, Katie. "The Return of the Technical McDonnell Douglas Paradigm." *Washington Law Review* 94 (2019): 967–1018.

Farber, Henry S. "Union Membership in the United States: The Divergence between the Public and Private Sectors." Working Paper 503. Princeton, NJ: Princeton University, September 2005.

Farrell, Michael B. "Cab Drivers Irate as Ban Against Livery App Reversed," *Boston Globe*, August 17, 2012. https://www.boston.com/news/technology/2012/08/17/cab-drivers-irate-as-ban-against-livery-app-reversed/.

"February 2023 Medicaid & CHIP Enrollment Data Highlights." Medicaid.gov. Accessed June 8, 2023. https://www.medicaid.gov/medicaid/program-information/medicaid-and-chip-enrollment-data/report-highlights/index.html.

Fede, Andrew. "Legitimized Violent Slave Abuse in the American South, 1619–1865: A Case Study in Six Southern States." *American Journal of Legal History* 29, no. 2 (April 1985): 93–150.

Feinman, Jay. "The Development of the Employment at Will Rule." *American Journal of Legal History* 20, no. 2 (April 1976): 118–35.

Fessenden, Stephen. "Present Status of Employers' Liability in the United States." *Bulletin of the Department of Labor* 31 (1900): 1157–61.

Finkin, Matthew. "Beclouded Work, Beclouded Workers in Historical Perspective." *Comparative Labor Law & Policy Journal* 37, no. 3 (Spring 2016): 603–18.

———. "Disloyalty! Does Jefferson Standard Stalk Still?" *Berkeley Journal of Employment & Labor Law* 28 (2007): 541–68.

———. "Shoring Up the Citadel (At-Will Employment)." *Hofstra Labor and Employment Law Journal* 24, no. 1 (Fall 2006): 1–30.

Finkleman, Paul. "Slaves as Fellow Servants: Ideology, Law, and Industrialization." *American Journal of Legal History* 31, no. 4 (October 1987): 269–305.

Fishback, Prince V., and Shawn Everett Kantor. "The Adoption of Workers' Compensation in the United States 1900-1930." *Journal of Law & Economic* 41, no. 2 (October 1998): 305–41.

Fisher, William, III. "Ideology and Imagery in the Law of Slavery." In *Slavery and the Law*, edited by Paul Finkelman, 43–85. Lanham, MD: Rowman & Littlefield, 1997.

Fisk, Catherine. "Removing the 'Fuel of Interest' from the 'Fire of Genius: Law and the Employee-Inventor, 1830–1930." *University of Chicago Law Review* 65 (1998): 1127-98.

———. *Working Knowledge: Employee Innovation and the Rise of Corporate Intellectual Property, 1800–1930.* Chapel Hill: University of North Carolina Press, 2009.

———. "Working Knowledge: Trade Secrets, Restrictive Covenants in Employment, and the Rise of Corporate Intellectual Property, 1800–1920." *Hastings Law Journal* 52 (2001): 441–536.

Foley, Ryan. "Iowa Finds No Violations at Tyson Plant with Deadly Outbreak." Associated Press, June 23, 2020. https://apnews.com/article/336ad340b0a01f9ab870aef1a32785f2.

———. "Tyson Fires 7 at Iowa Pork Plant After COVID Betting Inquiry." Associated Press, December 16, 2020. https://apnews.com/article/iowa-lawsuits-coronavirus-pandemic-lakes-meat-processing-af173a053c5ac8b31e2bd4cb6e8ab83f.

Foner, Eric. *Free Soil, Free Labor, Free Men: The Ideology of the Republican Party Before the Civil War.* New York: Oxford University Press, 1995 (ebook).

Forsythe, John S. "Legislative History of the Fair Labor Standards Act." *Law and Contemporary Problems* 6, no. 3 (Summer 1939): 464–90.

Foucault, Michel. *Discipline and Punish: The Birth of the Prison.* New York: Vintage Books, 1995.

Fox, James. "The Law of Many Faces: Antebellum Contract Law Background of Reconstruction-Era Freedom of Contract." *American Journal of Legal History* 49, no. 1 (January 2007): 61–112.

Franke, Katherine. *Repair: Redeeming the Promise of Abolition.* Chicago: Haymarket Books, 2019.

Franklin, John Hope. *Reconstruction After the Civil War.* Chicago: University of Chicago Press, 1994.

Freeman, Richard. "Contraction and Expansion: The Divergence of Private Sector and Public Sector Unionism in the United States." *Journal of Economic Perspectives* 2, no. 2 (1988): 63–88.

Freeman, Richard B. "Spurts in Union Growth: Defining Moments and Social Processes." In *The Defining Moment: The Great Depression and the American Economy in the Twentieth Century,* edited by Michael D. Bordo, Claudia Goldin, and Eugene White, 265–95. Chicago: University of Chicago Press, 1997.

———. "Unionism Comes to the Public Sector." National Bureau of Economic Research, Working Paper No. 1452. 1984. https://www.nber.org/papers/w1452.

Freeman, Steven. "Effects of ESOP Adoption and Employee Ownership: Thirty Years of Research and Experience." University of Pennsylvania Organizational Dynamics Working Papers. January 4, 2007.

Friedman, Lawrence. *A History of American Law.* New York: Simon & Schuster, 1973.

Fudge, Judy, and Owens, Rosemary. Introduction to *Precarious Work, Women and the New Economy: the Challenge to Legal Norms*, edited by Judy Fudge and Rosemary Owens, 3–28. Oxford: Hart Publishing, 2006.

Gansky, Lisa. *The Mesh: Why the Future of Business Is Sharing*. New York: Portfolio Penguin, 2010.

Garden, Charlotte. "Disrupting Work Law: Arbitration in the Gig Economy." *University of Chicago Legal Forum* 2017 (2017): 205–34.

———. "The Seattle Solution: Collective Bargaining by For-Hire Drivers & Prospects for Pro-Labor Federalism." *Harvard Law & Policy Review Online* 12 (2017): 1–21.

Garden, Charlotte, and Nancy Leong. "'So Closely Intertwined': Labor and Racial Solidarity." *George Washington Law Review* 81 (2013): 1135–1210.

Garner, Bryan A. *Black's Law Dictionary*. 11th ed. n.p.: Thompson Reuters, 2019.

Gary, Susan. "The Changing Landscape of Business Succession: How and Why Purpose Trusts Matter." *Ohio State Business Law Journal* 18 (2023): 42–96.

———. "The Oregon Stewardship Trust: A New Type of Purpose Trust That Enables Steward-Ownership of a Business," *University of Cincinnati Law Review* 88 no. 3 (2020): 707–33.

Gates, Henry Louis, Jr. *Stony the Road: Reconstruction, White Supremacy, and the Rise of Jim Crow*. New York: Penguin Press, 2019.

Genovese, Eugene. *Roll, Jordan, Roll: The World the Slaves Made*. New York: Vintage Books, 1976.

Gibson, Kate. "OSHA Has Failed to Protect Workers from COVID-19, Unions Say." *CBS News*, October 9, 2020. https://www.cbsnews.com/news/osha-covid-19-guidlines-protection-failed-unions-accuse/.

———. "Starbucks and Workers United Agree to Resume Contract Negotiations." *CBS News*, February 27, 2024. https://www.cbsnews.com/news/starbucks-workers-united-union-nlrb/.

Gillespie, Richard. *Manufacturing Knowledge: A History of the Hawthorn Experiments*. New York: Cambridge University Press, 1991.

Glenn, Evelyn Nakano. "From Servitude to Service Work: Historical Continuities in the Racial Division of Paid Reproductive Labor." *Signs* 18 (1992): 1–43.

———. *Unequal Freedom: How Race and Gender Shaped American Citizenship and Labor*. Cambridge, MA: Harvard University Press, 2002.

Glynn, Timothy. "The Limited Viability of Negligent Supervision, Retention and Intentional Infliction of Emotional Distress Claims in Employment Discrimination Cases in Minnesota." *William Mitchell Law Review* 24 (1998): 581–634.

Goldberg, Steven, Maren Fragala, and Jay Wohlgemuth. "Self-Insured Employer Health Benefits Strategy Established a Negative Cost Trend While Improving Performance." *Population Health Management* 22, no. 6 (December 2019): 547–54.

Goldfield, Michael. *The Decline of Organized Labor in the United States*. Chicago: University of Chicago Press, 1987.

Goldmark, Josephine Clara. *Fatigue and Efficiency: A Study in Industry.* New York: Russell Sage Foundation, 1912.

Gould, Elise, and Katherine DeCourcy. "Fastest Wage Growth over the Last Four Years Among Historically Disadvantaged Groups." March 21, 2024. https://www.epi.org/publication/swa-wages-2023/.

Grabell, Michael, and Bernice Yeung. "As COVID-19 Ravaged This Iowa City, Officials Discovered Meatpacking Executives Were the Ones in Charge." *ProPublica*, December 21, 2020. https://features.propublica.org/waterloo-meatpacking/as-covid-19-ravaged-this-iowa-city-officials-discovered-meatpacking-executives-were-the-ones-in-charge/.

Greene, Jamal. "The Anticanon." *Harvard Law Review* 125, no. 2 (December 2011): 379–475.

Griffith, Kati L. "The Fair Labor Standards Act at 80: Everything Old Is New Again." *Cornell Law Review* 104, no. 3 (March 2019): 557–606.

Groneman, Carol. "She Earns as a Child: She Pays as a Man." In *Class, Sex, and the Woman Worker*, edited by Milton Cantor & Bruce Laurie, 83–100. Westport, CT: Greenwood Press, 1977.

Groover, Heidi. "Lengthy Legal Fight Over Seattle's Uber Union Comes to an End." *Seattle Times*, April 13, 2020. https://www.seattletimes.com/seattle-news/transportation/lengthy-legal-fight-over-seattles-uber-unionization-law-comes-to-an-end/.

Gross, Ariela. *Double Character: Slavery and Mastery in the Antebellum Southern Courtroom.* Princeton, NJ: Princeton University Press, 2001.

———. "Slavery, Antislavery, and the Coming of the Civil War." In *The Cambridge History of Law in America*, edited by Michael Grossberg and Christopher Tomlins, 2:280–312. Cambridge: Cambridge University Press, 2007.

Grossman, Joanna L. "The First Bite Is Free: Employer Liability for Sexual Harassment." *Pittsburgh Law Review* 61, no. 3 (Spring 2000): 671–740.

Grossman, Jonathan. "Fair Labor Standards Act of 1938: Maximum Struggle for a Minimum Wage." *Monthly Labor Review* 101, no. 6 (June 1978): 22–30.

Gruber, Jonathan. "The Impacts of the Affordable Care Act: How Reasonable Are the Projections?" NBER Working Paper 17168. June 2011.

———. "The Tax Exclusion for Employer-Sponsored Health Insurance." *National Tax Journal* 64, no. 2 (June 2011): 511–30.

Gruber, Jonathan, and Michael Lettau. "How Elastic Is the Firms' Demand for Health Insurance?" *Journal of Public Economics* 88, nos. 7–8 (July 2004): 1273–93.

Gruber, Jonathan, and Brigitte C. Madrian, "Employment Separation and Health Insurance Coverage." *Journal of Public Economics* 66 (1997): 349–82.

Guendelsberger, Emily. *On the Clock: What Low-Wage Work Did to Me and How It Drives America Insane.* New York: Little, Brown, 2019.

Gurely, Lauren Kaori. "Amazon Is Forcing Its Warehouse Workers into Brutal 'Megacycle' Shifts." *VICE*, February 4, 2021. https://www.vice.com/en/article/y3gk3w/amazon-is-forcing-its-warehouse-workers-into-brutal-megacycle-shifts?utm_content=1612454786.

Hall, Kermit, William Wiecek, and Paul Finkelman. *American Legal History: Cases and Materials.* Oxford: Oxford University Press, 1991.

Harper, Michael, Samuel Estreicher and Joan Flynn. *Labor Law: Cases Materials and Problems.* 6th ed. Philadelphia: Wolters Kluwer, 2007.

Harris & Ewing, photographer. Photograph. *Hopkins Tells Mrs. Perkins About It: Washington, D.C., Jan. 7. Harry Hopkins, Secretary of Commerce, Stepped over to Labor Secretary Francis Perkins to Tell Her That He Likes His New Job . . . Was at the Jackson Day Dinner, 1/7/39.* Washington, DC. [January 7,] 1939. https://www.loc.gov/item/2016874728/.

Harris, Jonathan F. "Consumer Law as Work Law." *California Law Review* 112 (2024): 1–54.

Hattam, Victoria. "Courts and the Question of Class." In *Labor Law in America*, edited by Christopher Tomlins and Andrew King, 44–71. Baltimore, MD: Johns Hopkins University Press, 199.

———. *Labor Visions and State Power.* Princeton, NJ: Princeton University Press, 1993.

Hatton, Erin. *Coerced: Work Under Threat of Punishment.* Oakland: University of California Press, 2020.

———. *The Temp Economy: From Kelly Girls to Permatemps in Postwar America.* Philadelphia, PA: Temple University Press, 2011.

Heathcote, Jonathan, Fabrizio Perri, and Giovanni Violante. "Unequal We Stand: An Empirical Analysis of Economic Inequality in the United States 1967–2006." *Review of Economic Dynamics* 13, no. 1 (January 2010): 15–51.

Heggeness, Misty L., Jason Fields, Yazmin A. García Trejo, and Anthony Schulzetenberg. "Tracking Job Losses for Mothers of School-Age Children During a Health Crisis." U.S. Census Bureau, *Moms, Work and the Pandemic* (blog), March 3, 2021. https://www.census.gov/library/stories/2021/03/moms-work-and-the-pandemic.html.

Hernández, Tanya Katerí. *Multiracials and Civil Rights: Mixed-Race Stories of Discrimination.* New York: New York University Press, 2018.

Herod, Andrew. "Social Engineering Through Spatial Engineering." In *Company Towns in the Americas: Landscape, Power, and Working-Class Communities*, edited by Oliver Dininus and Angela Vergara, 21–44. Athens: University of Georgia Press, 2011.

Hirsch, Jeffrey, and Joseph Seiner. "A Modern Union for the Modern Economy." *Fordham Law Review* 86, no. 4 (March 2018): 1727–84.

Horwitz, Morton. *The Transformation of American Law, 1870–1960.* New York: Oxford University Press, 1992.

Howard, Christopher. *The Hidden Welfare State.* Princeton, NJ: Princeton University Press, 1997.

Hudson, Harry. *Working for Equality.* Edited by Randall L. Patton. Athens: University of Georgia Press, 2015.

Huffcut, Ernest. *The Law of Agency: Including the Law of Principal and Agent and the Law of Master and Servant.* Boston: Little, Brown, 1901.

Imai, Masaaki. *Gemba Kaizen: A Commonsense Low-Cost Approach to Management.* New York: McGraw-Hill, 1997.

———. *Kaizen (Ky'zen), the Key to Japan's Competitive Success*. New York: Random House, 1986.

"Industrial Problems, Welfare Work: United States, Ohio, Dayton; National Cash Register Company: Welfare Institutions of the National Cash Register Company, Dayton, Ohio; Advantages for Employees: Calisthenics: Social Museum Collection." Harvard Art Museums. 1904. https://hvrd.art/o/56750.

Internal Revenue Service. "Identifying Full-time Employees." January 22, 2021. https://www.irs.gov/affordable-care-act/employers/identifying-full-time-employees.

Ivanova, Irina. "Union Membership in the U.S. Hit Record Low in 2018." *CBS News*, January 21, 2019. https://www.cbsnews.com/news/union-membership-declined-in-2018/.

Jacoby, Sanford. *Employing Bureaucracy: Managers, Unions, and the Transformation of Work in the 20th Century*. Rev. ed. Lawrence Erlbaum Associates, 2004.

———. *Modern Manors: Welfare Capitalism Since the New Deal*. Princeton, NJ: Princeton University Press, 1997.

Jameson, Elizabeth. "Imperfect Unions." In *Class, Sex, and the Woman Worker*, edited by Milton Cantor and Bruce Laurie, 182. Westport, CT: Greenwood Press, 1977.

Jenkins, Sara, and Wil Chivers. "Can Cooperatives/Employee-Owned Businesses Improve 'Bad' Jobs? Evaluating Job Quality in Three Low-Paid Sectors." *British Journal of Industrial Relations* 60 (2022): 511–35.

Johnson, Judith J. "License to Harass Women: Requiring Hostile Environment Sexual Harassment to Be Severe or Pervasive Discriminates Among Terms and Conditions of Employment." *Maryland Law Review* 62, no. 1 (2003): 85–142.

Johnson, Roy, and Russell Lynch. *The Sales Strategy of John Patterson*. Chicago: The Dartnell Corp., 1932.

Jones, Jeffrey. "As Labor Day Turns 125, Union Approval Near 50-Year High." Gallup. August 28, 2019. https://news.gallup.com/poll/265916/labor-day-turns-125-union-approval-near-year-high.aspx.

Kahana, Jeffrey Steven. *The Unfolding of American Labor Law: Judges, Workers and Public Policy Across Two Political Generations, 1790–1850*. El Paso: LFB Scholarly Publishing, 2014.

Kaiser Family Foundation. "Employer Health Benefits, 2020 Annual Survey." 2020. https://www.kff.org/health-costs/report/2020-employer-health-benefits-survey/.

———. "Status of State Medicaid Expansion Decisions: Interactive Map." May 24, 2023. https://www.kff.org/medicaid/issue-brief/status-of-state-medicaid-expansion-decisions-interactive-map/.

Kalev, Alexandra, Frank Dobbin, and Erin Kelly. "Best Practices or Best Guesses? Assessing the Efficacy of Corporate Affirmative Action and Diversity Policies." *American Sociological Review* 71 (2006): 589–617.

Kalman, Laura. "The Constitution, the Supreme Court, and the New Deal." *American Historical Review* 110, no. 4 (October 2005): 1052–79.

Kanigel, Robert. *The One Best Way: Frederick Winslow Taylor and the Enigma of Efficiency*. Cambridge, MA: MIT Press, 2005.

Kantor, Jodi. "Working Anything but 9 to 5." *New York Times*, August 13, 2014. https://www.nytimes.com/interactive/2014/08/13/us/starbucks-workers-scheduling-hours.html.

Kantor, Jodi, and David Streitfeld. "Inside Amazon: Wrestling Big Ideas in a Bruising Workplace." *New York Times*, August 15, 2015.

Kantor, Jodi, Karen Weise, and Grace Ashford. "The Amazon That Customers Don't See." *New York Times*, June 15, 2021.

———. "Inside Amazon's Employment Machine." *New York Times*, June 15, 2021. https://www.nytimes.com/interactive/2021/06/15/us/amazon-workers.html.

Kantor, Shawn Evert, and Price V. Fishback. "Nonfatal Accident Compensation and the Common Law at the Turn of the Century." *Journal of Law, Economics, & Organization* 11, no. 2 (October 1995): 406–33.

Katznelson, Ira, Kim Geiger, and Daniel Kryder. "Limiting Liberalism: The Southern Veto in Congress, 1933–1950." *Political Science Quarterly* 108, no. 2 (1993): 286–306.

Kearney, Robert. "Death of a Rule." *UC Davis Business Law Journal* 16 (2015): 1–30.

Keckley, Elizabeth. *Behind the Scenes, or Thirty Years a Slave, and Four Years in the White House*. New York: G. W. Carleton, 1868. www.gutenberg.org (ebook 24968).

Keisler-Starkey, Katherine, and Lisa Bunch. "Health Insurance Coverage in the United States: 2021." United States Census Bureau. September 13, 2022. https://www.census.gov/library/publications/2022/demo/p60-278.html.

Kennedy, Elizabeth J. "Employed by an Algorithm: Labor Rights in the On-Demand Economy." *Seattle University Law Review* 40, no. 3 (Spring 2017): 987–1048.

Kessler-Harris, Alice. "Organizing the Unorganizable: Three Jewish Women and Their Union." In *Class, Sex, and the Woman Worker*, edited by Milton Cantor and Bruce Laurie, 144. Westport, CT: Greenwood Press, 1977.

———. "Where Are All the Organized Women Workers?" *Feminist Studies* 3, nos. 1/2 (1975): 92–110.

"Key Facts About the Uninsured Population." Kaiser Family Foundation. December 19, 2022. https://www.kff.org/uninsured/issue-brief/key-facts-about-the-uninsured-population/.

Kleinberg, Susan. "The Systematic Study of Urban Women." In *Class, Sex, and the Woman Worker*, edited by Milton Cantor & Bruce Laurie, 20–42. Westport, CT: Greenwood Press, 1977.

Klezmer, Randal M., and Nathan B. Maudlin. "3:22 Accidents." In *Indiana Worker's Compensation Law and Practice*. Indiana Practice Series No. 29, 2020–2021 ed.

Kruse, Douglas, et al. "Shared Capitalism in the U.S. Economy: Prevalence, Characteristics, and Employee Views of Financial Participation in Enterprises." NBER Working Paper Series. 2008. http://nber.org/papers/w14225.

Labatt, C. B. *Commentaries on the Law of Master and Servant: Including the Modern Laws on Workmen's Compensation, Arbitration, Employers' Liability Etc. Etc.* Rochester: The Lawyers Cooperative, 1913.

Lamb, Edward. *No Lamb for Slaughter*. New York: Harcourt, Brace & World, 1963.

*Laredo Morning Times*. "Obituary of José Luis Ayala." May 27, 2020. https://obituaries.lmtonline.com/obituary/jose-ayala-1083907657/.

Lebergott, Stanley. "Labor Force, Employment, and Unemployment, 1929–39: Estimating Methods." Bureau of Labor Statistics. July 1948. https://www.bls.gov/opub/mlr/1948/article/labor-force-employment-and-unemployment-1929-39-estimating-methods.htm.

Leuchtenburg, William. *The Supreme Court Reborn: The Constitutional Revolution in the Age of Roosevelt*. New York: Oxford University Press, 1995.

Levinson, Ariana. "Union Co-ops and the Revival of Labor Law." *Cardozo Journal of Conflict Resolution* 19 no. 3 (Spring 2018): 453–564.

Levinson, Ariana, and Chad Eisenback. "Cooperative Ownership and the Fair Labor Standards Act." *Michigan State Law Review* 2021, no. 1 (2021): 73–142.

Lewis, Ronald. *Coal, Iron and Slaves: Industrial Slavery in Maryland and Virginia, 1715–1865*. Westport, CT: Greenwood Press, 1979.

Linder, Marc. *The Employment Relationship in Anglo-American Law: A Historical Perspective*. Westport, CT: Greenwood Press, 1989.

———. "Farm Workers and the Fair Labor Standards Act: Racial Discrimination in the New Deal." *Texas Law Review* 65, no. 7 (June 1987): 1335–93.

———. *Moments Are the Elements of Profit: Overtime and the Deregulation of Working Hours Under the Fair Labor Standards Act*. Iowa City: Fănpìhuà Press, 2000.

Livingston, Gretchen, and Deja Thomas. "Among 41 Countries, Only U.S. Lacks Paid Parental Leave." Pew Research Center. December 16, 2019. https://www.pewresearch.org/fact-tank/2019/12/16/u-s-lacks-mandated-paid-parental-leave/.

Lobel, Orly. "The Law of the Platform." *Minnesota Law Review* 101, no. 1 (November 2016): 87–166.

Logue, John, and Jacquelyn Yates. *The Real World of Employee Ownership*. Ithaca, NY: ILR Press, 2001.

Lovell, Vicki, et al. "More Than Raising the Floor: The Persistence of Gender Inequalities in the Low-Wage Labor Market." In *The Sex of Class: Women Transforming American Labor*, edited by Dorothy Sue Cobble. Cornell University Press, 2011.

Lucas, Amelia. "Here's a Map of Starbucks Stores That Voted to Unionize." CNBC, December 9, 2022. https://www.cnbc.com/2022/12/09/map-of-starbucks-stores-that-voted-to-unionize.html.

MacKinnon, Catharine. *Sexual Harassment of Working Women: A Case of Sex Discrimination*. New Haven, CT: Yale University Press, 1979.

Madan, Udit. "Amazon Is Increasing the Average Total Compensation Package for Fulfillment and Transportation Employees in the US to over $29 per Hour." Amazon. September 18, 2024. https://www.aboutamazon.com/news/workplace/amazon-wage-increase-new-benefits-for-hourly-us-employees.

Magley, Vicki, et al. "Changing Sexual Harassment Within Organizations via Training Interventions: Suggestions and Empirical Data." In *The Fulfilling*

*Workplace: The Organization's Role in Achieving Individual and Organizational Health*, edited by Ronald Burke and Cary Cooper. Aldershot, UK: Gower Publishing, 2013.

Malamud, Deborah. "Engineering the Middle Classes: Class Line-Drawing in New Deal Hours Legislation." *Michigan Law Review* 96, no. 8 (August 1998): 2212–2321.

Markovits, Daniel. *The Meritocracy Trap*. New York: Penguin Press, 2019.

Marks, Mindy. "Minimum Wages, Employer-Provided Health Insurance, and the Non-Discrimination Law." *Industrial Relations* 50, no. 2 (April 2011): 241–62.

Martin, Natasha. "Immunity for Hire: How the Same-Actor Doctrine Sustains Discrimination in the Contemporary Workplace." *Connecticut Law Review* 40 (2008): 1117–74.

Matheny, Ken, and Marion Crain. "Disloyal Workers and the 'Un-American' Labor Law." *North Carolina Law Review* 82 (2004): 1711–12.

May, Martha. "Bread Before Roses: American Workingmen, Labor Unions and the Family Wage." In *Women, Work and Protest: A Century of US Women's Labor History*, 2nd ed., edited by Ruth Milkman, 1–21. New York: Routledge, 2013.

MBO Partners. "The Independent by Choice Movement: Authentic and Intentional, State of Independence in America 2024." Accessed March 10, 2025. https://www.mbopartners.com/state-of-independence/.

McCurdy, Charles W. "The Roots of Liberty of Contract Reconsidered: Major Premises in the Law of Employment, 1867–1937." *Yearbook: Supreme Court Historical Society* 1984 (1984): 20–33.

McGinley, Anne. "Reinventing Reality: The Impermissible Intrusion of After-Acquired Evidence in Title VII Litigation." *Connecticut Law Review* 26 (1993): 145–206.

McIntosh, Kriston, Emily Moss, Ryan Nunn, and Jay Shambaugh. "Examining the Black-White Wealth Gap." Brookings. February 27, 2020. https://www.brookings.edu/blog/up-front/2020/02/27/examining-the-black-white-wealth-gap/.

McKinsey & Company. "For Mothers in the Workplace, a Year (and Counting) Like No Other." May 5, 2021. https://www.mckinsey.com/featured-insights/diversity-and-inclusion/for-mothers-in-the-workplace-a-year-and-counting-like-no-other.

McMorris-Santoro, Evan, and Johana Bhuiyan. "How Obamacare Drives the Sharing Economy." *BuzzfeedNews*, October 14, 2014. https://www.buzzfeednews.com/article/evanmcsan/how-obamacare-drives-the-sharing-economy.

McMurtry-Chubb, Teri A. *Race Unequals: Overseer Contracts, White Masculinities, and the Formation of Managerial Identity in the Plantation Economy*. Lanham, MD: Lexington Books, 2021.

Means, Benjamin, and Joseph A. Seiner. "Navigating the Uber Economy." *University of California Davis Law Review* 49 (2016): 1511–46.

Mettler, Suzanne. "Federalism, Gender, & the Fair Labor Standards Act of 1938." *Polity* 26, no. 4 (Summer 1994): 635–54.

Meyer, Stephen, III. *The Five Dollar Day: Labor Management and Social Control in the Ford Motor Company, 1908–1921*. Albany: State University of New York Press, 1981.

Milkman, Ruth. "Two Worlds of Unionism: Women and the New Labor Movement." In *The Sex of Class: Women Transforming American Labor*, edited by Sue Cobble, 63–80. Ithaca, NY: Cornell University Press, 2011.

Mims, Christopher. "The Way Amazon Uses Tech to Squeeze Performance Out of Workers Deserves Its Own Name: Bezosism." *Wall St. Journal*, September 11, 2021.

Molla, Rani. "More Americans Are Taking Jobs Without Employer Benefits Like Health Care or Paid Vacation." *Vox*, September 3, 2021. https://www.vox.com/recode/22651953/americans-gig-independent-workers-benefits-vacation-health-care-inequality.

Morris, Thomas D. *Southern Slavery and the Law, 1619–1860*. Chapel Hill: University of North Carolina Press, 1996.

Morriss, Andrew. "Exploding Myths: An Empirical and Economic Reassessment of the Rise of Employment At-Will." *Missouri Law Review* 59, no. 1 (Winter 1994): 679–762.

Mulkeen, Patricia. "Private Household Workers and the Fair Labor Standards Act." *Connecticut Law Review* 5, no. 4 (Spring 1973): 623–38.

Murphy, Michael. "The ESOP at Thirty: A Democratic Perspective," *Willamette Law Review* 41 (2005): 655–706.

Mutari, Ellen. "Brothers and Breadwinners: Legislating Living Wages in the Fair Labor Standards Act of 1938." *Review of Social Economy* 62, no. 2 (June 2004): 129–48.

Nadasen, Premilla. "Citizenship Rights, Domestic Work, and the Fair Labor Standards Act." *Journal of Policy History* 24, no. 1 (January 2012): 74–94.

National Center for Employee Ownership. "Research on Employee Ownership." Accessed April 29, 2025. https://www.nceo.org/employee-ownership-data/academic-research.

———. "A Statistical Snapshot of ESOPs: Company and Participant Numbers, and Industry Distribution." Accessed April 29, 2025. https://www.esop.org/infographics/statistical-snapshot-esops.php.

National Women's Law Center, "Reporting Time Pay: A Key Solution to Curb Unpredictable and Unstable Scheduling Practices," January 2015. https://nwlc.org/wp-content/uploads/2015/08/reporting_time_pay_fact_sheet_jan_2015.pdf.

Neill, Charles Patrick. *Report on Conditions of Employment in the Iron and Steel Industry in the United States, Summary of the Wages and Hours of Labor*. Washington, DC: Government Printing Office, 1912.

Nelson, Daniel. *Frederick Taylor and the Rise of Scientific Management*. Madison: University of Wisconsin Press, 1980.

Nelson, William E. "The Impact of the Antislavery Movement upon Styles of Judicial Reasoning in Nineteenth Century America." *Harvard Law Review* 87, no. 3 (January 1974): 513–66.

"New HHS Data Show More Americans Than Ever Have Health Coverage Through the Affordable Care Act." Health and Human Services. June 5,

2021. https://www.cms.gov/newsroom/press-releases/new-hhs-data-show-more-americans-ever-have-health-coverage-through-affordable-care-act.

*New York Times.* Classified advertisements. January 1, 1966, 35(D). https://timesmachine.nytimes.com/timesmachine/1966/01/01/issue.html.

———. "Battle over Figures in the Rate Inquiry." September 9, 1910. https://www.nytimes.com/1910/09/09/archives/battle-over-figures-in-the-rate-inquiry-admission-made-that.html.

———. "Roads Could Save $1,000,000 a Day." November 22, 1910. https://www.nytimes.com/1910/11/22/archives/roads-could-save-1000000-a-day-brandeis-says-scientific-management.html.

Nielson, Laura Beth, and Robert Nelson. "Rights Realized—An Empirical Analysis of Employment Discrimination Litigation as a Claiming System." *Wisconsin Law Review* 2005, no. 2 (2005): 663–712.

Nolan, Hamilton. "Inside an Amazon Warehouse, the Relentless Need to 'Make Rate.'" *Gawker*, June 6, 2016. https://gawker.com/inside-an-amazon-warehouse-the-relentless-need-to-mak-1780800336.

O'Boyle, Ernest. "Employee Ownership and Firm Performance: A Meta-analysis." *Human Resource Management Journal*, no. 26 (2016): 425–48.

Olmstead, Frederick L. *The Cotton Kingdom.* Vol 1. New York: Mason Brothers, 1861.

Onwuachi-Willig, Angela. "What About #UsToo? The Invisibility of Race in the #MeToo Movement." *Yale Law Journal Forum* 128 (2018): 105–20.

Oppenheimer, David. "The Story of Green v. McDonnell Douglas." In *Employment Discrimination Stories*, 13–36, edited by Joel W. Friedman. St. Paul: West Academic, 2006.

Orren, Karen. *Belated Feudalism: Labor, the Law, and Liberal Development in the United States.* Cambridge: Cambridge University Press, 1991.

Painter, Nell Irvin. *Southern History Across the Color Line.* Chapel Hill: University of North Carolina Press, 2002.

———. *Standing at Armageddon: The United States 1877–1919.* New York: W. W. Norton, 1987.

Papanicolas, Irene, Liana Woskie, and Ashish Jha. "Health Care Spending in the United States and Other High-Income Countries." *Journal of the American Medical Association* 319, no. 10 (May 2018): 1024–39.

Parsons, Larry. "Title VII Remedies: Reinstatement and the Innocent Incumbent Employee." *Vanderbilt Law Review* 42, no. 5 (October 1989): 1441–68.

Patterson, Orlando. *Slavery and Social Death.* Cambridge: Harvard University Press, 1982.

Patton, Randall. *Lockheed, Atlanta and the Struggle for Racial Integration.* Athens: University of Georgia, 2019.

Paul, Sanjukta. "Uber as For-Profit Hiring Hall: A Price-Fixing Paradox and Its Implications." *Berkeley Journal of Employment and Labor Law* 38, no. 2 (2017): 233–64.

Penningroth, Dylan. "Race in Contract Law." *University of Pennsylvania Law Review* 170 (2022): 1199–1302.

Pepper, George Warton, and William Draper Lewis. *Pepper and Lewis' New Digest: A Digest of the Laws of Pennsylvania from 1700 to 1894.* Philadelphia: T. & J. W. Johnson, 1896.

Perea, Juan. "The Echoes of Slavery: Recognizing the Racist Origins of the Agricultural and Domestic Worker Exclusion from the National Labor Relations Act." *Ohio State Law Journal* 72, no. 1 (2011): 95–138.

Perkins, Frances. *The Roosevelt I Knew.* New York: Viking Press, 1946.

Pew Research Center. "Wealth Gaps Across Racial and Ethnic Groups." December 4, 2023. https://www.pewresearch.org/race-ethnicity/2023/12/04/wealth-gaps-across-racial-and-ethnic-groups/.

Pierce, Brooks. "Compensation Inequality." *Quarterly Journal of Economics* 116, no. 4 (2001): 1493–1525.

Plass, Stephen. "Dualism and Overlooked Class Consciousness in American Labor Laws." *Houston Law Review* 37, no. 3 (Fall 2000): 823–58.

Polk, Lee T. "Miscellaneous Fiduciary Issues—ESOPs." *ERISA Practice and Litigation* 1 (August 2023 update).

Pope, James. "The Workers' Freedom of Association Under the Thirteenth Amendment." In *The Promises of Liberty,* edited by Alexander Tsesis, 138–159 New York: Columbia University Press, 2010.

Posner, Eric, and Adrian Vermeule. "Reparations for Slavery and Other Historical Injustices." *Columbia Law Review* 103, no. 3 (April 2003): 689–747.

Post, Christopher W. "The Making of the Federal Company Town: Sunflower Village, Kansas." In *Company Towns in the Americas: Landscape, Power, and Working-Class Communities,* edited by Oliver J. Dinius and Angela Vergara, 111–13. Athens: University of Georgia Press, 2011.

"Present Law and Analysis." Joint Committee on Taxation, March 6, 2006. JCX-12-06.

"Program Statistics." Centers for Medicare and Medicaid Services. Accessed February 28, 2022. https://www.cms.gov/Rsearch-Statistics-Data-and-Systems/Statistics-Trends-and-Reports/CMSProgramStatistics/.

Quintanilla, Victor, and Cheryl Kaiser. "The Same-Actor Inference of Nondiscrimination: Moral Credentialing and the Psychological and Legal Licensing of Bias." *California Law Review* 104 (2016): 1–74.

Rasier, LLC. "Technology Services Agreement." 2015. https://www.documentcloud.org/documents/2645988-RASIER-Technology-Services-Agreement-Decmeber-10.

Raskin, A. H. "Negro Makes Job Gain in South Under Initial Drive and Lockheed." *New York Times,* June 18, 1961.

Reaves, Rhonda. "One of These Things Is Not Like the Other: Analogizing Ageism to Racism in Employment Discrimination Cases." *University of Richmond Law Review* 38, no. 4 (May 2004): 839–902.

Reder, Melvin. "The Rise and Fall of Unions: The Public Sector and the Private." *Journal of Economic Perspective* 2, no. 2 (1988): 89–110.

*Repair: Redeeming the Promise of Abolition.* Chicago: Haymarket Books, 2019.

"Reporting Time Pay: A Key Solution to Curb Unpredictable and Unstable Scheduling Practices." National Women's Law Center. January 2015. https://

nwlc.org/wp-content/uploads/2015/08/reporting_time_pay_fact_sheet_jan_2015.pdf.

Richter, Irving. "Four Years of the Fair Labor Standards Act of 1938: Some Problems of Enforcement." *Journal of Politic Economy* 51, no. 2 (April 1943): 95–111.

Rogers, Brishen. "Employment Rights in the Platform Economy: Getting Back to Basics." *Harvard Law and Policy Review* 10 (March 2016): 480–519.

Rogers, Joel. *Institutional Aspects of Postwar U.S. Union Decline*. Edited by Christopher Tomlins and Andrew King. Baltimore, MD: Johns Hopkins University Press, 1992.

Rosen, Judge Gerald, et al. "Coverage and Exemptions—In General." In *Federal Employment Litigation: Rutter Group Practice Guide* n.p.: Thompson Reuters, 2024.

Rosenfeld, Jake, and Patrick Denice. "What Do Government Unions Do? Public Sector Unions and Nonunion Wages, 1977–2015." *Social Science Research* 78 (2019): 41–56.

Rosenthal, Caitlin. *Accounting for Slavery: Masters and Management*. Cambridge, MA: Harvard University Press, 2018.

———. "Slavery's Scientific Management: Masters and Managers." In *Slavery's Capitalism*, edited by Sven Beckert and Seth Rockman, 62–86. Philadelphia: University of Pennsylvania, 2016.

Rowan, Regan. "Solving the Bluish Collar Problem: An Analysis of the DOL's Modernization of the Exemptions to the Fair Labor Standards Act." *University of Pennsylvania Journal of Labor and Employment Law* 7, no. 1 (Fall 2004): 119–38.

Rubenstein, Mitchell. "Employees, Employers, and Quasi-Employers: An Analysis of Employees and Employers Who Operate in the Borderland between an Employer-and-Employee Relationship." *University of Pennsylvania Journal of Business Law* 14, no. 3 (Spring 2012): 605–60.

Ruiz, Vicki. *Cannery Women, Cannery Lives*. Albuquerque: University of New Mexico Press, 1987.

Russell, Thomas D. "Slave Auctions on the Courthouse Steps: Court Sales of Slaves in Antebellum South Carolina." In *Slavery and the Law*, edited by Paul Finkelman, 329–64. Madison, WI: Madison House Publishers, 1997.

Sasaki, Satoshi. "The Introduction of Scientific Management by the Mitsubishi Electric Engineering Co. and the Formation of an Organised Scientific Management Movement in Japan in the 1920s and 1930s." *Business History* 34, no. 2 (April 1992): 12–27.

Schafer, Judith Kellere. "'Details Are of a Most Revolting Character': Cruelty to Slaves as Seen in Appeals to the Supreme Court of Louisiana." In *Slavery and the Law*, edited by Paul Finkelman, 241–267. Madison: Madison House Publishers, 1997.

Scheiber, Noam. "Starbucks Fall Short After Pledging Better Labor Practices." *Seattle Times*, September 23, 2015. https://www.seattletimes.com/business/starbucks-falls-short-after-pledging-better-labor-practices-2/.

Scheiber, Noam, and Cresswell, Julie. "Sexual Harassment Cases Show the Ineffectiveness of Going to H.R." *New York Times*, December 12, 2017.

https://www.nytimes.com/2017/12/12/business/sexual-harassment-human-resources.html.

Schmidt, James. *Free to Work: Labor Law, Emancipation, and Reconstruction, 1815–1880*. Athens: University of Georgia Press, 1998.

Seiner, Joseph. "Workplace Power." *Boston College Law Review* 65 (2024): 55–112.

Shad, Hamza, et al. "Ownership Trends in Private Equity: 2024." *Carta*, September 10, 2024. https://carta.com/data/ownership-trends-private-equity-2024/.

Shavers, Vickie, and Brenda Shavers. "Racism and Health Inequity Among Americans." *Journal of the National Medical Association* 98, no. 3 (March 2006): 386–96.

Sherwyn, David, Michael Heise, and Zev G. Eigen. "Don't Train Your Employees and Cancel Your '1-800' Harassment Hotline: An Empirical Examination and Correction of the Flaws in the Affirmative Defense to Sexual Harassment Charges." *Fordham Law Review* 69, no. 4 (March 2001): 1265–1304.

Shiflett, Crandall. *Coal Towns: Life, Work, and Culture in Company Towns of Southern Appalachia, 1880–1960*. Knoxville: University of Tennessee Press, 1994.

Slater, Joseph. "The 'American Rule' That Swallows the Exceptions." *Employee Rights and Employment Policy Journal* 11, no. 1 (2007): 53–110.

———. "Jeffrey Kahana, the Unfolding of American Labor Law: Judges, Workers, and Public Policy Across Two Political Generations, 1790–1850." *New York University Journal of Law & Liberty* 10, no. 1 (2016): 404–28.

———. *Public Workers: Government Employee Unions, the Law and the State, 1900–1962*. Ithaca, NY: ILR Press, 2004.

———. "Review: The Rise of Master-Servant and the Fall of Master Narrative: A Review of Labor Law in America." *Berkeley Journal of Employment and Labor Law* 15, no. 1 (1994): 141–71.

Smith, Charles Manley. *A Treatise on the Law of Master and Servant: Including Therein Masters and Workmen in Every Description of Trade and Occupation*. Philadelphia: T. & J.W. Johnson, 1852.

Smith, Mark M. *Mastered by the Clock: Time, Slavery and Freedom in the American South*. Chapel Hill: University of North Carolina Press, 1997.

Smith, Rebecca, and Maya Pinto. "Rewriting the Rules." In *Beyond the Algorithm: Qualitative Insights for Gig Work Regulation*, edited by Deepa Das Acevado, 189–207. Cambridge: Cambridge University Press, 2020.

Smith, Tovia. "When It Comes to Sexual Harassment Claims, Whose Side Is HR Really On?" *NPR*, November 15, 2017. https://www.npr.org/2017/11/15/564032999/when-it-comes-to-sexual-harassment-claims-whose-side-is-hr-really-on.

Solon, Olivia. "Amazon Patents Wristband That Tracks Warehouse Workers' Movements." *Guardian*, January 31, 2018. https://www.theguardian.com/technology/2018/jan/31/amazon-warehouse-wristband-tracking.

Souleles, Daniel. "Another Workplace Is Possible: Learning to Own and Changing Subjectivities in American Employee Owned Companies." *Critique of Anthropology* 40, no. 1 (2020): 28–48.

Sperino, Sandra. "Disbelief Doctrines." *Berkeley Journal of Employment & Labor Law* 39, no. 1 (2018): 231–52.

———. "Flying Without a Statutory Basis: Why McDonnell Douglas Is Not Justified by Any Statutory Construction Methodology." *Houston Law Review* 43, no. 3 (2006): 743–806.

Sperino, Sandra, and Suja Thomas. *Unequal: How America's Courts Undermine Discrimination Law.* Oxford: Oxford University Press, 2017.

Spieler, Emily. "(Re)Assessing the Grand Bargain: Compensation for Work Injuries in the United States, 1900–2017." *Rutgers University Law Review* 69, no. 3 (Spring 2017): 891–1014.

Stainback, Kevin, and Donald Tomaskovic-Devey. *Documenting Desegregation: Racial and Gender Segregation in Private-Sector Employment Since the Civil Rights Act.* New York: Russell Sage Foundation, 2012.

Stanley, Amy Dru. *From Bondage to Contract: Wage Labor, Marriage, and the Market in the Age of Slave Emancipation.* Cambridge: Cambridge University Press, 1998.

"The State of Paid Sick Time in the U.S. in 2023." The American Progress Institute. January 5, 2023. https://www.americanprogress.org/article/the-state-of-paid-sick-time-in-the-u-s-in-2023/.

Steinfeld, Robert. *The Invention of Free Labor: The Employment Relation in English and American Law and Culture, 1350–1870.* Chapel Hill: University of North Carolina Press, 1991.

Stone, Katherine V. W. "Legal Protections for Atypical Employees: Employment Law for Workers Without Workplaces and Employees Without Employers." *Berkeley Journal of Employment and Labor Law* 27, no. 2 (2006): 251–86.

Stone, Kerri Lynn. "Taking in Strays: A Critique of the Stray Comment Doctrine in Employment Discrimination Law." *Missouri Law Review* 77 (2012): 149–98.

Straker, David Augustus. *New South Investigated.* New York: Arno Press, 1973. First published 1888 by Ferguson Printing (Detroit).

Sullivan, Charles. "Circling Back to the Obvious: The Convergence of Traditional and Reverse Discrimination in Title VII Proof." *William & Mary Law Review* 46 (2004): 1031–36.

Sullivan, Charles A. "Mastering the Faithless Servant? Reconciling Employment Law, Contract Law, and Fiduciary Duty." *Wisconsin Law Review* 2011 (2011): 777–826.

Taifa, Nkechi. "Let's Talk About Reparations." Special issue, *Columbia Journal of Race and Law* 10, no. 1 (March 2020): 1–33.

"Tax Expenditures for Health Care." Joint Committee on Taxation. July 31, 2008. https://www.finance.senate.gov/imo/media/doc/073108ektest.pdf.

Taylor, Lisa Durham. "The Pro-Employee Bent of the Roberts Court." *Tennessee Law Review* 79, no. 4 (Summer 2012): 803–50.

Taylor, Fred W. "A Piece Rate System." *Economic Studies* 1, no. 2 (June 1896): 90–129.

Taylor, Frederick Winslow. *The Principles of Scientific Management.* New York: Harper & Bros., 1911.

Terborg-Penn, Rosalyn. "Survival Strategies Among African-American Workers." In *Women, Work and Protest: A Century of US Women's Labor History*, 2nd ed., edited by Ruth Milkman, 139–55. New York: Routledge, 2013.

Thomasson, Melissa. "The Importance of Group Coverage: How Tax Policy Shaped U.S. Health Insurance." NBER Working Paper Series, Working Paper 7543. 2003.

Thurman, Judith. "Eye of the Needle." *New Yorker* 49 (March 29, 2021).

Tippett, Elizabeth. "Employee Classification." In *Cambridge Handbook on Regulating the Sharing Economy*, edited by Nestor Davidson, Michele Finck, and John Infranca, 291–303. Cambridge: Cambridge University Press, 2018.

———. "Enslaved Agents: Business Transactions Negotiated by Slaves in the Antebellum South." *Arizona Law Review* 63, no. 4 (2021): 923–68.

———. "Harassment Trainings: A Content Analysis." *Berkeley Journal of Labor and Employment Law* 39, no. 2 (2018): 481–526.

———. "How Employers Profit from Digital Wage Theft Under the FLSA." *American Business Law Journal* 55, no. 2 (Summer 2018): 315–402.

———. "The Legal Implications of the #MeToo Movement." *Minnesota Law Review* 103, no. 1 (November 2018): 229–302.

———. "Opportunity Discrimination: A Hidden Liability That Employers Can Readily Fix." *Employee Rights and Employment Policy Journal* 23 (March 2019): 165–96.

———. "Robbing a Barren Vault: The Implications of Dukes v. Wal-Mart for Cases Challenging Subjective Employment Practices." *Hofstra Labor and Employment Law Journal* 29, no. 2 (Spring 2012): 433–84.

Tippett, Elizabeth, and Charlotte Alexander. "The Problem with Employee Scheduling Software." Oregon Law Lab. April 10, 2019. YouTube. https://youtu.be/8ikGVBSLKHc.

Tolbert, Jennifer, and Patrick Drake. "Key Facts About the Uninsured Population." Kaiser Family Foundation. December 19, 2022. https://www.kff.org/uninsured/issue-brief/key-facts-about-the-uninsured-population/.

Tolman, William Howe. *Industrial Betterment*. New York: Social Service Press, 1900.

Tomassetti, Julia. "Algorithmic Management, Employment, and the Self in Gig Work." In *Beyond the Algorithm: Qualitative Insights for Gig Work Regulation*, edited by Deepa Das Acevedo, 123–45. Cambridge: Cambridge University Press, 2020.

———. "From Hierarchies to Markets: Fedex Drivers and the Work Contract as Institutional Marker." *Lewis & Clark Law Review* 19 (2015): 1083–1152.

Tomlins, Christopher. "Law and Power in the Employment Relationship." In *Labor Law in America: Historical and Critical Essays*, edited by Christopher Tomlins and Andrew King. Baltimore, MD: Johns Hopkins University Press, 1992.

———. *Law, Labor, and Ideology in the Early American Republic*. Cambridge: Cambridge University Press, 1993.

———. *The State and the Unions: Labor Relations, Law, and the Organized Labor Movement in America, 1880–1960*. Cambridge: Cambridge University Press, 1985.

Torpy, Bill. "The 'Villain' in Gay Workers Rights Case Has Plenty to Say." *Atlanta Journal Constitution*, June 17, 2020.

Tracy, Lena Harvey. *How My Heart Sang: The Story of Pioneer Industrial Welfare Work.* New York: Richard R. Smith, 1950.
"Trends in the U.S. Uninsured Population, 2010–2020." Assistant Secretary for Planning and Evaluation. February 11, 2021. https://aspe.hhs.gov/system/files/pdf/265041/trends-in-the-us-uninsured.pdf.
Turner, Mary. Introduction to *From Chattel Slaves to Wage Slaves: The Dynamics of Labor Bargaining in the Americas*, edited by Mary Turner. Bloomington: Indiana University Press, 1995.
Tushnet, Mark. *The American Law of Slavery: 1810–1860: Considerations of Humanity and Interest.* Princeton, NJ: Princeton University Press, 1981.
U.S. Census Bureau. "Sex Race and Hispanic Origin: Annual Estimates of the Resident Population by Sex, Race, and Hispanic Origin for the United States: April 1, 2020 to July 1, 2022." NC-EST2022-SR11H. https://www.census.gov/data/datasets/time-series/demo/popest/2020s-national-detail.html.
U.S. Department of Agriculture, Food and Nutrition Service. "SNAP Work Requirements." Accessed April 29, 2025. https://www.fns.usda.gov/snap/work-requirements.
U.S. Department of Labor. "Unemployment Insurance Relief During COVID-19 Outbreak." Accessed April 29, 2025. https://www.dol.gov/coronavirus/unemployment-insurance.
U.S Equal Employment Opportunity Commission. *Legislative History of Titles VII and XI of Civil Rights Act of 1964.* Washington, DC: U.S. Government Printing Office, 1968.
U.S. Industrial Commission. *Report of the Industrial Commission on the Relations and Conditions of Capital and Labor.* Vol 14. Washington, DC: U.S. Government Printing Office, 1901.
U.S. Patent No. 9,881,276. "Ultrasonic Bracelet and Receiver for Detecting Position in 2d Plane." January 30, 2018. https://patents.justia.com/patent/9881277.
Vaas, Francis J. "Title VII: Legislative History." *Boston College Industrial and Commercial Law Review* 7, no. 3 (Spring 1966): 431–58.
Valdez, Inés. *Democracy and Empire: Labor, Nature and the Reproduction of Capitalism.* Cambridge: Cambridge University Press, 2023.
VanderVelde, Lea. "Anti-Republican Origins of the At-Will Doctrine." *American Journal of Legal History* 60, no. 4 (December 2020): 397–449.
———. "The Labor Vision of the Thirteenth Amendment." *University of Pennsylvania Law Review* 138, no. 2 (December 1989): 437–504.
———. "The Last Legally Beaten Servant in America: From Compulsion to Coercion in the American Workplace." *Seattle University Law Review* 39, no. 3 (Spring 2016): 727–86.
———. *Modern Employment Law: In Time and Place.* Eagan, MN: West Academic Publishing, 2022.
———. "Servitude & Captivity in the Common Law of Master-Servant: Judicial Interpretation of the Thirteenth Amendment's Labor Vision Immediately After its Enactment." *William & Mary Bill of Rights Journal* 27, no. 4 (2019): 1079–1112.

Villard, Oswalt Garrison. "Issues and Men: And a Woman—Frances Perkins." *Nation*, March 8, 1933.

Vinel, Jean-Christian. *The Employee: A Political History*. Philadelphia: University of Pennsylvania Press, 2013.

Vladeck, Bruce. "Universal Health Insurance in the United States: Reflections on the Past, the Present, and the Future." *American Journal of Public Health* 93, no. 1 (January 2003): 16–19. https://www.ncbi.nlm.nih.gov/pmc/articles/PMC1447684/.

Voinea, Anca. "US Department of Labor Launches Employee Ownership Initiative." *Co-op News*, September 6, 2024. https://www.thenews.coop/us-department-of-labour-launches-employee-ownership-initiative/.

Vosko, Leah F., John Grundy, Eric Tucker, Mark P. Thomas, Andrea M. Noack, Rebecca Casey, Mary Gellatly, and Jennifer Mussell. "The Compliance Model of Employment Standards Enforcement: An Evidence-Based Assessment of Its Efficacy in Instances of Wage Theft." *Industrial Relations Journal* 48, no. 3 (18 August 2017): 256–73.

Wahl, Jenny Bourne. "Legal Constraints on Slave Masters: The Problem of Social Cost." *American Journal of Legal History* 41, no. 1 (January 1997): 1–24.

Walker, Juliet. *History of Black Businesses in America: Capitalism, Race, Entrepreneurship*. 2nd ed. Chapel Hill: University of North Carolina Press, 2009.

Walker, Juliet E. K. *History of Black Business in America: Capitalism, Race, Entrepreneurship*. Chapel Hill: University of North Carolina Press, 1998.

Wallace, Julia. "Laredo Man's Death in Iowa Due to COVID Makes Waves Locally After His Story Goes Viral." *Laredo Morning Times*, June 15, 2020. https://www.lmtonline.com/local/article/Jose-Ayala-remembered-15340526.php.

"Walmart 2023 Associate Benefits Book: Summary Plan Descriptions." Walmart. May 1, 2023. https://one.walmart.com/content/uswire/en_us/me/link-page/benefitsbook.html.

Watkins, James L. *Production and Price of Cotton for One Hundred Years*. Miscellaneous Series, Bulletin No. 9. Washington, DC: United States Department of Agriculture, Division of Statistics, 1895.

Weil, David. *The Fissured Workplace: Why Work Became So Bad for So Many and What Can be Done to Improve It*. Cambridge, MA: Harvard University Press, 2017.

Weiler, Paul. *Governing the Workplace: The Future of Labor and Employment*. Cambridge, MA: Harvard University Press, 1990.

———. "Promises to Keep: Securing Workers' Rights to Self-Organization Under the NLRA." *Harvard Law Review* 96, no. 8 (June 1983): 1769–1827.

Welker, Kristen, et al. "Trump Orders Meat Processing Plants to Stay Open Amid Coronavirus Pandemic." *NBC News*, April 28, 2020. https://www.nbcnews.com/politics/white-house/trump-order-meat-processing-plants-stay-open-amid-coronavirus-pandemic-n1194536.

Were, Charles, and Richard Hodgetts. "Frederick Taylor's 1899 Pig Iron Observations: Examining Fact, Fiction, and Lessons for the New Millennium." *Academy of Management Journal* 43, no. 6 (2000): 1283–91.

Whittaker, William. "The Fair Labor Standards Act: A Historical Sketch of the Overtime Pay Requirements of Section 13(a)(1)." *CRS Report for Congress* 9 (May 9, 2005).

White, Brendan, and Ike Obi. "Workers and Industry in Muncie, Indiana, 1880–2012." https://cdn.knightlab.com/libs/timeline3/latest/embed/index.html?source=1S3fD1nW62GvrVywQPoS346uu8zg9gRw2gDy_zUTYDS0&font=Default&lang=en&initial_zoom=2&height=650.

Widiss, Deborah A. "Privatizing Family Leave Policy: Assessing the New Opt-in Insurance Model." *Seton Hall Law Review* 53, no. 5 (2023): 1543–76.

Wiefek, Nancy, and Nathan Nicholson. "S Corporation ESOPs and Retirement Security." National Center for Employee Ownership. December 2018. https://www.nceo.org/assets/pdf/articles/NCEO-S-ESOPs-Retirement-Dec-2018.pdf

Wigmore, John H. "Responsibility for Tortious Acts: Its History–II." *Harvard Law Review* 7, no. 7 (February 1894): 383–405.

Williams, Jamillah Bowman. "Maximizing #MeToo: Intersectionality & the Movement." *Boston College Law Review* 62, no. 6 (June 2021): 1797–1864.

———. "#MeToo as Catalyst: A Glimpse into 21st Century Activism." *University of Chicago Legal Forum* 2019 (2019): 371–94.

Williams, Jamillah Bowman, Elizabeth C. Tippett, and Anu Ramdin. "Legislative Approaches to Social Change During #MeToo." Unpublished manuscript, n.d., on file with author.

———. "Mind the Gap(s): Mitigating Harassment in a Post #MeToo Workplace." *University of Southern California Law Review*. Forthcoming.

Williams, Pamela N. "Historical Overview of the Fair Labor Standards Act." *Florida Coastal Law Review* 10, no. 4 (Summer 2009): 657–90.

Williston, Samuel. *Williston on Contracts*. 3rd ed. Mount Kisco, NY: Baker, Voorhis and Co., 1957.

Witt, John Fabian. *The Accidental Republic: Crippled Workingmen, Destitute Widows, and the Remaking of American Law*. Cambridge, MA: Harvard University Press, 2004.

Wood, Horace G. *A Treatise on the Law of Master and Servant: Covering the Relation, Duties and Liabilities of Employers and Employees*. Albany: John D. Parsons, 1877.

Wrege, Charles D., and Richard M. Hodgetts. "Frederick Taylor's 1899 Pig Iron Observations: Examining Fact, Fiction, and Lessons for the New Millennium." *Academy of Management Journal* 43, no. 6 (December 2000): 1283–91.

Yeginsu, Ceylan. "If Workers Slack Off, the Wristband Will Know." *New York Times*, February 1, 2018. https://www.nytimes.com/2018/02/01/technology/amazon-wristband-tracking-privacy.html.

Yglesias, Matthew. "When Is a Taxi Not a Taxi?" *Slate*, December 15, 2011. https://slate.com/technology/2011/12/uber-car-service-exposing-the-idiocy-of-american-city-taxi-regulations.html.

Zahavi, Gerald. *Workers, Managers, and Welfare Capitalism*. Champaign: University of Illinois Press, 1988.

Zatz, Noah D. "Does Work Have a Future If the Labor Market Does Not?" *Chicago-Kent Law Review* 91, no. 3 (August 2016): 1081–1116.

Zietlow, Rebecca. *Enforcing Equality: Congress, the Constitution and the Protection of Individual Rights*. New York: New York University Press, 2006.

———. *The Forgotten Emancipator: James Mitchell Ashley and the Ideological Origins of Reconstruction*. Cambridge: Cambridge University Press, 2018.

# Figure Credits and Sources

FIGURE 1. Harris & Ewing, photographer. *Hopkins tells Mrs. Perkins about it. Washington, D.C., Jan. 7. Harry Hopkins, Secretary of Commerce, stepped over to Labor Secretary Frances Perkins to tell her that he likes his new job . . . was at the Jackson Day Dinner, 1/7/39*. Washington, DC, [January 7], 1939. https://www.loc.gov/item/2016874728/.

FIGURE 2. Photograph by Warren K. Leffler, Library of Congress, https://www.loc.gov/item/2018650313/.

FIGURE 3. Photograph by Ian Meagher.

FIGURE 4. Photograph by Jessica Jaszewski.

FIGURE 5. Data for 1880–1995 from Richard B. Freeman, "Spurts in Union Growth: Defining Moments and Social Processes," in *The Defining Moment: The Great Depression and the American Economy in the Twentieth Century*, ed. Michael D. Bordo, Claudia Goldin, and Eugene White (University of Chicago Press, 1997). Data for 1996–2022 from Bureau of Labor Statistics, "Union Affiliation Data from the Current Population Survey," Data Viewer, Series ID LUU0204899600, https://beta.bls.gov/dataViewer/view/timeseries/LUU0204899600. Methodology from Brantly Callaway and William J. Collins, "Unions, Workers and Wages at the Peak of the American Labor Movement," NBER Working Paper Series, Working Paper 23516, 2017, http://www.nber.org/papers/w23516.

FIGURE 6. Constructed by the author using two different data series: a Bureau of Labor Statistics dataset illustrating public sector union density from 1983 to 2022; and a second series constructed using a 1979 Bureau of Labor Statistics publication that asked respondents about "union" membership between 1958 and 1968 and one that asked about both "unions" and "employee associations" from 1968 to 1978. The 1968–1978 data separated out the "union" data from "employee associations" data, suggesting that employee associations, on average, represented 45 percent of public sector union membership during that period. This 45 percent figure was used to estimate figures for the 1960s that included both unions and employee associations. The absence of that estimated data would otherwise suggest that union density suddenly doubled between 1966 and 1968, jumping from 16 to 32 percent. Data for 1956–1978 from Bureau of Labor Statistics, *Directory of National Unions and Employee Associations, 1979*, U.S. Department of Labor, September 1980, 66, http://fraser.stlouisfed.org (union membership data). This methodology was derived in part from a 1984 working paper by Richard Freeman, in which he uses the *Directory of National Unions* to construct a similar graph covering from 1958 to 1980, although he does not attempt to estimate the missing data on employee associations. Bureau of Labor Statistics, "Employment, Hours, and Earnings from the Current Economic Statistics Survey (Industry: Government)," Data Viewer, Series ID CES9000000001, https://beta.bls.gov/dataViewer/view/timeseries/CES9000000001 (public sector employment data). Data for 1983–2023 data from Bureau of Labor Statistics, "Union Affiliation Data from the Current Population Survey," Data Viewer, Series ID LUU0204922700, https://beta.bls.gov/dataViewer/view/timeseries/LUU0204922700(union membership data).

FIGURE 9. Courtesy of the Jefferson National Parks Association.

FIGURE 10. Data for management demographics from Equal Employment Opportunity Commission, "EEO-1 (Employer Information Report) Statistics," accessed January 25, 2024, https://www.eeoc.gov/data/job-patterns-minorities-and-women-private-industry-eeo-1-0 (management demographics). Data tool applied for job categories: "Exec/Sr. Officials & Managers" and "First/Mid Officials & Managers." U.S. Census Bureau, "Sex Race and Hispanic Origin: Annual Estimates of the Resident Population by Sex, Race, and Hispanic Origin for the United States: April 1, 2020 to July 1, 2022" NC-EST2022-SR11H, accessed January 25, 2024, https://www.census.gov/data/datasets/time-series/demo/popest/2020s-national-detail.html. The EEOC and Census Bureau apply racial and ethnic categories somewhat differently. Census treats Hispanic status independently of race (such that, for example, a respondent could choose both "White" and "Hispanic" or "Black" and "Hispanic"), while the EEOC data treat "Hispanic" as a race. For the purpose of the census data in figure 10, Hispanic respondents were treated as people of color.

FIGURE 11. Published in connection with Elizabeth Keckley's autobiography and touched up by the author in Adobe Photoshop from a scan of the image.

FIGURE 12. Courtesy of the Oregon Historical Society. Credit: Josh Binus, "Moving Camp," Oregon History Project, 2003, https://www.oregonhistoryproject.org/articles/historical-records/moving-camp/.

FIGURE 13. "Industrial Problems, Welfare Work: United States. Ohio. Dayton. National Cash Register Company: Welfare Institutions of the National Cash Register Company, Dayton, Ohio. Advantages for Employees: Calisthenics," Harvard Art Museums/Fogg Museum, 1903, https://hvrd.art/o/56966.

FIGURE 14. Oliveira v. New Prime Inc., Civil Action No. 1:15-cv-10603, Document 199 (Filed 10/16/2019), Exhibit 17, 123.

# Index

Cases and statutes appear in dedicated sections after the list of general terms. Cross-references are to general terms except as specified.

affirmative action, 85, 90, 213n22, 219nn32,34, 220n35, 224n117
AFL, 76, 207n40
AFL-CIO, 26
after-acquired evidence doctrine, 113, 224n114
agency, 24–26, 91–92, 213n22
agency law, 110
Amazon, 8, 61–65, 128–29, 201nn84,86,88–89, 202n94
antebellum, 7, 24, 29, 31–32, 34, 172nn69–70, 178n72, 184n24, 185n35, 186n47, 225nn1,4
antidiscrimination, 8, 86, 91, 100, 103, 139, 146, 154, 196n94, 222n95, 223n106
apprenticeship, 29, 74, 122, 133, 183n19, 232n7
arbitration, 77, 103, 135, 233n20

Ball State University, 1–2, 52, 163, 167nn1–2, 197n1, 198n10. See also *Vance v. Ball State University* under CASES
benefits. See employee benefits
Black Lives Matter, 160–61

*Black's Law Dictionary*, 4, 169n44
Bostock, Gerald, 101–2, 107–12, 114, 163–64, 218n10. See also *Bostock v. Clayton County* under CASES
Brandeis, Louis (Supreme Court justice), 54–55, 198n13, 199n28
but for cause, 112

capitalism, 5, 33, 36, 124, 224n1, 229n55, 230n85
certiorari, 2
Chisholm, Shirley, 48
collective bargaining, 6, 77, 81–82, 103, 122, 196n92, 206n37, 207nn38,40, 210n72, 213n27
commerce clause, 44
company store, 123, 137, 228n44
company town, 123, 137, 141
control test, 174–75n36
COVID-19, 13–14, 26, 142–44, 151, 157, 161. See also pandemic
craftsmen. See trades/tradespeople

deindustrialization, 80
deskilling, 74
disparate impact, 96–97

277

employee benefits, 121, 131, 135, 140, 156, 175n38, 230n95, 231n104
employee stock ownership plans (ESOP), 155, 241nn59,61
enticement, 75, 184n25
Equal Employment Opportunity Commission (EEOC) 2, 90–93, 99, 106, 215nn66–67,77, 219n33, 223n105
executive order, 83, 85–87, 91, 212n108, 218nn16,22
exemption, 47, 50–51, 183n20, 194n75, 196n97, 197n101

Faragher/Ellerth defense, 110, 115. See also *Burlington Industries, Inc. v. Ellerth* and *Faragher v. City of Boca Raton* under CASES
Federal Trade Commission (FTC), 160
fellow servant doctrine, 22, 179n103
feudalism, 4–6, 16, 43, 70, 119, 169n41, 170n51, 190n107, 205n21
fissuring, 136, 137
Ford Motor Company, 127
freedom of contract, 44, 46, 142, 190n6, 192n45
free labor, 22, 30, 122–23, 136, 141–42, 144, 184n24

gender stereotyping, 101, 111
gig economy, 9, 64, 136–38, 142, 148, 190n9
gig workers, 9, 138–40, 151, 153
Gompers, Samuel, 76
Gorsuch, Neil (Supreme Court justice), 6, 135, 140
Green, Percy, 97. See also *McDonnell Douglas Corp. v. Green* under CASES
Griffiths, Martha, 92

harassment, 2–3, 9, 52, 103–5, 109–10, 153–55, 160, 198n4
Hawthorne effect, 38
Hawthorne experiments, 8, 39, 190n3
hostile work environment, 52, 110
Hudson, Harry, 83–85, 99, 212nn1–2, 213nn5,12–15
human resources, 2, 9, 86, 99, 102–5, 109–11, 155, 220n36

industrialization, 54, 79, 187n56, 206n36
industrial welfare, 121, 124–26, 129, 201n102, 230n68
intellectual property, 6

intersectionality, 100, 198n4
Interstate Commerce Commission (ICC), 54

Jim Crow (laws), 36, 96
jurisdiction, 5, 16–19, 120, 169n36
just-in-time production, 8

kaizen, 8, 54, 59–62, 66
Keckley, Elizabeth, 117, 119, 225nn8–11

labor law, 2, 16, 44, 73, 77, 80, 128, 212n107
Lincoln, Mary Todd, 119
Lockheed Martin, 83–88, 90, 99, 104, 214n32
Lyft, 137–39, 233n29

Marshall, Thurgood (Supreme Court justice), 53, 96
McDonnell Douglas, 9, 97, 99, 100, 111, 154. See also *McDonnell Douglas Corp. v. Green* under CASES
medical care, 227n24
#MeToo movement, 105, 160–61
minimum wage, 39, 46–50, 57, 137, 139, 159, 193n66, 195n77, 196n87, 200n47, 231n103. See also wages/wage and hour
Mississippi Planter's College, 18
mixed motive proof, 111–14
moral turpitude, 31
muda, 59

National Association for the Advancement of Colored People (NAACP), 2, 86–88, 91, 93, 167n1, 213n27
National Cash Register Company (NCR), 124–26, 131, 229nn64,66, 229n70
National Labor Relations Board (NLRB), 69–70, 77–78, 80–81, 129, 152, 155, 204n15. See also National Labor Relations Act (NLRA) *under* STATUTES; *NLRB v. Mackay Radio & Telegraph Co.* under CASES
National Woman's Party (NWP), 92
negligence, 2–3, 17, 22, 30, 43, 52, 110, 179n103, 180n104, 227n25
New Deal Era, 48

Obamacare. See Affordable Care Act of 2010 *under* STATUTES
Occupational Safety and Health Administration (OSHA), 24–26, 146. See also Occupational Safety and Health Act *under* STATUTES

Oliveira, Dominic, 133, 164, 232nn1,5–6,12, 233n16–18, 236nn87–89, 237n93. See also *New Prime v. Oliveira* under CASES
overseers, 18–20, 31–32, 55, 109, 186nn39–40,42,45–46, 187n65, 199n24
overtime, 8, 39, 42, 47–48, 50, 57, 64–66, 78, 194n75, 197n101, 200n47, 203nn119–120

pandemic, 26, 62, 65, 120, 130, 136, 142–44, 157, 159. See also COVID-19
*parens patriae*, 4
paterfamilias, 43
paternalism, 16, 25, 121, 125–26, 130–31
Perkins, Frances (Secretary of Labor), 45, 192n52, 203n119
piece rate, 40–41, 47
Plan(s) for Progress, 88, 90, 215n60
police power, 43
PriceWaterhouse, 111
prima facie case, 97

reasonable care, 110
reparations, 157–58, 160, 243n82, 244n89
*Restatement of Employment Law*, 4, 175n40
Roberts, John (Supreme Court justice), 3, 53, 193n64

same actor defense, 113
Scalia, Antonin (Supreme Court justice), 3
segregation, 8, 31, 41, 44, 75–76, 83–91, 93–96, 100, 105, 123–24, 160, 179n101, 192n47
self-help, 16, 25, 78
sick leave, 9, 120, 129–30, 160. See also Family Medical Leave Act (FMLA) under STATUTES
slavery, 6–7, 9, 16–25, 29, 31–32, 36, 53, 61, 71, 74, 117, 121, 141, 157, 160, 162, 171n69, 172n70–73, 177n66, 185n36, 189n82, 224n1
sovereign/sovereignty, 5, 8–10, 17–19, 25, 28, 39–40, 43, 45, 142, 162
Straker, David Augustus, 75, 208n49
stray remarks doctrine, 113, 223n111
strict liability, 155
strikes, 25, 74–75, 77–78, 80, 103, 123, 153, 207n39, 209n66, 210n90, 229n66
Supplemental Nutrition Assistance Program, 120
symbolic structures, 104, 109, 113

tax expenditure, 149–50, 238nn21,23, 239n24
Taylor, Frederick Winslow, 41–42, 53–56, 191n18, 199n28, 223n104
Taylorism/Taylorists, 8, 42, 56, 60–61, 126, 201n88
Terrell, Mary Church, 75
ticker-tape system, 39
Title VII. See Civil Rights Act of 1964 under STATUTES
Tracy, Lena Harvey, 125–26, 229nn55,65
trades/tradespeople, 16, 21, 29, 40, 74–75, 99, 123, 179n100, 205n21, 205n26, 206nn28,30
Turner, Aletha, 122
Tyson Foods, 7, 13, 16, 159, 163, 173n1

Uber, 138–40, 148, 153, 233nn29–30, 240n42
unemployment insurance, 9, 15, 120, 139
unfair labor practice, 70, 80–82, 155. See also Fair Labor Standards Act (FLSA) under STATUTES
unions, 8, 22, 43, 45, 69–70, 73, 76–80, 102–3, 120–21, 123, 126, 128–29, 152–53, 161, 163, 190n3, 207nn38–40, 209nn57,63, 210nn82,90, 211nn91,93–94,106, 212n110, 213n27, 224n117, 229n66
universal health care, 150
U.S. Industrial Commission, 23

vagrancy/vagrants, 5, 119, 170n58
Vance, Maetta, 1–3, 52, 163, 167nn1–6, 168nn7–23,26–30, 198nn5,10. See also *Vance v. Ball State University* under CASES
vicarious liability, 15

wages/wage and hour, 4, 8, 15, 42, 44–47, 50, 57–58, 64, 70, 73, 85, 134, 139, 146, 180n115, 190n6, 194n71, 234n37. See also minimum wage
welfare, industrial, 121, 124–26, 129, 201n102, 230n68
welfare, social, 5, 9, 120, 140, 150–51, 159
welfare secretaries, 126
wellness, 131–32
whistleblower, 15
white collar workers, 30, 35, 50
Wonderlic test, 95–96
Wood, Horace G., 30, 32, 187nn49,65
workers' compensation, 15–17, 23–26, 137, 139, 145, 180n114, 181n129

## CASES

*Anderson v. Mt. Clemens Pottery Co.*, 328 U.S. 680 (1946), 8, 53, 57
*Bostock v. Clayton County*, 590 U.S. 644 (2020), 9, 101, 163
*Brewer v. Harris*, 5 Gratt. 285 (Va. 1848), 122
*Burlington Industries, Inc. v. Ellerth*, 524 U.S. 742 (1998), 52
*Dred Scott v. Sanford*, 60 U.S. 393 (1856), 18
*Faragher v. City of Boca Raton*, 524 U.S. 775 (1998), 52
*Farwell v. Boston and Worcester Rail Road Corp.*, 42 Met. 49 (Mass. 1842), 22
*Griggs v. Duke Power Co.*, 401 U.S. 424 (1971), 86, 93
*Guz v. Bechtel National, Inc.*, 24 Cal. 4th 317 (2000), 36–37
*Hammer v. Dagenhart*, 247 U.S. 251 (1918), 44
*Integrity Staffing Sol., Inc. v. Busk*, 574 U.S. 27 (2014), 65
*Koll v. Bush*, 6 Colo. App 294 (1895), 34–35
*Lochner v. New York*, 198 U.S. 45 (1905), 43, 47
*Martin v. Everett*, 11 Ala. 375 (1847), 31
*Matthews v. Park Bros*, 159 Pa. 579 (1894), 33
*McDonnell Douglas Corp. v. Green*, 411 U.S. 792 (1973), 86, 97
*Meritor Savings Bank v. Vinson*, 477 U.S. 57 (1986), 52
*Nationwide Mutual Ins. Co. v. Darden*, 503 U.S. 318 (1992), 4, 15
*New Prime v. Oliveira*, 139 S. Ct. 532 (2019), 4, 134
*NLRB v. Mackay Radio & Telegraph Co.*, 304 U.S. 333 (1938), 77–78
*Paul v. School Dist. No. 2 in Hartland*, 28 Vt. 575 (1856), 30
*Plessy v. Ferguson*, 163 U.S. 537 (1896), 36, 44, 75
*Scudder v. Woodbridge*, 1 Ga. 195 (1846), 23–24
*Vance v. Ball State University*, 570 U.S. 421 (2013), 2, 52, 163
*West Coast Hotel Co. v. Parish*, 300 U.S. 379 (1937), 46

## STATUTES

Affordable Care Act of 2010 (Obamacare), 64, 121, 146–47, 162
Civil Rights Act of 1964 (Title VII), 3, 8–9, 39–40, 51–52, 73, 85–86, 91–97, 99–103, 109–114, 130, 154, 157, 160, 173n77, 205n23, 213n19, 214n38, 215nn63–65,67,70,76,78–79,81, 216nn97,100,103, 220n42, 224n115, 241n55
Employee Retirement Income Security Act (ERISA), 15, 156, 242n73
Equal Pay Act, 51, 91, 154
Fair Labor Standards Act (FLSA), 8, 39–40, 47–51, 53, 56–58, 65–66, 69, 85–86, 91, 193n60, 194n71, 195nn78,80, 196n87, 200nn47,50,61,65, 203n120
Family Medical Leave Act (FMLA), 120
Federal Arbitration Act, 135, 233n22
National Industrial Recovery Act (NRA), 45, 162, 193n60, 196n93
National Labor Relations Act (NLRA), 8, 25, 39–40, 73, 77–78, 80–81, 103, 124, 153, 155, 160, 197n105, 205n25, 207n40, 210n86, 240nn39–40
Occupational Safety and Health Act (OSHA), 24, 146
Portal-to-Portal Act, 58–59, 65, 194n74, 200n65

Founded in 1893,
UNIVERSITY OF CALIFORNIA PRESS
publishes bold, progressive books and journals
on topics in the arts, humanities, social sciences,
and natural sciences—with a focus on social
justice issues—that inspire thought and action
among readers worldwide.

The UC PRESS FOUNDATION
raises funds to uphold the press's vital role
as an independent, nonprofit publisher, and
receives philanthropic support from a wide
range of individuals and institutions—and from
committed readers like you. To learn more, visit
ucpress.edu/supportus.

www.ingramcontent.com/pod-product-compliance
Lightning Source LLC
Chambersburg PA
CBHW021340230426
43666CB00006B/353